SUICIDE

SUICIDE

A STUDY IN SOCIOLOGY

By

EMILE DURKHEIM

Translated by
JOHN A. SPAULDING AND GEORGE SIMPSON
Edited with an Introduction by
GEORGE SIMPSON

First published in 1952 by
Routledge & Kegan Paul Ltd
Reprinted 1963, 1966, 1968, 1979

First published as a paperback 1970
Reprinted 1979, 1987

Reprinted 1989, 1992, 1993, 1996
by Routledge
11 New Fetter Lane,
London EC4P 4EE

© The Free Press 1951

Printed and bound in Great Britain
by Clays Ltd, St Ives PLC

ISBN 0-415-04587-8

To Those Who, with Durkheim, Understand the Life of Reason As Itself a Moral Commitment, and Especially to Arthur D. Gayer in Economics; Sol W. Ginsburg in Psychiatry; Robert S. Lynd in Sociology; and Arthur E. Murphy in Philosophy

CONTENTS

EDITOR'S PREFACE

Of the four major works of the renowned French sociologist, Emile Durkheim, only *Le Suicide* has remained to be translated. *The Elementary Forms of the Religious Life* was first published in English in 1915; the *Division of Labor in Society* in 1933 and *The Rules of Sociological Method* in 1938. Over half a century has gone by since the first edition of *Le Suicide,* yet far more than antiquarian interest attaches to it in the sociological, statistical, philosophical, and psychological disciplines. But the historical significance of the volume in social thought would be enough reason for presenting it to readers in the English-speaking world. As a milestone in social science and an indispensable part in understanding the work of the man who founded and firmly established academic sociology in France and influenced many others outside of France, it should have long since been available in translation.

Though our statistical material today is more refined and broader, and our socio-psychological apparatus better established than was Durkheim's, his work on suicide remains the prototype of systematic, rigorous and unrelenting attack on the subject with the data, techniques, and accumulated knowledge available at any given period. Indeed, *Le Suicide* is among the very first modern examples of consistent and organized use of statistical method in social investigation. In the last decade of the nineteenth century when Durkheim was conducting the investigations incorporated in this work, repositories (governmental or private) of statistical information on this, or any

other subject, were either rare, skimpy, or badly put together. With
characteristic energy and the aid of some of his students, especially
Marcel Mauss, Durkheim realigned the available statistics so as to
answer the question posed by the general problem and its internal
details. At the time, statistical techniques were little developed, and
Durkheim was forced at given points to invent them as he went
along. The elements of simple correlation were unknown except
among the pathfinders in statistical techniques like Galton and Pear-
son, as were those of multiple and partial correlation, yet Durkheim
establishes relationships between series of data by methodological
perseverence and inference.

The tables which Durkheim drew up have been left in the translation in their somewhat quaint form, with no attempt to set them up
according to present-day standards of statistical presentation. They
have that way an historical value, as well as a character of their own.
To embellish them would take away the atmosphere in which they
were literally forged through necessity. Though more recent data are
available, the kind of information Durkheim was trying to impart
through them is still the kind that sociologists and actuarialists are
interested in. Indeed, one table (on the effect of military life on
suicide) has been taken over bodily in one of the best general, recent
treatises on suicide.[2]

The maps which Durkheim placed in the text have been put in
Appendices here, along with a special table which Durkheim drew
up but could not use for reasons he gives in a footnote to it. The
maps have been reproduced as they are with the French titles and
statistical legends.

But in addition to its historical and methodological import, Le
Suicide is of abiding significance because of the problem it treats and
the sociological approach with which it is handled. For Durkheim
is seeking to establish that what looks like a highly individual and
personal phenomenon is explicable through the social structure and
its ramifying functions. And even the revolutionary findings in psychiatry and the refinement and superior competence of contemporary
actuarial statistics on this subject have yet to come fully to grips with
this. We shall have more to say of it in the introduction.

[2] Dublin, Louis I, and Bunzel, Bessie, *To Be or Not To Be*, New York, 1933,
p. 112-113.

There are those, moreover, who look upon *Le Suicide* as still an outstanding, if not the outstanding, work in what is called the study of social causation.[3] And in what has come to be known as the sociology of knowledge, Durkheim's attempts to relate systems of thought to states of the collective conscience involved in the currents of egoism, altruism, and anomy, in this volume, have been of no little influence.[4]

Finally, *Le Suicide* shows Durkheim's fundamental principles of social interpretation in action. His social realism, which sees society as an entity greater than the sum of its parts, with its accompanying concepts of collective representations and the collective conscience, is here applied to a special problem-area, and the results are some of the richest it has ever borne. For Durkheim not only enunciated methodological and heuristic principles (as pre-eminently in *The Rules of Sociological Method*); he also tested them in research of no mean scope. That his work would have to be supplemented, added to, revised, and our knowledge advanced, he would be the first to admit, since he rightly saw scientific endeavor as a great collective undertaking whose findings are handed on from generation to generation and improved upon in the process.

The translation has been made from the edition which appeared in 1930, thirteen years after Durkheim's death and thirty-three years after the first edition in 1897. This edition was supervised by Marcel Mauss. Professor Mauss, in his brief introductory note there, tells us that it was not possible, because of the method of reprinting, to correct the few typographical and editorial errors. With the aid of Dr. John A. Spaulding, I have sought by textual and statistical query, to rectify them wherever they could be discovered.

No index appeared in the French text, and none has been prepared here. Instead, the detailed table of contents which Durkheim drew up has been translated and placed at the back of this book.

For the version of the translation here, I must take full responsibility. Dr. Spaulding and I worked over the first draft, then we both re-worked the second draft. But the final changes I made alone.

Mr. Jerome H. Skolnick, a student of mine, aided in checking

[3] See especially, MacIver, R. M., *Social Causation*, New York, 1942.
[4] See, for example, Parsons, Talcott, *The Structure of Social Action*, Glencoe, Illinois, 1949.

the typescript and in proof-reading. He did not confine his work to routine, and many of his suggestions proved to be of great value to me.

GEORGE SIMPSON

The City College of New York
November 1, 1950.

EDITOR'S INTRODUCTION
THE AETIOLOGY OF SUICIDE

I

THE range of Emile Durkheim's analysis of the interconnectedness of suicide with social and natural phenomena is so wide and varied as to preclude treatment of all its avenues and by-roads in the short space of this introduction. Within the confines of one not over-long volume, Durkheim has treated or touched on normal and abnormal psychology, social psychology, anthropology (especially the concept of race), meteorological and other "cosmic" factors, religion, marriage, the family, divorce, primitive rites and customs, social and economic crises, crime (especially homicide) and law and jurisprudence, history, education, and occupational groups. But a short appraisal is still possible because throughout Durkheim's work on each and all of these topics subsidiary to suicide, is the basic theme that suicide which appears to be a phenomenon relating to the individual is actually explicable aetiologically with reference to the social structure and its ramifying functions.

The early chapters in Durkheim's work are devoted to the negation of doctrines which ascribe suicide to extra-social factors, such as mental alienation, the characteristics of race as studied by anthropology, heredity, climate, temperature, and finally to a negation of the doctrine of "imitation," particularly as represented in the works of Gabriel Tarde whose social theory at the time in France had many followers and against whom Durkheim waged unrelenting warfare within the bounds of scholarly and academic amenities. Here in these early chapters Durkheim is involved in a process of elimination: all theses which require resort to individual or other extra-social causes for suicide are dispatched, leaving only social causes to be considered. This is used as a foundation for reaffirming his thesis stated in his introduction that the suicide-rate is a phenomenon *sui generis;* that is, the *totality* of suicides in a society is a fact separate, distinct, and capable of study in its own terms.

Since, according to Durkheim, suicide cannot be explained by its individual forms, and since the suicide-rate is for him a distinct phenomenon in its own right, he proceeds to relate currents of suicide to social concomitants. It is these social concomitants of suicide which for Durkheim will serve to place any individual suicide in its proper aetiological setting.

From a study of religious affiliation, marriage and the family, and political and national communities, Durkheim is led to the first of his three categories of suicide: namely, egoistic suicide, which results from lack of integration of the individual into society. The stronger the forces throwing the individual onto his own resources, the greater the suicide-rate in the society in which this occurs. With respect to religious society, the suicide-rate is lowest among Catholics, the followers of a religion which closely integrates the individual into the collective life. Protestantism's rate is high and is correlate with the high state of individualism there. Indeed, the advancement of science and knowledge which is an accompaniment of the secularization process under Protestantism, while explaining the universe to man, nevertheless disintegrates the ties of the individual to the group and shows up in higher suicide-rates.

Egoistic suicide is also to be seen, according to Durkheim, where there is slight integration of the individual into family life. The greater the density of the family the greater the immunity of individuals to suicide. The individual characteristics of the spouses is unimportant in explaining the suicide-rate; it is dependent upon the structure of the family and the roles played by its members. In political and national communities, it is Durkheim's thesis that in great crises the suicide-rate falls because then society is more strongly integrated and the individual participates actively in social life. His egoism is restricted and his will to live strengthened.

Having established the variation of the suicide-rate with the degree of integration of social groups, Durkheim is led to consider the fact of suicide in social groups where there is comparatively great integration of the individual, as in lower societies. Here where the individual's life is rigorously governed by custom and habit, suicide is what he calls altruistic; that is, it results from the individual's taking his own life because of higher commandments, either those of religious sacrifice or unthinking political allegiance. This type of suicide Durkheim finds still existent in modern society in the army where ancient patterns of obedience are rife.

Egoistic suicide and altruistic suicide may be considered to be symptomatic of the way in which the individual is structured into the society; in the first case, inadequately, in the second case, over-adequately. But there is another form of suicide for Durkheim which results from lack of regulation of the individual by society. This he calls anomic suicide, and is in a chronic state in the modern economy. The individual's needs and their satisfaction have been regulated by society; the common beliefs and practices he has learned make him the embodiment of what Durkheim calls the collective conscience. When this regulation of the individual is upset so that his horizon is broadened beyond what he can endure, or contrariwise contracted unduly, conditions for anomic suicide tend toward a maximum. Thus, Durkheim instances sudden wealth as stimulative of suicide on the ground that the newly enriched individual is unable to cope with the new opportunities afforded him. The upper and lower limits of his desires, his scale of life, all are upset. The same type of situation occurs, according to Durkheim, in what he terms conjugal anomy exemplified by divorce. Here marital society no longer exercises its regulative influence upon the partners, and the suicide-rate for the divorced is comparatively high. This anomic situation is more severely reflected among divorced men than among divorced women, since it is the man, according to Durkheim, who has profited more from the regulative influence of marriage.

At this point in his analysis, Durkheim claims that the individual forms of suicide can be properly classified. Now that the three aetiological types—egoistic, altruistic, and anomic—have been established, it is possible, he says, to describe the individual behavior-patterns of those exemplifying these types. The other way around—seeking to find the causes of suicide by investigating the individual types— Durkheim had originally claimed to be fruitless. In addition to tabulating the individual forms of the three different types, Durkheim seeks to establish that there are individual forms of suicide which display mixed types, such as the ego-anomic, the altruist-anomic, the ego-altruist.

Thus, the statistics available to Durkheim he finds not correlated with biological or cosmic phenomena, but with social phenomena, such as the family, political and economic society, religious groups. This correlation he claims indicates decisively that each society has a collective inclination towards suicide, a rate of self-homicide which is fairly constant for each society so long as the basic conditions of its existence remain the same. This collective inclination conforms, Durkheim believes, to his definition of a social fact given in his treatise, *The Rules of Sociological Method*. That is, this inclination is a reality in itself, exterior to the individual and exercising a coercive effect upon him. In short, the individual inclination to suicide is explicable scientifically only by relation to the collective inclination, and this collective inclination is itself a determined reflection of the structure of the society in which the individual lives.

The aggregate of individual views on life is more than the sum of the individual views to Durkheim. It is an existence in itself; what he calls the collective conscience, the totality of beliefs and practices, of folkways and *mores*. It is the repository of common sentiments, a well-spring from which each individual conscience draws its moral sustenance. Where these common sentiments rigorously guide the individual, as in Catholicism, and condemn the taking of one's own life, there the suicide-rate is low; where these common sentiments lay great stress on individualism, innovation and free thought, the hold over the individual slackens, he is tenuously bound to society, and can the more easily be led to suicide. The latter is the case with Protestantism. In lower societies, the collective conscience, according to Durkheim, holds individual life of little value, and self-immolation through suicide is the reflection of the society at work in the individual. And in higher societies where sudden crises upset the adjustment to which the individual has become habituated through the common sentiments and beliefs, anomy appears which shows itself in a rising suicide-rate.

Suicide, like crime, is for Durkheim no indication of immorality *per se*. In fact, a given number of suicides are to be expected in a given type of society. But where the rate increases rapidly, it is symptomatic of the breakdown of the collective conscience, and of a basic flaw in the social fabric. But suicide and criminality are not correlative, as some criminologists had claimed, although both when excessive may indicate that the social structure is not operating normally.

The suicide-rate which Durkheim found increasing rapidly through the nineteenth century cannot be halted in its upward curve by education, exhortation, or repression, he says. For Durkheim all ameliorative measures must go to the question of social structure. Egoistic suicide can be reduced by reintegrating the individual into group-life, giving him strong allegiances through a strengthened collective conscience. This can be accomplished in no small part, he thinks, through the re-establishment of occupational groups, compact voluntary associations based on work-interests. This is the same recommendation he made in the second edition of his *Division of Labor in Society* apropos of the infelicitous workings of that phenomenon. The occupational group will also serve to limit the number of anomic suicides. In the case of conjugal anomy, his solution is in greater freedom and equality for women.

Thus, suicide for Durkheim shows up the deep crisis in modern society, just as the study of any other social fact would. No social fact to him has been explained until it has been seen in its full and complete nexus with all other social facts and with the fundamental structure of society.

II

Since Durkheim's work on suicide, the chief advances in our knowledge of the subject have come from actuarial statistics and psychoanalytic psychiatry. Durkheim's own approach has been carried forward, tested, and applied further by his student and friend, Maurice Halbwachs, in *Les Causes du Suicide*.[1] For the argument here, it must be noted (as Parsons has already pointed out) that Halbwachs saw that there is no antithesis such as Durkheim posited, between the social and the psychopathological explanations of suicide, but that they are complementary.[2]

The actuarialists have studied the overall extent and trends of suicide, related it to race and color incidence, age and sex distribu-

[1] Paris, 1930.
[2] Parsons, Talcott, *The Structure of Social Action*, New York, 1937, p. 326.

tion, urban and rural areas, seasonality (what Durkheim calls "cosmic" factors), economic conditions, religious affiliation, marital status. But the actuarialists have formulated no thorough-going, consistent and systematic hypothesis concerning the causes of suicide, which is what Durkheim is after. A sound compendium of actuarial work on this subject can be found in Louis I. Dublin's and Bessie Bunzel's book, *To Be or Not To Be*.[3] But for their interpretative framework, Dublin and Bunzel have had to fall back upon modern developments in psychiatry and mental hygiene.[4]

Durkheim is skeptical about the reliability of the statistics on suicide with regard to motives, on the ground that recording of motives is done by untrained enumerators in offices of vital statistics, as well as that the motives ascribed by suicides to their acts are unreliable. But the inadequacy of statistics on suicide generally has been even more trenchantly pointed up by psychoanalysts. Gregory Zilboorg has this to say: ". . . Statistical data on suicide as they are compiled today deserve little if any credence; it has been repeatedly pointed out by scientific students of the problem that suicide cannot be subject to statistical evaluation, since all too many suicides are not reported as such. Those who kill themselves through automobile accidents are almost never recorded as suicides; those who sustain serious injuries during an attempt to commit suicide and die weeks or months later of these injuries or of intercurrent infections are never registered as suicides; a great many genuine suicides are concealed by families; and suicidal attempts, no matter how serious, never find their way into the tables of vital statistics. It is obvious that under these circumstances the statistical data available cover the smallest and probably the least representative number of suicides; one is justified, therefore, in discarding them as nearly useless in a scientific evaluation of the problem."[5]

Moreover, Fenichel, following Brill and Menninger, has pointed

[3] New York, 1933.

[4] A similar situation holds with an earlier sociological study, Ruth S. Cavan's *Suicide* (Chicago, 1928). Here too actuarial and social statistics are presented, along with psychological case-histories, but the crucial relationship—that of the individual case-histories of suicide to the basic elements in the social structure—has been left relatively untouched.

[5] "Suicide Among Civilized and Primitive Races," *American Journal of Psychiatry*, vol. 92, 1935–36.

out the prevalence of "partial suicides," where death does not occur but which consist of "self-destructive actions, during melancholic states, carried out as self-punishment, as an expression of certain delusions or without any rationalization." The term, "partial suicides," Fenichel concludes, "is absolutely correct in so far as the underlying unconscious mechanisms are identical with those of suicide." [6] It is clear that these "partial suicides" never find their way into the statistics of suicide. From the aetiological standpoint, they are identical with consummated suicides; but of them all, Fenichel writes: "The factors, doubtlessly quantitative in nature, that determine whether or when the result is to be a suicide, a manic attack, or a recovery are still unknown." [7]

And even where statistical regularity appears to be ascertainable, a methodologist of science writes: "What makes the statistical regularity of long-run human conduct so striking is the fact that it shows itself in acts which are not the simple outcomes of a few mechanical forces, like the movements of spun coins, but in masses of close decisions of a very complex sort." He then goes on to instance the statistics of female suicides in New York City.[8]

It appears inescapable to state that until we have better records and more literate statistical classification in terms of psychiatric nomenclature, we can draw few binding conclusions concerning regularity in terms of age, ethnic groups, social status, etc. As an example, we may point out that Durkheim, Dublin and Bunzel, and others show little if any suicide among children, whereas Zilboorg has deemed it significant enough to make a special study.[9]

A further result of the unreliability of the statistics is that they have led to a conclusion that is fairly widespread that suicide grows as civilization advances. This thesis has been seriously challenged by Zilboorg. He concludes that suicide is evidently "as old as the human race, it is probably as old as murder and almost as old as natural death. *The lower the cultural niveau of the race, the more*

---

[6] Fenichel, Otto, *The Psychoanalytic Theory of Neurosis*, New York, W. W. Norton and Company, Inc., 1945, p. 401.

[7] *Ibid.*

[8] Larrabee, Harold A., *Reliable Knowledge*, Boston, Houghton Mifflin Company, 1945, p. 436.

[9] Zilboorg, Gregory, "Considerations on Suicide, with Particular Reference to that of the Young," *American Journal of Orthopsychiatry*, VIII, 1937.

deep-seated the suicidal impulse appears. [Italics not in original].
. . . The man of today, as far as suicide is concerned, is deficient, indeed, as compared with his forefathers who possessed a suicidal ideology, mythology, and an unsurpassed technique." [10] Zilboorg speaks of a traditional, almost instinctive bias, one of whose two chief elements is "the misconception that the rate of suicide increases with the development of our civilization, that in some unknown way civilization fosters suicidal tendencies within us." [11]

A statement of Steinmetz re-enforces Zilboorg's view. From his study of suicide among primitive people, Steinmetz reached the conclusion that "it seems probable from the data I have been able to collect that there is a greater propensity to suicide among savage than among civilized peoples." [12] Whether Steinmetz' conclusion would still hold if we had adequate data on suicides and partial suicides, will remain an unsolved question until we have broken through the thorny thickets of unreliable recording and squeamish acknowledgement.

III

Modern developments in motive-analysis and in the description of the fundamental characteristics of the emotional life were unknown to Durkheim, of course. Sigmund Freud had only just begun his investigations of the "unconscious" drives in human behavior when *Le Suicide* appeared, and it was to be more than a quarter of a century before his views were widely accepted after continual clinical confirmation, by which time Emile Durkheim was no longer among us. But today, over half a century since *Le Suicide* was first published, psychoanalytic psychiatry has done not overmuch to relate its revolutionary findings concerning human motives to sociological discoveries (with the exception of some ingenious references by Zilboorg). Indeed, there are psychoanalysts who appear to hold that the fundamental patterns of behavior set in infancy are not seriously affected by social factors at all, and that neuroses are not cured by social analysis. This view seems to rest on the postulate that since

[10] *American Journal of Psychiatry,* vol. 92, 1935–36, p. 1361, 1362.
[11] *Op. cit.,* p. 1351.
[12] Steinmetz, S. R., "Suicide Among Primitive People," *American Anthropologist,* 1894, quoted in Zilboorg, *op. cit.,* p. 1352.

therapy is and must be individual, and mental illness related back to the evolution of the psyche, there is no social aetiology ascribable to individual case-histories. Karl A. Menninger exemplifies this tendency.[13] From the wealth of case-history data and from his extensive and magistral clinical work, Menninger finds himself able to say only a few words in a concluding chapter titled "Social Techniques in the Service of Reconstruction," and even these few words end with the final conclusion that to the death-instinct there must be opposed the life-instinct, by calling forth from man his will to conquer his own self-annihilatory drives. But Menninger fails to analyze the relation between these self-annihilatory drives and the manner in which they are called forth by social factors, and also what social factors must be strengthened or called into being in order to overcome these drives.

IV

Though psychoanalytic psychiatry holds that within the corpus of its interpretative principles of behavior there are tools for ferreting out the causes of suicide, no one yet seems ready to commit himself unreservedly to a set of aetiological postulates, based either on empirical data or deduction from verified principles. Zilboorg writes: ". . . It is clear that the problem of suicide from the scientific point of view remains unsolved. Neither common sense nor clinical psychopathology has found a causal or even a strict empirical solution." [14]

In 1918 at a psychoanalytic symposium on suicide in Vienna, Sigmund Freud summarized the discussions as follows: "Despite the valuable material obtained in this discussion, we have not succeeded in arriving at any definite conclusion. . . . Let us therefore refrain from forming an opinion until the time comes when experience will have solved the problem." [15] Since then, extensive work has been done on suicide by expert, highly trained psychoanalysts including Freud, Zilboorg, Abraham, Menninger, Brill, and others.

But an important methodological obstacle must be pointed out, an obstacle which is almost impossible wholly to overcome at the pres-

[13] *Man Against Himself,* New York, Harcourt, Brace and Company, 1938.
[14] "Differential Diagnostic Types of Suicide," *Archives of Neurology and Psychiatry,* vol. 35, 1936, p. 271.
[15] Quoted by Zilboorg, citation note 14 above, p. 272.

ent time. Unless the individual who commits suicide has been under constant and long-time psychiatric examination (either through psychoanalysis or clinical study with full and copious life-history records), an interpretation and classification of his suicide becomes an *ex post facto* reconstruction of his life-history. This is extremely difficult, and probably impossible in most cases. Not even the most ardent opinion-poller or attitude-tester can go around interviewing suicides, and representative samples of a population can scarcely be investigated solely on the anticipatory ground that some of the items in the sample will commit suicide.

To some small degree this obstacle has been overcome by psychoanalytic psychiatrists who have re-examined the records of patients who were under treatment or examination and who committed suicide then or later, or of patients who attempted suicide unsuccessfully or toyed with the idea while under treatment. Zilboorg particularly concerned himself with this problem, in a close study of institutionalized cases, and his conclusions must therefore be looked upon as a fairly definitive statement of where psychoanalytic psychiatry stands in this regard. He found that suicide appeared in those suffering from depressive psychoses, compulsive neuroses, and schizophrenia, and was led to the conclusion: "Evidently there is no single clinical entity recognized in psychiatry that is immune to the suicidal drive." [16] Suicide, according to Zilboorg, "is to be viewed rather as a reaction of a developmental nature which is universal and common to the mentally sick of all types and probably also to many so-called normal persons." [17] He feels that "further psychoanalytic studies . . . will probably permit one later to subject the data to statistical tabulation and thus facilitate and probably corroborate the work on the clinical typology of suicides." [18]

V

But from the body of principles in psychoanalytic psychiatry we are led to certain aetiological principles concerning suicide. It is the basic hypothesis here that interrelating psychoanalytic discoveries on the motives for suicide with the social conditions under which sui-

[16] *Op. cit.*, p. 282.
[17] *Op. cit.*, p. 289.
[18] *Op. cit.*, p. 285.

cide occurs, offers the most fruitful method of advancing our knowledge of the phenomenon. This hypothesis leads to the forging of several subsidiary ones.

In attempting to arrive at such hypotheses, we must neglect the hortatory and speculative views on suicide expressed by some philosophers. Neither William James in his essay "Is Life Worth Living?" with his call to vital existence, nor Immanuel Kant in his ethical treatises with his rather prudish view that suicide is a violation of the moral law, can come to terms with modern scientific data. It is not enough to dislike the fact of suicide to assuage its havoc in human life. Nor does the defense by David Hume of the individual's right to commit suicide, nor the suicide's harmony with the denial of the will to live as in Schopenhauer, advance our scientific understanding. To announce that human beings have a social or philosophical right to commit suicide does not tell us why they do so. And until we know why they do so, we may condemn it as do James and Kant, or defend it as do Hume and Schopenhauer, but we cannot control it.

From the standpoint of psychoanalytic psychiatry, it may be said that every individual has what we may call a suicide-potential, a tendency to self-murder which varies in degree of intensity from individual to individual. To be sure, this intensity has never been measured by psychometricians, and the difficulty of measuring it is obvious and great. The degree of intensity of this potential is established in infancy and early childhood by the fears, anxieties, frustrations, loves and hatreds engendered in the individual by the family-environment in terms of eliminatory processes, weaning, sex-education, sibling rivalry, rejection or over-acceptance by the parents, degree of dependence. Where through excessive mother-love, father-rejection, inferiority induced by siblings, the individual is not readied for responsible adulthood according to the customs and mores of the society he is to participate in, the suicide-potential of an individual may be very high. At the other extreme, is the individual whose rearing has channeled the basic psychic configurations into work-activities or other activities, with no promises or rewards not possible in the world of reality; here the suicide-potential of the individual is slight. But slight as it may be, the woes, trials, and tribulations of adulthood may aggravate it to a point where self-murder becomes a possibility. Suicide is an ego-manifestation even though it is an annihilation of the ego. It is a pain inflicted on the ego, which, in being a compensation for guilt or a relief from anxiety, may be the only form of release, the utmost in going "beyond the pleasure principle."

Emotions therefore are not simple qualities of behavior explicable in terms of an immediate situation; they relate back to the life-history of the individual. Feelings of melancholia, depression, or any of the other states which Durkheim describes when he comes to classifying what he calls the morphological types of suicide in terms of their social causes, are not those of the moment of suicide; they have a long history in the individual, and although he may be stimulated to suicide by what looks like an immediate cause, no such stimulus would have resulted in the self-murder unless the underlying patterns of behavior had already been set. In the sense that all human beings have been subjected to the process of frustration and repression, of guilt and anxiety, to that extent suicide is a potential outlet under given kinds of emotional stress. That certain individuals resort to it requires investigation into the intensity with which these feelings are operative in them, as against their weaker operation in those who do not resort to it.

The most widely accepted view today in psychoanalysis is that suicide is most often a form of "displacement"; that is, the desire to kill someone who has thwarted the individual is turned back on the individual himself. Or technically stated: the suicide murders the introjected object and expiates guilt for wanting to murder the object. The ego is satisfied and the superego mollified through self-murder.

All of the emotions manifested in suicides are, then, explicable in terms of the life-history of the individual, particularly the channeling of the basic psychic configurations through the family. It may thus be possible to do what Durkheim thought was impossible—namely, classify suicides originally in terms of motives and what he calls morphologically. For the emotions of the suicide are psychogenic and unilateral in the sense that the individual emotion-structure has been laid down in infancy and childhood. It has been said that individual behavior must thus be construed not only as determined, but as *over-determined,* in the sense that it is relatively difficult to overcome the original structuring of the emotional life in the early years. But this recognition that behavior is what has been called over-determined can establish a situation where intelligence may redirect it.

Suicidal behavior is behavior which has not been redirected. The resurgence of old psychic wounds and frustrations more than offsets what life has to offer at present or in prospect. But it is important to investigate precisely what causes the resurgence, unless it is contended that no matter what life holds in store for the individual, his suicide-potential is so overwhelming that sooner or later it will win out. The struggle of the individual to win out over the death-instinct may thus be seen as a battle won, or partially or wholly lost, in infancy or childhood through the family and the schoolroom; or which is refought in the clinic or analytic room to a new stalemate or victory.

At this point, psychoanalytic psychiatry has failed to push the issue into the social realm. The basic reason for this failure lies in the preoccupation of psychoanalysis with therapy, that is, with the cure of mental illness. Now this type of therapy is obviously individual, and requires the recognition by the individual of his unconscious desires and wishes, the manner in which they have been frustrated and repressed, and the psychic toll they have taken of him. Through this recognition arrived at through "free association" in the analytic room (although on occasion possible also in clinic where depth-analysis proves unnecessary), the individual discovers why he behaves the way he does and is within the limits of the neurosis-intensity able to orient his behavior into new channels.

But though this type of therapy is necessarily individual and requires that the individual piece together the motivation-nexus for his conduct, this does not mean that social factors have not been causally involved in the neurosis. Neuroses, and suicide seems to present profound neurotic elements even when committed by a so-called normal person, must be treated medically as an individual phenomenon, but their causes may lie deep in the *social* life-history of the individual.

VI

The basic problem for social research must be to interrelate the life-histories of individual suicides and attempted suicides with sociological variables, on the hypothesis that certain social environments may (a) induce or (b) perpetuate or (c) aggravate the suicide-potential. If we can correlate for masses of data, suicides or attempted suicides with their having been induced, perpetuated, or aggravated by certain social environments, then we are in a position to establish laws of *generalized occurrence*.

It was Durkheim's contention that it was impossible to start an aetiological investigation of suicide as a *social* phenomenon by seeking to establish types of individual behavior in suicides. We now know better, and with the unflagging ability Durkheim always showed in utilizing the findings of psychologic science, there is every precedent in his work for believing that he would strive to bring his sociological analysis into harmony with psychoanalysis.

Below are offered some hypotheses for research today. Basic to all of these hypotheses is the underlying major hypothesis that suicidal behavior is a combination of psycho-instinctual impulse and social precipitation.

Problems of Collection of Data. We must investigate the possibility of getting matched samples so that individuals with the same social background may be compared—as to those who commit suicide and those who do not. This raises the intricate methodological problem whether there is any identity of social background on the emotional level. Reliable statistics on suicide cannot be compiled unless we have ready-at-hand accurate and painstakingly recorded psychiatric life-histories on all. This requires that the intimate life of the family be recorded in so far as it affects the individual, and that this be done from early age.

Hypotheses as Regards the Family. The emotional patterns of those attempting or committing suicide are laid down in infancy and early childhood by familial relationships. Socialization in the family is a process of frustration for all, and thus suicide is a potential outlet for everybody. It is necessary to find the relation of later social precipitants of suicide to the early emotional patterning.

Moreover, it is necessary to seek to interrelate the case-histories of suicides and attempted suicides with the type of family-rearing, including such variables as ethnic group, religious affiliation, income-group, size of family and place of the individual suicide in the family, educational level.

Suicide and Nationality. Suicide-rates differ from country to country. In part, this may be due to differences in record-keeping or quality of vital statistics. Countries of Germanic influence show high suicide-rates, and so does Japan. In Germanic countries this may be the result of religion. The effect of Lutheranism and Calvinism, which throw guilt-feelings back on the individual, and make frustration general with no compensating belief in the religious sanctity of such things as poverty, humility, and celibacy, must here be thoroughly investigated. The rates are not high for *Catholics* in Germanic countries.

The case of Japan (and certain segments of the population in India) involves investigation into family-life and social beliefs. The psychological development of the Japanese on the score of suicide appears to be completely inverted compared with that of our type of society. How can the same fundamental psychological mechanisms have such diametrically opposite results? This again raises the vexing problem of the relation of underlying instinctual patterns of behavior, and the different ways in which they can be objectified through social conditioning. Not to mention the manner in which patterns of social behavior are handed down from generation to generation. An interesting sidelight here is the effect which our attempt today to democratize Japan and change its people over to Western ways will have upon the Japanese suicide-rate.

Urban Life and Suicide. Present findings, that rates are high in urban areas, must be re-investigated in terms of the psychic aggravation of urban living. It is one thing to discover that urban rates are high because of aggravation and perpetuation of basic emotional patterns; it is quite another to hold that urban living *induces* suicide.

Suicide and Religious Affiliation. There is general agreement that the suicide-rate for Catholics is lowest of all religious groups. This requires investigation into the emotional outlets offered to Catholics for repressed instinctual desires, as against other religious groups.

This leads to inquiry into the causes of suicide among those Catholics who do commit it. These should show up as confirmatory of causes among non-Catholics. And what of the suicide-rate among Catholic *converts;* is this lower or higher than among other Catholics, and among other religious groups?

This in turn raises the problem whether suicides of Catholics are being accurately reported since the religious prohibition against suicide in the Catholic church may well lead to serious complications.

The suicide rates for Protestants everywhere shows itself as higher than that for Catholics, and often for the Jews. This has been ascribed by Morselli and Durkheim to the individualism emphasized by Protestantism and its emphasis upon reflective thinking and the individual conscience. If this holds true, then the most individualistic Protestant sects should show the highest suicide rates. For example, in the United States, Unitarians should show a very high rate, and high-church Episcopalians a very low rate. Do they? We do not know. Moreover, we have no data that relates psychiatric life-histories to religious affiliation. Where there has been emphasis in Unitarian churches on mental hygiene and the ministers have referred troubled members of their flock to psychoanalytic psychiatry as a general practice, the rate may be low.

Whereas in the nineteenth century, the suicide-rate for the Jews appeared to be lowest of the three main currents of religion in Western civilization, more recent figures (reflecting particularly political events in Europe under the Nazis) would probably show that it has increased beyond the other two.

The religious environment may be strictly linked with psychiatric interpretation of suicide. Durkheim's hypothesis of the comparative immunity of Catholics to suicide, which appears to be confirmed within the undoubtedly narrow limits of accuracy of contemporary actuarial and social statistics, may sink deep roots in psychiatric science. Durkheim ascribed Catholicism's immunity-giving power to the way in which it integrates the individual into the group, through a complete, thorough and all-encompassing body of common sentiments and beliefs. But to what do these common sentiments and beliefs refer? Catholic sentiments and beliefs seek to relieve the individual of guilt, make all sins expiable, establish an intricate, hierarchical system of father-substitutes, and an ingenious, poetic image of the mother.

And the less rigorous Protestant sects give no sublimatory outlet for infantile repression and frustration, through poetry, art, and ritual, and there is a rampaging of the sense of guilt which cannot be expiated through the confessional but which faces God and his elders' wrath in all its individual nakedness. Calvinism, and to no small degree, Lutheranism, deal with sin repressively and individualistically. In early Protestantism, the unconscious is thrown back upon itself, and later only exclusively non-religious social sanctions hold it in check.

Suicide and Sex. Consummated suicides are higher among men than among women, but it seems that attempted suicides are higher among women than among men. Laying aside the unreliability of the statistics, we may ask, is this because of the social position of women, or because of the emotional differences between men and women, or an interrelationship of both, and how and to what degree?

Suicide and Age. The suicide-rate is believed to increase with age. But is this not possibly because early frustrations are aggravated by failures in middle life? And what relation is there between middle-age suicide-rates and failure in intimate marital and familial relations?

The suicide-rate increases, according to the statistics we have, with advance in age. It is particularly high among the aged. Several problems arise here. First, is it that there is less reluctance to admit that death resulted from suicide when the individual is aged? Second, old-age is the time when degenerative diseases reach their mortal climax, and the affect upon the psyche may be immense. Third, shall we also call suicide the self-murder which is perpetrated in the knowledge that death is not far off anyhow? Fourth, is the *social* oblivion to which the aged are subjected an invitation to what the psychoanalysts call the desire for *maternal* oblivion; that is, a return to the kindly sleep of the unborn? These questions, and others, must obviously be to the forefront in the new branch of medicine called geriatrics, particularly in the light of what has been termed our aging population.

Suicide and Income-Groups. Suicide-rates are relatively high among the highest income-groups. Wealth, the touchstone of success in our type of society, is no assurance of immunity. Is this because of over-protection in infancy and youth? And what of suicides among self-made men? Dublin and Bunzel come to the conclusion that there is no simple causal relation between economic factors and suicide. Should, then, suicides among all economic groups show up confirmatory of the same emotional difficulties?

Suicide and War. In the midst of a shooting war, suicide-rates tend to decline; so the statistics say. But a shooting war offers for those in battle optimum opportunity for suicide to be committed without anyone being aware of it. What looks like courage may be suicidal proclivity; and anyway one may not contemplate suicide if the chances are greater that life may soon be over.

As far as the civilian population is concerned, the whole question of the impact of war upon psychic desiderata remains to be investigated.

Suicide and .Marital Status. Marital status and suicide are presumed to be strictly interrelated. Divorced men have a higher suicide-rate than the undivorced, divorced women a higher rate than undivorced women but lower than divorced men. What of suicide-rates among the divorced who have re-wed?

Among the widowed, childless marriages give high rates. But the interpretation of such phenomena seems to require generalization based on psychiatric case-histories, and some understanding of the relation of marital status to emotional life as patterned before marriage, divorce, or widowhood. And what of suicide-rates of the widowed who re-wed? If marriage protects against suicide, particularly fertile marriage, why does it not protect all such marriages? Is it that the suicide-potential overcomes even the devotion to spouse and family in the case of suicides? And if so, how did the suicide-potential get so powerful?

Suicide and the Negro. The rate for Negroes is very low compared to whites, in our society. There is obviously (if the statistics are correct) no correlation between Negro underprivilege and suicide, as might be expected. Is this because systematic oppression and underprivilege lead individuals to be adjusted to the misery and tragedy of human existence which is visited upon all? Expecting nothing of life, they may not be disappointed at how little it does offer them. But here a serious check must be made by studies of suicide among upper-class and well-educated Negroes, and among low-income and poorly educated Negroes. Do Negroes who are on the margin of upper-class white standards of living, materially and intellectually, commit suicide more than do other Negroes?

But Negro women have a rate somewhat closer to white women, than Negro men have to white men. Here intimate knowledge of the private lives of such Negro women would be of help. Also questions of high and low coloration may be necessarily involved throughout the problem of the relation of Negroes to suicide.

Suicide and Curative Therapy. Where, from analytic-room and clinic, the suicidal proclivity originally appeared high in given individuals, and curative therapy proved successful, what is the suicide-rate in later life among these individuals? Has the proclivity been redirected towards life? And what kind of life?

VII

To raise these hypotheses is certainly not to answer them.

Since the respect for human personality in our society is so great, we hold as a fundamental value an abhorrence of suicide. This in turn raises the problem of what to do about combatting suicide. From the psychiatric point of view, the answer would seem to be the vigorous training of parents and parents-to-be in the principles of mental hygiene, a rigorous training of nursery-school, grade-school, and high-school teachers in these principles, and an extensive system of psychiatric record-keeping in these "coming-of-age" organizations. Sociologically considered, it is necessary to assuage the suicidal proclivities of whatever social environments we find inducing and aggravating and perpetuating tendencies towards self-murder among individuals.

Some social scientists have for some time been chagrined by the increasing trend in professional guilds to establish programs for research, and not to give answers. Here, in the case of suicide, research has gone on for over fifty years, and some may feel that it is high time we had some answers. To this the answer is that it is only recently that we have found the key to this Pandora's box, but that this key itself can only open the box; it cannot quickly conquer the released wild and dark furies of irrationality to which human beings are heir.

All those who would enter this arena of research had better be prepared for the difficulties which await; and no ready cures should be expected. It is not administrative devices that will bring fewer suicides, but kindly ministration based on the tragedy of humanity in being imprisoned by irrational biology and psychology whose depths we have only just plumbed, and which in turn are nursed by prudery and squeamishness in acknowledging them as realities.

To fight irrationality, the findings of science and human reason must be incorporated into the social structure and the functioning of the individual in that structure. In the long tradition of Western thought, Durkheim joins with psychoanalysis in emphasizing that the life of reason has many enemies, the chief of which today is the failure to apply what we have discovered on sound evidence, to the social world about us. That he did not have our evidence at his disposal is an accident of birth and history; but, to use some of his own words in the preface to *Le Suicide:* "There is nothing necessarily discouraging in the incompleteness of the results thus far obtained; they should arouse new efforts, not surrender. . . . This makes possible some continuity in scientific labor,—continuity upon which progress depends."

GEORGE SIMPSON

SUICIDE

PREFACE

SOCIOLOGY has been in vogue for some time. Today this word, little known and almost discredited a decade ago, is in common use. Representatives of the new science are increasing in number and there is something like a public feeling favorable to it. Much is expected of it. It must be confessed, however, that results up to the present time are not really proportionate to the number of publications nor the interest which they arouse. The progress of a science is proven by the progress toward solution of the problems it treats. It is said to be advancing when laws hitherto unknown are discovered, or when at least new facts are acquired modifying the formulation of these problems even though not furnishing a final solution. Unfortunately, there is good reason why sociology does not appear in this light, and this is because the problems it proposes are not usually clear-cut. It is still in the stage of system-building and philosophical syntheses. Instead of attempting to cast light on a limited portion of the social field, it prefers brilliant generalities reflecting all sorts of questions to definite treatment of any one. Such a method may indeed momentarily satisfy public curiosity by offering it so-called illumination on all sorts of subjects, but it can achieve nothing objective. Brief studies and hasty intuitions are not enough for the discovery of the laws of so complex a reality. And, above all, such large and abrupt generalizations are not capable of any sort of proof. All that is accomplished is the occasional citation of some favorable examples illustrative of the hypothesis considered, but an illustration is not a proof. Besides, when so many various matters are dealt with, none is competently treated and only casual sources can be employed, with no means to make a critical estimate of them. Works of pure sociology are accordingly of little use to whoever insists on treating only definite questions, for most of them belong to no particular branch of research and in addition lack really authoritative documentation.

Believers in the future of the science must, of course, be anxious to put an end to this state of affairs. If it should continue, sociology would soon relapse into its old discredit and only the enemies of reason could rejoice at this. The human mind would suffer a grievous setback if this segment of reality which alone has so far denied or defied it should escape it even temporarily. There is nothing necessarily discouraging in the incompleteness of the results thus far obtained. They should arouse new efforts, not surrender. A science so recent cannot be criticized for errors and probings if it sees to it that their recurrence is avoided. Sociology should, then, renounce none of its aims; but, on the other hand, if it is to satisfy the hopes placed in it, it must try to become more than a new sort of philosophical literature. Instead of contenting himself with metaphysical reflection on social themes, the sociologist must take as the object of his research groups of facts clearly circumscribed, capable of ready definition, with definite limits, and adhere strictly to them. Such auxiliary subjects as history, ethnography and statistics are indispensable. The only danger is that their findings may never really be related to the subject he seeks to embrace; for, carefully as he may delimit this subject, it is so rich and varied that it contains inexhaustible and unsuspected tributary fields. But this is not conclusive. If he proceeds accordingly, even though his factual resources are incomplete and his formulae too narrow, he will have nevertheless performed a useful task for future continuation. Conceptions with some objective foundation are not restricted to the personality of their author. They have an impersonal quality which others may take up and pursue; they are transmissible. This makes possible some continuity in scientific labor,—continuity upon which progress depends.

It is in this spirit that the work here presented has been conceived. Suicide has been chosen as its subject, among the various subjects that we have had occasion to study in our teaching career, because few are more accurately to be defined and because it seemed to us particularly timely; its limits have even required study in a preliminary work. On the other hand, by such concentration, real laws are discoverable which demonstrate the possibility of sociology better than any dialectical argument. The ones we hope to have demonstrated will appear. Of course we must have made more than one error, must have overextended the facts observed in our inductions. But at least each proposition carries its proofs with it and we have tried to make them as numerous as possible. Most of all, we have striven in each case to separate the argument and interpretation from the facts interpreted. Thus the reader can judge what is relevant in our explanations without being confused.

Moreover, by thus restricting the research, one is by no means deprived of broad views and general insights. On the contrary, we think we have established a certain number of propositions concerning marriage, widowhood, family life, religious society, etc., which, if we are not mistaken, are more instructive than the common theories of moralists as to the nature of these conditions or institutions. There will even emerge from our study some suggestions concerning the causes of the general contemporary maladjustment being undergone by European societies and concerning remedies which may relieve it. One must not believe that a general condition can only be explained with the aid of generalities. It may appertain to specific causes which can only be determined if carefully studied through no less definite manifestations expressive of them. Suicide as it exists today is precisely one of the forms through which the collective affection from which we suffer is transmitted; thus it will aid us to understand this.

Finally, in the course of this work, but in a concrete and specific form, will appear the chief methodological problems elsewhere stated and examined by us in greater detail.[1] Indeed, among these questions there is one to which the following work makes a contribution too important for us to fail to call it immediately to the attention of the reader.

Sociological method as we practice it rests wholly on the basic principle that social facts must be studied as things, that is, as reali-

---

[1] *Les regles de la Methode sociologique*, Paris, F. Alcan, 1895. (Translated into English as *The Rules of Sociological Method*, and published by the Free Press, Glencoe, Illinois, 1950.)

ties external to the individual. There is no principle for which we have received more criticism; but none is more fundamental. Indubitably for sociology to be possible, it must above all have an object all its own. It must take cognizance of a reality which is not in the domain of other sciences. But if no reality exists outside of individual consciousness, it wholly lacks any material of its own. In that case, the only possible subject of observation is the mental states of the individual, since nothing else exists. That, however, is the field of psychology. From this point of view the essence of marriage, for example, or the family, or religion, consists of individual needs to which these institutions supposedly correspond: paternal affection, filial love, sexual desire, the so-called religious instinct, etc. These institutions themselves, with their varied and complex historical forms, become negligible and of little significance. Being superficial, contingent expressions of the general characteristics of the nature of the individual, they are but one of its aspects and call for no special investigation. Of course, it may occasionally be interesting to see how these eternal sentiments of humanity have been outwardly manifested at different times in history; but as all such manifestations are imperfect, not much importance may be attached to them. Indeed, in certain respects, they are better disregarded to permit more attention to the original source whence flows all their meaning and which they imperfectly reflect. On the pretext of giving the science a more solid foundation by establishing it upon the psychological constitution of the individual, it is thus robbed of the only object proper to it. *It is not realized that there can be no sociology unless societies exist, and that societies cannot exist if there are only individuals.* Moreover, this view is not the least of the causes which maintain the taste for vague generalities in sociology. How can it be important to define the concrete forms of social life, if they are thought to have only a borrowed existence?

But it seems hardly possible to us that there will not emerge, on the contrary, from every page of this book, so to speak, the impression that the individual is dominated by a moral reality greater than himself: namely, collective reality. When each people is seen to have its own suicide-rate, more constant than that of general mortality, that its growth is in accordance with a coefficient of acceleration characteristic of each society; when it appears that the variations through which it passes at different times of the day, month, year, merely reflect the rhythm of social life; and that marriage, divorce, the family, religious society, the army, etc., affect it in accordance with definite laws, some of which may even be numerically expressed —these states and institutions will no longer be regarded simply as characterless, ineffective ideological arrangements. Rather they will be felt to be real, living, active forces which, because of the way they determine the individual, prove their independence of him; which, if the individual enters as an element in the combination whence these forces ensue, at least control him once they are formed. Thus it will appear more clearly why sociology can and must be objective, since it deals with realities as definite and substantial as those of the psychologist or the biologist.[2]

We must, finally, acknowledge our gratitude to our two former pupils, Professor N. Ferrand of the Ecole primaire supérieure at Bordeaux and M. Marcel Mauss, agrégé de philosophie, for their generous aid and assistance. The former made all the maps contained in this book; the latter has enabled us to combine the elements necessary for Tables XXI and XXII, the importance of which will appear later. For this purpose the records of some 26,000 suicides had to be studied to classify separately their age, sex, marital status, and the presence or absence of children. M. Mauss alone performed this heavy task.

These tables have been drawn up from documents of the Ministry of Justice not appearing in the annual reports. They have been most kindly submitted to us by M. Tarde, Chief of the Bureau of Legal Statistics. His assistance is most gratefully acknowledged.

EMILE DURKHEIM

[2] Nevertheless on page 325, footnote, we shall show that this way of looking at it, far from ruling out all liberty, is the only means of reconciling liberty with the determinism revealed by the statistical data.

INTRODUCTION

I

S INCE the word "suicide" recurs constantly in the course of conversation, it might be thought that its sense is universally known and that definition is superfluous. Actually, the words of everyday language, like the concepts they express, are always susceptible of more than one meaning, and the scholar employing them in their accepted use without further definition would risk serious misunderstanding. Not only is their meaning so indefinite as to vary, from case to case, with the needs of argument, but, as the classification from which they derive is not analytic, but merely translates the confused impressions of the crowd, categories of very different sorts of fact are indistinctly combined under the same heading, or similar realities are differently named. So, if we follow common use, we risk distinguishing what should be combined, or combining what should be distinguished, thus mistaking the real affinities of things, and accordingly misapprehending their nature. Only comparison affords explanation. A scientific investigation can thus be achieved only if it deals with comparable facts, and it is the more likely to succeed the more certainly it has combined all those that can be usefully compared. But these natural affinities of entities cannot be made clear safely by such superficial examination as produces ordinary terminology; and so the scholar cannot take as the subject of his research roughly assembled groups of facts corresponding to words of common usage. He himself must establish the groups he wishes to study in order to give them the homogeneity and the specific meaning necessary for them to be susceptible of scientific treatment. Thus the botanist, speaking of flowers or fruits, the zoologist of fish or insects, employ these various terms in previously determined senses.

Our first task then must be to determine the order of facts to be studied under the name of suicides. Accordingly, we must inquire whether, among the different varieties of death, some have common qualities objective enough to be recognizable by all honest observers, specific enough not to be found elsewhere and also sufficiently kin to those commonly called suicides for us to retain the same term without breaking with common usage. If such are found, we shall combine under that name absolutely all the facts presenting these distinctive characteristics, regardless of whether the resulting class fails to include all cases ordinarily included under the name or includes others usually otherwise classified. The essential thing is not to express with some precision what the average intelligence terms suicide, but to establish a category of objects permitting this classification, which are objectively established, that is, correspond to a definite aspect of things.

Among the different species of death, some have the special quality of being the deed of the victim himself, resulting from an act whose author is also the sufferer; and this same characteristic, on the other hand, is certainly fundamental to the usual idea of suicide. The intrinsic nature of the acts so resulting is unimportant. Though suicide is commonly conceived as a positive, violent action involving some muscular energy, it may happen that a purely negative attitude or mere abstention will have the same consequence. Refusal to take food is as suicidal as self-destruction by a dagger or fire-arm. The subject's act need not even have been directly antecedent to death for death to be regarded as its effect; the causal relation may be indirect without that changing the nature of the phenomenon. The iconoclast, committing with the hope of a martyr's palm the crime of high treason known to be capital and dying by the executioner's hand, achieves his own death as truly as though he had dealt his own death-blow; there is, at least, no reason to classify differently these two sorts of voluntary death, since only material details of their execution differ. We come then to our first formula: the term suicide is applied to any death which is the direct or indirect result of a positive or negative act accomplished by the victim himself.

But this definition is incomplete; it fails to distinguish between two very different sorts of death. The same classification and treatment cannot be given the death of a victim of hallucination, who throws himself from an upper window thinking it on a level with the ground, and that of the sane person who strikes while knowing what he is doing. In one sense, indeed, few cases of death exist which are not immediately or distantly due to some act of the subject. The causes of death are outside rather than within us, and are effective only if we venture into their sphere of activity.

Shall suicide be considered to exist only if the act resulting in death was performed by the victim to achieve this result? Shall only he be thought truly to slay himself who has wished to do so, and suicide be intentional self-homicide? In the first place, this would define suicide by a characteristic which, whatever its interest and significance, would at least suffer from not being easily recognizable, since it is not easily observed. How discover the agent's motive and whether he desired death itself when he formed his resolve, or had some other purpose? Intent is too intimate a thing to be more than approximately interpreted by another. It even escapes self-observation. How often we mistake the true reasons for our acts! We constantly explain acts due to petty feelings or blind routine by generous passions or lofty considerations.

Besides, in general, an act cannot be defined by the end sought by the actor, for an identical system of behavior may be adjustable to too many different ends without altering its nature. Indeed, if the intention of self-destruction alone constituted suicide, the name suicide could not be given to facts which, despite apparent differences, are fundamentally identical with those always called suicide and which could not be otherwise described without discarding the term. The soldier facing certain death to save his regiment does not wish to die, and yet is he not as much the author of his own death as the manufacturer or merchant who kills himself to avoid bankruptcy? This holds true for the martyr dying for his faith, the mother sacrificing herself for her child, etc. Whether death is accepted merely as an unfortunate consequence, but inevitable given the purpose, or is actually itself sought and desired, in either case the person renounces existence, and the various methods of doing so can be only varieties of a single class. They possess too many essential similarities not to be combined in one generic expression, subject to distinction as the species of the genus thus established. Of course, in common terms, suicide is pre-eminently the desperate act of one who does not care to live. But actually life is none the less abandoned because one desires it at the moment of renouncing it; and there are common traits clearly essential to all acts by which a living being thus renounces the possession presumably most precious of all. Rather, the diversity of motives capable of actuating these resolves can give rise only to secondary differences. Thus, when resolution entails certain sacrifice of life, scientifically this is suicide; of what sort shall be seen later.

The common quality of all these possible forms of supreme renunciation is that the determining act is performed advisedly; that at the moment of acting the victim knows the certain result of his conduct, no matter what reason may have led him to act thus. All mortal facts thus characterized are clearly distinct from all others in which the victim is either not the author of his own end or else only its unconscious author. They differ by an easily recognizable feature, for it is not impossible to discover whether the individual did or did not know in advance the natural results of his action. Thus, they form a definite, homogeneous group, distinguishable from any other and therefore to be designated by a special term. Suicide is the one appropriate; there is no need to create another, for the vast majority of occurrences customarily so-called belong to this group. We may then say conclusively: the term *suicide is applied to all cases of death resulting directly or indirectly from a positive or negative act of the victim himself, which he knows will produce this result*. An attempt is an act thus defined but falling short of actual death.

This definition excludes from our study everything related to the suicide of animals. Our knowledge of animal intelligence does not really allow us to attribute to them an understanding anticipatory of their death nor, especially, of the means to accomplish it. Some, to be sure, are known to refuse to enter a spot where others have been killed; they seem to have a presentiment of death. Actually, however, the smell of blood sufficiently explains this instinctive reaction. All cases cited at all authentically which might appear true suicides may be quite differently explained. If the irritated scorpion pierces itself with its sting (which is not at all certain), it is probably

from an automatic, unreflecting reaction. The motive energy aroused
by his irritation is discharged by chance and at random; the creature
happens to become its victim, though it cannot be said to have had
a preconception of the result of its action. On the other hand, if some
dogs refuse to take food on losing their masters, it is because the
sadness into which they are thrown has automatically caused lack
of hunger; death has resulted, but without having been foreseen.
Neither fasting in this case nor the wound in the other have been
used as means to a known effect. So the special characteristics of
suicide as defined by us are lacking. Hence in the following we shall
treat human suicide only.[1]

But this definition not only forestalls erroneous combinations and
arbitrary exclusions; it also gives us at once an idea of the place of
suicide in moral life as a whole. It shows indeed that suicides do not
form, as might be thought, a wholly distinct group, an isolated class
of monstrous phenomena, unrelated to other forms of conduct, but
rather are related to them by a continuous series of intermediate
cases. They are merely the exaggerated form of common practices.
Suicide, we say, exists indeed when the victim at the moment he
commits the act destined to be fatal, knows the normal result of it
with certainty. This certainty, however, may be greater or less.
Introduce a few doubts, and you have a new fact, not suicide but
closely akin to it, since only a difference of degree exists between
them. Doubtless, a man exposing himself knowingly for another's
sake but without the certainty of a fatal result is not a suicide, even
if he should die, any more than the daredevil who intentionally
toys with death while seeking to avoid it, or the man of apathetic
temperament who, having no vital interest in anything, takes no
care of health and so imperils it by neglect. Yet these different ways
of acting are not radically distinct from true suicide. They result
from similar states of mind, since they also entail mortal risks not
unknown to the agent, and the prospect of these is no deterrent;
the sole difference is a lesser chance of death. Thus the scholar who

[1] A very small but highly suspicious number of cases may not be explicable in
this way. For instance as reported by Aristotle, that of a horse, who, realizing that
he had been made to cover his dam without knowing the fact and after repeated
refusals, flung himself intentionally from a cliff (*History of Animals*, IX, 47).
Horse-breeders state that horses are by no means averse to incest. On this whole
question see Westcott, *Suicide*, p. 174-179.

dies from excessive devotion to study is currently and not wholly unreasonably said to have killed himself by his labor. All such facts form a sort of embryonic suicide, and though it is not methodologically sound to confuse them with complete and full suicide, their close relation to it must not be neglected. For suicide appears quite another matter, once its unbroken connection is recognized with acts, on the one hand, of courage and devotion, on the other of imprudence and clear neglect. The lesson of these connections will be better understood in what follows.

II

But is the fact thus defined of interest to the sociologist? Since suicide is an individual action affecting the individual only, it must seemingly depend exclusively on individual factors, thus belonging to psychology alone. Is not the suicide's resolve usually explained by his temperament, character, antecedents and private history?

The degree and conditions under which suicides may be legitimately studied in this way need not now be considered, but that they may be viewed in an entirely different light is certain. If, instead of seeing in them only separate occurrences, unrelated and to be separately studied, the suicides committed in a given society during a given period of time are taken as a whole, it appears that this total is not simply a sum of independent units, a collective total, but is itself a new fact *sui generis,* with its own unity, individuality and consequently its own nature—a nature, furthermore, dominantly social. Indeed, provided too long a period is not considered, the statistics for one and the same society are almost invariable, as appears in Table I. This is because the environmental circumstances attending the life of peoples remain relatively unchanged from year to year. To be sure, more considerable variations occasionally occur; but they are quite exceptional. They are also clearly always contemporaneous with some passing crisis affecting the social state.[2] Thus, in 1848 there occurred an abrupt decline in all European states.

If a longer period of time is considered, more serious changes are observed. Then, however, they become chronic; they only prove that the structural characteristics of society have simultaneously suffered profound changes. It is interesting to note that they do not take place

[2] The numbers applying to these exceptional years we have put in parentheses.

with the extreme slowness that quite a large number of observers has attributed to them, but are both abrupt and progressive. After a series of years, during which these figures have varied within very narrow limits, a rise suddenly appears which, after repeated vacillation, is confirmed, grows and is at last fixed. This is because every breach of social equilibrium, though sudden in its appearance, takes

TABLE I—Stability of Suicide in the Principal European Countries (absolute figures)

Years	France	Prussia	England	Saxony	Bavaria	Denmark
1841	2,814	1,630		290		377
1842	2,866	1,598		318		317
1843	3,020	1,720		420		301
1844	2,973	1,575		335	244	285
1845	3,082	1,700		338	250	290
1846	3,102	1,707		373	220	376
1847	(3,647)	(1,852)		377	217	345
1848	(3,301)	(1,649)		398	215	(305)
1849	3,583	(1,527)		(328)	(189)	337
1850	3,596	1,736		390	250	340
1851	3,598	1,809		402	260	401
1852	3,676	2,073		530	226	426
1853	3,415	1,942	.	431	263	419
1854	3,700	2,198		547	318	363
1855	3,810	2,351		568	307	399
1856	4,189	2,377		550	318	426
1857	3,967	2,038	1,349	485	286	427
1858	3,903	2,126	1,275	491	329	457
1859	3,899	2,146	1,248	507	387	451
1860	4,050	2,105	1,365	548	339	468
1861	4,454	2,185	1,347	(643)		
1862	4,770	2,112	1,317	557		
1863	4,613	2,374	1,315	643		
1864	4,521	2,203	1,240	(545)		411
1865	4,946	2,361	1,392	619		451
1866	5,119	2,485	1,329	704	410	443
1867	5,011	3,625	1,316	752	471	469
1868	(5,547)	3,658	1,508	800	453	498
1869	5,114	3,544	1,588	710	425	462
1870		3,270	1,554			486
1871		3,135	1,495			
1872		3,467	1,514			

time to produce all its consequences. Thus, the evolution of suicide is composed of undulating movements, distinct and successive, which occur spasmodically, develop for a time, and then stop only to begin again. On the above table one of these waves is seen to have occurred almost throughout Europe in the wake of the events of 1848, or about the years 1850–1853 depending on the country; another began in Germany after the war of 1866, in France somewhat earlier, about 1860 at the height of the imperial government, in England about 1868, or after the commercial revolution caused by contemporary commercial treaties. Perhaps the same cause occasioned the new recrudescence observable in France about 1865. Finally, a new forward movement began after the war of 1870 which is still evident and fairly general throughout Europe.[3]

At each moment of its history, therefore, each society has a definite aptitude for suicide. The relative intensity of this aptitude is measured by taking the proportion between the total number of voluntary deaths and the population of every age and sex. We will call this numerical datum *the rate of mortality through suicide, characteristic of the society under consideration.* It is generally calculated in proportion to a million or a hundred thousand inhabitants.

Not only is this rate constant for long periods, but its invariability is even greater than that of leading demographic data. General mortality, especially, varies much more often from year to year and the variations it undergoes are far greater. This is shown assuredly by comparing the way in which both phenomena vary in several periods. This we have done in Table II. To manifest the relationship, the rate for each year of both deaths and suicides, has been expressed as a proportion of the average rate of the period, in percentage form. Thus the differences of one year from another or with reference to the average rate are made comparable in the two columns. From this comparison it appears that at each period the degree of variation is much greater with respect to general mortality than to suicide; on the average, it is twice as great. Only the minimum difference between two successive years is perceptibly the same in each case during the last two periods. However, this minimum is exceptional in the column of mortality, whereas the annual variations of suicides differ from it rarely. This may be seen by a comparison of the average differences.[4]

To be sure, if we compare not the successive years of a single period but the averages of different periods, the variations observed in the rate of mortality become almost negligible. The changes in one or the other direction occurring from year to year and due to temporary and accidental causes neutralize one another if a more extended unit of time is made the basis of calculation; and thus disappear from the average figures which, because of this elimination,

[3] In the table, ordinary figures and heavy type figures represent respectively the series of numbers indicating these different waves of movement, to make each group stand out in its distinctiveness.

[4] Wagner had already compared mortality and marriage in this way. (*Die Gesetzmässigkeit,* etc., p. 87.)

TABLE II—Comparative Variations of the Rate of Mortality by Suicide and the Rate of General Mortality

A. ABSOLUTE FIGURES

Period 1841–46	Suicides per 100,000 Inhabitants	Deaths per 1,000 Inhabitants	Period 1849–55	Suicides per 100,000 Inhabitants	Deaths per 1,000 Inhabitants	Period 1856–60	Suicides per 100,000 Inhabitants	Deaths per 1,000 Inhabitants
1841	8.2	23.2	1849	10.0	27.3	1856	11.6	23.1
1842	8.3	24.0	1850	10.1	21.4	1857	10.9	23.7
1843	8.7	23.1	1851	10.0	22.3	1858	10.7	24.1
1844	8.5	22.1	1852	10.5	22.5	1859	11.1	26.8
1845	8.8	21.2	1853	9.4	22.0	1860	11.9	21.4
1846	8.7	23.2	1854	10.2	27.4			
			1855	10.5	25.9			
Averages	8.5	22.8	Averages	10.1	24.1	Averages	11.2	23.8

B. ANNUAL RATE RELATED TO THE AVERAGE IN PERCENTAGE FORM

1841	96	101.7	1849	98.9	113.2	1856	103.5	97
1842	97	105.2	1850	100	88.7	1857	97.3	99.3
1843	102	101.3	1851	98.9	92.5	1858	95.5	101.2
1844	100	96.9	1852	103.8	93.3	1859	99.1	112.6
1845	103.5	92.9	1853	93	91.2	1860	106.0	89.9
1846	102.3	101.7	1854	100.9	113.6			
			1855	103	107.4			
Averages	100	100	Averages	100	100	Averages	100	100

C. DEGREE OF DIFFERENCE

	Between Two Consecutive Years			Above and Below the Average	
	Greatest Difference	Least Difference	Average Difference	Greatest Below	Greatest Above
			Per. 1841–46		
General mortality	8.8	2.5	4.9	7.1	4.0
Suicide-rate	5.0	1	2.5	4	2.8
			Per. 1849–55		
General mortality	24.5	0.8	10.6	13.6	11.3
Suicide-rate	10.8	1.1	4.48	3.8	7.0
			Per. 1856–60		
General mortality	22.7	1.9	9.57	12.6	10.1
Suicide-rate	6.9	1.8	4.82	6.0	4.5

show much more invariability. For example, in France from 1841 to
1870, it was in each successive ten-year period 23.18; 23.72; 22.87.
But, first, it is already remarkable that from one year to its successor
suicide is at least as stable, if not more so, than general mortality
taken only from period to period. The average rate of mortality,

50 SUICIDE

furthermore, achieves this regularity only by being general and impersonal, and can afford only a very imperfect description of a given society. It is in fact substantially the same for all peoples of approximately the same degree of civilization; at least, the differences are very slight. In France, for example, as we have just seen, it oscillates, from 1841 to 1870, around 23 deaths per 1,000 inhabitants; during the same period in Belgium it was successively 23.93, 22.5, 24.04; in England, 22.32, 22.21, 22.68; in Denmark, 22.65 (1845–49), 20.44 (1855–59), 20.4 (1861–68). With the exception of Russia, which is still only geographically European, the only large European countries where the incidence of mortality differs somewhat more widely from the above figures are Italy, where even between 1861 and 1867 it rose to 30.6, and Austria, where it was yet greater (32.52).[5] On the contrary, the suicide-rate, while showing only slight annual changes, varies according to society by doubling, tripling, quadrupling, and even more (Table III below). Accordingly, to a much higher degree than the death-rate, it is peculiar to each social group where it can be considered as a characteristic index. It is even so closely related to what is most deeply constitutional in each national temperament that the order in which the different societies

TABLE III—Rate of Suicides per Million Inhabitants in the Different European Countries

| | Period | | | Numerical Position in the | | |
	1866–70	1871–75	1874–78	1 period	2 period	3 period
Italy	30	35	38	1	1	1
Belgium	66	69	78	2	3	4
England	67	66	69	3	2	2
Norway	76	73	71	4	4	3
Austria	78	94	130	5	7	7
Sweden	85	81	91	6	5	5
Bavaria	90	91	100	7	6	6
France	135	150	160	8	9	9
Prussia	142	134	152	9	8	8
Denmark	277	258	255	10	10	10
Saxony	293	267	334	11	11	11

appear in this respect remains almost exactly the same at very different periods. This is proved by examining this same table. During the three periods there compared, suicide has everywhere increased, but in this advance the various peoples have retained their respective

[5] According to Bertillon, article *Mortalité* in the *Dictionnaire Encyclopedique des sciences medicals*, V. LXI, p. 738.

distances from one another. Each has its own peculiar coefficient of acceleration.

The suicide-rate is therefore a factual order, unified and definite, as is shown by both its permanence and its variability. For this permanence would be inexplicable if it were not the result of a group of distinct characteristics, solidary one with another, and simultaneously effective in spite of different attendant circumstances; and this variability proves the concrete and individual quality of these same characteristics, since they vary with the individual character of society itself. In short, these statistical data express the suicidal tendency with which each society is collectively afflicted. We need not state the actual nature of this tendency, whether it is a state *sui generis* of the collective mind,[6] with its own reality, or represents merely a sum of individual states. Although the preceding considerations are hard to reconcile with the second hypothesis, we reserve this problem for treatment in the course of this work.[7] Whatever one's opinion on this subject, such a tendency certainly exists under one heading or another. Each society is predisposed to contribute a definite quota of voluntary deaths. This predisposition may therefore be the subject of a special study belonging to sociology. This is the study we are going to undertake.

We do not accordingly intend to make as nearly complete an inventory as possible of all the conditions affecting the origin of individual suicides, but merely to examine those on which the definite fact that we have called the social suicide-rate depends. The two questions are obviously quite distinct, whatever relation may nevertheless exist between them. Certainly many of the individual conditions are not general enough to affect the relation between the total number of voluntary deaths and the population. They may perhaps cause this or that separate individual to kill himself, but not give society as a whole a greater or lesser tendency to suicide. As they do not depend on a certain state of social organization, they have no social repercussions. Thus they concern the psychologist, not the sociologist. The latter studies the causes capable of affecting not

---

[6] By the use of this expression we of course do not at all intend to hypostasize the collective conscience. We do not recognize any more substantial a soul in society than in the individual. But we shall revert to this point.

[7] Bk. III, Chap. 1.

separate individuals but the group. Therefore among the factors of suicide the only ones which concern him are those whose action is felt by society as a whole. The suicide-rate is the product of these factors. This is why we must limit our attention to them.

Such is the subject of the present work, to contain three parts.

The phenomenon to be explained can depend only on extra-social causes of broad generality or on causes expressly social. We shall search first for the influence of the former and shall find it non-existent or very inconsiderable.

Next we shall determine the nature of the social causes, how they produce their effects, and their relations to the individual states associated with the different sorts of suicide.

After that, we shall be better able to state precisely what the social element of suicide consists of; that is, the collective tendency just referred to, its relations to other social facts, and the means that can be used to counteract it.[8]

[8] Whenever necessary, the special bibliography of the particular questions treated will be found at the beginning of each chapter. Below are references on the general bibliography of suicide:

I. Official statistical publications forming our principal sources: Oesterreichische Statistik (Statistik des Sanitätswesens).—Annuaire statistique de la Belgique.—Zeitschrift des Koeniglisch Bayerischen statistischen Bureau.—Preussische Statistik (Sterblichkeit nach Todesursachen und Altersklassen der Gestorbenen).—Würtembürgische Jahrbücher für Statistik und Landeskunde.—Badische Statistik.—Tenth Census of the United States. Report on the mortality and vital statistics of the United States, 1880, 11th part.—Annuario statistico Italiano.—Statistica delle cause delle Morti in tutti i communi del Regno.—Relazione medico-statistica sulle conditione sanitarie dell' Exercito Italiano.—Statistische Nachrichten des Grossherzogthums Oldenburg.—Compte-rendu general de l'administration de la justice criminelle en France.

Statistisches Jahrbuch der Stadt Berlin.—Statistik der Stadt Wien.—Statistisches Handbuch für den Hamburgischen Staat.—Jahrbuch für die amtliche Statistik der Bremischen Staaten.—Annuaire statistique de la ville de Paris.

Other useful information will be found in the following articles: Platter, Ueber die Selbstmorde in Oesterreich in den Jahren 1819–1872. In Statist. Monatsh , 1876.—Brattassevic, Die Selbstmorde in Oesterreich in den Jahren 1873–77, in Stat. Monatsh., 1878, p. 429.—Ogle, Suicides in England and Wales in relation to Age, Sex, Season and Occupation. In Journal of the Statistical Society, 1886.—Rossi, Il Suicidio nella Spagna nel 1884. Arch. di psychiatria, Turin, 1886.

II. Studies on suicide in general: De Guerry, Statistique morale de la France, Paris, 1835, and Statistique morale comparée de la France et de l'Angleterre, Paris, 1864.—Tissot, De la manie du suicide et de l'esprit de révolte, de leurs causes et de leurs remèdes, Paris, 1841.—Etoc-Demazy, Recherches statistiques sur le suicide, Paris, 1844.—Lisle, Du suicide, Paris, 1856.—Wappäus, Allgemeine Bevölkerungsstatistik,

Leipzig, 1861.—Wagner, *Die Gesetzmässigkeit in den scheinbar willkürlichen menschlichen Handlungen*, Hamburg, 1864, Part 2.—Brierre de Boismont, *Du suicide et de la folie-suicide*, Paris, Germer Bailliere, 1865.—Douay, *Le suicide ou la mort volontaire*, Paris, 1870.—Leroy, *Etude sur le suicide et les maladies mentales dans le department de Seine-et-Marne*, Paris, 1870.—Oettingen, *Die Moralstatistik*, 3rd Ed., Erlangen, 1882, p. 786-832 and accompanying tables 103-120.—By the same, *Ueber acuten und chronischen Selbstmord*, Dorpat, 1881.—Morselli, *Il suicidio*, Milan, 1879.—Legoyt, *Le suicide ancien et moderne*, Paris, 1881.—Masaryk, *Der Selbstmord als sociale Massenerscheinung*, Vienna, 1881.—Westcott, *Suicide, its history, literature*, etc., London, 1885.—Motta, *Bibliografia del Suicidio*, Bellinzona, 1890.—Corre, *Crime et suicide*, Paris, 1891.—Bonomelli, *Il suicidio*, Milan, 1892. —Mayr, *Selbstmordstatistik*, In *Handwörterbuch der Staatswissenschaften, herausgegeben von Conrad, Erster Supplementband*, Jena, 1895.—Hauviller, D., *Suicide*, thesis, 1898–99.

BOOK ONE
EXTRA-SOCIAL FACTORS

CHAPTER 1
SUICIDE AND PSYCHOPATHIC STATES[1]

THERE are two sorts of extra-social causes to which one may, *a priori,* attribute an influence on the suicide-rate; they are organic-psychic dispositions and the nature of the physical environment. In the individual constitution, or at least in that of a significant class of individuals, it is possible that there might exist an inclination, varying in intensity from country to country, which directly leads man to suicide; on the other hand, the action of climate, temperature, etc., on the organism, might indirectly have the same effects. Under no circumstances can the hypothesis be dismissed unconsidered. We shall examine these two sets of factors successively, to see whether they play any part in the phenomenon under study and if so, what.

I

The annual rate of certain diseases is relatively stable for a given society though varying perceptibly from one people to another. Among these is insanity. Accordingly, if a manifestation of insanity

[1] Bibliography.—Falret, *De l'hypochondrie et du suicide,* Paris, 1822.—Esquirol, *Des maladies mentales,* Paris, 1838 (V. I, p. 526-676) and the article *Suicide,* in *Dictionnaire de médécine,* in 60 vols.—Cazauvieilh, *Du suicide et de l'aliénation mentale,* Paris, 1840—Etoc-Demazy, *De la folie dans la production du suicide,* in *Annales medico-psych.,* 1844.—Bourdin, *Du suicide considéré comme maladie,* Paris, 1845.—Dechambre, *De la monomanie homicide-suicide,* in Gazette Medic., 1852.—Jousset, *Du suicide et de la monomanie suicide,* 1858.—Brierre de Boismont, *op. cit.*—Leroy, *op. cit.—Art. Suicide,* in *Dictionnaire de médecine et de chirurgie pratique,* V. XXXIV, p. 117.—Strahan, *Suicide and Insanity,* London, 1894.

Lunier, *De la production et de la consommation des boissons alcooliques en France,* Paris, 1877.—By the same, art. in *Annales medico-psych.,* 1872; *Journal de la Soc. de stat.,* 1878.—Prinzing, *Trunksucht und Selbstmord,* Leipzig, 1895.

were reasonably to be supposed in every voluntary death, our problem
would be solved; suicide would be a purely individual affliction.[2]

This thesis is supported by a considerable number of alienists.
According to Esquirol: "Suicide shows all the characteristics of mental alienation." [3]—"A man attempts self-destruction only in delirium
and suicides are mentally alienated." [4] From this principle he concluded that suicide, being involuntary, should not be punished by
law. Falret [5] and Moreau de Tours use almost the same terms. The
latter, to be sure, in the same passage where he states his doctrine,
makes a remark which should subject it to suspicion: "Should suicide
be regarded in all cases as the result of mental alienation? Without
wishing to dispose here of this difficult question, let us say generally
that one is instinctively the more inclined to the affirmative the
deeper the study of insanity which he has made, the greater his
experience and the greater the number of insane persons whom he
has examined." [6] In 1845 Dr. Bourdin, in a brochure which at once
created a stir in the medical world, had enunciated the same opinion
even more unreservedly.

This theory may be and has been defended in two different ways.
Suicide itself is either called a disease in itself, *sui generis,* a special
form of insanity; or it is regarded, not as a distinct species, but
simply an event involved in one or several varieties of insanity, and
not to be found in sane persons. The former is Bourdin's thesis;
Esquirol is the chief authority holding the other view. "From what
has preceded," he writes, "suicide may be seen to be for us only a
phenomenon resulting from many different causes and appearing
under many different forms; and it is clear that this phenomenon is
not characteristic of a disease. From considering suicide as a disease
sui generis, general propositions have been set up which are belied
by experience." [7]

The second of these two methods of proving suicide to be a manifestation of insanity is the less rigorous and conclusive, since because

---

[2] In so far as insanity itself is purely individual. Actually it is partly a social
phenomenon. We shall return to this point.
[3] *Maladies mentales,* v. 1, p. 639.
[4] *Ibid.,* v. 1, p. 665.
[5] *Du suicide,* etc., p. 137.
[6] In *Annales medico-psych.,* v. VII, p. 287.
[7] *Maladies mentales,* v. I, p. 528.

of it negative experiences are impossible. A complete inventory of all cases of suicide cannot indeed be made, nor the influence of mental alienation shown in each. Only single examples can be cited which, however numerous, cannot support a scientific generalization; even though contrary examples were not affirmed, there would always be possibility of their existence. The other proof, however, if obtainable, would be conclusive. If suicide can be shown to be a mental disease with its own characteristics and distinct evolution, the question is settled; every suicide is a madman.

But does suicidal insanity exist?

II

Since the suicidal tendency is naturally special and definite if it constitutes a sort of insanity, this can be only a form of partial insanity, limited to a single act. To be considered a delirium it must bear solely on this one object; for, if there were several, the delirium could no more be defined by one of them than by the others. In traditional terminology of mental pathology these restricted deliria are called monomanias. A monomaniac is a sick person whose mentality is perfectly healthy in all respects but one; he has a single flaw, clearly localized. At times, for example, he has an unreasonable and absurd desire to drink or steal or use abusive language; but all his other acts and all his other thoughts are strictly correct. Therefore, if there is a suicidal mania it can only be a monomania, and has indeed been usually so called.[8]

On the other hand, if this special variety of disease called monomanias is admitted, it is clear why one readily includes suicide among them. The character of these kinds of afflictions, according to the definition just given, is that they imply no essential disturbance of intellectual functions. The basis of mental life is the same in the monomaniac and the sane person; only, in the former, a specific psychic state is prominently detached from this common basis. In short, monomania is merely one extreme emotion in the order of impulses, one false idea in the order of representations, but of such intensity as to obsess the mind and completely enslave it. Thus, ambition, from being normal, becomes morbid and a monomania of grandeur when it assumes such proportions that all other cerebral

[8] See Brierre de Boismont, p. 140.

functions seem paralyzed by it. A somewhat violent emotional access
disturbing mental equilibrium is therefore enough to cause the monomania to appear. Now suicides generally seem influenced by some
abnormal passion, whether its energy is abruptly expended or gradually developed; it may thus even appear reasonable that some such
force is always necessary to offset the fundamental instinct of self-
preservation. Moreover, many suicides are completely indistinguish-
able from other men except by the particular act of self-destruction;
and there is therefore no reason to impute a general delirium to them.
This is the reasoning by which suicide, under the appellation of
monomania, has been considered a manifestation of insanity.

But, do monomanias exist? For a long time this was not questioned; alienists one and all concurred without discussion in the
theory of partial deliria. It was not only thought confirmed by clinical
observation but regarded as corollary to the findings of psychology.
The human intelligence was supposed to consist of distinct faculties
and separate powers which usually function cooperatively but may
act separately; thus it seemed natural that they might be separately
affected by disease. Since human intelligence may be manifested
without volition and emotion without intelligence, why might there
not be affections of the intelligence or will without disturbances of
the emotions and *vice versa?* Applied to the specialized forms of
these faculties, the same principle led to the theory that a lesion may
exclusively affect an impulse, an action or an isolated idea.

Today however this opinion has been universally discarded. The
non-existence of monomanias cannot indeed be proved from direct
observation, but not a single incontestable example of their existence
can be cited. Clinical experience has never been able to observe a
diseased mental impulse in a state of pure isolation; whenever there
is lesion of one faculty the others are also attacked, and if these
concomitant lesions have not been observed by the believers in monomania, it is because of poorly conducted observations. "For example,"
writes Falret, "take an insane person obsessed by religious ideas who
would be classified among religious monomaniacs. He declares himself divinely inspired; entrusted with a heavenly mission he brings
a new religion to the world. . . . This idea will be said to be wholly
insane; yet he reasons like other men except for this series of religious
thoughts. Question him more carefully, however, and other morbid

ideas will soon be discovered; for instance, you will find a tendency to pride parallel to the religious ideas. He believes himself called upon to reform not only religion but also to reform society; perhaps he will also imagine the highest sort of destiny reserved for himself. . . . If you have not discovered tendencies to pride in this patient, you will encounter ideas of humility or tendencies to fear. Preoccupied with religious ideas he will believe himself lost, destined to perish, etc." [9] All of these forms of delirium will, of course, not usually be met with combined in a single person, but such are those most commonly found in association; if not existing at the same moment in the illness they will be found in more or less quick succession.

Finally, apart from these special manifestations, there always exists in these supposed monomaniacs a general state of the whole mental life which is fundamental to the disease and of which these delirious ideas are merely the outer and momentary expression. Its essential character is an excessive exaltation or deep depression or general perversion. There is, especially, a lack of equilibrium and coordination in both thought and action. The patient reasons, but with lacunas in his ideas; he acts, not absurdly, but without sequence. It is incorrect then to say that insanity constitutes a part, and a restricted part of his mental life; as soon as it penetrates the understanding it totally invades it.

Moreover, the principle underlying the hypothesis of monomania contradicts the actual data of science. The old theory of the faculties has few defenders left. The different sorts of conscious activity are no longer regarded as separate forces, disunited, and combined only in the depths of a metaphysical substance, but as interdependent functions; thus one cannot suffer lesion without the others being affected. This interpenetration is even closer in mental life than in the rest of the organism; for psychic functions have no organs sufficiently distinct from one another for one to be affected without the others. Their distribution among the different regions of the brain is not well defined, as appears from the readiness with which its different parts mutually replace each other, if one of them is prevented from fulfilling its task. They are too completely interconnected for insanity to attack certain of them without injury to the

[9] *Maladies mentales*, 437.

others. With yet greater reason it is totally impossible for insanity to alter a single idea or emotion without psychic life being radically changed. For representations and impulses have no separate existence; they are not so many little substances, spiritual atoms, constituting the mind by their combination. They are merely external manifestations of the general state of the centers of consciousness, from which they derive and which they express. Thus they cannot be morbid without this state itself being vitiated.

But if mental flaws cannot be localized, there are not, there cannot be monomanias properly so-called. The apparently local disturbances given this name always derive from a more extensive perturbation; they are not diseases themselves, but particular and secondary manifestations of more general diseases. If then there are no monomanias, there cannot be a suicidal monomania and, consequently, suicide is not a distinct form of insanity.

III

It remains possible, however, that suicide may occur only in a state of insanity. If it is not by itself a special form of insanity, there are no forms of insanity in connection with which it may not appear. It is only an episodic syndrome of them, but one of frequent occurrence. Perhaps this frequency indicates that suicide never occurs in a state of sanity, and that it indicates mental alienation with certainty?

The conclusion would be hasty. For though certain acts of the insane are peculiar to them and characteristic of insanity, others are common to them and to normal persons, though assuming a special form in the case of the insane. There is no reason, *a priori,* to place suicide in the first of the two categories. To be sure, alienists state that most of the suicides known to them show all the indications of mental alienation, but this evidence could not settle the question, for the reviews of such cases are much too summary. Besides, no general law could be drawn from so narrowly specialized an experience. From the suicides they have known, who were, of course, insane, no conclusion can be drawn as to those not observed, who, moreover, are much more numerous.

The only methodical procedure consists of classifying according to their essential characteristics the suicides committed by insane persons, thus forming the principal types of insane suicide, and then trying to learn whether all cases of voluntary death can be included under these systematically arranged groups. In other words, to learn whether suicide is an act peculiar to the insane one must fix the forms it assumes in mental alienation and discover whether these are the only ones assumed by it.

In general, specialists have paid little heed to classifying the suicides of the insane. The four following types, however, probably include the most important varieties. The essential elements of the classification are borrowed from Jousset and Moreau de Tours.[10]

1. *Maniacal suicide.*—This is due to hallucinations or delirious conceptions. The patient kills himself to escape from an imaginary danger or disgrace, or to obey a mysterious order from on high, etc.[11] But the motives of such suicide and its manner of evolution reflect the general characteristics of the disease from which it derives— namely, mania. The quality characteristic of this condition is its extreme mobility. The most varied and even conflicting ideas and feelings succeed each other with intense rapidity in the maniac's consciousness. It is a constant whirlwind. One state of mind is instantly replaced by another. Such, too, are the motives of maniacal suicide; they appear, disappear, or change with amazing speed. The hallucination or delirium which suggests suicide suddenly occurs; the attempt follows; then instantly the scene changes, and if the attempt fails it is not resumed, at least, for the moment. If it is later repeated it will be for another motive. The most trivial incident may cause these sudden transformations. One such patient, wishing to kill himself, had leaped into a river—one that was generally shallow. He was seeking a place where submersion was possible when a customs officer, suspecting his intention, took aim and threatened to fire if he did not leave the water. The man went peaceably home at once, no longer thinking of self-destruction.[12]

2. *Melancholy suicide.*—This is connected with a general state of extreme depression and exaggerated sadness, causing the patient no longer to realize sanely the bonds which connect him with people and things about him. Pleasures no longer attract; he sees everything

[10] See article, *Suicide,* in *Dictionnaire de médecine et de chirurgie pratique.*

[11] These hallucinations must not be confused with those tending to deceive the patient as to the risks he runs; for example, to make him mistake a window for a door. In the latter case, there is no suicide as defined above, but accidental death.

[12] Bourdin, *op. cit.,* p. 43.

as through a dark cloud. Life seems to him boring or painful. As these feelings are chronic, so are the ideas of suicide; they are very fixed and their broad determining motives are always essentially the same. A young girl, daughter of healthy parents, having spent her childhood in the country, has to leave at about the age of fourteen, to finish her education. From that moment she contracts an extreme disgust, a definite desire for solitude and soon an invincible desire to die. "She is motionless for hours, her eyes on the ground, her breast laboring, like someone fearing a threatening occurrence. Firmly resolved to throw herself into the river, she seeks the remotest places to prevent any rescue." [13] However, as she finally realizes that the act she contemplates is a crime she temporarily renounces it. But after a year the inclination to suicide returns more forcefully and attempts recur in quick succession.

Hallucinations and delirious thoughts often associate themselves with this general despair and lead directly to suicide. However, they are not mobile like those just observed among maniacs. On the contrary they are fixed, like the general state they come from. The fears by which the patient is haunted, his self-reproaches, the grief he feels are always the same. If then this sort of suicide is determined like its predecessor by imaginary reasons, it is distinct by its chronic character. And it is very tenacious. Patients of this category prepare their means of self-destruction calmly; in the pursuit of their purpose they even display incredible persistence and, at times, cleverness. Nothing less resembles this consistent state of mind than the maniac's constant instability. In the latter, passing impulses without durable cause; in the former, a persistent condition linked with the patient's general character.

3. *Obsessive suicide.*—In this case, suicide is caused by no motive, real or imaginary, but solely by the fixed idea of death which, without clear reason, has taken complete possession of the patient's mind. He is obsessed by the desire to kill himself, though he perfectly knows he has no reasonable motive for doing so. It is an instinctive need beyond the control of reflection and reasoning, like the needs to steal, to kill, to commit arson, supposed to constitute other varieties of monomania. As the patient realizes the absurdity of his wish he tries at first to resist it. But throughout this resistance he is sad,

[13] Falret, *Hypochondrie et suicide,* p. 299-307.

depressed, with a constantly increasing anxiety oppressing the pit of his stomach. Hence, this sort of suicide has sometimes been called *anxiety-suicide*. Here is the confession once made by a patient to Brierre de Boismont, which perfectly describes the condition: "I am employed in a business house. I perform my regular duties satisfactorily but like an automaton, and when spoken to, the words sound to me as though echoing in a void. My greatest torment is the thought of suicide, from which I am never free. I have been the victim of this impulse for a year; at first it was insignificant; then for about the last two months it has pursued me everywhere, *yet I have no reason to kill myself*. . . . My health is good; no one in my family has been similarly afflicted; I have had no financial losses, my income is adequate and permits me the pleasures of people of my age." [14] But as soon as the patient has decided to give up the struggle and to kill himself, anxiety ceases and calm returns. If the attempt fails it is sometimes sufficient, though unsuccessful, to quench temporarily the morbid desire. It is as though the patient had voided this impulse.

4. *Impulsive or automatic suicide.*—It is as unmotivated as the preceding; it has no cause either in reality or the patient's imagination. Only, instead of being produced by a fixed idea obsessing the mind for a shorter or longer period and only gradually affecting the will, it results from an abrupt and immediately irresistible impulse. In the twinkling of an eye it appears in full force and excites the act, or at least its beginning. This abruptness recalls what has been mentioned above in connection with mania; only the maniacal suicide has always some reason, however irrational. It is connected with the patient's delirious conceptions. Here on the contrary the suicidal tendency appears and is effective in truly automatic fashion, not preceded by any intellectual antecedent. The sight of a knife, a walk by the edge of a precipice, etc. engender the suicidal idea instantaneously and its execution follows so swiftly that patients often have no idea of what has taken place. "A man is quietly talking with his friends; suddenly he leaps, clears a parapet and falls into the water. Rescued immediately and asked for the motives of his behaviour, he knows nothing of them, he has yielded to irresistible force." [15] "The

---

[14] *Suicide et folie-suicide*, p. 397.
[15] Brierre, *op. cit.*, p. 574.

strange thing is," another says, "that I can't remember how I climbed the casement and my controlling idea at the time; for I had no thought of killing myself, or, at least I have no memory of such a thought today." [16] To a lesser degree, patients feel the impulse growing and manage to escape the fascination of the mortal instrument by fleeing from it immediately.

In short, all suicides of the insane are either devoid of any motive or determined by purely imaginary motives. Now, many voluntary deaths fall into neither category; the majority have motives, and motives not unfounded in reality. Not every suicide can therefore be considered insane, without doing violence to language. Of all the suicides just characterized, that which may appear hardest to detect of those observed among the sane is melancholy suicide; for very often the normal person who kills himself is also in a state of dejection and depression like the mentally alienated. But an essential difference between them always exists in that the state of the former and its resultant act are not without an objective cause, whereas in the latter they are wholly unrelated to external circumstances. In short, the suicides of the insane differ from others as illusions and hallucinations differ from normal perceptions and automatic impulses from deliberate acts. It is true that there is a gradual shading from the former to the latter; but if that sufficed to identify them one would also, generally speaking, have to confuse health with sickness, since the latter is but a variety of the former. Even if it were proved that the average man never kills himself and that only those do so who show certain anomalies, this would still not justify considering insanity a necessary condition of suicide; for an insane person is not simply a man who thinks or acts somewhat differently from the average.

Thus, suicide has been so closely associated with insanity only by arbitrarily restricting the meaning of the words. "That man does not kill himself," Esquirol exclaims, "who, obeying only noble and generous sentiments, throws himself into certain peril, exposes himself to inevitable death, and willingly sacrifices his life in obedience to the laws, to keep pledged faith, for his country's safety." [17] He cites the examples of Decius, of Assas, etc. Falret likewise refuses to

[16] *Ibid.*, p. 314.
[17] *Maladies mentales.* v. I, p. 529.

consider Curtius, Codrus or Aristodemus as suicides.[18] Bourdin excepts in this manner all voluntary deaths inspired not only by religious faith or political conviction but even by lofty affection. But we know that the nature of the motives immediately causing suicide cannot be used to define it, nor consequently to distinguish it from what it is not. All cases of death resulting from an act of the patient himself with full knowledge of the inevitable results, whatever their purpose, are too essentially similar to be assigned to separate classes. Whatever their cause, they can only be species of a single genus; and to distinguish among them, one must have other criteria than the victim's more or less doubtful purpose. This leaves at least a group of suicides unconnected with insanity. Once exceptions are admitted, it is hard to stop. For there is only a gradual shading between deaths inspired by usually generous feelings and those from less lofty motives. An imperceptible gradation leads from one class to the other. If then the former are suicides, there is no reason for not giving the same name to the latter.

There are therefore suicides, and numerous ones at that, not connected with insanity. They are doubly identifiable as being deliberate and as springing from representations involved in this deliberation which are not purely hallucinatory. This often debated question may therefore be solved without requiring reference to the problem of freedom. To learn whether all suicides are insane, we have not asked whether or not they act freely; we have based ourselves solely on the empirical characteristics observable in the various sorts of voluntary death.

IV

Since the suicides of insane persons do not constitute the entire genus but only a variety of it, the psychopathic states constituting mental alienation can give no clue to the collective tendency to suicide in its generality. But between mental alienation properly so-called and perfect equilibrium of intelligence, an entire series of intermediate stages exist; they are the various anomalies usually combined under the common name of neurasthenia. Let us therefore see whether they, in cases devoid of insanity, do not have an important role in the origin of the phenomenon we are studying.

[18] *Hypochondrie et suicide*, p. 3.

The very existence of insane suicide suggests the question. In fact, if a deep affection of the nervous system is enough to create suicide, a lesser affection ought to exercise the same influence to a lesser degree. Neurasthenia is a sort of elementary insanity; it must therefore have the same effects in part. It is also a much more widespread condition than insanity; it is even becoming progressively more general. The total of abnormalities thus termed may therefore be one of the factors with which the suicide-rate varies.

Besides, neurasthenia may reasonably predispose to suicide; for by temperament neurasthenics seem destined to suffer. It is well known that pain, in general, results from too violent a shock to the nervous system; a too intense nervous wave is usually painful. But this maximum intensity beyond which pain begins varies with individuals; it is highest among those whose nerves have more resistance, less in others. The painful zone begins earlier, therefore, among the latter. Every impression is a source of discomfort for the neuropath, every movement an exertion; his nerves are disturbed at the least contact, being as it were unprotected; the performance of physiological functions which are usually most automatic is a source of generally painful sensations for him. On the other hand, it is true that the zone of pleasure itself also begins at a lower level; for the excessive penetrability of a weakened nervous system makes it a prey to stimuli which would not excite a normal organism. Thus insignificant occurrences may cause such a person excessive pleasures. Seemingly he must gain on one side all that he loses on the other and, thanks to this compensatory action, he should not be less well armed than others to sustain the conflict. This is not the case however, and his inferiority is real; for current impressions, sensations most frequently reproduced by the conditions of average life, are always of a definite intensity. Life therefore is apt to be insufficiently tempered for this sufferer. To be sure, he may live with a minimum of suffering when he can live in retirement and create a special environment only partially accessible to the outer tumult; thus he sometimes is seen to flee the world which makes him ill and to seek solitude. But if forced to enter the melée and unable to shelter his tender sensitivity from outer shocks, he is likely to suffer more pain than pleasure. Such organisms are thus a favorite field for the idea of suicide.

Nor does this situation alone make life difficult for the neuropath.

Due to this extreme sensitivity of his nervous system, his ideas and feelings are always in unstable equilibrium. Because his slightest impressions have an abnormal force, his mental organization is utterly upset at every instant, and under the hammer of these uninterrupted shocks cannot become definitely established. It is always in process of becoming. For it to become stable past experiences would have to have lasting effects, whereas they are constantly being destroyed and swept away by abruptly intervening upheavals. Life in a fixed and constant medium is only possible if the functions of the person in question are of equal constancy and fixity. For living means responding appropriately to outer stimuli and this harmonious correspondence can be established only by time and custom. It is a product of experiments, sometimes repeated for generations, the results of which have in part become hereditary and which cannot be gone through all over again everytime there is necessity for action. If, however, at the moment of action everything has to be reconstructed, so to speak, it is impossible for this action to be what it should be. We require this stability not only in our relations with the physical environment, but also with the social environment. The individual can maintain himself in a society definitely organized only through possessing an equally definite mental and moral constitution. This is what the neuropath lacks. His state of disturbance causes him to be constantly taken by surprise by circumstances. Unprepared to respond, he has to invent new forms of conduct; whence comes his well-known taste for novelty. When, however, he has to adapt himself to traditional situations, improvised contrivances are inadequate against those derived from experience; and they therefore usually fail. Thus the more fixed the social system, the more difficult is life there for so mobile a person.

This psychological type is therefore very probably the one most commonly to be found among suicides. What share has this highly individual condition in the production of voluntary deaths? Can it alone, if aided by circumstances, produce them, or does it merely make individuals more accessible to forces exterior to them and which alone are the determining causes of the phenomenon?

To settle the question directly, the variations of suicide would have to be compared with those of neurasthenia. Unfortunately, the latter has not been statistically studied. But the difficulty may be indirectly solved. Since insanity is only the enlarged form of nervous degeneration, it may be granted without risk of serious error that the number of nervous degenerates varies in proportion to that of the insane, and consideration of the latter may be used as a substitute in the case of the former. This procedure would also make it possible to establish a general relation of the suicide-rate to the total of mental abnormalities of every kind.

One fact might lead us to attribute to them an undue influence; the fact that suicide, like insanity, is commoner in cities than in the country. It seems to increase and decrease like insanity, a fact which might make it seem dependent on the latter. But this parallelism does not necessarily indicate a relation of cause to effect; it may very well be a mere coincidence. The latter hypothesis is the more plausible in that the social causes of suicide are, as we shall see, themselves closely related to urban civilization and are most intense in these great centers. To estimate the possible effect of psychopathic states on suicide, one must eliminate cases where they vary in proportion to the social conditions of the latter; for when these two factors tend in the same direction the share of each cannot be determined in the final result. They must be considered only where they are in inverse proportion to one another; only when a sort of conflict exists between them can one learn which is decisive. If mental disorders are of the decisive importance sometimes attributed to them, their presence should be shown by characteristic effects, even when social conditions tend to neutralize them; and, inversely, the latter should be unable to appear when individual conditions contradict them. The following facts show that the opposite is the rule:

1. All statistics prove that in insane asylums the female inmates are slightly more numerous than the male. The proportion varies by

| | Year | No. of Men and Women to 100 Insane | |
		Men	Women
Silesia	1858	49	51
Saxony	1861	48	52
Wurtemberg	1853	45	55
Denmark	1847	45	55
Norway	1855	45 *	56 *
New York	1855	44	56
Massachusetts	1854	46	54
Maryland	1850	46	54
France	1890	47	53
France	1891	48	52

* As in Durkheim's original, though equaling more than 100 together.—Ed.

countries, but as appears in the table on the preceding page, it is in general 54 or 55 for the women to 46 or 45 for the men.

Koch has compared the results of the census taken of the total insane population in eleven different states. Among 166,675 insane of both sexes, he found 78,584 men and 88,091 women, or 1.18 insane per 1,000 male and 1.30 per 1,000 female inhabitants.[19] Mayr has discovered similar figures.

There is the question, to be sure, whether the excess of women is not simply due to the mortality of the male being higher than that of the female insane. In France, certainly, of every 100 insane who die in asylums, about 55 are men. The larger number of women recorded at a given time would therefore not prove that women have a greater tendency to insanity, but only that, in this condition as in all others, they outlive men. It is none the less true that the actual insane population includes more women than men; if, then, as seems reasonable, we apply the argument from the insane to the nervous, more neurasthenics must be admitted to exist at a given moment among females than among men. So, if there were a causal relation between the suicide-rate and neurasthenia, women should kill themselves more often than men. They should do so at least as often. For, even considering their lower mortality and correcting the

TABLE IV *—Share of Each Sex in the Total Number of Suicides

	Absolute Numbers of Suicides		To 100 Suicides Number of	
	Men	Women	Men	Women
Austria (1873–77)	11,429	2,478	82.1	17.9
Prussia (1831–40)	11,435	2,534	81.9	18.1
Prussia (1871–76)	16,425	3,724	81.5	18.5
Italy (1872–77)	4,770	1,195	80	20
Saxony (1851–60)	4,004	1,055	79.1	20.9
Saxony (1871–76)	3,625	870	80.7	19.3
France (1836–40)	9,561	3,307	74.3	25.7
France (1851–55)	13,596	4,601	74.8	25.2
France (1871–76)	25,341	6,839	79.7	21.3
Denmark (1845–56)	3,324	1,106	75.0	25.0
Denmark (1870–76)	2,485	748	76.9	23.1
England (1863–67)	4,905	1,791	73.3	26.7

* According to Morselli.

census figures accordingly, our only conclusion would be that they have a predisposition to insanity at least as great as that of men; their lower figure of mortality and their numerical superiority in all

[19] Koch, *Zur Statistik der Geisteskrankheiten*, Stuttgart, 1878, p. 73.

censuses of the insane almost exactly cancel each other. But far from
their aptitude for voluntary death being either higher or equal to
that of men, suicide happens to be an essentially male phenomenon.
To every woman there are on the average four male suicides (Table
IV, p. 71). Each sex has accordingly a definite tendency to suicide
which is even constant for each social environment. But the intensity
of this tendency does not vary at all in proportion to the psychopathic factor, whether the latter is estimated by the number of new
cases registered annually or by that of census subjects at a given
moment.

2. Table V shows the comparative strength of the tendency to
insanity among the different faiths.

**TABLE V *—Tendency to Insanity Among the Different Re-
ligious Faiths**

	Number of Insane per 1,000 Inhabitants of Each Faith		
	Protestants	Catholics	Jews
Silesia (1858)	0.74	0.79	1.55
Mecklenburg (1862)	1.36	2.00	5.33
Duchy of Baden (1863)	1.34	1.41	2.24
Duchy of Baden (1873)	0.95	1.19	1.44
Bavaria (1871)	0.92	0.96	2.86
Prussia (1871)	0.80	0.87	1.42
Wurtemberg (1832)	0.65	0.68	1.77
Wurtemberg (1853)	1.06	1.06	1.49
Wurtemberg (1875)	2.18	1.86	3.96
Grand Duchy of Hesse (1864)	0.63	0.59	1.42
Oldenburg (1871)	2.12	1.76	3.37
Canton of Bern (1871)	2.64	1.82	...

* According to Koch, *op. cit.*, p. 108-119.

Insanity is evidently much more frequent among the Jews than
among the other religious faiths; we may therefore assume that the
other affections of the nervous system are likewise in the same proportion among them. Nevertheless, the tendency to suicide among
the Jews is very slight. We shall even show later that it is least
prominent in this religion.[20] *In this case accordingly suicide varies
in inverse proportion to psychopathic states,* rather than being consistent with them. Doubtless this does not prove that nervous and
cerebral weaknesses have ever been preservatives against suicide; but
they must have very little share in determining it, since it can reach
so low a figure at the very point where they reach their fullest
development.

[20] See below, Bk. II, Chap. 2.

If Catholics alone are compared with Protestants, the inverse proportion is less general; yet it is very frequent. The tendency of Catholics to insanity is only one-third lower than that of Protestants and the difference between them is therefore very slight. On the other hand, in Table XVIII (see p. 154), we shall see that the former kill themselves much less often than the latter, without exception anywhere.

3. It will be shown later (see Table IX, p. 101), that in all countries the suicidal tendency increases regularly from childhood to the most advanced old age. If it occasionally retrogresses after the age of 70 or 80, the decrease is very slight; it still remains at this time of life from two to three times greater than at maturity. On the other hand, insanity appears most frequently at maturity. The danger is greatest at about 30; beyond that it decreases, and is weakest by far in old age.[21] Such a contrast would be inexplicable if the causes of the variation of suicide and those of mental disorders were not different.

If the suicide-rate at each age is compared, not with the relative frequency of new cases of insanity appearing during this same period, but with the proportional number of the insane population, the lack of any parallelism is just as clear. The insane are most numerous in relation to the total population at about the age of 35. The proportion remains about the same to approximately 60; beyond that it rapidly decreases. It is minimal, therefore, when the suicide-rate is maximal, and prior to that no regular relation can be found between the variations of the two.[22]

4. If different societies are compared from the double point of view of suicide and insanity, no greater relation is found between the variations of these two phenomena. True, statistics of mental alienation are not compiled accurately enough for these international comparisons to be very strictly exact. Yet it is notable that the two following tables, taken from two different authors, offer definitely concurring conclusions.

Thus the countries with the fewest insane have the most suicides; the case of Saxony is especially striking. In his excellent study on suicide in Seine-et-Marne, Dr. Leroy had already observed the same

[21] Koch, op. cit., p. 139-146.
[22] Koch, op. cit., p. 81.

TABLE VI—Relations of Suicide and Insanity in Different European Countries

A

	No. Insane per 100,000 Inhabitants	No. Suicides per 1,000,000 Inhabitants	Ranking Order of Countries for	
			Insanity	Suicide
Norway	180 (1855)	107 (1851–55)	1	4
Scotland	164 (1855)	34 (1856–60)	2	8
Denmark	125 (1847)	258 (1846–50)	3	1
Hannover	103 (1856)	13 (1856–60)	4	9
France	99 (1856)	100 (1851–55)	5	5
Belgium	92 (1858)	50 (1855–60)	6	7
Wurtemburg	92 (1853)	108 (1846–56)	7	3
Saxony	67 (1861)	245 (1856–60)	8	2
Bavaria	57 (1858)	73 (1846–56)	9	6

B *

	No. Insane per 100,000 Inhabitants	No. Suicides per 1,000,000 Inhabitants	Averages of Suicides
Wurtemburg	215 (1875)	180 (1875)	107
Scotland	202 (1871)	35	
Norway	185 (1865)	85 (1866–70)	63
Ireland	180 (1871)	14	
Sweden	177 (1870)	85 (1866–70)	
England and Wales	175 (1871)	70 (1870)	
France	146 (1872)	150 (1871–75)	164
Denmark	137 (1870)	277 (1866–70)	
Belgium	134 (1868)	66 (1866–70)	
Bavaria	98 (1871)	86 (1871)	153
Cisalpine Austria	95 (1873)	122 (1873–77)	
Prussia	86 (1871)	133 (1871–75)	
Saxony	84 (1875)	272 (1875)	

* The first part of the table is borrowed from the article, "*Alienation mentale,*" in the *Dictionnaire* of Dechambre (v. III, p. 34); the second from Oettingen, *Moralstatistik*, Table appendix 97.

fact. "Usually," he writes, "the places with a large number of mental diseases also have many suicides. However these two maxima may be completely distinct. I should even be inclined to believe that, side by side with some countries fortunate enough to have neither mental diseases nor suicides . . . there are others where mental diseases only are found." The reverse occurs in other localities.[23]

Morselli, to be sure, reaches slightly different conclusions.[24] But this is because, first, he has combined the insane proper and idiots under the common name of alienated.[25] Now, the two afflictions

[23] *Op. cit.*, p. 238.

[24] *Op. cit.*, p. 404.

[25] Morselli does not expressly say so, but it appears from the figures he gives. They are too high to represent cases of insanity only. Cf. the Table given in Dechambre's *Dictionnaire* where the distinction is made. Morselli has evidently given the total of the insane and the idiots.

are very different, especially in regard to the influence upon suicide provisionally attributed to them. Far from predisposing to suicide, idiocy seems rather a safeguard against it; for idiots are much more numerous in the country than in the city, while suicides are much rarer in the country. Two such different conditions must therefore be distinguished in seeking to determine the share of different neuropathic disorders in the rate of voluntary deaths. But even by combining them no regular parallelism is found between the extent of mental alienation and that of suicide. If indeed, accepting Morselli's figures unreservedly, the principal European countries are separated into five groups according to the importance of their alienated population (idiots and insane being combined in the same classification), and if then the average of suicides in each of these groups is sought, the following table is obtained:

	Mentally Alienated per 100,000 Inhabitants	Suicides per 1,000,000 Inhabitants
1st Group (3 countries)	from 340 to 280	157
2nd Group (3 countries)	from 261 to 245	195
3rd Group (3 countries)	from 185 to 164	65
4th Group (3 countries)	from 150 to 116	61
5th Group (3 countries)	from 110 to 100	68

On the whole it appears that there are many suicides where the insane and idiots are numerous, and that the inverse is true. But there is no consistent agreement between the two scales which would show a definite causal connection between the two sets of phenomena. The second group, which should show fewer suicides than the first, has more; the fifth, which from the same point of view should be less than all the others, is on the contrary larger than the fourth and even than the third. Finally, if for Morselli's statistics of mental alienation those of Koch are substituted, which are much more complete and apparently more careful, the lack of parallelism is much more pronounced. The following in fact is the result: [26]

	Insane and Idiots per 100,000 Inhabitants	Average of Suicides per 1,000,000 Inhabitants
1st Group (3 countries)	from 422 to 305	76
2nd Group (3 countries)	from 305 to 291	123
3rd Group (3 countries)	from 268 to 244	130
4th Group (3 countries)	from 223 to 218	227
5th Group (4 countries)	from 216 to 146	77

[26] We have omitted only Holland from the European countries reported upon by Koch, the information given concerning the intensity of the tendency to suicide there not seeming sufficient.

Another comparison made by Morselli between the different provinces of Italy is by his own admission very inconclusive.[27]

5. In short, as insanity is agreed to have increased regularly for a century [28] and suicide likewise, one might be tempted to see proof of their interconnection in this fact. But what deprives it of any conclusive value is that in lower societies where insanity is rare, suicide on the contrary is sometimes very frequent, as we shall show below.[29]

The social suicide-rate therefore bears no definite relation to the tendency to insanity, nor, inductively considered, to the tendency to the various forms of neurasthenia.

If in fact, as we have shown, neurasthenia may predispose to suicide, it has no such necessary result. To be sure, the neurasthenic is almost inevitably destined to suffer if he is thrust overmuch into active life; but it is not impossible for him to withdraw from it in order to lead a more contemplative existence. If then the conflicts of interests and passions are too tumultuous and violent for such a delicate organism, he nevertheless has the capacity to taste fully the rarest pleasures of thought. Both his muscular weakness and his excessive sensitivity, though they disqualify him for action, qualify him for intellectual functions, which themselves demand appropriate organs. Likewise, if too rigid a social environment can only irritate his natural instincts, he has a useful role to play to the extent that society itself is mobile and can persist only through progress; for he is superlatively the instrument of progress. Precisely because he rebels against tradition and the yoke of custom, he is a highly fertile source of innovation. And as the most cultivated societies are also those where representative functions are the most necessary and most developed, and since, at the same time, because of their very great complexity, their existence is conditional upon almost constant change, neurasthenics have most reason for existence precisely when they are the most numerous. They are therefore not essentially a-social types, self-eliminating because not born to live in the environment in which they are put down. Other causes must supervene upon their special organic condition to give it this twist and develop it in this

[27] *Op. cit.*, p. 403.
[28] Completely conclusive proof of it, to be sure, has never been given. Whatever the increase has been, the coefficient of acceleration is not known.
[29] See Bk. II, Chap. IV.

direction. Neurasthenia by itself is a very general predisposition, not necessarily productive of any special action, but capable of assuming the most varied forms according to circumstances. It is a field in which most varied tendencies may take root depending on the fertilization it receives from social causes. Disgust with life and inert melancholy will readily germinate amongst an ancient and disoriented society, with all the fatal consequences which they imply; contrariwise, in a youthful society an ardent idealism, a generous proselytism and active devotion are more likely to develop. Although the degenerate multiply in periods of decadence, it is also through them that States are established; from among them are recruited all the great innovators. Such an ambiguous power [30] could not therefore account for so definite a social fact as the suicide-rate.

V

But there is a special psychopathic state to which for some time it has been the custom to attribute almost all the ills of our civilization. This is alcoholism. Rightly or wrongly, the progress of insanity, pauperism and criminality have already been attributed to it. Can it have any influence on the increase of suicide? *A priori* the hypothesis seems unlikely, for suicide has most victims among the most cultivated and wealthy classes and alcoholism does not have its most numerous followers among them. But facts are unanswerable. Let us test them.

If the French map of suicides is compared with that of prosecutions for alcoholism,[31] almost no connection is seen between them. Characteristic of the former is the existence of two great centers of contamination, one of which is in the Ile-de-France, extending from

[30] A striking example of this ambiguity is seen in the similarities and differences between French and Russian literature. The sympathy accorded the latter in France shows that it does not lack affinity with our own. In the writers of both nations, in fact, one perceives a morbid delicacy of the nervous system, a certain lack of mental and moral equilibrium. But what different social consequences flow from this identical condition, at once biological and psychological! Whereas Russian literature is excessively idealistic, whereas its peculiar melancholy originating in active pity for human suffering is the healthy sort of sadness which excites faith and provokes action, ours prides itself on expressing nothing but deep despair and reflects a disquieting state of depression. Thus a single organic state may contribute to almost opposite social ends.

[31] According to the *Compte général de l'administration de la justice criminelle*, tor 1887. See Appendix I.

78									SUICIDE

there eastward, while the other lies on the Mediterranean, stretching from Marseilles to Nice. The light and dark areas on the maps of alcoholism have quite a different distribution. Here three chief centers appear, one in Normandy, especially in Seine-Inférieure, another in Finisterre and the Breton departments in general, and the third in the Rhone and the neighboring region. From the point of view of suicide, on the other hand, the Rhone is not above the average, most of the Norman departments are below it and Brittany is almost immune. So the geography of the two phenomena is too different for us to attribute to one an important share in the production of the other.

The same result is obtained by comparing suicide not with criminal intoxication but with the nervous or mental diseases caused by alcoholism. After grouping the French departments in eight classes according to their rank in suicides, we examined the average number of cases of insanity due to alcoholism in each class, using Dr. Lunier's figures.[32] We got the following result:

	Suicides per 100,000 Inhabitants (1872-76)	Alcoholic Insane per 100 Admissions (1867-69 and 1874-76)
1st Group (5 departments)	Below 50	11.45
2nd Group (18 departments)	From 51 to 75	12.07
3rd Group (15 departments)	From 76 to 100	11.92
4th Group (20 departments)	From 101 to 150	13.42
5th Group (10 departments)	From 151 to 200	14.57
6th Group (9 departments)	From 201 to 250	13.26
7th Group (4 departments)	From 251 to 300	16.32
8th Group (5 departments)	Above	13.47

The two columns do not correspond. Whereas suicides increase sixfold and over, the proportion of alcoholic insane barely increases by a few units and the growth is not regular; the second class surpasses the third, the fifth the sixth, the seventh the eighth. Yet if alcoholism affects suicide as a psychopathic condition it can do so only by the mental disturbance it causes. The comparison of the two maps confirms that of the averages.[33]

At first sight there seems to be a closer relation between the quantity of alcohol consumed and the tendency to suicide, at least for our country. Indeed most alcohol is drunk in the northern departments and it is also in this same region that suicide shows its

[32] De la production et de la consommation des boissons alcooliques en France, p. 174-175.
[33] See Appendix I.

greatest ravages. But, first, the two areas have nothing like the same outline on the two maps. The maximum of one appears in Normandy and the North and diminishes as it descends toward Paris; that of alcoholic consumption. The other is most intense in the Seine and neighboring departments; it is already lighter in Normandy and does not reach the North. The former tends westward, and reaches the Atlantic coast; the other has an opposite direction. It ends abruptly in the West, at Eure and Eure-et-Loir, but has a strong easterly tendency. Moreover, the dark area on the map of suicides formed in the Midi by Var and Bouches-du-Rhone does not appear at all on the map of alcoholism. (See Appendix I).

In short, even to the extent that there is some coincidence it proves nothing, being random. Leaving France and proceeding farther North, for example, the consumption of alcohol increases almost regularly without the appearance of suicide. Whereas only 2.84 liters of alcohol per inhabitant were consumed on the average in France in 1873, the figure rises in Belgium to 8.56 for 1870, in England to 9.07 (1870–71), in Holland to 4 (1870), in Sweden to 10.34 (1870), in Russia to 10.69 (1866) and even, at Saint Petersburg to 20 (1855). And yet whereas, in the corresponding periods, 150 suicides per million inhabitants occurred in France, Belgium had only 68, Great Britain 70, Sweden 85, Russia very few. Even at Saint Petersburg from 1864 to 1868 the average annual rate was only 68.8. Denmark is the only northern country where there are both many suicides and a large consumption of alcohol (16.51 liters in 1845).[34] If then our northern departments are distinguished both by their tendency to suicide and their addiction to alcohol, it is not because the former arises from the latter and is explained by it. The conjunction is accidental. In general, much alcohol is drunk in the North because of the local rarity of wine and its cost,[35] and perhaps because a special nourishment calculated to maintain the organism's temperature is more necessary there than elsewhere; and on the other hand the originating causes of suicide are especially concentrated in the same region of our country.

[34] See Lunier, *op. cit.*, p. 180 ff. Similar figures applying to other years are to be found in Prinzing, *op. cit.*, p. 58.

[35] The consumption of wine indeed varies rather inversely to suicide. Most wine is drunk in the Midi where suicides are least numerous. Wine is, however, not to be regarded as a guarantee against suicide for this reason.

ALCOHOLISM AND SUICIDE IN GERMANY

	Consumption of Alcohol (1884-86) Liters per Capita	Average of Suicides per 1,000,000 Inhabitants	Country
1st Group	13 to 10.8	206.1	Posnania, Silesia, Brandenburg, Pomerania
2nd Group	9.2 to 7.2	208.4	East and West Prussia, Hanover, Province of Saxony, Thuringia, Westphalia
3rd Group	6.4. to 4.5	234.1	Mecklenburg, Kingdom Saxony, Schleswig-Holstein, Alsace, Grand Duchy Hesse
4th Group	4 and less	147.9	Rhine provinces, Baden, Bavaria Wurtemburg

The comparison of the different states of Germany confirms this conclusion. If they are classified both in regard to suicide and to alcoholic consumption,[36] (see above), it appears that the group showing most suicidal tendency (the third) is one of those where least alcohol is consumed. Genuine contrasts are even found in certain details: the province of Posen is almost the least affected by suicide of the entire Empire (96.4 cases per million inhabitants), yet it is the one where most alcoholism is found (13 liters per capita); in Saxony, where suicide is almost four times as common (348 per million), only half as much alcohol is consumed. It is to be noted, finally, that the fourth group, that of the lowest consumption of alcohol, is composed almost exclusively of southern states. From another standpoint, if suicide occurs there less than in the rest of Germany, this is because its population is either Catholic or contains large Catholic minorities.[37]

[36] See Prinzing, op. cit., p. 75.

[37] To illustrate the influence of alcohol the example of Norway has occasionally been cited, where alcoholic consumption and suicide have shown a parallel decline since 1830. But in Sweden alcoholism has diminished also and proportionately, while suicide has continued to increase (115 cases per million in 1886-88, instead of 63 in 1821-30). The situation is the same in Russia.

To give the reader all sides of the question we must add that the proportion of suicides ascribed to occasional or habitual drunkenness by French statistics rose from 6.69 in 1849 to 13.41 per cent in 1876. But first, by no means all such cases are attributable to alcoholism properly so-called, nor must this be confused with simple intoxication nor frequentation of a bar. Whatever the exact meaning of these figures,

Thus no psychopathic state bears a regular and indisputable relation to suicide. A society does not depend for its number of suicides on having more or fewer neuropaths or alcoholics. Although the different forms of degeneration are an eminently suitable psychological field for the action of the causes which may lead a man to suicide, degeneration itself is not one of these causes. Admittedly, under similar circumstances, the degenerate is more apt to commit suicide than the well man; but he does not necessarily do so because of his condition. This potentiality of his becomes effective only through the action of other factors which we must discover.

moreover, they do not prove that the abuse of spiritous liquors plays a large role in the suicide-rate. Finally, it will be shown later why no great value can be attached to the information thus given by statistics concerning the presumptive causes of suicide.

CHAPTER 2

SUICIDE AND NORMAL PSYCHOLOGICAL
STATES—RACE, HEREDITY

But it might be that the tendency to suicide is based on the constitution of the individual without special dependence on the abnormal states just considered. It might consist of purely psychological phenomena without necessarily being associated with any perversion of the nervous system. Why should there not occur among men a tendency to renounce existence, which is neither a monomania nor a form of mental alienation or neurasthenia? It might even be considered an established fact if, as several writers on suicide have declared,[1] each race had a characteristic suicide-rate of its own. For a race is defined and differentiated from others only by organic-psychic characteristics. If then suicide really varied with races, it would be established that it is closely connected with some organic disposition.

But does this relation exist?

I

First, what is a race? A definition is especially necessary because not merely the layman but anthropologists themselves use the word in quite varying senses. Yet underneath the different formulae suggested for it, two basic ideas are usually found: the ideas of resemblance and filiation. One or the other occupies the first place according to different schools.

Recently race has been understood to mean an aggregate of individuals with clearly common traits, but traits furthermore due to deri-

[1] Notably Wagner, *Gesetzmässigkeit,* etc., p. 165 ff.; Morselli, p. 158; Oettingen, *Moralstatistik,* p. 760.

82

vation from a common stock. Whenever, under the influence of any cause, one or more members of the same sexual generation display a variation separating them from the rest of the species, and this variation, instead of disappearing in the next generation, becomes progressively established in the organism through heredity, it gives birth to a race. In this sense M. de Quatrefages could define race as "the total of similar individuals of the same species who transmit characteristics of a primitive sort by sexual propagation." [2] Thus understood, race would differ from species in that the original couples from whom the different races of one species derive, would in turn all be derived from a single couple. The concept would thus be clearly circumscribed and defined by the special method of filiation to which it owes its source.

Unfortunately, if this formula is accepted, the existence and area of a race can be established only by historical and ethnographic research, the results of which are always uncertain; for only very uncertain probabilities can be determined in questions of origin. Moreover, it is not certain that there are today human races answering to this definition; for, due to crossings in every direction, each of the existing varieties of our species comes from very different origins. Without any other criterion being given, it would therefore be very hard to discover the relations of the various races to suicide, for no one could say with accuracy where they begin and end. Besides, M. de Quatrefages' concept errs in prejudging the solution of a problem as yet by no means scientifically settled. It assumes in fact that racial characteristics are formed through evolution, that they are fixed in the organism only through heredity. This is contested by a whole school of anthropology that has taken the name of polygenists. According to this school, instead of being derived as a whole from one and the same couple, in the manner of biblical tradition, humanity has appeared either simultaneously or successively at different points on the globe. As these primitive stocks were formed independently of one another and in different environments, they differed from the beginning; hence, each of them would be a race. Therefore, the principal races would not have been formed by a progressive fixation of acquired differences, but from the beginning and all at once.

Since this large question is still unsettled, it would be contrary to

[2] *L'espèce humaine*, p. 28. Paris, Felix Alcan.

sound method to introduce into the notion of race the idea of filiation or kinship. It is better defined by its immediate qualities, directly
available to the observer, and without reference to the whole question
of origin. Only two characteristics are left to mark race. First, it is a
group of individuals who resemble one another. But so do members
of a single faith or profession. The distinguishing characteristic is
that the resemblances are hereditary. It is a type which, however
originally formed, is now hereditarily transmissible. In this sense,
Prichard wrote: "By the term race is understood any collection of
individuals with a greater or less number of common characteristics
transmissible by heredity, regardless of the origin of these characteristics." M. Broca uses about the same terms: "The varieties of human
kind," he writes, "have received the name of races, which suggests
the idea of a more or less direct filiation between the individuals
of the same variety, but this neither affirmatively nor negatively
determines the question of kinship between individuals of different
varieties." [3]

Put thus, the question of the constitution of races becomes soluble
but the word is then taken in such an extended sense that it becomes
illusive. It no longer represents merely the most general branches of
the species, the natural and relatively unchangeable divisions of humanity, but every sort of type. In fact, from this point of view each
group of nations the members of which, due to their centuries-
long intimate mutual relations, show partially hereditable similarities,
would constitute a race. Thus we sometimes speak of a Latin race,
an Anglo-Saxon race, etc. Only in this sense indeed can races still be
regarded as concrete, living factors of historical development. In the
mingling of peoples, in the melting-pot of history, the great primitive and fundamental races have finally become so blended with each
other that they have lost almost all individuality. If they have not
totally disappeared, at least only vague features and scattered traits
are found in imperfect combination with one another, forming no
characteristic physiognomies. A human type thus constituted merely
by the aid of often indefinite data as to height and cranial structure
is not sufficiently consistent and fixed to have attributed to it much
influence on the course of social phenomena. The more specialized
and smaller types called races in the broad sense of the word are

[3] Article, *Anthropologie*, in Dechambre's *Dictionnaire*, vol. V.

more clearly marked and necessarily have an historical role, since they are less the products of nature than of history. But they are far from objectively defined. We know little, for instance, of the exact differences between the Latin and the Anglo-Saxon races. Everybody speaks of them in his own way with little scientific exactness.

These introductory remarks give warning that the sociologist must be very careful in searching for the influence of races on any social phenomenon. For to solve such problems the different races and their distinctions from each other must be known. This caution is the more essential because this anthropological uncertainty might well be due to the fact that the word "race" no longer corresponds to anything definite. Indeed, on the one hand, the original races have only a paleontological interest, and on the other the narrower groups so designated today seem to be only peoples or societies of peoples, brothers by civilization rather than by blood. Thus conceived, race becomes almost identical with nationality.

II

Yet let us agree that there are certain great types in Europe the most general characteristics of which can be roughly distinguished and among whom the peoples are distributed, and agree to give them the name of races. Morselli distinguishes four: the *Germanic type,* including as varieties the German, the Scandinavian, the Anglo-Saxon, the Flemish; the *Celto-Roman type* (Belgians, French, Italians, Span-iards); the *Slav type* and the *Ural-Altaïc type.* We mention the last only by courtesy, since it has too few representatives in Europe for its relations to suicide to be ascertainable. In fact only the Hungarians, the Finns and the people of some Russian provinces can be assigned to it. The other three races would be classified as follows according to the decreasing order of their aptitude for suicide: first the Germanic peoples, then the Celto-Romans, and finally the Slavs.[4]

But can these differences really be imputed to the effects of race?

The hypothesis would be plausible if each group of peoples thus combined under a single name had an equally strong tendency to suicide. But the greatest differences exist between nations of the same race. While in general the Slavs have little inclination to self-de-

---

[4] We shall not mention the classifications proposed by Wagner and Oettingen; Morselli himself has criticized them decisively. (p. 160)

struction, Bohemia and Moravia are exceptions. The former has 158 suicides per million inhabitants and the second 136, while Carniola has only 46, Croatia 30, Dalmatia 14. Similarly, of all the Celto-Roman peoples, France stands out by the size of its contribution, 150 suicides per million, while in the same period Italy had only about 30 and Spain still fewer. It is hard to agree with Morselli that so great a difference is explained by the greater number of Germanic elements in France than in the other Latin countries. Granted especially that the peoples thus distinguished among their kindred are also the most civilized, it is possible to assume that what differentiates societies and so-called ethnic groups is rather their unequal degree of civilization.

Among the Germanic peoples the variety is yet greater. Of the four groups associated with this stock, three of them are much less inclined to suicide than the Slavs and Latins. These are the Flemish, numbering only 50 suicides (per million), the Anglo-Saxons with only 70; [5] as for the Scandinavians, Denmark, to be sure, has the high number of 268 suicides, but Norway has only 74.5 and Sweden only 84. So it is impossible to attribute the Danish suicide-rate to race, since it produces opposite effects in the two countries where this race is purest. In short, of all the Germanic peoples, only the Germans are in general strongly inclined to suicide. If then the terms were strictly used, it would be a question not of race but of nationality. Yet, since the existence of a German type in part, at least, hereditary, has not been disproved, the sense of the word may be stretched to the extreme extent of saying that suicide is more developed among the peoples of German race than among most Celto-Roman, Slavic or even Anglo-Saxon and Scandinavian societies. But that is all that may be concluded from the above figures. In any case, this is the only instance where a certain influence of ethnic characteristics might possibly be suspected. Even here we shall find that in reality race plays no part.

To attribute the German inclination to suicide to this cause, it is not enough to prove that it is general in Germany; for this might be due to the special nature of German civilization. But the inclination would have to be shown to be connected with an hereditary state of

[5] To explain these facts Morselli assumes, with no proof, that there are numerous Celtic elements in England and invokes the influence of climate for the Flemish.

the German organism, and that this is a permanent trait of the type, persisting even under change of social environment. Only thus could we regard it as a racial product. Let us see whether the German retains this sad primacy outside Germany, in the midst of the life of other peoples and acclimatized to different civilizations.

Austria offers us a complete laboratory for answering this question. In differing proportions in the various provinces, the Germans are mixed with a population of totally different ethnic origins. Let us see whether their presence effects an increase in the number of suicides. Table VII shows for each province the average suicide-rate for the quinquennium 1872–77 together with the numerical weight of the German elements. The races have been distinguished by their use of language; though this is not an absolutely exact standard, it is nevertheless the surest that can be employed.

TABLE VII—Comparison of Austrian Provinces with Respect to Suicide and Race

		No. of Germans per 100 Inhabitants	Suicide-rate per Million		
Provinces purely German	Lower Austria	95.90	254		
	Upper Austria	100	110	Average	
	Salzburg	100	120	106	
	Transalpine Tyrol	100	88		
Majority German	Carinthia	71.40	92		
	Styria	62.45	94	Average	
	Silesia	53.37	190	125	
Important German minority	Bohemia	37.64	158		
	Moravia	26.33	136	Average	
	Bukovina	9.06	128	140	
Small German minority	Galicia	2.72	82		Average of two Groups 86
	Cisalpine Tyrol	1.90	88		
	Littoral	1.62	38		
	Carniola	6.20	46		
	Dalmatia	.....	14		

In this table, taken from Morselli himself, not the least trace of German influence can be seen. Bohemia, Moravia and Bukovina, containing only from 37 to 9 per cent of Germans, have a higher average of suicides (140) than Styria, Carinthia and Silesia (125), where the Germans are in the great majority. The latter provinces likewise, though containing an important Slav minority, in respect to suicide exceed the only three where the population is entirely German, Upper Austria, Salzburg and Transalpine Tyrol. To be sure, Lower Austria has many more suicides than the other regions; but its excess in this respect cannot be attributed to German elements, since Germans are more numerous in Upper Austria, Salzburg and Transalpine Tyrol where there are one-half or one-third as many suicides. The real reason for the high figure is that Lower Austria's metropolis, Vienna, like all capitals has an enormous annual number of suicides; in 1876, 320 were committed per million inhabitants. The part played by the metropolis must not be attributed to race. Inversely, the small number of suicides of the Littoral, Carniola and Dalmatia is not due to the lack of Germans; for in Cisalpine Tyrol and in Galicia, where there are just as few Germans, there are from two to five times as many voluntary deaths. Even if the average suicide-rate for all eight provinces with German minorities is taken, we get the figure 86 or as much as in Transalpine Tyrol where there are only Germans, and more than in Carinthia and Styria, where they are very numerous. Thus, when the German and the Slav live in the same social environment, their tendency to suicide is approximately the same. Accordingly, the difference observed between them under other circumstances is not one of race.

It is the same with the difference noted between the German and the Latin. The two races are both found in Switzerland. Fifteen cantons are wholly or in part German. Their average of suicides is *186* (1876). Five have a French majority (Valais, Fribourg, Neufchâtel, Geneva, Vaud). Their average of suicides is *255*. The canton where fewest are committed, Valais (10 per 1 million), is the very one containing most Germans (319 per 1,000 inhabitants); on the other hand, Neufchâtel, Geneva and Vaud where the population is almost wholly Latin have respectively 486, 321 and 371 suicides.

To show more clearly the influence of the ethnic factor, if there is one, we have sought to eliminate the religious factor by which it might be obscured. To accomplish this we have compared German and French cantons of the same confession. The results of this calculation only confirm those above:

SWISS CANTONS

| German Catholics | 87 suicides | German Protestants | 293 suicides |
| French Catholics | 83 suicides | French Protestants | 456 suicides |

Among Catholics there is no perceptible difference between the races; and among Protestants, the French have the greater number.

Facts thus concur in showing that Germans commit suicide more than other peoples not because of their blood but because of the civilization in which they are reared. However, one of Morselli's proofs to establish the influence of race might at first glance seem more conclusive. The French people consists of a mixture of two principal races, the Celts and the Cymry, who from the beginning have been distinct from each other in regard to height. From the times of Julius Caesar the Cymry have been known for their great stature. Thus Broca was able to determine by the height of the inhabitants how these two races are distributed today over our territory, and he found populations of Celtic origin preponderant to the South of the Loire and those of Cymric origin to the North. This ethnographic map thus offers a certain similarity to that of suicide; for we know that suicides are concentrated largely in the northern part of the country and are, contrariwise, at their minimum in the Center and the Midi. But Morselli has gone further. He thought that he could prove the regular variation of French suicides according to the distribution of ethnic groups. To do so, he formed six groups of departments, calculated the average suicides for each, and also that of drafted soldiers exempted for insufficient height; which is an indirect way of measuring the average height of the corresponding population, because average height increases as the number of exempted men decreases. These two series of averages are found to vary inversely with one another; the fewer men exempted for insufficient height, that is, the greater the average height, the greater the number of suicides is found to be.[6]

So exact a correspondence, if established, could scarcely be explained by anything but the action of race. But Morselli's way of reaching this result forbids us to consider it final. As basis for his comparison, he took the six ethnic groups defined by Broca [7] according to the assumed degree of purity of the two races, Celts or Cymry. Despite this scholar's authority, these ethnographic questions are much too complex and still leave too much room for a variety of interpretations and contradictory hypotheses, for his proposed classification to be considered as certain. The number of more or less unverifiable historical conjectures with which he had to support it

[6] Morselli, *op. cit.*, p. 189.
[7] *Mémoires d'anthropologie*, vol. I, p. 320.

need only be considered for it to appear that though this research proves the presence in France of two clearly distinct anthropological types, the reality of the intermediate and variously shaded types which he believed he had discovered is much more doubtful.[8] If we disregard this systematic but somewhat overingenious scheme, and merely classify the departments by the average stature characteristic of each (that is, by the average number of men exempted for insufficient height), and if we confront each of these averages with that of suicide, results, quite different from Morselli's, are obtained. (See Table VIII, p. 91).

The suicide-rate does not increase in regular proportion to the relative importance of the real or supposed Cymric elements; for the first group with highest stature has fewer suicides than the second and scarcely more than the third. Likewise the last three groups are on approximately the same level,[9] however unequal in respect to height. All that these figures show is that France is divided into two halves as regards both suicides and stature, one northern with numerous suicides and high stature, the other central with lower stature and fewer suicides, but that these two progressions are not exactly paral-

[8] The existence of two great regional masses seems indisputable, one consisting of 15 northern departments in which tall stature predominates (only 39 exempt among a thousand drafted men), the other of 24 central and western departments where short stature is common (from 98 to 130 exemptions per thousand). Is this difference a result of race? This is a much more difficult question. Considering that the average stature in France has perceptibly changed within thirty years, that the number of exempt for this reason has dropped from 92.80 per thousand in 1831 to 59.40 in 1860, we have reason to doubt whether so changeable a characteristic is a very sure criterion for proving the existence of these relatively stable types called races. But, in any case, the constitution of the intermediate groups interposed between the two extreme types by Broca, their denomination and association with either the Cymric or the other stock, appears to leave place for even more doubt. Morphological reasons are impossible here. Anthropology may indeed determine the average stature in a given region, but not the crossings from which this average results. Now these intermediate statures may quite as well be due to crossings of the Celts with men of greater stature as to alliances of the Cymry with smaller men than themselves. Nor may geographical distribution be considered, for these mixed groups occur very sporadically, in the North-West (Normandy and the Lower Loire), the South-West (Aquitaine), the South (the Roman Province), in the East (Lorraine), etc. Historical arguments then remain which can only be very conjectural. Little is known historically as to how, when, and in what conditions and proportions the various invasions and infiltrations of peoples took place. Still less can history help to determine their influence on the organic constitution of these peoples.

[9] Especially if the Seine is disregarded, which, because of the exceptional conditions there, is not exactly comparable with the other departments.

TABLE VIII

DEPARTMENTS WITH HIGH STATURE

	No. of Exempt	Average Suicide-rate
1st group (9 departments)	Below 40 per 1,000 examined	180
2nd group (8 departments)	From 40 to 50	249
3rd group (17 departments)	From 50 to 60	170
General average	Below 60 per 1,000 examined	191

DEPARTMENTS WITH LOW STATURE

	No. of Exempt	Average Suicide-rate
1st group (22 departments)	From 60 to 80 per 1,000 examined	115 (without Seine, 101)
2nd group (12 departments)	From 80 to 100	88
3rd group (14 departments)	Above 100	90
General average	Above 60 per 1,000 examined	103 (with Seine) 93 (without Seine)

lel. In other words, the two great regional masses found on the ethnographic map are also found on that of suicides; but the coincidence is only broadly and generally accurate. It does not appear in the detailed variations shown by the two subjects compared.

Once the coincidence has thus been reduced to its true proportions, it is no longer a decisive proof of the ethnic elements; for it is merely a curious fact inadequate to prove a law. It may well be a mere encounter of independent factors. The hypothesis attributing it to the action of race would at least require confirmation, even demonstration, by other facts. On the contrary, it is contradicted by the following facts:

1. It would be surprising if such a collective type as the Germans, incontestably real and with so strong an affinity for suicide, should cease to show this affinity at the first modification of social conditions, and if a somewhat problematic type like the Celts or the ancient Belgians, of whom only rare vestiges remain, should exert an effective influence on this same tendency. There is too great a difference between the extremely general characteristics which memorialize this type and the complex and special character of such a tendency.

2. We shall see below that suicide was common among the ancient Celts.[10] Therefore, if it is rare today in populations of supposedly

[10] See below, Bk. II, Chap. 4.

Celtic origin, it cannot be due to a congenital characteristic of the race but to changed external circumstances.

3. Celts and Cymry are not pure primitive races; they were related "by blood, language and beliefs." [11] Both are only varieties of the tall, blond race which gradually spread throughout Europe by mass invasions or successive thrusts. The only ethnographic difference between them is that the Celts became more differentiated from the common type through crossings with the smaller, darker races of the Midi. Thus, if the greater aptitude for suicide of the Cymry has ethnic causes, it is because in them the primitive race has changed less. In that case, however, suicide should be found to increase the more, even outside of France, the more the distinctive characteristics of this race have been unaltered. This is not so. The greatest statures in Europe (1.72 m.) are found in Norway and, besides, the type probably originates in the North, especially on the Baltic coast; it is supposed also to be best preserved there. Yet the suicide-rate has not risen in the Scandinavian peninsula. The same race is said to have preserved its purity better in Holland, Belgium and England than in France,[12] and yet the last-named country shows many more suicides than the other three.

But this geographical distribution of French suicides may be explained without the necessity of introducing the obscure operations of race. Our country is known to be divided morally as well as ethnologically into two parts as yet not wholly combined. The peoples of the Center and the Midi have retained their own temperament, a characteristic way of life, and for this reason resist the ideas and manners of the North. Now the center of French civilization is in the North; it has remained essentially northern in character. Since, on the other hand, as will be seen later, this civilization contains the principal causes which lead Frenchmen to suicide, the geographical limits of its sphere of action are also those of the zone most fertile in suicides. Thus, if the people of the North commit suicide more than those of the Midi, it is not because they are more predisposed to it by their ethnic temperament, but simply that the social causes of suicide are more specially located north rather than south of the Loire.

As for the origin and persistence of this twofold moral character

---

[11] Broca, *op. cit.*, vol. I, p. 394.
[12] See Topinard, *Anthropologie*, p. 464.

of our country, this is an historical question not adequately to be solved by ethnographic considerations. It is not, or at least not only, racial differences which may have been the cause of it; for very distinct races may blend and disappear in one another. There is no such antagonism between the northern and southern types that centuries of common life have not been able to overcome. The native of Lorraine was as different from the Norman as the Provencal from the inhabitant of Ile-de-France. But for historical reasons the provincial spirit and local traditionalism have remained much stronger in the Midi, while in the North the need of facing common enemies, a closer solidarity of interests and more frequent contacts have brought the peoples together and blended their history much sooner. And just this moral levelling, by increasing the circulation of persons, ideas and things has made the latter region the birthplace of an intense civilization.[13]

III

The theory that sees race as an important factor in the inclination to suicide also implies that it is hereditary; for it can be an ethnic characteristic only on this condition. But has the heredity of suicide been proved? The question deserves close examination because of an interest of its own besides its relation to the one just considered. If indeed it were proved that the tendency to suicide is genetically transmitted, it would follow that it depends closely on a definite organic state.

But the meaning of the words must first be defined. When suicide is said to be hereditary, is it meant merely that the children of suicides by inheriting their parents' disposition are inclined in like circumstances to behave like them? In this sense the proposition is incontestable but without bearing, for then it is not suicide which is hereditary; what is transmitted is simply a certain general temperament which, in a given case, may predispose persons to the act but

---

[13] The same remark applies to Italy. There, too, suicides are more numerous in the North than in the South, and, on the other hand, the average height of the people of the North is slightly greater than that of the South. But present-day Italian civilization is Piedmontese in origin and, on the other hand, the Piedmontese are slightly taller than the people of the South. The difference, however, is slight. The maximum found in Tuscany and Venetia is 1.65 m., the minimum, in Calabria, is 1.60, at least for continental Italy. In Sardinia height diminishes to 1.58 m.

without forcing them, and is therefore not a sufficient explanation of their determination. In fact, the individual constitution which favors its appearance most, namely neurasthenia in its various forms, has been seen to offer no reason for the variations shown by the suicide-rate. But psychologists have very often spoken of heredity in quite another sense. According to this, it is the tendency to self-destruction which passes directly and wholly from parents to children and which, once transmitted, gives birth wholly automatically to suicide. It would then be a sort of psychological mechanism, semi-autonomous, not very different from a monomania and probably corresponding to a no less definite physiological mechanism. Thus it would depend essentially on individual causes.

Does observation show the existence of such an heredity? Certainly, suicide sometimes reappears in a given family with terrible regularity. Gall cites one of the most striking examples: "A certain Mr. G——, a landowner, leaves seven children and a legacy of two millions; six remain in Paris or the neighborhood and retain their share of the father's fortune; some even increase it. None have misfortunes; all enjoy good health. . . . All seven brothers committed suicide within forty years." [14] Esquirol knew a merchant, the father of six children, four of whom killed themselves; a fifth made repeated attempts.[15] In other instances, parents, children and grandchildren yield successively to the same impulse. But the example of physiologists should teach us not to draw hasty conclusions in these questions of heredity which have to be treated very carefully. Thus, there are certainly many cases where tuberculosis attacks successive generations and yet scholars still hesitate to admit that it is hereditary. The opposite seems to be the prevalent conclusion. This repetition of a disease in the same family may indeed be due not to the hereditary character of tuberculosis itself but to that of a general temperament calculated to receive and on occasion propagate the bacillus causing the disease. Here what is transmitted is not the affliction itself but only a field such as to favor its development. To have the right to reject the last explanation peremptorily, one must at least have proven that the Koch bacillus is often found in the foetus; until this has been proved the solution is doubtful. Like caution is required in

14 *Sur les fonctions du cerveau*, Paris, 1825.
15 *Maladies mentales*, vol. I, p. 582.

the problem before us. To solve it, therefore, it is not enough to cite certain facts favorable to the thesis of heredity. These facts must also be numerous enough not to be attributable to accidental circumstances —not to permit another explanation—to be contradicted by no other fact. Do they satisfy this triple condition?

To be sure, they are considered common. But to conclude that the nature of suicide is hereditary, their greater or less frequency is not enough. One must also be able to show their proportion relative to the total of voluntary deaths. If hereditary antecedents were shown for a relatively high fraction of the total number of suicides, it might be admitted that a relation of causality exists between the two facts, that suicide tends to be hereditarily transmissible. But lacking this proof it is always possible that the cases cited are due to chance combinations of various causes. Now the observations and comparisons which alone would solve this question have never been made on a large scale. Rarely is more than a certain number of interesting anecdotes adduced. Our slight information on this particular matter is in no sense conclusive; it is even somewhat contradictory. Among 39 insane cases with a more or less pronounced tendency to suicide observed by Dr. Luys in his hospital and on which he had collected fairly complete data, he found only a single case where the same tendency had already been found in the patient's family.[16] Of 265 insane, Brierre de Boismont found only 11, or 4 per cent, whose parents had committed suicide.[17] The proportion given by Cazauvieilh is much higher; he is said to have found hereditary antecedents in 13 patients out of 60, making 28 per cent.[18] According to Bavarian statistics, the only ones recording hereditary influence, it has been found about 13 in 100 times from 1857–66.[19]

Indecisive as these facts may be, if they could be accounted for only by admitting a special suicidal heredity, this hypothesis would receive a certain authority from the sheer impossibility of accounting for it otherwise. But there are at least two other causes which, especially in conjunction, may produce the same effect.

First, almost all these observations were made by alienists and,

[16] *Suicide,* p. 197.
[17] Quoted by Legoyt, p. 242.
[18] *Suicide,* pp. 17-19.
[19] See Morselli, p. 410.

consequently, among the insane. Of all diseases, insanity is perhaps the one most commonly transmitted. One may therefore question whether what is hereditary is the tendency to suicide rather than the insanity of which it is a frequent but nevertheless accidental symptom. Doubt is the more justified because according to all observers it is especially, if not exclusively, among insane suicides that cases favorable to the heredity-hypothesis occur.[20] Even under such conditions, doubtless, heredity plays an important role; but it is no longer the heredity of suicide. What is transmitted is the general mental affliction, the nervous weakness of which suicide is a contingent result, though one always to be apprehended. In this case heredity has nothing more to do with the tendency to suicide than with hemoptysis in cases of hereditary tuberculosis. If the unfortunate, with both insane persons and suicides in his family, kills himself, it is not because his parents had done the same but because they were insane. Thus, as mental sickness alters in transmission, as for example the melancholy of the progenitors becomes the chronic delirium or instinctive madness of the descendants, several members of the same family may kill themselves and all these suicides resulting from different sorts of insanity may consequently be of different types.

This primary cause, however, is not enough to explain all the facts. For it is not also proved, on the one hand, that suicide never repeats itself except among families of the insane; and on the other, the remarkable fact remains that in some of these families suicide seems to be in an endemic state, although insanity does not necessarily imply such a result. Not every insane person is impelled to self-destruction. How does it happen, then, that there are families of insane apparently predestined to it? The abundance of such cases evidently presupposes another factor than the one just mentioned, but which may be accounted for without attributing it to heredity. The contagious power of example is enough to cause it.

In fact, we shall see in one of the following chapters that suicide is very contagious. This contagiousness is specially common among individuals constitutionally very accessible to suggestion in general and especially to ideas of suicide; they are inclined to reproduce not only all that impresses them but, above all, to repeat an act toward which they have already some inclination. This twofold condition is

[20] Brierre de Boismont, *op. cit.*, p. 59; Cazauvieilh, *op. cit.*, p. 19.

found among insane or merely neurasthenic persons whose parents have committed suicide. For their nervous weakness makes them susceptible to hypnosis and simultaneously predisposes them to ready reception of the idea of self-destruction. It is not astonishing then that the memory or sight of the tragic end of their kinfolk becomes for them the source of an obsession or irresistible impulse.

Not only is this explanation as satisfactory as that of heredity, but it alone can interpret certain facts. In families where repeated suicides occur, they are often performed almost identically. They take place not only at the same age but even in the same way. In one case hanging is preferred, in another asphyxiation or falling from a high place. In a case often quoted, the resemblance is yet greater; the same weapon served a whole family at intervals of several years.[21] One more proof of heredity has been seen in these resemblances. Yet, if there are good reasons for not regarding suicide as a distinct psychological entity, how much more difficult to admit the existence of a tendency to suicide by hanging or shooting! Do not these facts rather show the great contagious influence of suicides, already recorded in their family history, on the minds of the survivors? For they must be besieged and persecuted by these memories to be persuaded to repeat the act of their predecessors so faithfully.

This explanation is made yet more probable by numerous cases of the same character where heredity is not in question and where contagion is the only source of the evil. In the epidemics to be mentioned again below, different suicides almost always resemble one another to an astonishing degree. They seem copies of one another. There is the well-known story of the fifteen patients who hung themselves in swift succession in 1772 from the same hook in a dark passage of the hospital. Once the hook was removed there was an end of the epidemic. Likewise, at the camp of Boulogne, a soldier blew out his brains in a sentry-box; in a few days others imitated him in the same place; but as soon as this was burned, the contagion stopped. All these facts show the overpowering influence of obsession, because they cease with the disappearance of the material object which evoked the idea. Thus, when suicides, obviously springing from one another, all seem to follow the same model, they may fairly be attributed to the same cause, the more so because the latter must have maximum

21 Ribot, L'hérédité, p. 145. Paris, Felix Alcan.

effect in families where everything combines to augment its power.

Furthermore, many persons feel that by imitating their parents they yield to the prestige of example. Such was the case of a family observed by Esquirol: "The youngest (brother) of between 26 and 27 years became melancholy and threw himself from the roof of his house; a second who was caring for him reproached himself with the death, made several attempts at suicide, and died a year later from prolonged and repeated self-starvation. . . . A fourth brother, a doctor, killed himself. Two years before, he had told me with terrifying despair that he would not escape his fate." [22] Moreau cites the following: an insane person whose brother and paternal uncle had committed suicide was influenced by the suicidal tendency. A brother who visited him at Charenton was appalled by the horrible thoughts he brought away and could not resist the conviction that he, too, would finally succumb.[23] A patient made the following confession to Brierre de Boismont: "Until the age of 53 I had good health; I had no troubles; my temperament was quite cheerful when, three years ago, I began to have gloomy thoughts. . . . For the past three months they have persecuted me constantly and I am tempted to kill myself at every moment. I will not conceal that my brother committed suicide at the age of 60; I had never thought seriously of it, but on reaching my fifty-sixth year the memory recurred to me more vividly and now it never leaves me." But one of the most conclusive facts is reported by Falret. A young girl of 19 learned that "an uncle on the father's side had intentionally killed himself. The news affected her greatly: she had heard it said that insanity was hereditary, and the thought that some day she might lapse into this sad condition soon obsessed her. . . . When she was in this sad state her father killed himself. From that time she felt herself absolutely destined to violent death. She had no other thought than the impending end and repeated incessantly: 'I must perish like my father and my uncle! Thus is my blood tainted!' She made an attempt. Now the man whom she thought her father was not really so. To free her from her fears her mother confessed the truth and obtained an interview for her with her real father. The great physical resemblance caused the patient's

[22] Lisle, *op. cit.*, p. 195.
[23] Brierre, *op. cit.*, p. 57.

doubts to disappear instantly. She at once gave up all idea of suicide; her cheerfulness steadily returned and she recovered her health." [24]

Thus, on one hand, the cases most favorable to the heredity of suicide do not suffice to prove its existence, and on the other, they readily admit of a different explanation. But in addition, certain statistical facts, the importance of which psychologists seem to have missed, are inconsistent with the hypothesis of hereditary transmission properly so called. They are as follows:

1. If there is an organic-psychic determinism of hereditary origin which predestines people to suicide it must have approximately equal effect upon both sexes. For as suicide by itself is in no sense sexual, there is no reason why inheritance should afflict men rather than women. Now, actually, the suicides of females are known to be very few, only a slight fraction of those of males. This would not be so if heredity had the influence attributed to it.

Shall we say that women inherit the tendency to suicide as much as men, but that it is usually offset by the social conditions peculiar to the female sex? What then shall one think of an heredity which remains latent in most cases, except that it is a vague potentiality of a wholly unproven reality?

2. Speaking of the heredity of tuberculosis, M. Grancher writes as follows: "We may recognize heredity in such a case (one of pronounced tuberculosis in a three-month old child); we are fully justified in doing so. . . . It is much less certain that tuberculosis dates from the intra-uterine period when it appears fifteen or twenty months after birth, when nothing could suggest the existence of latent tuberculosis. . . . What shall we say of tuberculosis appearing fifteen, twenty or thirty years after birth? Even supposing that a lesion existed at the beginning of life, would it not have lost its virulence after so long a time? Is it natural to accuse these fossil microbes rather than decidedly living bacilli of all the evil . . . to which the person is exposed in the course of his life?" [25] In fact, lacking the peremptory proof of being shown the germ in the foetus or the newborn child, the right to declare an affection hereditary at least requires proof that it often occurs among young children. This is why

[24] Luys, *op. cit.*, p. 201.
[25] *Dictionnaire encyclopédique des sciences méd.*, art. *Phtisie*, vol. LXXVI, p. 542.

heredity has been called the basic cause of the special madness appearing in earliest infancy and known for this reason as hereditary
insanity. Koch has even shown that where insanity is influenced by
heredity, though not completely its result, it has a much greater tendency to precocity than where it has no known antecedents.[26]

Characteristics are cited, to be sure, which are considered hereditary
and which, nevertheless, appear only at a more or less advanced age:
the beard, horns of animals, etc. But this delay is explicable under the
hypothesis of heredity only if they depend on an organic state itself
capable of development only through the evolution of the individual;
for example, heredity can evidently produce no demonstrable effects
relating to the sexual functions until puberty. But if the transmitted
characteristic is possible at any age, it should appear at once. Thus,
the longer it takes in appearing, the more clearly must heredity be
considered only a weak stimulus to its existence. It is not clear why
the tendency to suicide should share one phase of organic development rather than another. If it constitutes a definite mechanism,
capable of being transmitted fully organized, it should become active
during the very first years.

But the opposite actually takes place. Suicide is extremely rare
among children. From 1861–75 according to Legoyt, there were in
France per million children under 16 years of age 4.3 suicides by
boys, 1.8 suicides by girls. According to Morselli, the figures are
lower in Italy: they are not above 1.25 for the former and 0.33 for
the latter sex (period from 1866–75), and the proportion is essentially the same in all countries. The earliest suicides are committed at
five years and are wholly exceptional. But no proof exists that these
extraordinary facts must be attributed to heredity. It must be remembered that the child too is influenced by social causes which may
drive him to suicide. Even in this case their influence appears in the
variations of child-suicide according to social environment. They are
most numerous in large cities.[27] Nowhere else does social life commence so early for the child, as is shown by the precocity of the little
city-dweller. Introduced earlier and more completely than others to
the current of civilization, he undergoes its effects more completely

[26] *Op. cit.,* pp. 170-172.
[27] See Morselli, p. 329 ff.

and earlier. This also causes the number of child-suicides to grow with pitiful regularity in civilized lands.[28]

But in addition, not only is suicide very rare during childhood but it reaches its height only in old age, and during the interval grows steadily from age to age.

TABLE IX *—Suicides at Different Ages (per million of each age)

	France (1835–44)		Prussia (1873–75)		Saxony (1847–58)		Italy (1872–76)		Denmark (1845–56) Men & Women Combined
	Men	Women	Men	Women	Men	Women	Men	Women	
Below 16 years	2.2	1.2	10.5	3.2	9.6	2.4	3.2	1.0	113
16 to 20	56.5	31.7	122.0	50.3	210	85	32.3	12.2	272
20 to 30	130.5	44.5	231.1	60.8	396	108	77.0	18.9	307
30 to 40	155.6	44.0	235.1	55.6			72.3	19.6	426
40 to 50	204.7	64.7	347.0	61.6	551	126	102.3	26.0	576
50 to 60	217.9	74.8					140.0	32.0	702
60 to 70	274.2	83.7	529.0	113.9	906	207	147.8	34.5	
70 to 80	317.3	91.8			917	297	124.3	29.1	785
Above	345.1	81.4					103.8	33.8	642

* The elements of this table are taken from Morselli.

With some shades of difference these relations are the same in all countries. Sweden is the only society in which the maximum comes between 40 and 50 years. Everywhere else, it occurs only in the last or next to the last period of life and, everywhere alike, with very slight exceptions due perhaps to errors of tabulation,[29] the increase to this extreme limit is continuous. The decrease observable beyond 80 years is not absolutely general and in any case is very slight. The contingent of this age is somewhat below that of the septuagenarians, but is above the others or, at least, most of them. How therefore can one attribute to heredity a tendency appearing only in the adult *and which, from that period on, continues to increase with the advance of age?* How consider an affliction congenital which, non-existent or very

---

[28] See Legoyt, p. 158 ff. Paris, Felix Alcan.

[29] For men only one case, that of Italy, is known to us where a stationary phase occurs between 30 and 40 years. For women there is a moment of pause at the same age, which is general and must therefore be real. It marks a stage in female life. As it is peculiar to the unmarried, it probably corresponds to the intermediate period when disappointments and frustrations caused by celibacy begin to be less felt, and when the moral isolation felt by the unmarried woman when alone in the world at a more advanced age does not yet produce all its effects.

weak during childhood, develops constantly and reaches its maximum intensity only among the aged?

The law of homochronous heredity cannot be invoked for the species. It practically states that under certain circumstances the inherited characteristic appears among the descendants at approximately the same age as among the parents. This is not true of suicide, which, beyond 10 or 15 years, is common to all ages. Its character is not to appear at a definite moment in life but to progress steadily from age to age. This constant progression shows that its cause itself develops as a man grows older. Heredity does not fulfill this condition; for by definition heredity is what it is and what it may be immediately on full fecundation. Does the suicidal tendency then exist latently from birth, but appear only under the influence of other forces which emerge late and develop progressively? This would indeed reduce hereditary influence at most to a very general, vague predisposition; for, if it requires the aid of another factor so much that its action is felt only with and in proportion to the occurrence of this factor, the latter must be regarded as the true cause.

In short, the variation of suicide with age shows that no organic-psychic state can possibly be its determining cause. For everything organic, being subject to the vital rhythm, successively experiences phases of growth, stoppage and, finally, regression. No biological or psychological characteristic progresses indefinitely; all, having reached a moment of climax, become decadent. Suicide, on the contrary, achieves its culminating point only at the final limits of human existence. Even the decrease often observed at about 80 years of age is not only slight and not absolutely general, but only relative, since nonagenarians commit suicide as much or more than sexagenarians and, especially, more than men in full maturity. Does not this prove that the cause of the variations of suicide cannot be a congenital and invariable impulse, but the progressive action of social life? Just as suicide appears more or less early depending on the age at which men enter into society, it grows to the extent that they are more completely involved in it.

We are thus referred back to the conclusion of the preceding chapter. Doubtless, suicide is impossible if the individual's constitution is opposed to it. But the individual state most favorable to it is not a definite and automatic tendency (except in the case of the insane), but a general, vague aptitude, which may assume various forms according to circumstances, permitting but not necessarily implying suicide and therefore giving no explanation for it.

CHAPTER 3
SUICIDE AND COSMIC FACTORS[1]

B UT if individual predispositions are not by themselves the determining causes of suicide, perhaps they are more active in combination with certain cosmic factors. Just as the material environment at times causes the appearance of diseases which, without it, would remain dormant, it might be capable of activating the general and merely potential natural apitudes of certain persons for suicide. In that case, the suicide-rate need not be regarded as a social phenomenon; due to the cooperation between certain physical causes and an organic-psychic state, it would spring wholly or chiefly from abnormal psychology. It might, to be sure, be hard to explain how, in such cases, suicide can be so intimately typical in each social group; for the cosmic environment does not greatly differ from country to country. One important fact, however, would have been seized: that at least some of the variations connected with this phenomenon might be accounted for without reference to social causes.

Among such factors an influence on suicide has been attributed to only two: climate and seasonal temperature.

I

Suicides are distributed as follows on the map of Europe, according to the varying degrees of latitude:

[1] *Bibliography.*—Lombroso, *Pensiero e Meteore;* Ferri, *Variations thermométriques et criminalité.* In *Archives d'Anth, criminelle,* 1887; Corre, *Le délit et le suicide à Brest.* In *Arch. d'Anth. crim.,* 1890, p. 109 ff., 259 ff.; by the same, *Crime et suicide,* pp. 605-639; Morselli, pp. 103-157.

36th-43rd degree of latitude	21.1 suicides per million inhabitants
43rd-50th degree of latitude	93.3 suicides per million inhabitants
50th-55th degree of latitude	172.5 suicides per million inhabitants
Beyond 55th degree of latitude	88.1 suicides per million inhabitants

Suicide is therefore at a minimum in the South and North of Europe; it is most developed in the Center. More exactly, Morselli has stated that the space between the 47th and 57th degrees of latitude, on the one hand, and the 20th and 40th of longitude on the other, was the area most favorable to suicide. This zone coincides approximately with the most temperate region of Europe. Is this coincidence to be regarded as an effect of climatic influences?

Morselli advanced this thesis, though somewhat hesitantly. Indeed, the relation is not readily discernible between temperate climate and the tendency to suicide; to require such an hypothesis the facts must be in unusual agreement. Now, far from there being a relation between suicide and a given climate, we know suicide to have flourished in all climates. Italy is today relatively exempt; but it was very frequent there at the time of the Empire when Rome was the capital of civilized Europe. It has also been highly developed at certain epochs under the burning sun of India.[2]

The very shape of this zone shows that climate is not the cause of the numerous suicides committed there. The area formed by it on the map is not a single, fairly equal and homogeneous strip, including all the countries having the same climate, but two distinct areas: one having Ile-de-France and neighboring departments as a center, the other Saxony and Prussia. They therefore coincide with the two principal centers of European civilization, not with a clearly defined climatic region. We must therefore seek the cause of the unequal inclination of peoples for suicide, not in the mysterious effects of climate but in the nature of this civilization, in the manner of its distribution among the different countries.

Another fact, already mentioned by Guerry, and confirmed through new observations by Morselli, which is fairly general though not without exceptions, may be similarly explained. In the countries outside the central zone, their regions closest to it, whether North or South, are those most stricken with suicide. Thus, it is most developed in

[2] See below, Bk. II, Chap. 4.

Italy in the North, while in England and Belgium it is more so in the South. But there is no reason to ascribe these facts to the proximity to the temperate climate. Is it not more probable that the ideas and sentiments, in short, the social currents so strongly influencing the inhabitants of Northern France and of Northern Germany to suicide, reappear in the neighboring countries of a somewhat similar way of life, but with less intensity? Another fact shows the great influence of social causes upon this distribution of suicide. Until 1870 the northern provinces of Italy showed most suicides, then the center and thirdly the south. But the difference between North and Center has gradually diminished and their respective ranks have been finally reversed (See Table X). Yet the climate of the different regions has remained the same. The change consists in the movement of the Italian capital to the center of the country as a result of the conquest of Rome in 1870. Scientific, artistic and economic activity shifted in the same manner. Suicides followed along.

One need dwell no further on an hypothesis proved by nothing and disproved by so many facts.

TABLE X—Regional Distribution of Suicide in Italy

	Suicides per Million Inhabitants			Ratio of Each Region Expressed in Terms of the North Represented by 100		
	1866–67	1864–76	1884–86	1866–67	1864–76	1884–86
North	33.8	43.6	63	100	100	100
Center	25.6	40.8	88	75	93	139
South	8.3	16.5	21	24	37	33

II

The influence of seasonal temperature seems better demonstrated. The facts are invariable though they may be variously interpreted.

If without reference to them one were to try to foretell logically what season should be most favorable to suicide, one might easily assume the season when the sky is darkest, and the temperature lowest or most humid. Does not the desolate appearance of nature at such times tend to incline men to revery, awaken unhappy passions, provoke melancholy? Moreover, this is the time when life is most difficult, because a more abundant sustenance is necessary to replace the lack of natural warmth, and because this is harder to obtain. For this very reason Montesquieu considered cold, foggy countries most favorable to the development of suicide, and this opinion was long

held. Applying it to the seasons, one would expect the height of suicide to occur in autumn. Although Esquirol had already expressed
doubts as to the exactness of this theory, Falret still accepted it in
principle.[3] Today statistics have definitely refuted it. Neither in winter nor in autumn does suicide reach its maximum, but during the
fine season when nature is most smiling and the temperature mildest.
Man prefers to abandon life when it is least difficult. If the year is
divided into two halves representing respectively the six warmest
months (from March to August inclusive) and the six coldest, the
former always include more suicides. *Not one country is an exception
to this law.* The proportion is everywhere almost exactly the same.
Of 1,000 annual suicides from 590 to 600 are committed during the
fine season and only 400 during the remainder of the year.

The relation of suicide to the variations of temperature may be determined even more precisely.

If it is agreed to call winter the three months from December to
February inclusive, spring the three months from March to May,
summer, from June to August and autumn the three following
months, and if these four seasons are classified according to the importance of their suicide-mortality, summer is found to have the first
place almost everywhere. Morselli was able from this point of view
to compare 34 different periods among 18 European states, and has
established that in 30 cases, or 88 per cent, the maximum of suicides
occurs during the summer season, in only three cases in spring, and in
only one case in autumn. This last irregularity, observed only in the
Grand-Duchy of Baden and at a single moment of its history, is
valueless, for it results from a calculation bearing on too brief a period; besides, it never recurred. The other three exceptions are
scarcely more significant. They occur in Holland, Ireland and Sweden.
For the first two countries the available figures which were the base
for the seasonal averages are too uncertain for anything positive to be
concluded; there are only 387 cases for Holland and 755 for Ireland.
In general, the statistics for these two peoples are not wholly authoritative. For Sweden, finally, the fact has been noted only for the period 1835–51. If we consider only the states concerning which there
are authentic figures, the law may be held to be absolute and universal.

[3] *De l'hypochondrie*, etc., p. 28.

The period of the minimum is no less regular: 30 times out of 34, or 88 per cent it occurs in winter; the other four times in autumn. The four countries departing from the rule are Ireland and Holland (as in the case above), the canton of Berne, and Norway. We know the import of the first two anomalies; the third has still less value, having been observed only from among 97 suicides in all. In short, 26 out of 34 times, or 76 per cent, the seasons come in the following order: summer, spring, autumn, winter. This relation is true without exception for Denmark, Belgium, France, Prussia, Saxony, Bavaria, Wurttemberg, Austria, Switzerland, Italy and Spain.

Not only are the seasons identically ranked, but the proportional share of each barely differs from country to country. To emphasize this uniformity, we have shown in Table XI the share of each season in the principal European states in relation to the annual total considered as 1,000. The same series of numbers is seen to recur almost identically in each column.

From these incontestable facts, Ferri and Morselli have concluded that temperature had a direct influence on the tendency to suicide; that heat by its mechanical action on the cerebral functions stimulated a person to suicide. Ferri even tried to explain how it produced this

TABLE XI—Proportional Share of Each Season in the Annual Total of the Suicides of Each Country

	Denmark (1858–65)	Belgium (1841–49)	France (1835–43)	Saxony (1847–58)	Bavaria (1858–65)	Austria (1858–59)	Prussia (1869–72)
Summer	312	301	306	307	308	315	290
Spring	284	275	283	281	282	281	284
Autumn	227	229	210	217	218	219	227
Winter	177	195	201	195	192	185	199
	1,000	1,000	1,000	1,000	1,000	1,000	1,000

effect. On the one hand, he says, heat increases the excitability of the nervous system; on the other, since in the warm season the organism does not need to consume as much material to maintain its own temperature at the desired degree, there results an accumulation of available energy naturally tending to seek employment. During summer, for this twofold reason, there is a surplus of activity, an abundance of life demanding expenditure and able to find manifestation only in violent action. Suicide is one of these manifestations, homicide another, and thus voluntary deaths increase during this season simultaneously with sanguinary crime. Moreover, insanity in all its forms is supposed to develop at this period; thus, he says, suicide naturally develops in the same way, as a result of its relation to insanity.

This theory, of tempting simplicity, at first seems in agreement with the facts. It even seems that it is merely their direct expression. Actually, it is a long way from accounting for them.

III

First, this theory implies a most debatable conception of suicide. It assumes that its constant psychological antecedent is a state of over-excitement, that it consists in a violent act and is only possible by a great exertion of energy. On the contrary, it very often results from extreme depression. Granted that excited or exasperated suicide occurs, suicide from unhappiness is as frequent; we shall have occasion to prove this. But heat cannot possibly act in the same way on both; if it stimulates the former, it must make the latter less frequent. Its possibly aggravating influence on certain persons would be offset and discounted by its moderating influence on others; hence it could not appear through the data of statistics, especially in any perceptible fashion. The seasonal variations shown by the statistics must therefore have another cause. To accept the explanation that sees in them a mere consequence of similar, simultaneous variations of insanity, a more direct and closer connection between suicide and insanity would have to be conceded than exists. Besides, it is not even proved that the seasons affect the two phenomena identically,[4] and even if this parallelism were certain, the question would still remain whether it is the seasonal changes of temperature which cause the curve of

[4] The distribution of the cases of insanity among the seasons can be estimated only by the number of admissions to the asylums. Such a standard is very inadequate; for families intern invalids not immediately but some time after the outbreak of the disease. Also such data as we have are a long way from showing perfect agreement between the seasonal variations of insanity and those of suicide. According to figures of Cazauvieilh, the share of each season in 1,000 annual admissions to Charenton is as follows: Winter, 222; Spring, 283; Summer, 261; Autumn, 231. The same calculation for the total of insane admitted to institutions of the Seine gives analogous results: Winter, 234; Spring, 266; Summer, 249; Autumn, 248. It appears, first, that the maximum occurs in Spring and not in Summer; moreover, the fact must be kept in mind that for the reasons indicated the real maximum has to be earlier; and secondly that the seasonal differences are very slight. They are much more marked for suicides.

insanity to rise and fall. Causes of a very different sort may possibly produce or contribute to this result.

But, however this influence attributed to heat is explained, let us examine its reality.

Certain observations do seem to show that too great heat excites man to kill himself. During the Egyptian campaign, the number of suicides in the French army seems to have increased and this growth was attributed to the rise in temperature. In the tropics men are often seen to throw themselves abruptly into the ocean under the direct rays of the sun. Dr. Dietrich relates that in a trip around the world from 1844–47 by Count Charles de Gortz he noticed an irresistible impulse among the sailors, called by him *the horrors*, which he describes as follows: "The affliction usually appears in Winter when the sailors, landing after a long voyage, group themselves incautiously about a hot stove and, as is customary, indulge in all sorts of excesses. On returning on board the symptoms of the terrible *horrors* appear. Those stricken by it are irresistibly impelled to throw themselves into the water, whether overcome by dizziness in the midst of work at the mast-tops, or during sleep, from which they start up violently with frightful cries." The *sirocco,* likewise, which produces a stifling heat, has been observed to have a similar effect on suicide.[5]

But this effect is not peculiar to heat; violent cold has the same result. Thus, during the retreat from Moscow our armies are said to have been stricken by numerous suicides. Such facts therefore cannot be used to explain the usually greater number of voluntary deaths in Summer than in Autumn and in Autumn than in Winter; for all that can be drawn from them is that extreme temperatures of whatever sort favor the development of suicide. Clearly, moreover, all sorts of excesses, abrupt and violent changes in physical environment, disturb the organism, derange the normal play of functions and thus cause species of deliria during which the idea of suicide may arise and be put into effect, if not checked. But these unusual, abnormal disturbances bear no likeness to the gradual changes of temperature in the course of every year. The question then is unsolved. Its solution must be sought by the analysis of statistical data.

If temperature were the basic cause of the variations noted, suicide would vary regularly with it. This is not true. Far more suicides

[5] We take these facts from Brierre de Boismont, *op. cit.,* pp. 60-62.

occur in Spring than in Autumn, although it is a little colder in Spring:

	France		Italy	
	Proportion of 1,000 Annual Suicides in Each Season	Average Temperature of the Seasons *	Proportion of 1,000 Annual Suicides in Each Season	Average Temperature of the Seasons *
Spring	284	50.36 degrees	297	55.22 degrees
Autumn	227	51.98 degrees	196	55.58 degrees

* Fahrenheit. Durkheim gives the figures in centigrade.—Ed.

Thus, while the thermometer is rising 1.62 F. degrees in France and .36 F. degrees in Italy, the number of suicides decreases by 21 per cent in the former country and 35 per cent in the latter. Likewise, in Italy the winter temperature is much lower than that of Autumn (36.14 F. degrees instead of 55.58 F.) and yet suicide-mortality is about the same in both seasons (196 cases as against 194). Everywhere the difference between Spring and Summer is very slight for suicides but very high for temperature. In France the difference is 78 per cent for the one and only 8 per cent for the other; in Prussia it is 121 per cent and 4 per cent.

This independence as regards temperature is still more noticeable if the monthly, not seasonal, variations of suicide are observed. In fact, these monthly variations obey the following law, found in all European countries: *Beginning with January inclusive, the incidence of suicide increases regularly from month to month until about June and regularly decreases from that time to the end of the year.* Usually, in 62 per cent of the cases, the maximum occurs in June, 25 per cent in May and 12 per cent in July. The minimum has occurred in 60 per cent of the cases in December, 22 per cent in January, 15 per cent in November and 3 per cent in October. The greatest irregularities, moreover, usually appear in series too small to be very significant. Wherever, as in France, the development of suicide can be followed over a long extent of time, it is seen to increase till June, then decrease until January, and the distance between the extremes averages not less than from 90 to 100 per cent. Suicide therefore does not reach its height in the hottest months which are August or July; on the contrary, beginning with August it starts to diminish perceptibly. In most cases, likewise, it reaches its lowest point not in January, the coldest month, but in December. Table XII (see p. 112) shows for

each month that the agreement between variations of the thermometer
and of suicide are quite irregular and intermittent.

In one and the same country, months with an essentially similar
temperature produce a very different proportion of suicides (for instance, May and September, April and October in France, June and
September in Italy, etc.). The reverse is no less common; January and
October, February and August in France have a like number of suicides in spite of great differences in temperature, and the same
holds true for April and July in Italy and Prussia. Moreover, the proportional figures are almost exactly the same for each month in these
different countries, although the temperature of the respective months
varies greatly from one to another country. Thus May, whose temperature is 50.84 F. degrees in Prussia, 57.56 F. in France and
64.4 F. in Italy, has 104 suicides in the first, 105 in the second

TABLE XII *

	France (1866–70)		Italy (1883–88)			Prussia (1876–78, 80–82, 85–89)	
	Average Temperature	No. of Suicides Monthly per 1,000 Annual	Average Temp. Rome	Naples	No. of Suicides Monthly per 1,000 Annual	Average Temperature (1848–77)	No. of Suicides Monthly per 1,000 Annual
January	36.12	68	44.24	47.12	69	32.50	61
February	39.20	80	46.76	48.74	80	33.31	67
March	43.52	86	50.72	51.26	81	37.93	78
April	50.18	102	56.30	57.20	98	44.22	99
May	57.56	105	64.40	63.61	103	50.84	104
June	62.96	107	71.42	70.70	105	57.29	105
July	66.12	100	76.82	75.74	102	59.39	99
August	65.30	82	75.74	75.56	93	58.48	90
September	60.26	74	70.16	71.70	75	52.88	83
October	52.34	70	61.34	62.68	65	46.02	78
November	43.70	66	51.62	53.96	63	37.27	70
December	38.66	61	46.22	49.10	61	33.08	61

* All the months in this table have been reduced to 30 days. The figures relative to tem-
perature are taken for France from l'Annuaire du bureau des longitudes, and for Italy from
Annali dell' Ufficio centrale de Meteorologia. [Temperatures are here given in Fahrenheit;
Durkheim's original figures are in Centigrade.—Ed.]

and 103 in the third.[6] The same holds true for almost all the other
months. The case of December is especially significant. Its share in
the annual total of suicides is exactly the same for the three societies
compared (61 per thousand); and yet at this time of year the thermometer registers on the average 46.22 F. degrees at Rome, 49.10 F.
at Naples, while in Prussia it never rises above 33.20 F. Not only

[6] This stability of the proportional figures cannot be too much emphasized and we
shall revert to its significance below (Bk. III, Chap. I.)

are the monthly temperatures not the same but they vary according to different laws in the different countries; thus, in France, the thermometer rises more from January to April than from April to June, while the reverse holds true for Italy. The thermometric variations and those of suicide are without any relation to one another.

Moreover, if the temperature had the supposed influence, it should be felt equally in the geographic distribution of suicides. The hottest countries should be those most stricken. The deduction is so evident that the Italian school itself refers to it when undertaking to show that the homicidal tendency also increases with the heat. Lombroso and Ferri have tried to show that, as murders are more frequent in Summer than in Winter, they are also more numerous in the South than in the North. Unfortunately, in the case of suicide the evidence refutes the Italian criminologists: for it is least developed in the southern countries of Europe. Italy has only one fifth as much as France; Spain and Portugal are almost immune. On the French suicide map, the only white area of any extent consists of the departments south of the Loire. Of course, we do not mean that this situation is really an effect of temperature; but whatever its cause, it is a fact inconsistent with the theory that heat is a stimulant to suicide.[7]

The perception of these difficulties and contradictions made Lombroso and Ferri slightly modify the school's doctrine, without relinquishing it in principle. According to Lombroso, whose opinion Morselli follows, it is not so much the intensity of heat which provokes suicide as the incidence of the first warm weather, the contrast between the departing cold and the beginning of the hot season. The latter is supposed to shock the organism as yet unaccustomed to this new temperature. But a glance at Table XII is enough to show that this explanation is devoid of all foundation. If it were correct, the curve representing the monthly variations of suicide should remain horizontal during Autumn and Winter, then rise abruptly precisely at the appearance of the first warm weather, the cause of all the

---

[7] It is true that, according to these authors, suicide is only a variety of homicide. The absence of suicides in southern countries would thus be merely apparent, being offset by an excess of homicides. We shall see later what this fusion amounts to. But is it not already clear that this argument turns against its authors? If the excess of homicides observed in hot countries offsets the lack of suicides, why does not the same offset occur during the warm season as well? Why is the latter fertile both in self-murder and in the murder of others?

trouble, and fall as suddenly, as soon as the organism has had time to acclimatize itself. On the contrary, its course is perfectly regular; while the rise lasts it is practically the same from one month to another. It rises from December to January, from January to February, from February to March, that is, throughout the months when the first hot weather is yet distant, and descends steadily from September to December, when the warm weather has so long since disappeared that this decrease cannot be attributed to its disappearance. Besides, when does the warm weather occur? It is generally assumed to begin in April. Actually, the thermometer rises from March to April from 33.52 F. degrees to 50.18 F.; the increase is thus 57 per cent, while it is only 40 per cent from April to May, 21 per cent from May to June. An unusual increase of suicides should therefore be observed in April. Actually, the increase at that time is no higher than that found from January to February (18 per cent). In short, as this increase not only persists but rises, though more slowly, until June and even July, it seems very difficult to ascribe it to the action of Spring, unless this season is prolonged to the end of Summer, exclusive only of the month of August.

Besides, if the first hot weather were so deleterious, the first cold weather should have the same effect. It also suddenly attacks the unprepared organism and disturbs vital functions until readaptation is accomplished. But no rise occurs in Autumn even faintly resembling that observed in Spring. It is thus not clear how Morselli could add, after recognizing that according to his theory the change from hot to cold should have the same effect as the reverse change: "This action of the first cold weather is verifiable in our statistical tables, or even better in the second rise of all our curves in Autumn, in the months of October and November, that is, when the change from the hot to the cold season is most sharply felt by the human organism and especially by the nervous system." [8] A mere reference to Table XII will show that this assertion is wholly contrary to the facts. From Morselli's own figures the number of suicides in almost every country is shown not to increase from October to November, but rather to diminish. Exceptions exist only for Denmark, Ireland and for one period in Austria (1851–54), and the increase is negligible in all

[8] *Op. cit.,* p. 148.

three cases.[9] In Denmark the numbers rise from 68 per thousand to 71, in Ireland from 62 to 66, in Austria from 65 to 68. There are likewise in October increases in only eight of thirty-one cases observed, namely during one period in Norway, one in Sweden, one in Saxony, one in Bavaria, Austria, the Duchy of Baden, and two in Wurttemberg. In all others there is a decrease or no change. To summarize, in twenty-one cases out of thirty-one, or 67 per cent, there is a regular diminution from September to December.

The perfect continuity of the curve, both in its progressive and its regressive phases, thus proves that the monthly variations of suicide cannot result from a brief organic crisis, occurring once or twice annually as a sudden, temporary interruption of equilibrium. They can depend only on causes themselves varying with the same continuity.

IV

It is now possible to perceive the nature of these causes.

If the proportional share of each month in the total of annual suicides is compared with the average length of the day at the same time

TABLE XIII—Comparison of the Monthly Variations of Suicides with the Average Length of Day in France

	Length of Day * Hr.	Min.	Increase and Diminution Increase	No. of Suicides per Month in 1,000 Annual Suicides	Increase and Diminution Increase
January	9	19		68	
February	10	56	From Jan. to	80	From Jan. to
March	12	47	April, 55%	86	April, 50%
April	14	29		102	
May	15	48	From April to	105	From April
June	16	3	June, 10%	107	to June, 5%
			Diminution		Diminution
July	15	4	From June to	100	From June to
August	13	25	Aug., 17%	82	Aug., 24%
September	11	39	From Aug. to	74	From Aug. to
October	9	51	Oct., 27%	70	Oct., 27%
November	8	31	From Oct. to	66	From Oct. to
December	8	11	Dec., 17%	61	Dec., 13%

* The indicated length is that of the last day of the month.

[9] We omit the figures for Switzerland. They are calculated for one year only (1876) and consequently nothing can be concluded from them. Moreover, the rise from October to November is very slight. Suicides increase from 83 per thousand to 90.

of the year, the two numerical series thus obtained vary in exactly the same way. (See Table XIII).

The parallelism is perfect. The maximum occurs at the same moment in each case and the minimum likewise; during the interval, the two orders of facts progress *pari passu*. When the days grow longer quickly, suicides increase greatly (January to April); when the increase of the former slows down, so does that of the latter (April to June). The same correspondence reappears during the time of decrease. Even the different months when days are of approximately the same length have approximately the same number of suicides (July and May, August and April).

So regular and precise a correspondence cannot be accidental. There must be some relation between the progress of the day and that of suicide. This hypothesis not only follows directly from Table XIII, it explains a fact which we have previously noted. We have seen that in the chief European societies suicides are distributed in a manner rigorously similar among the various portions of the year, seasons or months.[10] The theories of Ferri and Lombroso could afford no explanation of this curious uniformity, for the temperature varies greatly in the different European countries and evolves differently. On the contrary, the length of the day is appreciably the same for all European countries we have compared.

But what definitely proves the reality of this relation is the fact that in every season the majority of suicides occurs during the daytime. Brierre de Boismont was able to examine the records of 4,595 suicides committed in Paris from 1834 to 1843. Out of the 3,518 cases the moment of which could be determined, 2,094 had been committed by day, 766 during the evening and 658 at night. Those of the daytime and evening therefore are four-fifths of the sum total, and the former alone, three-fifths.

Prussian statistics have assembled more voluminous data on this subject. They refer to 11,822 cases occurring in the years 1869–72. They only confirm the conclusions of Brierre de Boismont. As the

[10] This uniformity relieves us of making Table XIII more involved. It is not necessary to compare the monthly variations of the day and those of suicide in other countries than France, since both are everywhere appreciably the same, unless one compares countries of very different latitude.

relations are appreciably the same each year, we will give, for brevity's sake, only those of 1871 and 1872:

TABLE XIV—Number of Suicides at Each Time of Day Among 1,000 Daily Suicides

	1871		1872	
Early morning *	35.9		35.9	
Later morning	158.3 ⎫		159.7 ⎫	
Middle of day	73.1 ⎬ 375		71.5 ⎬ 391.9	
Afternoon	143.6 ⎭		160.7 ⎭	
Evening	53.5		61.0	
Night	212.6		219.3	
Time unknown	322		291.9	
	1,000		1,000	

* This term means the time of day immediately succeeding sunrise.

The preponderance of suicides by day is obvious. Therefore, if daytime is richer in suicides than night, the suicides naturally grow more numerous as the day lengthens.

But what causes this diurnal influence?

To explain it one could certainly not refer to the action of the sun and the temperature. Actually, suicides committed in the middle of the day, that is, at the moment of greatest heat, are far fewer than those of the afternoon [11] or later morning. It will even appear below that a considerable decrease occurs at full noon. This explanation being discarded, we have but one other possible, namely, that day favors suicide because this is the time of most active existence, when human relations cross and recross, when social life is most intense.

Whatever information is available as to how suicide is distributed among the different hours of the day or the different days of the week confirms this view. On the basis of 1,993 cases observed by Brierre de Boismont for Paris and 548 covering all of France assembled by Guerry, the following are the chief oscillations of suicide during the twenty-four hours:

Paris	Hourly Number of Suicides	France	Hourly Number of Suicides
From midnight to 6	55	From midnight to 6	30
From 6 to 11	108	From 2 to 6	61
From 11 to noon	81	From noon to 2	32
From noon to 4	105	From 6 to noon	47
From 4 to 8	81	From 6 to midnight	38
From 8 to midnight	61		

[11] The French text here reads "evening." But those committed in the evening are not more numerous than those committed in the middle of the day. A look at Table XIV makes it indubitable that Durkheim meant "afternoon."—Ed.

There are clearly two climactic periods of suicide; those when existence is most active, morning and afternoon. Between the two periods is one of rest when general activity is briefly interrupted; suicide pauses momentarily. This calm occurs in Paris at about eleven and at about noon in the other departments of France. It is longer and more definite in the departments than in the capital through the simple fact that non-Parisians take their chief meal then; the pause of suicide is accordingly longer and more definite there. The data of Prussian statistics given above would confirm this view.[12]

Moreover, Guerry, having determined for 6,587 cases the day of week on which they happened, constructed the scale reproduced in Table XV. This shows that suicide diminishes toward the end of the week beginning with Friday. Prejudices concerning Friday are known to retard public activity. On this day railroad travel is much less than

TABLE XV

	Share in Per Cent of Each Day in 1,000 Weekly Suicides	Proportional Share of Each Sex	
		Per Cent Men	Per Cent Women
Monday	15.20	69	31
Tuesday	15.71	68	32
Wednesday	14.90	68	32
Thursday	15.68	67	33
Friday	13.74	67	33
Saturday	11.19	69	31
Sunday	13.57	64	36

on others. On this day of ill omen people hesitate to make contacts and undertake business. An initial slackness commences on Saturday afternoon; in certain districts idleness is widespread; the prospect of the next day also perhaps has a calming effect on the mind. Finally, on Sunday economic activity stops completely. If activities of another sort did not replace those that have ceased, and recreation areas fill as studios, offices and shops empty, the decrease of suicide might conceivably be yet more noticeable on Sunday. This, it will be noted, is the day when woman's relative share is greatest; then also she most

---

[12] Another proof that social life experiences a rhythm of rest and activity at the different times of day is the variations of accidents by hours. They are distributed as follows according to the Prussian Bureau of Statistics:

From 6 to noon 1,011 accidents per average hour
From noon to 2   686 accidents per average hour
From 2 to 6   1,191 accidents per average hour
From 6 to 7   979 accidents per average hour

frequently departs from indoors, her shelter during the rest of the week, and mingles somewhat with the life of others.[13]

Thus everything proves that if daytime is the part of the twenty-four hours most favorable to suicide, it is because it is also the time when social life is at its height. Then we have a reason why the number of suicides increases, the longer the sun remains above the horizon. The mere lengthening of the days seems to offer wider latitude to collective life. Its time of rest begins later and is sooner over. It has more space to operate in. Thus its accompanying effects must develop simultaneously and, since suicide is one of them, it must increase.

But this is the first, not the only cause. If public activity is greater in Summer than in Spring and in Spring than in Autumn and Winter, this is not merely because its setting enlarges as the year progresses, but because this activity is directly aroused for other reasons.

For the countryside, Winter is a time of rest approaching stagnation. All life seems to stop; human relations are fewer both because of atmospheric conditions and because they lose their incentive with the general slackening of activity. People seem really asleep. In Spring, however, everything begins to awake; activity is resumed, relations spring up, interchanges increase, whole popular migrations take place to meet the needs of agricultural labor. Now these special conditions of rural life must have a great influence on the monthly distribution of suicides, since more than half the total of voluntary deaths comes from the country; in France, from 1873 to 1878, the country accounted for 18,470 cases out of a total of 36,365. They therefore naturally occur more often as the inclement season becomes remote. They reach their maximum in June or July, when activity is

[13] It is noteworthy that this contrast between the first and second parts of the week recurs during the month. The following, according to Brierre de Boismont, *op. cit.*, p. 424, is the distribution of 4,595 Parisian suicides:

> During the first ten days of the month 1,727
> During the next ten days of the month 1,488
> During the last ten days of the month 1,380

The numerical inferiority of the last ten days is even greater than the figures show; for because of the 31st day it often includes 11 days instead of 10. The rhythm of social life seems to reproduce the calendar's divisions; there seems to be renewed activity whenever a new period is entered and a sort of slackening as it draws to an end.

greatest in the country. In August when everything begins to settle down, suicides diminish. They do so rapidly only beginning with October and especially November; perhaps because several harvests do not occur until Autumn.

The same reasons also affect the entire land, though to a lesser extent. City life itself is more active during the fine season. Communications being easier then, people travel more readily and inter-social relations increase. Below are the seasonal receipts of our great railroad lines, for express service only (for 1887): [14]

Winter	71.9 million francs
Spring	86.7 million francs
Summer	105.1 million francs
Autumn	98.1 million francs

The inner life of every city exhibits the same phases. During this same year, 1887, the number of passengers travelling from one point in Paris to another regularly increased from January (655,791) to June (848,831), then decreased as steadily to December (659,960).[15]

A final instance confirms this interpretation of the facts. If, for reasons just indicated, urban life must be more intense in Summer and in Spring than during the rest of the year, nevertheless the difference between seasons should be less marked there than in the country. For trade and industry, art and science as well as fashionable activities are less interrupted in Winter than agriculture. The occupations of city-dwellers may continue with approximate regularity throughout the year. The greater or lesser length of days especially should have little effect in great centers, because artificial lighting there restricts darkness more than elsewhere. If then the monthly and seasonal variations of suicide depend on the irregular intensity of collective life, they should be less noticeable in great cities than in the country as a whole. The facts strictly confirm this

[14] See the *Bulletin du ministère des travaux publics.*

[15] *Ibid.* The following may be added to all the other facts showing the increase of social activity during the Summer; namely, that accidents are commoner during the fine season than at other times. Here is their distribution in Italy:

	1886	1887	1888
Spring	1,370	2,582	2,457
Summer	1,823	3,290	3,085
Autumn	1,474	2,560	2,780
Winter	1,190	2,748	3,032

If from this point of view Winter sometimes numerically follows Summer, this is merely because falls are commoner due to ice and because the cold itself produces special accidents. If we discount such accidents, the seasons assume the same order as for suicides.

conclusion. Table XVI (see below) shows that whereas in France, Prussia, and Austria there is a difference of 52, 45 and even of 68 per cent between the minimum and the maximum, at Paris, Berlin, Hamburg, etc., this averages from 20 to 25 per cent and even reaches 12 per cent (at Frankfurt).

It is clear, moreover, that the maximum generally occurs in Spring in great cities, unlike the rest of society. Even where Spring is surpassed by Summer (Paris and Frankfurt), the increase in the latter season is slight. This is because during the fine season a veritable

TABLE XVI—Seasonal Variations of Suicide in Several Large Cities Compared with Those of the Whole Country

	Paris	Berlin	Hamburg	Vienna	Frankfurt	Geneva	France	Prussia	Austria
	(1888–92)	(1882–85–87–89–90)	(1887–91)	(1871–72)	(1867–75)	(1838–47) (1852–54)	(1835–43)	(1869–72)	(1858–59)
				PROPORTIONAL FIGURES FOR 1,000 ANNUAL SUICIDES					
Winter	218	231	239	234	239	232	201	199	185
Spring	262	287	289	302	245	288	283	284	281
Summer	277	248	232	211	278	253	306	290	315
Autumn	241	232	258	253	238	227	210	227	219
			PROPORTIONAL FIGURES FOR EACH SEASON EXPRESSED IN TERMS OF THE WINTER FIGURE REDUCED TO 100						
	Paris	Berlin	Hamburg	Vienna	Frankfurt	Geneva	France	Prussia	Austria
Winter	100	100	100	100	100	100	100	100	100
Spring	120	124	120	129	102	124	140	142	151
Summer	127	107	107	90	112	109	152	145	168
Autumn	100	100.3	103	108	99	97	104	114	118

migration of the chief public personages takes place and public life accordingly shows a slight tendency to slow down.[16]

To recapitulate: we first showed that the direct action of cosmic factors could not explain the monthly or seasonal variations of suicide. We now see the nature of its real causes, the direction in which they must be sought, and this positive result confirms the conclusions of our abstract analysis. If voluntary deaths increase from January to

[16] It should also be noticed that the proportional figures of the different seasons are substantially the same in the great cities compared, though different from those of the countries to which these cities belong. Thus, the suicide-rate is found everywhere stable in the same social environments. The suicidal tendency varies in like manner at different times of the year in Berlin, Vienna, Geneva, Paris, etc. One thus realizes in some measure the full extent of its reality.

July, it is not because heat disturbs the organism but because social life is more intense. To be sure, this greater intensity derives from the greater ease of development of social life in the Summer than in the Winter, owing to the sun's position on the ecliptic, the state of the atmosphere, etc. But the physical environment does not stimulate it directly; above all, it has no effect on the progression of suicide. The latter depends on social conditions.

Of course, we are yet uncertain how collective life can have this effect. But it already appears that if it contains the causes of the variation of the suicide-rate, the latter must increase or decrease as social life becomes more or less active. To determine these causes more exactly will be the purpose of the following book.

CHAPTER 4
IMITATION[1]

Bᴜᴛ before searching for the social causes of suicide, a final psychological factor remains, the influence of which must be determined because of the great importance attributed to it with respect to the origin of social facts in general and of suicide in particular. This factor is imitation.

That imitation is a purely psychological phenomenon appears clearly from its occurrence between individuals connected by no social bond. A man may imitate another with no link of either one with the other or with a common group on which both depend, and the imitative function when exercised has in itself no power to form a bond between them. A cough, a dance-motion, a homicidal impulse may be transferred from one person to another even though there is only chance and temporary contact between them. They need have no intellectual or moral community between them nor exchange services nor even speak the same language, nor are they any more related after the transfer than before. In short, our method of imitating human beings is the same method we use in reproducing natural sounds, the shapes of things, the movements of non-human beings. Since the latter group of cases contains no social element, there is none in the former case. It originates in certain qualities of our representational life not based upon any collective influence. If, therefore,

[1] *Bibliography.*—Lucas, *De l'imitation contagieuse,* Paris, 1833.—Despine, *De la contagion morale,* 1870. *De l'imitation,* 1871.—Moreau de Tours (Paul), *De la contagion du suicide,* Paris, 1875.—Aubry, *Contagion du meurtre,* Paris, 1888.— Tarde, *Les Lois de l'imitation* (*passim*). *Philosophie pénale,* p. 319 and ff. Paris, F. Alcan.—Corre, *Crime et suicide,* p. 207 and ff.

imitation were shown to help in determining the suicide-rate, the latter would depend directly either in whole or in part upon individual causes.

I

But before examining the facts, let us determine the meaning of the word. Sociologists so commonly use terms without defining them, neither establishing nor methodically circumscribing the range of things they intend to discuss, that they constantly but unconsciously allow a given expression to be extended from the concept originally or apparently envisaged by it to other more or less kindred ideas. Thus, the idea finally becomes too ambiguous to permit discussion. Having no clear outline, it is changeable almost at will according to momentary needs of argument without the possibility of critical foreknowledge of all its different potential aspects. Such is notably the case with what is called the instinct of imitation.

This word is currently used to mean simultaneously the three following groups of facts:

1. In the midst of the same social group, all the elements of which undergo the action of a single cause or number of similar causes, a sort of levelling occurs in the consciousness of different individuals which leads everyone to think or feel in unison. The name of imitation has very often been given the whole number of operations resulting in this harmony. It then designates the quality of the states of consciousness simultaneously felt by a given number of different persons leading them so to act upon one another or combine among themselves as to produce a new state. Using the word in this sense, we mean that this combination results from reciprocal imitation of each of them by all and of all by each.[2] "In the noisy gatherings of our cities, in the great scenes of our revolutions," [3] it has been said, best appears the nature of imitation thus defined. There one sees best how men in union can mutually transform one another by their reciprocal influence.

2. The same name has been given the impulse which drives us to seek harmony with the society to which we belong, and, with this purpose, to adopt the ways of thought or action which surround us. Thus we follow manners and customs, and—as legal and moral prac-

---

[2] Bordier, *Vie des sociétés*, Paris, 1887, p. 77—Tarde, *Philosophie pénale*, p. 321.
[3] Tarde, *Ibid.*, pp. 319-320.

tices are merely defined and well-established customs—we usually act thus when we act morally. Whenever we are ignorant of the reasons for the moral maxim we obey, we conform solely because it possesses social authority. In this sense the imitation of manners is distinguished from that of customs, depending on whether our models are our ancestors or our contemporaries.

3. Finally, we may happen to reproduce an act which has occurred in our presence or to our knowledge, just because it has occurred in our presence or because we have heard it spoken of. It has no intrinsic character of its own causing us to repeat it. We copy it just to copy it, not because we think it useful nor to be in harmony with a model. Our conception of it automatically determines the movements which recreate it. Thus we yawn, laugh, weep, because we see someone yawn,, laugh or weep. Thus also the thought of homicide passes from one to another consciousness. It is ape-like imitation for its own sake.

Now these three sorts of facts are very different from one another.

To begin with, *the first cannot be confused with the others, because it involves no act of genuine reproduction,* but syntheses *sui generis* of different states or at least of states of different origins. The term "imitation" cannot therefore be used in speaking of it without losing all clear meaning.

Let us analyze the phenomenon. A number of men in assembly are similarly affected by the same occurrence and perceive this at least partial unanimity by the identical signs through which each individual feeling is expressed. What happens then? Each one imperfectly imagines the state of those about him. Images expressing the various manifestations emanating, with their different shades, from all parts of the crowd, are formed in the minds of all. Nothing to be called imitation has thus far occurred; there have been merely perceptible impressions, then sensations wholly identical with those produced in us by external bodies.[4] What happens then? Once aroused in my consciousness, these various representations combine with one another

---

[4] In attributing these images to a process of imitation, would we mean that they are mere copies of the states they express? First, this would be a very crude metaphor, taken from the old inacceptable theory of perceptible types. Also, if we use the word imitation thus, it must be extended to all our sensations and ideas indiscriminately; for of all we may say, using the same metaphor, that they reproduce the object to which they refer. Thereupon all intellectual life becomes a product of imitation.

and with my own feeling. A new state is thus formed, less my own than its predecessor, less tainted with individuality and more and more freed, by a series of repeated elaborations analogous to the foregoing, from all excessive particularity. Such combinations could also not be called facts of imitation, unless the name were accepted for all intellectual activity through which two or more similar states of consciousness appeal to one another by their likeness, then blend and fuse in a compound absorbing them but different from them. True, all definitions of words are permissible. But this, it must be recognized, would be extremely arbitrary and could thus be only a source of confusion, since it leaves the word none of its customary meaning. One should say creation rather than imitation, since this combination of forces results in something new. This is indeed the only procedure by which the mind has the power of creation.

This creation may be said to amount merely to an intensification of the original state. But first, a quantitative change need not fail to be a novelty. Moreover, the quantity of things cannot change without changing their quality; a feeling alters its nature completely on becoming two or three times as violent. We know in fact that the mutual reactions of men in assembly may transform a gathering of peaceful citizens into a fearful monster. What a strange imitation to produce such metamorphoses! A term so inadequate to express the phenomenon can have been used only by vaguely imagining that each individual feeling models itself after somebody else's feelings. Actually, there are here neither models nor copies. There is a penetration, a fusion of a number of states within another, distinct from them: that is the collective state.

To be sure, the cause of this state might properly be called imitation if a leader were admitted always to have inspired the crowd with it. But not only has this assertion never even begun to be proved, and not only is it contradicted by very many cases, where the leader is clearly the product of the crowd rather than its informing cause; but, indeed, in so far as this directive action is real, it has no relation to what is called reciprocal imitation, being unilateral; thus there can be no question of imitation in this sense. We must guard most carefully against those confusions of meaning which have so obscured the subject. Similarly, if one said that an assemblage always contains persons who cling to the common opinion, not through spontaneous impulse but through its imposition upon them, this would undeniably be true. We even believe that there is no individual consciousness in such cases which does not feel such constraint to some degree. But since this constraint originates in the force *sui generis* investing common practices or beliefs, once they are constituted, it belongs to the second category of facts distinguished above. Let us examine this, therefore, and see how far it deserves to be called imitation.

At least it differs from its predecessor in implying a reproduction. In following a manner or observing a custom one does what others have done and do, daily. But the definition itself implies that this repetition is not owing to the so-called instinct of imitation, but on the one hand, to the sympathy constraining us not to wound the feelings of our fellows, lest we forfeit their intercourse, and on the other, to the respect we feel for collective ways of acting and thinking and the direct or indirect pressure exerted on us by this collectivity to avoid dissension and maintain in us this sense of respect. The act is not reproduced because it took place in our presence or to our knowledge and because we like the reproduction in and for itself, but because it seems obligatory to us and to some extent useful. We perform it not merely because it has been performed but because it bears a social stamp and because we defer to this necessarily on pain of serious inconvenience. That is, *to act through respect or fear of opinion is not to act through imitation.* Such acts differ little from those we agree upon whenever we innovate. They occur in fact because of a quality inherent in them—a quality which makes us consider them as necessary to do. But when instead of following customs we revolt, we are moved in the same way; if we adopt a new idea or an original practice, it is because of its intrinsic qualities making us feel that it should be adopted. Certainly, our motives are not the same in both cases; but the psychological mechanism is exactly the same. In each, an intellectual operation intrudes between the representation and the execution of the act, consisting of a clear or unclear, rapid or slow awareness of the determining characteristic, whatever it may be. Our way of conforming to the morals or manners of our country has nothing in common,[5] therefore, with the mechanical, ape-like repeti-

---

[5] In these particular cases, a manner or tradition may indeed be reproduced through mere ape-like imitation; but then it is not reproduced as a manner or tradition as such.

tion causing us to reproduce motions which we witness. Between the
two ways of acting, is all the difference between reasonable, deliberate behaviour and automatic reflex. The former has motives even
when not expressed as explicit judgments. The latter has not; it results directly from the mere sight of an act, with no other mental
intermediary.

It is thus clear what mistakes arise when two such different sets of
facts are given the same name. Let us be on our guard; when we
speak of imitation the phenomenon of contagion is implicitly understood, and reasonably enough we pass from one idea to the other very
readily. But what is contagious in the accomplishment of a moral
precept, in deference to the authority of tradition or to public opinion?
Thus, while thinking that we have reduced two realities to one we
have actually only confused very distinct ideas. In pathological biology, a disease is called contagious when it rises wholly or mainly
from the development of a germ introduced into the organism from
outside. Inversely, in so far as this germ has been able to develop
thanks only to the active cooperation of the field in which it has
taken root, the term "contagion" becomes inexact. Likewise, for an
act to be attributed to a moral contagion it is not enough that the
idea be inspired by a similar act. Once introduced into the mind, it
must automatically and of itself have become active. Then contagion
really exists, because the external act is reproduced by itself, entering
into us by way of a representation. Imitation likewise exists, since the
new act is wholly itself by virtue of the model it copies. But if the
impression upon us of the latter takes effect only through our consent
and participation, contagion is only figuratively present and the figure
is inexact. For the reasons making us consent are the determining
causes of our action, not the example before our eyes. We are its
authors, even though not its inventors.[6] Consequently, all these oft-
repeated expressions about imitative propagation and contagious expansion are inapplicable and must be discarded. They deform instead
of defining the facts; they obscure rather than clarify the question.

In short, if we are to think clearly we cannot use one and the same

---

[6] To be sure, everything not original invention is sometimes called imitation. As
such, almost all human acts are clearly acts of imitation; for true inventions are very
rare. But the term imitation then has no definite meaning, just because it means almost everything. Such terminology can only breed confusion.

name for the process by which a collective sentiment develops among a gathering, for the process causing our adhesion to common or traditional rules of behavior, and, finally, for the one causing Panurge's sheep to cast themselves into the water because one of them began it. It is one thing to share a common feeling, another to yield to the authority of opinion, and a third to repeat automatically what others have done. No reproduction occurs in the first case; in the second it results only from logical operations,[7] judgments and reasonings, implicit or explicit, but themselves the essence of the phenomenon; and thus reproduction cannot be the definition. It becomes all embracing only in the third case. There it is all-comprehensive; the new act is a mere echo of the original. Not merely does it repeat, but this repetition has no cause for existence outside itself, only the total of characteristics which make us imitative creatures under certain circumstances. The name of imitation must then be reserved solely for such facts if it is to have clear meaning, and we shall say: *Imitation exists when the immediate antecedent of an act is the representation of a like act, previously performed by someone else; with no explicit or implicit mental operation which bears upon the intrinsic nature of the act reproduced intervening between representation and execution.*

So, when we ask what is the influence of imitation on the suicide-rate, we must use the word in this sense.[8] If its sense is not thus defined, we risk mistaking a purely verbal expression for an explanation. In fact, when a way of acting or thinking is called an act of imitation we mean that imitation explains it and thus think we have told everything by uttering this magical word. Actually, only in cases

---

[7] It is true there is a so-called logical imitation (See Tarde, *Lois de l'imitation,* I. ed., p. 158); this reproduces an act because it serves a definite end. But such imitation obviously has nothing to do with the imitative impulse; facts due to one must be carefully distinguished from those due to the other. They have quite different explanations. On the other hand, as we have just shown, manner-imitation and custom-imitation are as logical as the others, although having their special logic in some respects.

[8] Acts imitated because of the moral or intellectual prestige of the original actor, whether individual or collective, that serves as a model, belong rather to the second class. For such imitation has no automatic quality. It implies reasoning: one acts like a person possessing one's confidence because his recognized superiority guarantees the propriety of his acts. One has the same reasons to follow him as to respect him. No explanation has therefore been given of such acts when they are said merely to have been imitated. What matters is the cause of the confidence or respect determining this obedience.

of automatic reproduction does it have this quality. There imitation itself may be a sufficient explanation,[9] because all that takes place results from imitative contagion. But when a custom is followed, a moral practice conformed to, the reasons for docility are found in the nature of this practice, the special qualities of the custom and the feelings they inspire. Thus when imitation is mentioned apropos of this sort of act, nothing is explained; we are told simply that the fact we reproduce is not new, that is, that it is reproduced, without being told at all why it was produced nor why we reproduce it. Much less can this word take the place of analysis of the complex process whence come collective sentiments and of which we have been able to supply only a conjectural and approximate description above.[10] Thus the misuse of the term may be thought to offer a solution or partial solution of these questions, whereas it has merely succeeded in concealing them.

Only on condition of defining imitation thus, shall we also have the right to consider it a psychological factor of suicide. Actually, so-called reciprocal imitation is a highly social phenomenon, since it is cooperative elaboration of a common sentiment. The repetition of customs and traditions is similarly a result of social causes, being due to the obligatory nature and special prestige investing collective beliefs and practices by virtue of the very fact of their being collective beliefs and practices. Insofar, therefore, as suicide is admittedly disseminated by one or the other of these methods, it would be dependent on social causes and not on individual conditions.

Having thus defined the terms of the problem, let us examine the facts.

[9] Yet imitation itself alone, as we shall see below, is a sufficient explanation only in rare instances.

[10] For we must confess that we have only a vague idea of what it is. Exactly how the combinations occur resulting in the collective state, what are its constituent elements, how the dominant state is produced are questions too complex to be solved solely by introspection. Manifold experiments and observations would be required and have not been made. We know little as yet how and according to what laws mental states of even the single individual combine; much less do we know of the mechanism of the far more complicated combinations produced by group-existence. Our explanations are often mere metaphors. Our words are therefore not meant as an exact expression of the phenomenon; we have tried only to show that there is something else here than imitation.

II

The idea of suicide may undoubtedly be communicated by contagion. The corridor has already been mentioned where fifteen invalids hung themselves in succession and also the famous sentry-box of the camp at Boulogne, the scene of several suicides in quick succession. Such facts have often been observed in the army: in the 4th regiment of chasseurs at Provins in 1862, in the 15th of the line in 1864, in the 41st, first at Montpellier, then at Nîmes, in 1868, etc. In 1813 in the little village of Saint-Pierre-Monjau, a woman hanged herself from a tree and several others did likewise at a little distance away. Pinel tells of a priest's hanging himself in the neighborhood of Etampes; some days later two others killed themselves and several laymen imitated them.[11] When Lord Castlereagh threw himself into Vesuvius, several of his companions followed his example. The tree of Timon of Athens has become proverbial. The frequency of such cases of contagion in prisons is likewise affirmed by many observers.[12]

Certain facts, however, usually referred to this class and ascribed to imitation seem to us to have a different origin. Such is notably the case with what has sometimes been called the suicides of the besieged. In his *History of the War of the Jews against the Romans*,[13] Josephus relates that during the assault on Jerusalem some of the besieged committed suicide with their own hands. More especially forty Jews, having taken refuge underground, decided to choose death and killed one another. According to Montaigne, the Xanthians, besieged by Brutus, "rushed about pell-mell, men, women and children, with such a furious longing to die, that nothing can be done to fly from death which they did not do to fly from life; so that Brutus had much difficulty in saving a small number of them." [14] It does not appear that these *mass suicides* originated in one or two individual cases which they merely repeated. They seem to spring from a collective resolve, a genuine social consensus rather than a simple contagious impulse. The idea does not spring up in one particular person and then spread to others; but is developed by the whole group which,

---

[11] See the detailed facts in Legoyt, *op. cit.*, p. 227 ff.
[12] See similar facts in Ebrard, *op. cit.*, p. 376.
[13] III, 26.
[14] *Essais*, II, 3. [Translation from vol. I, p. 40, *The Essays of Michel de Montaigne*, New York, 1934.—Ed.]

in a situation desperate for all, collectively decides upon death. Such is the course of events whenever a social group, of whatever nature, reacts in common under the influence of a common pressure. The agreement is no different because of being arrived at in a passionate impulse; it would be substantially the same if it were more methodical and deliberate. One cannot therefore properly speak of imitation.

We might say as much of several other similar facts. Thus Esquirol reports: "Historians declare that the Peruvians and Mexicans, rendered desperate by the destruction of their religious worship . . . killed themselves in such numbers that more perished by their own hands than by the swords and muskets of their barbarous conquerors." In a wider sense, to justify the appeal to imitation, numerous suicides must not only be shown to occur at the same time and place. For they may be due to a general state of the social environment resulting in a collective group disposition that takes the form of multiple suicide. Finally, it would perhaps be interesting, to make the terminology precise, to distinguish moral epidemics from moral contagions; these two words used carelessly for one another actually denote two very different sorts of things. An epidemic is a social fact, produced by social causes; contagion consists only in more or less repeated repercussions of individual phenomena.[15]

Once admitted, such a distinction would certainly reduce the list of suicides imputable to imitation; yet they are, it is true, very numerous. Perhaps no other phenomenon is more readily contagious. Not even the homicidal impulse is so apt to spread. Cases where it spreads automatically are less frequent, and the role of imitation especially is generally less prominent; contrary to common opinion, the instinct of self-preservation would seem less strongly rooted in consciousness than the fundamental moral sentiments, since it shows less resistance to the same influences. But granted this, the question proposed at the beginning of this chapter is unsolved. It does not follow a priori from the fact that suicide may be communicated from person to person that this contagious quality has social effects, that is, that it affects the social suicide-rate, our object of study. Undeniable as it is, it may

[15] It will appear below that there is always and normally, in every society, a collective disposition taking the form of suicide. This differs from what we shall call epidemic by being chronic and a normal element of the moral temper of the society. Epidemics are also collective dispositions, but which rarely make their appearance, since they come from abnormal and usually transient causes.

have only individual, sporadic consequences. The above observations accordingly do not solve the problem; but they make its extent clearer. If, as has been said, imitation is really an original and specially fecund source of social phenomena, it should show its influence especially in suicide since no field exists over which it has more sway. Suicide will thus help us to verify by decisive experience the reality of the wonderful power ascribed to imitation.

III

If this influence exists, it must appear above all in the geographic distribution of suicides. In certain cases, the rate characteristic of a country or locality should be transmitted, so to speak, to neighboring localities. We must thus consult the map. But methodically.

Certain authors have felt that they might appeal to imitation whenever two or more contiguous departments showed an equally strong tendency to suicide. Yet this diffusion within a single region may well spring from an equal diffusion of certain causes favorable to the development of suicide, and from the fact that the social environment is the same throughout the region. To be assured that imitation causes the spread of a tendency or idea, one must see it leave the environments of its birthplace and invade regions not themselves calculated to encourage it. For, as we have shown, imitative propagation exists only where the fact imitated, and it alone, determines the acts that reproduce it, automatically and without assistance from other factors. A criterion less simple than that often accepted is therefore needed to prove the share of imitation in the phenomenon under investigation.

First of all, no imitation can exist without a model to imitate; no contagion without a central hearth in which it necessarily displays its maximum intensity. Nor can the suicidal tendency justifiably be declared to pass from one part of society to another unless observation uncovers the existence of certain centers of radiation. By what tokens shall they be known?

First, they must have greater aptitude for suicide than all surrounding points; they must show a deeper tinge on the map than neighboring regions. Since, as is natural, imitation acts simultaneously with causes truly productive of suicide, cases must be more numerous there. Secondly, for these centers to play the part ascribed to them and justify reference of events occurring outside their sphere to their influence, each must be something of a cynosure for outlying districts. Clearly, it cannot be imitated without being seen. If attention swerves elsewhere, no matter how many the suicides, they will be as good as non-existent because ignored; so they will not be reproduced. Peoples' eyes can be thus fixed only on a point of importance to the regional life. In other words, phenomena of contagion are bound to be most pronounced near capitals and large cities. They may even be more anticipated there because in this case the propagative power of imitation is assisted and reenforced by such other factors as the moral authority of great centers, which at times gives such expansive power to their ways of acting. There, accordingly, imitation must have social effects if anywhere. Finally, since as is commonly held, other things being equal, the power of example weakens with distance, surrounding regions should be less afflicted the further they are from the focal hearth, and inversely. The map of suicides must at least satisfy these three conditions to have its contour even partially ascribed to imitation. There will always be occasion to question also whether or not this geographical disposition is not due to a parallel distribution of living condition, conducive to suicide.

Having established these rules, let us apply them.

The customary maps, where, so far as France is concerned, the suicide-rate is indicated only by departments, are inadequate for this investigation. They do not actually permit the observation of the possible effects of imitation where they must be most perceptible, among the different portions of a single department. Moreover, the presence of a district (arrondissement) more or less fertile in suicides may artificially raise or lower the departmental average and thus cause an apparent discontinuity between the other districts and those of neighboring departments, or even, contrariwise, conceal a real discontinuity. Finally, the influence of great cities is too much obscured in this manner to be easily perceived. So we have drawn a map by districts specially for the study of this question, referring to the five-year period 1887–1891. Its study has given most unexpected results.[16]

What is first noticeable is the presence toward the North of a large area, the greater part of which occupies the place of the former Ile-de-France, but which enters deep into Champagne and extends into

16 See Appendix II.

Lorraine. If it were due to imitation, its focus would have to be in Paris, the only conspicuous center of the entire area. Indeed, it is usually imputed to the influence of Paris; Guerry even declared that starting from any point in the periphery of the country (with the exception of Marseilles) and moving toward the capital, suicides are found to increase more and more the nearer one comes. But if the map by departments might seem to confirm this view, the map by districts thoroughly belies it. The Seine, indeed, is found to have a suicide-rate less than all neighboring arrondissements. It has only 471 per million inhabitants, while Coulommiers has 500, Versailles 514, Melun 518, Meaux 525, Corbeil 559, Pontoise 561, Provins 562. Even the districts of Champagne far surpass those most adjacent to the Seine: Reims has 501 suicides, Epernay 537, Arcis-sur-Aube 548, Château-Thierry 623. In his study, *Le suicide en Seine-et-Marne,* Dr. Leroy had already noted with surprise that the district of Meaux had relatively more suicides than the Seine.[17] Here are his figures:

	Period 1851–63	Period 1865–66
Arrondissement of Meaux	1 suicide to 2,418 inhabitants	1 to 2,547 inhabitants
Seine	1 suicide to 2,750 inhabitants	1 to 2,822 inhabitants

And the district of Meaux was not alone in this respect. *The same author tells us the names of 166 communes of the same department where suicide at this time was more frequent than in Paris.* A strange center, to be so inferior to the secondary centers it is supposed to nourish! Yet with the exception of the Seine no other center of radiation can be discovered. For it is still more difficult to make Paris a satellite of Corbeil or Pontoise.

A little further north appears another area, less evenly distributed but still deeply shaded; it corresponds to Normandy. If it were due to contagious expansion, it would therefore have to have Rouen as its center, the provincial capital and a very important city. Now, the two points of this region where suicide is most widespread are the district of Neufchâtel (509 suicides) and that of Pont-Audemer (537 per million inhabitants); and they are not even contiguous. Yet

[17] *Op. cit.,* p. 213.—According to the same author, even the entire departments of Marne and of Seine-et-Marne surpassed the Seine in 1865–66. Marne, he declares, then to have had 1 suicide to 2,791 inhabitants; Seine-et-Marne, 1 to 2,768; the Seine 1 to 2,822.

the moral constitution of the province can certainly not be due to their influence.

Far to the South-East, along the Mediterranean shores, we find a strip of territory reaching from the farthest limits of the Bouches-du-Rhône to the Italian frontier, where suicides are also very numerous. Here there is a genuine metropolis, Marseilles, and at the other end a great center of fashionable life, Nice. Yet the most stricken districts are those of Toulon and Forcalquier. No one will say, however, that Marseilles is influenced by them. On the west coast likewise, Rochefort alone stands out with its rather dark shade from the elongated mass of the two Charentes, though a much larger city, Angoulême, lies within them. In general, there are a great many departments where it is not the district of the principal town which leads the way. In the Vosges we have Remirement and not Épinal; in Haute-Saône, Gray, a stagnant or semi-stagnant town, and not Vesoul; in Doubs, Dôle and Poligny, not Besançon; in Gironde, not Bordeaux but La Réole and Bazas; in Maine-et-Loire, Saumur instead of Angers; in Sarthe, Saint-Calais instead of Le Mans; in Nord, Avesnes instead of Lille, etc. Yet in none of these cases does the district which thus surpasses the metropolis include the most important city of the department.

It would be interesting to continue this comparison, not only from district to district but from commune to commune. Unfortunately, a map of suicides by communes cannot be made for the entire country. But in his interesting monograph Dr. Leroy performed this task for the department of Seine-et-Marne. Having classified all the communes of this department according to their suicide-rates, beginning with the highest, he reached the following results: "La Ferté-sous-Jouarre (4,482 inhabitants) the first important town on the list, is the 124th; Meaux (10,762 inhabitants), is 130th; Provins (7,547 inhabitants) is 135th; Coulommiers (4,628 inhabitants) is 138th. Comparison of the rank of these cities representing their place in the series even suggests, curiously enough, a common influence upon them all.[18] Lagny (3,468 inhabitants) and so near Paris is only the

[18] Of course, there is no question of contagious influence. These are three principal towns in the districts, of nearly equal importance, separated by many communes of very different rates. All the comparison proves is that social groups of like dimensions and with sufficiently similar living conditions, have a like suicide-rate without necessarily influencing one another.

219th; Montereau-Faut-Yonne (6,217 inhabitants), 245th; Fontaine-
bleau (11,939 inhabitants), 247th. . . . Finally Melun (11,170 inhabitants), principal town of the department, is only the 279th. On
the other hand, examining the 25 communes at the head of the list,
one will find all but 2 of very small population." [19]

Outside of France we shall make identical discoveries. The part of
Europe most infested with suicide is that including Denmark and
central Germany. Now in this vast zone the country leading all others
by far is the Kingdom of Saxony; it has 311 suicides per million
inhabitants. The Duchy of Saxe-Altenburg follows next (303 suicides), while Brandenburg has only 204. These two little states,
however, are far from being centers of importance in Germany.
Neither Dresden nor Altenburg set the tone for Hamburg or Berlin.
Of all the Italian provinces, likewise, Bologna and Livorno have proportionally most suicides (88 and 84); Milan, Genoa, Turin and
Rome follow only at a distance according to averages reached by
Morselli for the years 1864–1876.

In short, all the maps show us that suicide, far from being
grouped more or less concentrically around certain centers from
which it radiates more and more weakly, occurs in great roughly
(but only roughly) homogeneous masses and with no central nucleus.
Such a configuration indicates nothing with respect to the influence
of imitation. It merely shows that suicide is not restricted to local
circumstances varying from city to city, but that its determining conditions are always of a certain general nature. There are here neither

---

[19] *Op. cit.*, pp. 193-194. The very small commune at the head (Lesche) has 1 suicide to 630 inhabitants, or 1,587 suicides per million, four to five times as many as
Paris. Nor are these cases peculiar to Seine-et-Marne. We are indebted to Dr. Legou-
pils of Trouville for the information concerning three tiny communes of the district
of Pont-l'Evêque, Villerville (978 inhabitants), Cricqueboeuf (150 inhabitants) and
Pennedepie (333 inhabitants). The suicide-rates calculated for periods ranging from
14 to 25 years are respectively 429,800 and 1,081 per million inhabitants.

Of course, it is true that large cities generally have more suicides than small ones
or country districts. But the proposition is only broadly true and has many exceptions. Besides, the preceding facts which seem to contradict it may be reconciled
with it. We need only agree that large cities are formed and develop under the influence of the same causes which themselves determine the development of suicide
more than the cities do themselves. Thus these cities are naturally numerous in
regions rich in suicides, but without having any monopoly in them; such cities are
few, on the contrary, where suicides are few without the small number of the latter
being due to their absence. Thus their average rate would generally be superior to
that of country districts, though inferior to it in certain cases.

imitators nor imitated, but relative identity in the effects, due to relative identity in the causes. And this is readily understandable if, as is foreshadowed by all the preceding remarks, suicide depends essentially on certain states of the social environment. For the latter generally retains the same constitution over very considerable areas. Thus, wherever it is the same, it naturally has the same consequences without contagion having anything to do with it. This is why the suicide-rate in a given region usually remains at very much the same level. On the other hand, since its generating causes can never be quite evenly distributed, inevitably it occasionally shows more or less important variations, from one place to another, from one district to a neighboring district such as those we have indicated.

The proof that this explanation is true is that the suicide-rate changes abruptly and completely whenever there is an abrupt change in social environment. Never does the environment exert influence beyond its natural limits. Never does a country very predisposed to suicide by special conditions cast its influence over its neighbors by dint of mere example, unless the same or similar conditions exist there to the same extent. Thus in Germany suicide is endemic and its ravages have been mentioned; we shall show later that Protestantism is the chief cause of this exceptional aptitude. Yet three regions are exceptions to the general rule; the Rhenish provinces with Westphalia, Bavaria and especially Bavarian Swabia, and finally Posnania. These alone in all Germany have less than 100 suicides per million inhabitants. On the map [20] they seem like three lost islands and their clear areas contrast with the surrounding darker shades. They are all three Catholic. Thus the very intense suicidal current which flows about them, has no influence upon them; it stops at their frontiers simply because it fails to find conditions favorable to its development beyond. Likewise the entire South of Switzerland is Catholic; all Protestant elements are in the North. From the contrast of these two districts on the map [21] of suicides, one would think that they belonged to different societies. Although they are everywhere contiguous and in uninterrupted relations with one another, each maintains its individuality with respect to suicide. The average is as low on

[20] See Appendix III.
[21] See Appendix III and for details of figures by cantons, Bk. II, Chap. V, Table XXVI.

one hand as it is high on the other. Likewise, within northern Switzerland, Lucern, Uri, Unterwalden, Schwyz and Zug, Catholic cantons, have at most 100 suicides per million, though surrounded by Protestant cantons having many more.

Another experiment might be attempted which should, we believe, confirm the above proofs. Moral contagion can be spread in only two ways: either the event which serves as a model is spread orally by what we call public report, or the newspapers disseminate it. Generally the latter are blamed; undoubtedly they do form a powerful diffusive instrument. If imitation plays a part in the development of suicide, therefore, suicides should vary with the importance that newspapers have in public opinion.

Unfortunately this importance is quite hard to determine. Not the number of papers but rather that of their readers is the measure of the extent of their influence. In a relatively decentralized country like Switzerland, papers may be numerous because each locality has its own and yet, since each is little read, its power of propagation is slight. On the contrary, a single journal such as the *London Times,* the *New York Herald,* the *Petit Journal,* etc., affects an immense public. It even seems that the press can hardly have the influence attributed to it without a certain centralization. For where each region has its own way of life, less interest is felt for what passes beyond its small horizon; distant facts are less observed and, consequently, are read more carelessly. Thus there are fewer examples to stimulate imitation. Quite otherwise is the case where a wider field of action is open to sympathy and curiosity by the levelling of local environments and where, accordingly, great papers daily report all important events of their own and neighboring countries, distributing the news in all directions. The accumulating examples reenforce each other. But, of course, one cannot compare the reading public of the different European newspapers and especially evaluate the more or less local character of their news. Yet without being able positively to prove our statement, we doubt that France and England are inferior in these two respects to Denmark, Saxony and even the various districts of Germany. Yet suicides are far fewer in the two countries first named. Nor can it be supposed that within France far fewer papers are read south than north of the Loire; but the difference with respect to suicide between these two regions

is known. Without wishing to attach more importance than it deserves to an argument that we cannot rest on established facts, we
nevertheless believe it has enough probability to merit some attention.

IV

In short, certain as the contagion of suicide is from individual to
individual, imitation never seems to propagate it so as to affect the
social suicide-rate. Imitation may give rise to more or less numerous
individual cases, but it does not contribute to the unequal tendency
in different societies to self-destruction, or to that of smaller social
groups within each society. Its radiating influence is always very
restricted; and what is more, intermittent. Its attainment of a certain
degree of intensity is always brief.

But a more general reason explains why the effects of imitation
are imperceptible in statistics. It is because imitation all by itself
has no effect on suicide. Except in the very rare instances of a more
or less complete "fixed idea," the thought of an act is not sufficient
to produce a similar act itself in an adult, unless he is a person
himself specially so inclined. "I have always noticed," writes Morel,
"that, powerful as the influence of imitation is, neither it nor the
impression left by the recital or reading of an unusual crime proved
strong enough to provoke similar acts among persons of perfectly
sound mind." [22] Likewise, Dr. Paul Moreau of Tours thought his
personal observations proved that contagious suicide occurs only
among individuals strongly predisposed to it.[23]

To be sure, as this predisposition seemed to him to depend essentially on organic causes, he found it hard to explain certain cases
not referable to this origin without admitting combinations of quite
improbable, fairly miraculous causes. How improbable that the fifteen patients above referred to were all simultaneously afflicted with
nervous weakness! And so with the contagious events so often
noticed in the army or in prisons. But the facts are easily explicable
once it is acknowledged that the suicidal tendency can be created
by the social environment. Then they may well be attributed not to a
blind chance which from all points of the compass assembled in one
barracks or penitentiary a fairly large number of persons all with

[22] *Traité des maladies mentales,* p. 243.
[23] *De la contagion du suicide,* p. 42.

the same mental affliction, but to the influence of the common environment in which they live. In fact we shall see that a collective state exists in prisons and in regiments disposing the soldiers and prisoners as directly to suicide as the most violent neurosis. An example furnishes the occasion which causes the impulse to break out, but it does not create the impulse and would have no effect if it did not exist.

With very rare exceptions, then, it may be said that imitation is not an original factor of suicide. It only exposes a state which is the true generating cause of the act and which probably would have produced its natural effect even had imitation not intervened; for the predisposition must be very strong to enable so slight a matter to translate it into action. It is not surprising, therefore, that the acts fail to show the stamp of imitation, since it has no influence of its own, and what it does exert is very slight.

A practical remark may serve as corollary to this conclusion.

Certain authors, ascribing to imitation a power it does not possess, have demanded that the printing of reports of suicides and crimes in the newspapers be prohibited.[24] Such a prohibition might possibly succeed in slightly reducing the annual total of such acts. But it could hardly modify their social rate. The strength of the collective tendency would be unchanged, since the moral state of the groups would be unaffected by this. Weighing the doubtful and very slight possible advantages of such a measure against the serious objections to the suppression of all judicial publicity, the legislator may well hesitate to follow the advice of such specialists. Actually, what may contribute to the growth of suicide or murder is not talking of it but how it is talked of. Where such acts are loathed, the feelings they arouse penetrate the recital of them and thus offset rather than encourage individual inclinations. But inversely, when society is morally decadent, its state of uncertainty inspires in it an indulgence for immoral acts frankly expressed whenever they are discussed, and which obscures their immorality. Then example becomes truly dangerous not as example but because the revulsion it should inspire is reduced by social tolerance or indifference.

But what this chapter chiefly shows is the weakness of the theory that imitation is the main source of all collective life. No fact is

---

[24] See especially Aubry, *Contagion du meurtre*, 1st ed., p. 87.

more readily transmissible by contagion than suicide, yet we have just seen that this contagiousness has no social effects. If imitation is so much without social influence in this case, it cannot have more in others; the virtues ascribed to it are therefore imaginary. Within a narrow circle it may well occasion the repetition of a single thought or action, but never are its repercussions sufficiently deep or extensive to reach and modify the heart of society. Thanks to the almost unanimous and generally ancient predominance of collective states, they are far too resistant to be offset by an individual innovation. How could an individual, who is nothing more than an individual,[25] be strong enough to mould society to his image? If we were not still reduced to conceiving of the social world almost as crudely as the primitive does the physical world; if, regardless of all scientific induction, we were not still reduced at least tacitly and unconsciously to admitting that social phenomena are not proportionate to their causes, we would not even pause to consider a conception which, though of biblical simplicity, is at the same time in flagrant contradiction to the fundamental principles of thought. We no longer believe that zoological species are only individual variations hereditarily transmitted; [26] it is equally inadmissible that a social fact is merely a generalized individual fact. But most untenable of all is the idea that this generalization may be due to some blind contagion or other. We should even be amazed at the continuing necessity of discussing an hypothesis which, aside from the serious objections it suggests, has never even begun to receive experimental proof. For it has never been shown that imitation can account for a definite order of social facts and, even less, that it alone can account for them. The proposition has merely been stated as an aphorism, resting on vaguely metaphysical considerations. But sociology can only claim to be treated as a science when those who pursue it are forbidden to dogmatize in this fashion, so patently eluding the regular requirements of proof.

[25] By this, we mean an individual stripped of all power possibly acquired by collective confidence or admiration. Clearly, a functionary or a popular man embodies not merely his individually inherited powers but social powers resulting from the collective sentiments of which they are the object, which give him influence over the progress of society. But only in so far as he is more than an individual does he possess this influence.

[26] See Delage, *La structure du protoplasme et les théories de l'hérédité*, Paris, 1895, p. 813 ff.

BOOK TWO
SOCIAL CAUSES AND SOCIAL TYPES

CHAPTER 1
HOW TO DETERMINE SOCIAL CAUSES
AND SOCIAL TYPES

T HE results of the preceding book are not wholly negative. We have in fact shown that for each social group there is a specific tendency to suicide explained neither by the organic-psychic constitution of individuals nor the nature of the physical environment. Consequently, by elimination, it must necessarily depend upon social causes and be in itself a collective phenomenon; some of the facts examined, especially the geographic and seasonal variations of suicide, had definitely led us to this conclusion. We must now study this tendency more closely.

I

To accomplish this it would seem to be best to inquire first whether the tendency is single and indestructible or whether it does not rather consist of several different tendencies, which may be isolated by analysis and which should be separately studied. If so, we should proceed as follows. As the tendency, single or not, is observable only in its individual manifestations, we should have to begin with the latter. Thus we should observe and describe as many as possible, of course omitting those due to mental alienation. If all were found to have the same essential characteristics, they should be grouped in a single class; otherwise, which is much more likely—for they are too different not to include several varieties—a certain number of species should be determined according to their resemblances and differences. One would admit as many suicidal currents as there were distinct types, then seek to determine their causes and respective importance. We have pursued some such method in our brief study of the suicide of insanity.

Unfortunately, no classification of the suicides of sane persons can be made in terms of their morphological types or characteristics, from almost complete lack of the necessary data. To be attempted, it would require good descriptions of many individual cases. One would have to know the psychological condition of the suicide at the moment of forming his resolve, how he prepared to accomplish it, how he finally performed it, whether he were agitated or depressed, calm or exalted, anxious or irritated, etc. Now we have such data practically only for some cases of insane suicide, and just such observations and descriptions by alienists have enabled us to establish the chief types of suicide where insanity is the determining cause. We have almost no such information for others. Brierre de Boismont alone has tried to do this descriptive work for 1,328 cases where the suicide left letters or other records summarized by the author in his book. But, first, this summary is much too brief. Then, the patient's revelations of his condition are usually insufficient, if not suspect. He is only too apt to be mistaken concerning himself and the state of his feelings; he may believe that he is acting calmly, though at the peak of nervous excitement. Finally, besides being insufficiently objective, these observations cover too few facts to permit definite conclusions. Some very vague dividing lines are perceptible and their suggestions may be utilized; but they are too indefinite to provide a regular classification. Furthermore, in view of the manner of execution of most suicides, proper observations are next to impossible.

But our aim may be achieved by another method. Let us reverse the order of study. Only in so far as the effective causes differ can there be different types of suicide. For each to have its own nature, it must also have special conditions of existence. The same antecedent or group of antecedents cannot sometimes produce one result and sometimes another, for, if so, the difference of the second from the first would itself be without cause, which would contradict the principle of causality. Every proved specific difference between causes therefore implies a similar difference between effects. Consequently, we shall be able to determine the social types of suicide by classifying them not directly by their preliminarily described characteristics, but by the causes which produce them. Without asking why they differ from one another, we will first seek the social conditions responsible for them; then group these conditions in a number of separate classes by their resemblances and differences, and we shall be sure that a specific type of suicide will correspond to each of these classes. In a word, instead of being morphological, our classification will from the start be aetiological. Nor is this a sign of inferiority, for the nature of a phenomenon is much more profoundly got at by knowing its cause than by knowing its characteristics only, even the essential ones.

The defect of this method, of course, is to assume the diversity of types without being able to identify them. It may prove their existence and number but not their special characteristics. But this drawback may be obviated, at least in a certain measure. Once the nature of the causes is known we shall try to deduce the nature of the effects, since they will be both qualified and classified by their attachment to their respective sources. Of course, if this deduction were not at all guided by facts, it might be lost in purely imaginary constructions. But with the aid of some data on the morphology of suicides it may be made clearer. Alone, these data are too incomplete and unsure to provide a principle of classification; but once the outlines of this classification are found, the data may be used. They will indicate what direction the deduction should take and, by the examples they offer, the deductively established species may be shown not to be imaginary. Thus we shall descend from causes to effects and our aetiological classification will be completed by a morphological one which can verify the former and vice versa.

In all respects this reverse method is the only fitting one for the special problem that we have set ourselves. Indeed we must not forget that what we are studying is the social suicide-rate. The only types of interest to us, accordingly, are those contributing to its formation and influencing its variation. Now, it is not sure that all individual sorts of voluntary death have this quality. Some, though general to a certain degree, are not bound or not sufficiently bound to the moral temper of society to enter as a characteristic element into the special physiognomy of each people with respect to suicide. For instance, we have seen that alcoholism is not a determining factor of the particular aptitude of each society, yet alcoholic suicides evidently exist and in great numbers. No description, however good, of particular cases will ever tell us which ones have a sociological character. If one wants to know the several tributaries of suicide as a collective phenomenon one must regard it in its collective form, that is, through statistical data, from the start. The social rate must be taken directly as the object of analysis; progress must be from the whole to the parts. Clearly, it can only be analyzed with reference to its different causes, for in themselves the units composing it are homogeneous, without qualitative difference. We must then immediately discover its causes and later consider their repercussions among individuals.

II

But how reach these causes?

The legal establishments of fact always accompanying suicide include the motive (family trouble, physical or other pain, remorse, drunkenness, etc.), which seems to have been the determining cause, and in the statistical reports of almost all countries is found a special table containing the results of these inquiries under the title: *presumptive motives of suicides*. It seems natural to profit by this already accomplished work and begin our study by a comparison of such records. They apparently show us the immediate antecedents of different suicides; and is it not good methodology for understanding the phenomenon we are studying to seek first its nearest causes, and then retrace our steps further in the series of phenomena if it appears needful?

But as Wagner long ago remarked, what are called statistics of the motives of suicides are actually statistics of the opinions concerning such motives of officials, often of lower officials, in charge of this information service. Unfortunately, official establishments of fact are known to be often defective even when applied to obvious material facts comprehensible to any conscientious observer and leaving no room for evaluation. How suspect must they be considered when applied not simply to recording an accomplished fact but to its interpretation and explanation! To determine the cause of a phenomenon is always a difficult problem. The scholar requires all sorts of observations and experiments to solve even one question. Now, human volition is the most complex of all phenomena. The value of improvised judgments, attempting to assign a definite origin for each special case from a few hastily collected bits of information is, therefore, obviously slight. As soon as some of the facts commonly supposed to lead to despair are thought to have been discovered in the victim's past, further search is considered useless, and his drunkenness or domestic unhappiness or business troubles are blamed, depending on whether he is supposed recently to have lost money, had home troubles or indulged a taste for liquor. Such uncertain data cannot be considered a basis of explanation for suicide.

Moreover, even if more credible, such data could not be very useful, for the motives thus attributed to the suicides, whether rightly or wrongly, are not their true causes. The proof is that the proportional numbers of cases assigned by statistics to each of these presumed causes remain almost identically the same, whereas the absolute figures, on the contrary, show the greatest variations. In France, from 1856 to 1878, suicide rises about 40 per cent, and more than 100 per cent in Saxony in the period 1854–1880 (1,171 cases in place of 547). Now, in both countries each category of motives retains the same respective importance from one period to another. This appears in Table XVII on page 150.

If we consider that the figures here reported are, and can be, only grossly approximate and therefore do not attach too much importance to slight differences, they will clearly appear to be practically stable. But for the contributory share of each presumed reason to remain proportionally the same while suicide has doubled its extent, each must be supposed to have doubled its effect. It cannot be by coincidence that all at the same time become doubly fatal. The conclusion is forced that they all depend on a more general state, which all more or less faithfully reflect. This it is which makes them more or less productive of suicide and which is thus the truly determining cause of it. We must then investigate this state without wasting time on its distant repercussions in the consciousness of individuals.

Another fact, taken from Legoyt,[1] shows still better the worth of the causal action ascribed to these different motives. No two occupations are more different from each other than agriculture and the liberal professions. The life of an artist, a scholar, a lawyer, an officer, a judge has no resemblance whatever to that of a farmer.

[1] *Op. cit.*, p. 358.

TABLE XVII—Share of Each Category of Motives in 100 Annual Suicides of Each Sex

FRANCE *

	Men		Women	
	1856–60	1874–78	1856–60	1874–78
Poverty and losses	13.30	11.79	5.38	5.77
Family troubles	11.68	12.53	12.79	16.00
Love, jealousy, debauchery, misconduct	15.48	16.98	13.16	12.20
Various types of distress	23.70	23.43	17.16	20.22
Mental sickness	25.67	27.09	45.75	41.81
Remorse, fear of criminal sentence	0.84	.....	0.19	.....
Other causes and unknown causes	9.33	8.18	5.51	4.00
Totals	100.00	100.00	100.00	100.00

SAXONY †

	Men		Women	
	1854–78	1880	1854–78	1880
Physical pain	5.64	5.86	7.43	7.98
Family troubles	2.39	3.30	3.18	1.72
Losses and poverty	9.52	11.28	2.80	4.42
Debauchery, gambling	11.15	10.74	1.59	0.44
Remorse, fear of prosecution, etc.	10.41	8.51	10.44	6.21
Unhappy love	1.79	1.50	3.74	6.20
Mental troubles, religious mania	27.94	30.27	50.64	54.43
Anger	2.00	3.29	3.04	3.09
Disgust with life	9.58	6.67	5.37	5.76
Unknown causes	19.58	18.58	11.77	9.75
Totals	100.00	100.00	100.00	100.00

* According to Legoyt, p. 342.
† According to Oettingen, *Moralstatistik*, Tables appended, p. 110.

It is practically certain, then, that the social causes for suicide are not the same for both. Now, not only are the suicides of these two categories of persons attributed to the same reasons, but the respective importance of these different reasons is supposed to be almost exactly the same in both. Following are the actual percentile shares of the chief motives for suicide in these two occupations in France during the years 1874–78:

	Agriculture	Liberal Professions
Loss of employment, financial losses, poverty	8.15	8.87
Family troubles	14.45	13.14
Disappointed love, jealousy	1.48	2.01
Intoxication and drunkenness	13.23	6.41
Suicides of criminals or minor offenders	4.09	4.73
Physical sufferings	15.91	19.89
Mental sickness	35.80	34.04
Disgust with life, varied disappointments	2.93	4.94
Unknown causes	3.96	5.97
	100.00	100.00

Except for intoxication and drunkenness, the figures, especially those of most numerical importance, differ little from column to column. Thus, through consideration of motives only, one might think that the causes of suicide are not, to be sure, of the same intensity but of the same sort in both cases. Yet actually, the forces impelling the farm laborer and the cultivated man of the city to suicide are widely different. The reasons ascribed for suicide, therefore, or those to which the suicide himself ascribes his act, are usually only apparent causes. Not only are the reasons merely individual repercussions of a general state, but they express the general state very unfaithfully, since they are identical while it is not. They may be said to indicate the individual's weak points, where the outside current bearing the impulse to self-destruction most easily finds introduction. But they are no part of this current itself and consequently cannot help us to understand it.

We therefore do not regret that certain countries like England and Austria are abandoning the collection of such supposed causes of suicide. Statistical efforts should take quite a different direction. Instead of trying to solve these insoluble problems of moral casuistry, they should notice more carefully the social concomitants of suicide. For our own part, at least, we make it a rule not to employ in our studies such uncertain and uninstructive data; no law of any interest has in fact ever been drawn from them by students of suicide. We shall thus refer to them only rarely, when they seem to have special meaning and to offer special assurance. We shall try to determine the productive causes of suicide directly, without concerning ourselves with the forms they can assume in particular individuals. Disregarding the individual as such, his motives and his ideas, we shall seek directly the states of the various social environments (religious confessions, family, political society, occupational groups, etc.), in terms of which the variations of suicide occur. Only then returning to the individual, shall we study how these general causes become individualized so as to produce the homicidal results involved.

CHAPTER 2
EGOISTIC SUICIDE

First let us see how the different religious confessions affect suicide.

I

If one casts a glance at the map of European suicide, it is at once clear that in purely Catholic countries like Spain, Portugal, Italy, suicide is very little developed, while it is at its maximum in Protestant countries, in Prussia, Saxony, Denmark. The following averages compiled by Morselli confirm this first conclusion:

	Average of Suicides per Million Inhabitants
Protestant states	190
Mixed states (Protestant and Catholic)	96
Catholic states	58
Greek Catholic states	40

The low proportion of the Greek Catholics cannot be surely attributed to religion; for as their civilization is very different from that of the other European nations, this difference of culture may be the cause of their lesser aptitude. But this is not the case with most Catholic or Protestant societies. To be sure, they are not all on the same intellectual and moral level; yet the resemblances are sufficiently essential to make it possible to ascribe to confessional differences the marked contrast they offer in respect to suicide.

Nevertheless, this first comparison is still too summary. In spite of undeniable similarities, the social environments of the inhabitants of these different countries are not identical. The civilizations of Spain and Portugal are far below that of Germany and this inferiority may conceivably be the reason for the lesser development of suicide which we have just mentioned. If one wishes to avoid this source of error and determine more definitely the influence of Catholicism and Protestantism on the suicidal tendency, the two religions must be compared in the heart of a single society.

Of all the great states of Germany, Bavaria has by far the fewest suicides. There have been barely 90 per million inhabitants yearly since 1874, while Prussia has 133 (1871–75), the duchy of Baden 156, Wurttemberg 162, Saxony 300. Now, Bavaria also has most Catholics, 713.2 to 1,000 inhabitants. On the other hand, if one com-

Bavarian Provinces (1867–75) *

Provinces w. Catholic Minority (less than 50%)	Suicides per Million Inhabitants	Provinces w. Catholic Majority (50 to 90%)	Suicides Per Million Inhabitants	Provinces w. More Than 90% Catholic	Suicides Per Million Inhabitants
Rhenish Palatinate	167	Lower Franconia	157	Upper Palatinate	64
Central Franconia	207	Swabia	118	Upper Bavaria	114
Upper Franconia	204			Lower Bavaria	19
Average	192	Average	135	Average	75

* The population below 15 years has been omitted.

pares the different provinces of Bavaria, suicides are found to be in direct proportion to the number of Protestants and in inverse proportion to that of Catholics (See Table above). Not only the proportions of averages to one another confirm the law but all the numbers of the first column are higher than those of the second and those of the second higher tnan those of the third without exception.

It is the same with Prussia:

Prussian Provinces (1883–90)

Provinces with More Than 90% Protestant	Suicides per Million Inhabitants	Provinces with from 89 to 68% Protestant	Suicides per Million Inhabitants
Saxony	309.4	Hanover	212.3
Schleswig	312.9	Hesse	200.3
Pomerania	171.5	Brandenburg and Berlin	296.3
		E. Prussia	171.3
Average	264.6	Average	220.0

Provinces with from 40 to 50% Protestant	Suicides per Million Inhabitants	Provinces with from 32 to 28% Protestant	Suicides per Million Inhabitants
W. Prussia	123.9	Posen	96.4
Silesia	260.2	Rhineland	100.3
Westphalia	107.5	Hohenzollern	90.1
Average	163.6	Average	95.6

There are only two slight irregularities among the 14 provinces thus compared, so far as detail is concerned; Silesia, which because of its relatively high number of suicides should be in the second category, is only in the third, while on the contrary Pomerania would be more in its place in the second than in the first colum.

Switzerland forms an interesting study from this same point of view. For as both French and German populations exist there, the influence of the confession is observable separately on each race. Now, its influence is the same on both. Catholic cantons show four and five times fewer suicides than Protestant, of whichever nationality.

French Cantons		German Cantons		Total of Cantons of All Nationalities	
Catholics	83 suicides per million inhabitants	Catholics	87 suicides	Catholics	86.7 suicides
				Mixed	212.0 suicides
Protestants	453 suicides per million	Protestants	293 suicides	Protestants	326.3 suicides

Confessional influence is therefore so great as to dominate all others.

Besides, in a fairly large number of cases the number of suicides per million inhabitants of the population of each confession has been directly determined. The following figures were obtained by various observers:

TABLE XVIII—Suicides in Different Countries per Million Persons of Each Confession

		Protestants	Catholics	Jews	Names of Observers
Austria	(1852–59)	79.5	51.3	20.7	Wagner
Prussia	(1849–55)	159.9	49.6	46.4	Id.
Prussia	(1869–72)	187	69	96	Morselli
Prussia	(1890)	240	100	180	Prinzing
Baden	(1852–62)	139	117	87	Legoyt
Baden	(1870–74)	171	136.7	124	Morselli
Baden	(1878–88)	242	170	210	Prinzing
Bavaria	(1844–56)	135.4	49.1	105.9	Morselli
Bavaria	(1884–91)	224	94	193	Prinzing
Wurttemberg	(1846–60)	113.5	77.9	65.6	Wagner
Wurttemberg	(1873–76)	190	120	60	Durkheim
Wurttemberg	(1881–90)	170	119	142	Id.

Thus, everywhere without exception,[1] Protestants show far more suicides than the followers of other confessions. The difference varies

[1] We have no data on confessional influence in France, Leroy, however, tells us the following in his study on Seine-et-Marne: in the communes of Quincy, Nanteuil-les-Meaux, Mareuil, Protestants show one suicide to 310 inhabitants, Catholics 1 to 678 (op. cit., p. 203).

between a minimum of 20 to 30 per cent and a maximum of 300 per cent. It is useless to invoke with Mayr [2] against such a unanimous agreement of facts, the isolated case of Norway and Sweden which, though Protestant, have only an average number of suicides. First, as we noted at the beginning of this chapter, these international comparisons are not significant unless bearing on a considerable number of countries, and even in this case are not conclusive. There are sufficiently great differences between the peoples of the Scandinavian peninsula and those of Central Europe for it to be reasonable that Protestantism does not produce exactly the same effects on both. But furthermore, if the suicide-rate is not in itself very high in these two countries, it seems relatively so if one considers their modest rank among the civilized peoples of Europe. There is no reason to suppose that they have reached an intellectual level above Italy, to say the least, yet self-destruction occurs from twice to three times as often (90 to 100 suicides per million inhabitants as against 40). May Protestantism not be the cause of this relatively higher figure? Thus the fact not only does not tell against the law just established on the basis of so many observations, but rather tends to confirm it.[3]

The aptitude of Jews for suicide is always less than that of Protestants; in a very general way it is also, though to a lesser degree, lower than that of Catholics. Occasionally however, the latter relation is reversed; such cases occur especially in recent times. Up to the middle of the century, Jews killed themselves less frequently than Catholics in all countries but Bavaria; [4] only towards 1870 do they begin to lose their ancient immunity. They still very rarely greatly exceed the rate for Catholics. Besides, it must be remembered that Jews live more exclusively than other confessional groups in cities and are in intellectual occupations. On this account they are more inclined to suicide than the members of other confessions, for reasons other than their religion. If therefore the rate for Judaism is so low, in spite of this

[2] *Handwörterbuch der Staatswissenschaften*, Supplement, Vol. I, p. 702.
[3] The case of England is exceptional, a non-Catholic country where suicide is infrequent. It will be explained below.
[4] Bavaria is still the only exception: Jews there kill themselves twice as often as Catholics. Is there something exceptional about the position of Judaism in this country? We do not know.

aggravating circumstance, it may be assumed that other things being equal, their religion has the fewest suicides of all.

These facts established, what is their explanation?

II

If we consider that the Jews are everywhere in a very small minority and that in most societies where the foregoing observations were made, Catholics are in the minority, we are tempted to find in these facts the cause explaining the relative rarity of voluntary deaths in these two confessions.[5] Obviously, the less numerous confessions, facing the hostility of the surrounding populations, in order to maintain themselves are obliged to exercise severe control over themselves and subject themselves to an espcially rigorous discipline. To justify the always precarious tolerance granted them, they have to practice greater morality. Besides these considerations, certain facts seem really to imply that this special factor has some influence. In Prussia, the minority status of Catholics is very pronounced, since they are only a third of the whole population. They kill themselves only one third as often as the Protestants. The difference decreases in Bavaria where two thirds of the inhabitants are Catholics; the voluntary deaths of the latter are here only in the proportion of 100 to 275 of those of Protestants or else of 100 to 238, according to the period. Finally, in the almost entirely Catholic Empire of Austria, only 155 Protestant to 100 Catholic suicides are found. It would seem then that where Protestantism becomes a minority its tendency to suicide decreases.

But first, suicide is too little an object of public condemnation for the slight measure of blame attaching to it to have such influence, even on minorities obliged by their situation to pay special heed to public opinion. As it is an act without offense to others, it involves no great reproach to the groups more inclined to it than others, and is not apt to increase greatly their relative ostracism as would certainly be the case with a greater frequency of crime and misdemeanor. Besides, when religious intolerance is very pronounced, it often produces an opposite effect. Instead of exciting the dissenters to respect opinion more, it accustoms them to disregard it. When one feels himself an object of inescapable hostility, one abandons the idea of con-

[5] Legoyt, *op. cit.*, p. 205: Oettingen, *Moralstatistik*, p. 654.

ciliating it and is the more resolute in his most unpopular observances. This has frequently happened to the Jews and thus their exceptional immunity probably has another cause.

Anyway, this explanation would not account for the respective situation of Protestants and Catholics. For though the protective influence of Catholicism is less in Austria and Bavaria, where it is in the majority, it is still considerable. Catholicism does not therefore owe this solely to its minority status. More generally, whatever the proportional share of these two confessions in the total population, wherever their comparison has been possible from the point of view of suicide, Protestants are found to kill themselves much more often than Catholics. There are even countries like the Upper Palatinate and Upper Bavaria, where the population is almost wholly Catholic (92 and 96 per cent) and where there are nevertheless 300 and 423 Protestant suicides to 100 Catholic suicides. The proportion even rises to 528 per cent in Lower Bavaria where the reformed religion has not quite one follower to 100 inhabitants. Therefore, even if the prudence incumbent on minorities were a partial cause of the great difference between the two religions, the greatest share is certainly due to other causes.

We shall find these other causes in the nature of these two religious systems. Yet they both prohibit suicide with equal emphasis; not only do they penalize it morally with great severity, but both teach that a new life begins beyond the tomb where men are punished for their evil actions, and Protestantism just as well as Catholicism numbers suicide among them. Finally, in both cults these prohibitions are of divine origin; they are represented not as the logical conclusion of correct reason, but God Himself is their authority. Therefore, if Protestantism is less unfavorable to the development of suicide, it is not because of a different attitude from that of Catholicism. Thus, if both religions have the same precepts with respect to this particular matter, their dissimilar influence on suicide must proceed from one of the more general characteristics differentiating them.

The only essential difference between Catholicism and Protestantism is that the second permits free inquiry to a far greater degree than the first. Of course, Catholicism by the very fact that it is an idealistic religion concedes a far greater place to thought and reflection than Greco-Latin polytheism or Hebrew monotheism. It is not restricted to mechanical ceremonies but seeks the control of the conscience. So it appeals to conscience, and even when demanding blind submission of reason, does so by employing the language of reason. None the less, the Catholic accepts his faith ready made, without scrutiny. He may not even submit it to historical examination since the original texts that serve as its basis are proscribed. A whole hierarchical system of authority is devised, with marvelous ingenuity, to render tradition invariable. All *variation* is abhorrent to Catholic thought. The Protestant is far more the author of his faith. The Bible is put in his hands and no interpretation is imposed upon him. The very structure of the reformed cult stresses this state of religious individualism. Nowhere but in England is the Protestant clergy a hierarchy; like the worshippers, the priest has no other source but himself and his conscience. He is a more instructed guide than the run of worshippers but with no special authority for fixing dogma. But what best proves that this freedom of inquiry proclaimed by the founders of the Reformation has not remained a Platonic affirmation is the increasing multiplicity of all sorts of sects so strikingly in contrast with the indivisible unity of the Catholic Church.

We thus reach our first conclusion, that the proclivity of Protestantism for suicide must relate to the spirit of free inquiry that animates this religion. Let us understand this relationship correctly. Free inquiry itself is only the effect of another cause. When it appears, when men, after having long received their ready made faith from tradition, claim the right to shape it for themselves, this is not because of the intrinsic desirability of free inquiry, for the latter involves as much sorrow as happiness. But it is because men henceforth need this liberty. This very need can have only one cause: the overthrow of traditional beliefs. If they still asserted themselves with equal energy, it would never occur to men to criticize them. If they still had the same authority, men would not demand the right to verify the source of this authority. Reflection develops only if its development becomes imperative, that is, if certain ideas and instinctive sentiments which have hitherto adequately guided conduct are found to have lost their efficacy. Then reflection intervenes to fill the gap that has appeared, but which it has not created. Just as reflection disappears to the extent that thought and action take the form of automatic habits, it awakes only when accepted habits become disorganized. It asserts its rights against public opinion only when the latter loses strength, that is, when it is no longer prevalent to the same extent. If these assertions occur not merely occasionally and as passing crises, but become chronic; if individual consciences keep reaffirming their autonomy, it is because they are constantly subject to conflicting impulses, because a new opinion has not been formed to replace the one no longer existing. If a new system of beliefs were constituted which seemed as indisputable to everyone as the old, no one would think of discussing it any longer. Its discussion would no longer even be permitted; for ideas shared by an entire society draw from this consensus an authority that makes them sacrosanct and raises them above dispute. For them to have become mc:e tolerant, they must first already have become the object of less general and complete assent and been weakened by preliminary controversy.

Thus, if it is correct to say that free inquiry once proclaimed, multiplies schisms, it must be added that it presupposes them and derives from them, for it is claimed and instituted as a principle only in order to permit latent or half-declared schisms to develop more freely. So if Protestantism concedes a greater freedom to individual thought than Catholicism, it is because it has fewer common beliefs and practices. Now, a religious society cannot exist without a collective *credo* and the more extensive the *credo* the more unified and strong is the society. For it does not unite men by an exchange and reciprocity of services, a temporal bond of union which permits and even presupposes differences, but which a religious society cannot form. It socializes men only by attaching them completely to an identical body of doctrine and socializes them in proportion as this body of doctrine is extensive and firm. The more numerous the manners of action and thought of a religious character are, which are accordingly removed from free inquiry, the more the idea of God presents itself in all details of existence, and makes individual wills converge to one identical goal. Inversely, the greater concessions a confessional group makes to individual judgment, the less it dominates lives, the less its cohesion and vitality. We thus reach the conclusion that the superiority of Protestantism with respect to suicide results from its being a less strongly integrated church than the Catholic church.

This also explains the situation of Judaism. Indeed, the reproach to which the Jews have for so long been exposed by Christianity has

created feelings of unusual solidarity among them. Their need of re-
sisting a general hostility, the very impossibility of free communication with the rest of the population, has forced them to strict union
among themselves. Consequently, each community became a small,
compact and coherent society with a strong feeling of self-conscious-
ness and unity. Everyone thought and lived alike; individual divergences were made almost impossible by the community of existence and the close and constant surveillance of all over each. The
Jewish church has thus been more strongly united than any other,
from its dependence on itself because of being the object of intolerance. By analogy with what has just been observed apropos of
Protestantism, the same cause must therefore be assumed for the
slight tendency of the Jews to suicide in spite of all sorts of circumstances which might on the contrary incline them to it. Doubtless
they owe this immunity in a sense to the hostility surrounding them.
But if this is its influence, it is not because it imposes a higher morality but because it obliges them to live in greater union. They are
immune to this degree because their religious society is of such solidarity. Besides, the ostracism to which they are subject is only one of
the causes producing this result; the very nature of Jewish beliefs
must contribute largely to it. Judaism, in fact, like all early religions,
consists basically of a body of practices minutely governing all the
details of life and leaving little free room to individual judgment.

III

Several facts confirm this explanation.

First, of all great Protestant countries, England is the one where
suicide is least developed. In fact, only about 80 suicides per million
inhabitants are found there, whereas the reformed societies of Germany have from 140 to 400; and yet the general activity of ideas and
business seems no less great there than elsewhere.[6] Now, it happens
at the same time that the Anglican church is far more powerfully integrated than other Protestant churches. To be sure, England has
been customarily regarded as the classic land of individual freedom;

---

[6] To be sure, the statistics of English suicides are not very exact. Because of the
penalties attached to suicide, many cases are reported as accidental death. However,
this inexactitude is not enough to explain the extent of the difference between this
country and Germany.

but actually many facts indicate that the number of common, obligatory beliefs and practices, which are thus withdrawn from free inquiry by individuals, is greater than in Germany. First, the law still sanctions many religious requirements: such as the law of the observance of Sunday, that forbidding stage representations of any character from Holy Scripture; the one until recently requiring some profession of faith from every member of political representative bodies, etc. Next, respect for tradition is known to be general and powerful in England: it must extend to matters of religion as well as others. But a highly developed traditionalism always more or less restricts activity of the individual. Finally, the Anglican clergy is the only Protestant clergy organized in a hierarchy. This external organization clearly shows an inner unity incompatible with a pronounced religious individualism.

Besides, England has the largest number of clergymen of any Protestant country. In 1876 there averaged 908 church-goers for every minister, compared with 932 in Hungary, 1,100 in Holland, 1,300 in Denmark, 1,440 in Switzerland and 1,600 in Germany.[7] The number of priests is not an insignificant detail nor a superficial characteristic but one related to the intrinsic nature of religion. The proof of this is that the Catholic clergy is everywhere much more numerous than the Protestant. In Italy there is a priest for every 267 Catholics, in Spain for 419, in Portugal for 536, in Switzerland for 540, in France for 823, in Belgium for 1,050. This is because the priest is the natural organ of faith and tradition and because here as elsewhere the organ inevitably develops -in exact proportion to its function. The more intense religious life, the more men are needed to direct it. The greater the number of dogmas and precepts the interpretation of which is not left to individual consciences, the more authorities are required to tell their meaning; moreover, the more numerous these authorities, the more closely they surround and the better they restrain the individual. Thus, far from weakening our theory, the case of England verifies it. If Protestantism there does not produce the same results as on the continent, it is because religious society there is much more strongly constituted and to this extent resembles the Catholic church.

[7] Oettingen, *Moralstatistik*, p. 626.

162 SUICIDE

Here, however, is a more general proof in confirmation of our thesis.

The taste for free inquiry can be aroused only if accompanied by that for learning. Knowledge is free thought's only means of achieving its purposes. When irrational beliefs or practices have lost their hold, appeal must be made, in the search for others, to the enlightened consciousness of which knowledge is only the highest form. Fundamentally, these two tendencies are one and spring from the same source. Men generally have the desire for self-instruction only in so far as they are freed from the yoke of tradition; for as long as the latter governs intelligence it is all-sufficient and jealous of any rival. On the other hand, light is sought as soon as customs whose origins are lost in obscurity no longer correspond to new necessities. This is why philosophy, the first, synthetic form of knowledge, appears as soon as religion has lost its sway, and only then; and is then followed progressively by the many single sciences with the further development of the very need which produced philosophy. Unless we are mistaken, if the progressive weakening of collective and customary prejudices produces a trend to suicide and if Protestantism derives thence its special pre-disposition to it, the two following facts should be noted: 1, the desire for learning must be stronger among Protestants than among Catholics; 2, in so far as his denotes a weakening of common beliefs it should vary with suicide, fairly generally. Do facts confirm this twofold hypothesis?

If Catholic France is compared with Protestant Germany merely at their highest levels, that is, if only the upper classes of both are compared, it seems that France may bear the comparison. In the great centers of our country, knowledge is no less honored or widespread than among our neighbors; we even decidedly outdistance several Protestant countries in this respect. But if the desire for learning is equally felt in the upper reaches of the two societies, it is not so on their lower levels; and whereas the maximal intensity is approximately the same in both, the average intensity is less among us. The same is true of the aggregate of Catholic nations compared with Protestant nations. Even assuming that the highest culture of the former is about the same as the latter's, the situation is quite otherwise as regards popular education. Whereas among the Protestant peoples of Saxony, Norway, Sweden, Baden, Denmark and Prussia, from

1877–1878 among 1,000 children of school age, that is, from 6 to 12 years, an average of 957 attended school, the Catholic peoples, France, Austria-Hungary, Spain and Italy, had only 667, or 31 per cent less. Proportions are the same for the periods of 1874–75 and 1860–61.[8] Prussia, the Protestant country having the lowest figure here, is yet far above France at the head of the Catholic countries; the former has 897 pupils per 1,000 children, the latter only 766.[9] In all of Germany, Bavaria has most Catholics and also most illiterates. Of all Bavarian provinces, the Upper Palatinate is one of the most profoundly Catholic and has also the most conscripted men who do not know how to read or write (15 per cent in 1871). In Prussia the same is true for the duchy of Posen and the province of Prussia.[10] Finally, in the whole kingdom there numbered in 1871, 66 illiterates to every 1,000 Protestants and 152 to 1,000 Catholics. The relation is the same for the women of both faiths.[11]

Perhaps it will be objected that primary instruction can be no measure of general education. The degree of a people's education, it is often said, does not depend on the greater or smaller number of illiterates. Let us agree to this qualification, though the various degrees of education are perhaps more closely interrelated than seems to be the case and the development of one is difficult without the simultaneous growth of the others.[12] In any case, although the level of primary instruction may only imperfectly reflect that of scientific culture, it has a certain reference to the extent of the desire for knowledge of a people as a whole. A people must feel this need very keenly to try to spread its elements even among the lowest classes. Thus to place the means of learning within everyone's reach, and even legally to forbid ignorance, shows a national awareness of the indispensability of broadened and enlightened intelligence of the individual for the nation's own existence. Actually, Protestant nations have so stressed primary instruction because they held that each individual must be able to understand the Bible. Our present search is

[8] Oettingen, *Moralstatistik*, p. 586.
[9] Bavaria slightly exceeds Prussia in one of these periods (1877–78); but only this once.
[10] Oettingen, *ibid.*, p. 582.
[11] Morselli, *op. cit.*, p. 223.
[12] Moreover it will appear below that both secondary and higher education are more developed among Protestants than among Catholics.

for the average intensity of this need, the value attached by each people to knowledge, not the standing of its scholars and their discoveries. From this special point of view, the state of advanced learning and truly scientific production would be a poor criterion; for it would show only what goes on in a limited sector of society. Popular and general education is a more accurate index.

Having thus proved our first proposition, let us attack the second. Does the craving for knowledge to the degree that it corresponds to a weakening of common faith really develop as does suicide? The very facts that Protestants are better educated and commit suicide more than Catholics is a first presumption for this. But the law can not only be verified by comparison of one faith with the other but also be observed within each religious confession.

Italy is wholly Catholic. Public instruction and suicide are identically distributed (See Table XIX).

TABLE XIX *—Comparison of Italian Provinces with Reference to Suicide and Education

First Group of Provinces	Per Cent of Marriages with Both Husband and Wife Literate	Suicides per Million Inhabitants
Piedmont	53.09	35.6
Lombardy	44.29	40.4
Liguria	41.15	47.3
Rome	32.61	41.7
Tuscany	24.33	40.6
Averages	39.09	41.1
Second Group of Provinces		
Venice	19.56	32.0
Emilia	19.31	62.9
Umbria	15.46	30.7
Marches	14.46	34.6
Campania	12.45	21.6
Sardinia	10.14	13.3
Averages	15.23	32.5
Third Group of Provinces		
Sicily	8.98	18.5
Abruzzi	6.35	15.7
Apulia	6.81	16.3
Calabria	4.67	8.1
Basilicata	4.35	15.0
Averages	6.23	14.7

* The figures for literate couples are from Oettingen, *Moralstatistik*, supplement, Table 85; they refer to the years 1872–78, suicides to the period 1864–76.

Not only do the averages correspond exactly, but the agreement extends to details. There is a single exception; Emilia, where under the influence of local causes suicides have no relation to the extent of literacy. Similar observations may be made in France. The departments containing most illiterate couples (above 20 per cent) are Corrèze, Corsica, Côtes-du-Nord, Dordogne, Finisterre, Landes, Morbihan, Haute-Vienne; all relatively free from suicides. More generally, among departments with more than 10 per cent of couples unable either to read or write, not one belongs to the northeastern region which is classical territory for French suicides.[13]

If Protestant countries are compared with one another, the same parallelism will be found. More suicides occur in Saxony than in Prussia; Prussia has more illiterates than Saxony (5.52 per cent compared with 1.3 in 1865). Saxony is even peculiar in that the school population is above the legal requirement. For 1,000 children of school age in 1877–78, 1,031 attended school: that is, many children continued their studies after the required time. The fact is not met with in any other country.[14] Finally England, as we know, is the one Protestant country with the fewest suicides; it also most resembles Catholic countries with respect to education. In 1865 there were still 23 per cent of naval seamen who could not read and 27 per cent unable to write.

Still other facts may be compared with the foregoing and confirm them.

The liberal professions and in a wider sense the well-to-do classes are certainly those with the liveliest taste for knowledge and the most active intellectual life. Now, although the statistics of suicide by occupations and classes cannot always be obtained with sufficient accuracy, it is undeniably exceptionally frequent in the highest classes of society. In France from 1826 to 1880 the liberal professions lead, with 550 suicides per million of the professional group, while servants, immediately following, have only 290.[15] In Italy, Morselli succeeded in computing the groups exclusively devoted to letters and found that they far surpass all others in their relative contribution. Indeed, for 1868–76, he estimates it as 482.6 per million members of this profession; the army follows with only 404.1 and the general average of the country is only 32. In Prussia (1883–90) the corps of

---

[13] See *Annuaire statistique de la France*, 1892–94, p. 50 and 51.
[14] Oettingen, *Moralstatistik*, p. 586.
[15] General report of criminal justice for 1882, p. CXV.

public officials, which is most carefully recruited and forms an intellectual elite, surpasses all other professions with 832 suicides; the
health services and public instruction, though much lower, still have
very high figures (439 and 301). Bavaria shows the same picture.
Omitting the army, the position of which is exceptional from the
point of view of suicide for reasons to be given below, public officials hold second place with 454 suicides and almost achieve first
place, for they are barely exceeded by business, with the rate of 465;
the arts, literature and the press follow closely with 416.[16] To be
sure, the educated classes in Belgium and Wurttemberg seem less
gravely afflicted; but professional nomenclature in these countries is
too imprecise to permit much importance being attributed to the two
irregularities.

Further, we have seen that in all the countries of the world women
commit suicide much less than men. They are also much less educated. Fundamentally traditionalist by nature, they govern their conduct by fixed beliefs and have no great intellectual needs. In Italy,
between 1878–79, there were 4,808 married men out of 10,000 who
could not sign their marriage contract; of 10,000 married women,
7,029 could not.[17] In France, the proportion in 1879 was 199 husbands and 310 wives per 1,000 couples. In Prussia the same difference is found between the sexes, among Protestants as well as among
Catholics.[18] In England it is much less than in other European countries. In 1879, 138 illiterate husbands were found per thousand to
185 wives, and since 1851 the proportion has been practically the
same.[19] But England is also the country where women come closer to
men with respect to suicide. To 1,000 suicides of women there were
2,546 of men in 1858–60, 2,745 in 1863–67, 2,861 in 1872–76,
while everywhere else [20] suicides of women are four, five or six times
less frequent than those of men. Finally, circumstances are almost
reversed in the United States, which makes them particularly instruc-

[16] See Prinzing, *op. cit.*, pp. 28-31. It is noteworthy that in Prussia journalism
and the arts show a rather ordinary figure (279 suicides).
[17] Oettingen, *Moralstatistik,* supplement, Table 83.
[18] Morselli, p. 223.
[19] Oettingen, *ibid.*, p. 577.
[20] Except Spain. But not only is the accuracy of Spanish statistics open to doubt,
but Spain cannot compare with the great nations of Central and Northern Europe.

tive. Negro women, it seems, are equally or more highly educated than their husbands. Several observers report [21] that they are also very strongly predisposed to suicide, at times even surpassing white women. The proportion in certain places is said to be 350 per cent.

There is one case, however, in which our law might seem not to be verified.

Of all religions, Judaism counts the fewest suicides, yet in none other is education so general. Even in elementary education the Jews are at least on a level with the Protestants. In fact, in Prussia (1871), to 1,000 Jews of each sex there were 66 illiterate men and 125 women; for the Protestants the numbers were practically the same, 66 and 114. But the Jews participate proportionally more, particularly in secondary and higher learning, than the members of other religions, as the following figures taken from Prussian statistics (years 1875–76) [22] show

	Catholics	Protestants	Jews
Share of each religion in 100 inhabitants of all sorts	33.8	64.9	1.3
Share of each religion in 100 secondary school pupils	.17.3	73.1	9.6

Taking into account differences of population, Jews attend Gymnasia, *Realschulen,* etc., about 14 times as often as Catholics and 7 times as often as Protestants. It is the same with higher education. Among 1,000 young Catholics attending institutions of learning of every sort, there are only 1.3 at a university; among 1,000 Protestants, 2.5; for the Jews the proportion increases to 16. [23]

But if the Jew manages to be both well instructed and very disinclined to suicide, it is because of the special origin of his desire for knowledge. It is a general law that religious minorities, in order to protect themselves better against the hate to which they are exposed or merely through a sort of emulation, try to surpass in knowledge the populations surrounding them. Thus Protestants themselves show more desire for knowledge when they are a minority of the general

[21] Baly and Boudin. We quote from Morselli, p. 225.

[22] According to Alwin Petersilie, *Zur Statistik der höheren Lehranstalten in Preussen.* In Zeitschr. d. preus. stat. Bureau, 1887, p. 109 ff.

[23] *Zeitschr. d. pr. stat. Bureau,* 1889, p. XX.

population.[24] The Jew, therefore, seeks to learn, not in order to replace his collective prejudices by reflective thought, but merely to be better armed for the struggle. For him it is a means of offsetting the unfavorable position imposed on him by opinion and sometimes by law. And since knowledge by itself has no influence upon a tradition in full vigor, he superimposes this intellectual life upon his habitual routine with no effect of the former upon the latter. This is the reason for the complexity he presents. Primitive in certain respects, in others he is an intellectual and man of culture. He thus combines the advantages of the severe discipline characteristic of small and ancient groups with the benefits of the intense culture enjoyed by our great societies. He has all the intelligence of modern man without sharing his despair.

Accordingly, if in this case intellectual development bears no relation to the number of voluntary deaths, it is because its origin and significance are not the usual ones. So the exception is only apparent; it even confirms the law. Indeed, it proves that if the suicidal tendency is great in educated circles, this is due, as we have said, to the weakening of traditional beliefs and to the state of moral individualism resulting from this; for it disappears when education has another cause and responds to other needs.

IV

Two important conclusions derive from this chapter.

First, we see why as a rule suicide increases with knowledge. Knowledge does not determine this progress. It is innocent; nothing

[24] In fact, the following shows the variation of Protestant enrollment in secondary schools in the different provinces of Prussia:

Proportion of Protestant Population to Total			Average Proportion of Protestant Pupils to Total No. of Pupils	Difference Between First and Second
1st group	98.7-87.2%	Average 94.6	90.8	— 3.8
2nd group	80 -50 %	Average 70.3	75.3	+ 5
3rd group	50 -40 %	Average 46.4	56.0	+ 10.4
4th group	Below 40%	Average 29.2	61.0	+ 31.8

Thus, where Protestantism is in a great majority, its scholastic population is not in proportion to its total population. With the increase of the Catholic minority, the difference between the two populations, from being negative, becomes positive, and this positive difference becomes larger in proportion as the Protestants become fewer. The Catholic faith also shows more intellectual curiosity when in the minority. (See Oettingen, *Moralstatistik*, p. 650).

is more unjust than to accuse it, and the example of the Jews proves this conclusively. But these two facts result simultaneously from a single general state which they translate into different forms. Man seeks to learn and man kills himself because of the loss of cohesion in his religious society; he does not kill himself because of his learning. It is certainly not the learning he acquires that disorganizes religion; but the desire for knowledge wakens because religion becomes disorganized. Knowledge is not sought as a means to destroy accepted opinions but because their destruction has commenced. To be sure, once knowledge exists, it may battle in its own name and in its own cause, and set up as an antagonist to traditional sentiments. But its attacks would be ineffective if these sentiments still possessed vitality; or rather, would not even take place. Faith is not uprooted by dialectic proof; it must already be deeply shaken by other causes to be unable to withstand the shock of argument.

Far from knowledge being the source of the evil, it is its remedy, the only remedy we have. Once established beliefs have been carried away by the current of affairs, they cannot be artificially reestablished; only reflection can guide us in life, after this. Once the social instinct is blunted, intelligence is the only guide left us and we have to reconstruct a conscience by its means. Dangerous as is the undertaking there can be no hesitation, for we have no choice. Let those who view anxiously and sadly the ruins of ancient beliefs, who feel all the difficulties of these critical times, not ascribe to science an evil it has not caused but rather which it tries to cure! Beware of treating it as an enemy! It has not the dissolvent effect ascribed to it, but is the only weapon for our battle against the dissolution which gives birth to science itself. It is no answer to denounce it. The authority of vanished traditions will never be restored by silencing it; we shall be only more powerless to replace them. We must, to be sure, be equally careful to avoid seeing a self-sufficient end in education, whereas it is only a means. If minds cannot be made to lose the desire for freedom by artificially enslaving them, neither can they recover their equilibrium by mere freedom. They must use this freedom fittingly.

Secondly, we see why, generally speaking, religion has a prophylactic effect upon suicide. It is not, as has sometimes been said, because it condemns it more unhesitatingly than secular morality, nor because the idea of God gives its precepts exceptional authority which subdues the will, nor because the prospect of a future life and the terrible punishments there awaiting the guilty give its proscriptions a greater sanction than that of human laws. The Protestant believes in God and the immortality of the soul no less than the Catholic. More than this, the religion with least inclination to suicide, Judaism, is the very one not formally proscribing it and also the one in which the idea of immortality plays the least role. Indeed, the Bible contains no law forbidding man to kill himself [25] and, on the other hand, its beliefs in a future life are most vague. Doubtless, in both matters, rabbinical teaching has gradually supplied the omissions of the sacred book; but they have not its authority. The beneficent influence of religion is therefore not due to the special nature of religious conceptions. If religion protects man against the desire for self-destruction, it is not that it preaches the respect for his own person to him with arguments *sui generis;* but because it is a society. What constitutes this society is the existence of a certain number of beliefs and practices common to all the faithful, traditional and thus obligatory. The more numerous and strong these collective states of mind are, the stronger the integration of the religious community, and also the greater its preservative value. The details of dogmas and rites are secondary. The essential thing is that they be capable of supporting a sufficiently intense collective life. And because the Protestant church has less consistency than the others it has less moderating effect upon suicide.

[25] The only penal proscription known to us is that mentioned by Flavius Josephus in his *History of the War of the Jews against the Romans* (III, 25), which says simply that "the bodies of those who kill themselves voluntarily remain unburied until after sunset, although those who have been killed in battle may be buried earlier." This is not even definitely a penal measure.

CHAPTER 3
EGOISTIC SUICIDE
(continued)

BUT if religion preserves men from suicide only because and in so far as it is a society, other societies probably have the same effect. From this point of view let us consider the family and political society.

I

If one consults only the absolute figures, unmarried persons seem to commit suicide less than married ones. Thus in France, during the period 1873–78, there were 16,264 suicides of married persons while unmarried persons had only 11,709. The former number is to the second as 132 to 100.[1] As the same proportion appears at other periods and in other countries, certain authors had once taught that marriage and family life multiply the chances of suicide. Certainly, if in accordance with current opinion one regards suicide primarily as an act of despair caused by the difficulties of existence, this opinion has all the appearance of probability. An unmarried person has in fact an easier life than a married one. Does not marriage entail all sorts of burdens and responsibilities? To assure the present and future of a family, are not more privations and sufferings required than to meet the needs of a single person?[2] Nevertheless, clear as it seems, this a priori reasoning is quite false and the facts only seem to support it because of being poorly analyzed. The elder Bertillon

[1] Durkheim's figure of 132 appears to be a misprint. The figure works out to 139.—Ed.
[2] See Wagner, *Die Gesetzmässigkeit,* etc., p. 177.

first established this by an ingenious calculation which we shall reproduce.[3]

Really to appreciate the figures given above, we must remember that a very large number of unmarried persons are less than 16 years old, while all married persons are older. Up to 16 years the tendency to suicide is very slight, due to age, without considering other factors. In France only one or two suicides per million inhabitants are found at this time of life; at the following period there are twenty times as many. The inclusion of many children below 16 among unmarried persons thus unduly reduces the average aptitude of the latter, since the reduction is due to age, not celibacy. If they seem to contribute fewer suicides, it is not because they are unmarried but because many of them are yet immature. So, if one tries to compare the two populations to determine the influence of marital status and that alone, one must rid oneself of this disturbing element and compare with married persons only the unmarried above 16. When this subtraction is made, it appears that between 1863–68 there were on the average 173 suicides in a million unmarried persons above 16 years and 154.5 for a million married persons. The ratio of the first to the second number is that of 112 to 100.

There is thus a certain accretion due to celibacy. But it is much greater than the preceding figures show. Actually, we have assumed that all unmarried persons above 16 years and all married persons were of the same average age. This is not true. The majority of unmarried men in France, exactly 58 per cent, are between 15 and 20 years; the majority of unmarried women, exactly 57 per cent are less than 25 years. The average age of all unmarried men is 26.8, of all unmarried women 28.4. The average age of married persons, on the contrary, is between 40 and 45 years. For both sexes combined, suicide develops according to age as follows:

From 16 to 21 years	45.9 suicides per million inhabitants
From 21 to 30 years	97.9 suicides per million inhabitants
From 31 to 40 years	114.5 suicides per million inhabitants
From 41 to 50 years	164.4 suicides per million inhabitants

[3] See article, *Mariage*, in *Dictionnaire encyclopédique des sciences médicales*, 2nd series. See p. 50 ff.—On this question *cf.* J. Bertillon, Jr., *Les célibataires, les veufs et les divorcés au point de vue du mariage in Revue scientifique*, February, 1879.— Also an article in the *Bulletin de la société d'anthropologie*, 1880, p. 280 ff.— Durkheim, *Suicide et natalité*, in *Revue philosophique*, November 1888.

These figures refer to the years 1848–57. If age were the only influence, the aptitude of unmarried persons for suicide could not be above 97.9 and that of married persons would be between 114.5 and 164.4, or about 140 suicides per million inhabitants. Suicides of married persons would be to those of unmarried as 100 to 69. The latter would be only two-thirds of the former whereas we know that they are actually more numerous. The effect of family life is thus to reverse the relation. Whereas without the effect of family life married persons should kill themselves half again as often as unmarried by virtue of their age, they do so perceptibly less. Thus marriage may be said to reduce the danger of suicide by about half or, more exactly, non-marriage produces an increase expressed by the proportion 112/69, or 1.6. Thus, if we represent the suicidal tendency of married persons by unity, that of unmarried persons of the same average age must be estimated as 1.6.

The relationships are practically the same in Italy. Due to their age, married persons (years 1873–77) should show 102 suicides per million and the unmarried above 16 years only 77; the first number is to the second as 100 to 75.[4] Actually, married persons commit fewer suicides; they show only 71 cases to 86 of unmarried persons or 100 to 121. The aptitude of the unmarried is thus in the proportion of 121 to 75 for that of married persons, or 1.6, as in France. Similar figures might be obtained in other countries. The rate of married persons is everywhere to some degree below that of unmarried persons,[5] whereas it ought, by virtue of age, to be higher. In Wurttemberg, from 1846 to 1860, these two figures were to one another as 100 to 143, in Prussia from 1873 to 1875 as 100 to 111.

But if, with the data available, this method of calculation is the only one applicable in almost all cases, and if consequently it must be used to establish the general situation, its results can be only roughly approximate. Of course, it suffices to show that non-marriage increases the tendency to suicide; but it gives only a very inexact idea of the extent of this increase. Indeed, to distinguish the influence of age and that of marital status, we have taken as our starting point

---

[4] We assume that the average age of these groups is the same as in France. The error which may result from this assumption is very slight.
[5] If the two sexes are considered combined. The importance of this remark will appear below (Bk. II, Ch. 5, Par. 3).

the relation between the suicide-rate at 30 years and that at 45. Unfortunately, the influence of marital status has already left its own mark on this relation; for the contingent of each of the two ages was calculated for unmarried and married persons taken together. Of course, if the proportion of married and unmarried men were the same at the two periods, as well as that of unmarried and married women, they would compensate each other and the effect of age alone would be apparent. But this is not so. While at 30 unmarried men are slightly more numerous than married men (746,111 for the former, 714,278 for the latter according to the census for 1891), at 45 years, on the contrary, the former are only a slight minority (333,-033 to 1,864,401 married men); it is the same with the other sex. Because of this unequal distribution, their great aptitude for suicide does not produce the same effects in both cases. It increases the former rate much more than the latter. The latter is consequently relatively too slight and the numerical superiority which it would show over the former if age alone were involved is artificially reduced. In other words, the difference as regards suicide, *due merely to the fact of age,* between the population of from 25 to 30 years and that of from 40 to 45 is certainly greater than appears from this way of figuring. Now the extent of this difference forms almost all the relative immunity of married people. This immunity thus appears less than it is in reality.

This method has caused even greater errors. Thus, to determine the influence of widowhood on suicide, the rate of widowed persons has sometimes merely been compared with that of persons of every marital status of the same average age, or about 65 years. Now a million widowers in 1863–68 showed 628 suicides; a million men aged 65 (of every marital status combined) about 461. From these figures one might judge that at the same age widowed persons kill themselves considerably more often than any other class of the population. In this way the assumption has arisen that widowhood is the most unlucky of all states from the point of view of suicide.[6] Actually, if the population of 65 years does not show more suicides, it is because it is almost entirely composed of married persons (997,198 to 134,238 unmarried). So if this comparison suffices to prove that

[6] See Bertillon, art., *Mariage,* in *Dict. Encycl.,* 2d series, see p. 52. Morselli, p. 348.—Corre, *Crime et suicide,* p. 472.

widowed persons kill themselves more than married persons of the same age, it shows nothing as to their tendency to suicide compared with that of unmarried persons.

In short, when only averages are compared, the facts and their relations to one another appear only approximately. Thus it may very well be true that married persons kill themselves in general less often than unmarried persons, and that nevertheless this proportion may be exceptionally reversed at certain ages; in fact we shall see that this is so. Now these exceptions, possibly instructive for the explanation of the phenomenon, could not be shown by the preceding method. There may also be changes from age to age, which without achieving complete inversion, have nevertheless an importance of their own and which should therefore be shown.

The only way to avoid these difficulties is to determine the rate of each group separately, at each age. Under such conditions one may, for example, compare unmarried persons of from 25 to 30 years with married and widowed persons of the same age and similarly for other periods; the influence of marital status will thus be isolated from all the other influences and all its possible variations will appear. Besides, this is the method which Bertillon first applied to mortality and the marriage rate. Unfortunately, official publications do not contain the necessary data for this comparison.[7] Actually, they show the age of suicides independently of their marital status. The only publication which to our knowledge has followed a different practice is that of the grand-duchy of Oldenburg (including the principalities of Lübeck and Birkenfeld).[8] For the years 1871–85 this publication gives us the distribution of suicides by age for each category of marital status considered separately. But this little State had only 1,369 suicides during these fifteen years. As nothing certain can be concluded from so few cases, we undertook to do the work ourselves for France with the aid of unpublished documents in the possession of the Ministry of Justice. We studied the years 1889, 1890 and 1891. We classified about 25,000 suicides in this way.

[7] Yet the labor of assembling these data, considerable if undertaken by an individual, might easily be accomplished by the official bureaus of statistics. All sorts of valueless information is given and only that omitted which, as will be seen below, might show the state of family life in the different European societies.

[8] There are, to be sure, Swedish statistics reproduced in the *Bulletin de démographie internationale*, 1878. p. 195, giving these data. But they are useless. In the

Not only is such a figure sufficiently important in itself to serve as a
basis for induction, but we assured ourselves that there was no need

first place, widowed persons are there combined with unmarried persons, making
the co parison relatively insignificant, for such different conditions must be distinguished. Moreover, we believe these statistics to be inexact. Here for example are
some of their figures:

SUICIDES PER 100,000 INHABITANTS OF EACH SEX, OF LIKE MARITAL STATUS AND AGE

	Years of Age						
	16-25	26-35	36-45	46-55	56-65	66-75	Above 75
			Men				
Married	10.51	10.58	18.77	24.08	26.29	20.76	9.48
Non-married (widowed included)	5.69	25.73	66.95	90.72	150.08	229.27	333.35
			Women				
Married	2.63	2.76	4.15	5.55	7.09	4.67	7.64
Non-married	2.99	6.14	13.23	17.05	25.98	51.93	34.69

HOW MUCH MORE FREQUENT ARE SUICIDES OF UNMARRIED THAN OF MARRIED PERSONS OF SAME SEX AND AGE

	16-25	26-35	36-45	46-55	56-65	66-75	Above 75
Men	0.5	2.4	3.5	3.7	5.7	11	37
Women	1.13	2.22	3.18	3.04	3.66	11.12	4.5

These figures have from the first seemed suspicious with regard to the tremendous degree of relative immunity enjoyed by married persons of advanced age, since
they differ so from all facts known to us. To achieve verification that we deem indispensable, we have examined the absolute numbers of suicides committed by each
age-group in Sweden at the same period. For men they are as follows:

	16-25	26-35	36-45	46-55	56-65	66-75	Above 75
Married	16	220	567	640	383	140	15
Non-married	283	519	410	269	217	156	56

Comparing these figures with the proportional numbers given above, the error
committed becomes obvious. Actually, from 66 to 75 years, married and non-married
persons show almost the same absolute number of suicides, whereas per 100,000 the
former are supposed to kill themselves eleven times less often than the latter. For
this to be true there would have to be at this age about ten times (exactly, 9.2
times) more married than non-married persons, that is, than widowed and unmarried combined. For the same reason, the married population above 75 should be
exactly 10 times more numerous than the other. But that is impossible. At these
advanced ages widowed persons are very numerous and, combined with unmarried
persons, they are equal or even greater in number than married persons. This suggests what error has probably been committed. The suicides of unmarried and widowed persons must have been added together and the resulting total divided only
by the figure for the unmarried population alone, while the suicides of married persons were divided by one for the widowed and married populations combined. What
makes this probable is that the degree of immunity of married persons is extraordinary only at the advanced ages, or when the number of widowed persons becomes
great enough seriously to falsify the resulting calculation. And the improbability is
greatest after 75 years, or when widowed persons are very numerous.

to extend our observations over a longer period. From one year to another the contingent of each age remains approximately the same in each group. There is therefore no need to fix the averages for a greater number of years.

Tables XX and XXI contain these different figures. To make their meaning clearer we have placed for each age, beside the figure expressing the rate for widowed persons and that for married persons, what we call the *coefficient of preservation,* either of the latter by comparison with the former or of both by comparison with unmarried persons. By this phrase we mean the number show-

TABLE XX—Grand-duchy of Oldenburg: Suicides Committed, by Each Sex, per 10,000 Inhabitants of Each Age and Marital Status Group Throughout the Period 1871–85 *

| | | | | Coefficients of Preservation of | | |
| | | | | Married | | Widowed |
Age	Unmarried	Married	Widowed	With Reference to Unmarried	With Reference to Widowed	With Reference to Unmarried
			Men			
From 0 to 20	7.2	769.2	....	0.09	....	....
20 to 30	70.6	49.0	285.7	1.40	5.8	0.24
30 to 40	130.4	73.6	76.9	1.77	1.04	1.69
40 to 50	188.8	95.0	285.7	1.97	3.01	0.66
50 to 60	263.6	137.8	271.4	1.90	1.90	0.97
60 to 70	242.8	148.3	304.7	1.63	2.05	0.79
Above 70	266.6	114.2	259.0	2.30	2.26	1.02
			Women			
From 0 to 20	3.9	95.2	....	0.04	....	....
20 to 30	39.0	17.4	....	2.24	....	....
30 to 40	32.3	16.8	30.0	1.92	1.78	1.07
40 to 50	52.9	18.6	68.1	2.85	3.66	0.77
50 to 60	66.6	31.1	50.0	2.14	1.60	1.33
60 to 70	62.5	37.2	55.8	1.68	1.50	1.12
Above 70	....	120	91.4	....	1.31	....

* These figures therefore refer not to the average year but to the total of suicides committed during these fifteen years.

ing how many times less frequent suicide is in one group than in another at the same age. Thus, when we say that the coefficient of preservation of husbands of the age of 25 in relation to unmarried men is 3, we mean that if the tendency to suicide of married persons at this time of life is represented by 1, that of unmarried persons the same period must be represented by 3. Of course, when the coefficient of preservation sinks below unity, it really becomes a coefficient of aggravation.

The laws derived from these tables may be formulated thus:

1. *Too early marriages have an aggravating influence on suicide, especially as regards men.* This result, to be sure, being calculated from a very small number of cases, should be confirmed; in France, from 15 to 20 years, in the average year barely one suicide is committed among married persons, exactly 1.33. However, as the fact is

TABLE XXI—France (1889-1891): Suicides Committed per 1,000,000 Inhabitants of Each Age and Marital Status Group, Average Year

Ages	Unmarried	Married	Widowed	Married Coefficients of Preservation of With Reference to Unmarried	Married With Reference to Widowed	Widowed With Reference to Unmarried
Men						
15 to 20	113	500	....	0.22	....	....
20 to 25	237	97	142	2.40	1.45	1.66
25 to 30	394	122	412	3.20	3.37	0.95
30 to 40	627	226	560	2.77	2.47	1.12
40 to 50	975	340	721	2.86	2.12	1.35
50 to 60	1,434	520	979	2.75	1.88	1.46
60 to 70	1,768	635	1,166	2.78	1.83	1.51
70 to 80	1,983	704	1,238	2.81	1.82	1.54
Above 80	1,571	770	1,154	2.04	1.49	1.36
Women						
15 to 20	79.4	33	333	2.39	10	0.23
20 to 25	106	53	66	2.00	1.05	1.60
25 to 30	151	68	178	2.22	2.61	0.84
30 to 40	126	82	205	1.53	2.50	0.61
40 to 50	171	106	168	1.61	1.58	1.01
50 to 60	204	151	199	1.35	1.31	1.02
60 to 70	189	158	257	1.19	1.62	0.77
70 to 80	206	209	248	0.98	1.18	0.83
Above 80	176	110	240	1.60	2.18	0.79

likewise observed in the grand-duchy of Oldenburg, and even for women, it is probably not accidental. Even the Swedish statistics quoted above,[9] show the same aggravation, at least for the male sex. If, now, for the reasons mentioned, we believe these statistics inexact for the advanced ages, we have no reason to doubt them for the first periods of life, when there are as yet no widowed persons. Besides, the mortality of very young husbands and wives is known to considerably exceed that of unmarried men and women of the same age. A thousand unmarried men between 15 and 20 give 8.9 deaths each

[9] See above p. 176.—To be sure, one might think that this unfavorable situation of married persons from 15 to 20 years is due to their average age being above that of unmarried persons in the same age-group. But what proves that there is a real aggravation is that the ratio of married persons of the following age-group (20 to 25 years) is five times less.

year, a thousand married men of the same age, 51 deaths or 473 per cent more. The difference is less for the other sex, 9.9 deaths for wives, 8.3 for unmarried women; the former number is to the second only as 119 to 100.[10] This greater mortality of young married persons is evidently due to social reasons, for if its principal cause were the immaturity of the organism this would be more marked in the female sex, due to the dangers involved in parturition. Thus everything tends to prove that premature marriages bring about a harmful moral state, especially to men.

2. *From 20 years, married persons of both sexes enjoy a coefficient of preservation in comparison with unmarried persons.* It is above that calculated by Bertillon. The figure 1.6 indicated by that observer is a minimum rather than an average.[11]

This coefficient changes with age. It soon reaches a maximum between 25 and 30 years in France, between 30 and 40 in Oldenburg; from then on it decreases till the final period of life when a slight rise sometimes occurs.

3. *The coefficient of preservation of married persons by comparison with unmarried persons varies with the sexes.* In France it is men who are in the favorable position and the difference between the sexes is considerable; for married men the average is 2.73 while for married women it is only 1.56, or 43 per cent less. But in Oldenburg the opposite is true; the average for women is 2.16 and for men only 1.83. It is to be noted that at the same time the disproportion is less; the second number is only 16 per cent lower than the first. We shall say therefore that *the sex enjoying the higher coefficient of preservation in the state of marriage varies from society to society and that the extent of the difference between the rates of the sexes itself varies to the extent that the coefficient of preservation favors the favored sex.* In the course of our work we shall encounter facts confirming this law.

4. *Widowhood diminishes the coefficient of married persons of each sex, but it rarely eliminates it entirely.* Widowed persons kill

[10] See Bertillon, art. *Mariage,* p. 43 ff.
[11] There is a single exception; women of from 70 to 80 years, whose coefficient descends slightly below unity. The cause of this variation is the influence of the department of the Seine. In other departments (see Table XXII, p. 196), the coefficient of women of this age is above unity; but it must be noted that even in the provinces it is less than that of other ages.

themselves more often than married persons but generally less than unmarried persons. Their coefficient in certain cases even rises to 1.60 and 1.66. Like that of married persons it changes with age, but following an irregular evolution the law of which cannot be determined.

Just as for married persons, *the coefficient of preservation of widowed persons compared with unmarried persons varies with the sex.* In France men are in the favored position; their average coefficient is 1.32 while for widows it falls below unity, 0.84, or 37 per cent less. But in Oldenburg women are favored, as in marriage; they have an average coefficient of 1.07, while that of widowers is below unity, 0.89, or 17 per cent less. As in the state of marriage, when it is women who are most favored, the difference between the sexes is less than where men have the advantage. So we may say in the same terms that *the sex enjoying the higher coefficient of preservation in the state of widowhood varies from society to society, and that the extent of the difference between the rates of the sexes, itself varies to the extent that the coefficient of preservation favors the favored sex.*

Facts being thus determined, let us seek explanations.

II

The immunity enjoyed by married persons can be attributed only to one of the two following causes:

It may be due to the influence of the domestic environment. It would then be the influence of the family which neutralized the suicidal tendency or prevented its outburst.

Or this immunity is due to what may be called matrimonial selection. Marriage in fact does make for some sort of selection among the population at large. Not everyone who wants to, gets married; one has little chance of founding a family successfully without certain qualities of health, fortune and morality. People without them, unless through a conjunction of exceptionally favorable circumstances, are thus involuntarily relegated to the unmarried class which consequently includes the human dregs of the country. The sick, the incurable, the people of too little means or known weakness are found here. Hence, if this part of the population is so far inferior to the other, it naturally proves this inferiority by a higher mortality, a greater criminality, and finally by a stronger suicidal tendency. According to this hypothesis, it would not be the family which was a protection against suicide, crime or sickness; the privileged position of married persons would be theirs simply because only those are admitted to family life who already provide considerable guarantees of physical and moral health.

Bertillon seems to have vacillated between the two explanations and to have admitted both at once. Since then, M. Letourneau, in his *Évolution du mariage et de la famille*,[12] has categorically chosen the second. He refuses to acknowledge that the undeniable superiority of the married population is a result and proof of the superiority of marital life. He would have judged less precipitously had he observed the facts less hastily.

Of course, it is quite probable that married people generally have a physical and moral constitution somewhat better than that of unmarried persons. Matrimonial selection, however, does not bar all but the elite of the population from wedlock. It is especially doubtful that persons without means and position marry much less than others. As has been noted,[13] they usually have more children than the people with assured incomes. If, then, no forethought limits the imprudent increase of their family, why should it prevent their founding one? Besides, repeated proof will be given below that poverty is not one of the factors on which the social suicide-rate depends. As for the infirm, not merely are infirmities overlooked for many reasons, but it is not at all certain that suicides are most numerous among the infirm. The organic-psychic temperament most predisposing man to kill himself is neurasthenia in all its forms. Now today neurasthenia is rather considered a mark of distinction than a weakness. In our refined societies, enamoured of things intellectual, nervous members constitute almost a nobility. Only the clearly insane are apt to be refused admittance to marriage. This limited exclusion is not enough to account for the extensive immunity of married persons.[14]

[12] Paris, 1888, p. 436.
[13] J. Bertillon, Jr., article cited in the *Revue scientifique*.
[14] To reject the hypothesis that the privileged position of married persons is due to matrimonial selection, the aggravation, which is supposed to result from widowhood, is sometimes mentioned. But we have just seen that no such aggravation exists by comparison with unmarried persons. Widowed persons kill themselves much less than non-married persons. Thus the argument does not carry.

Besides these somewhat *a priori* considerations, numerous facts show that the respective immunity of married and unmarried persons is due to quite other causes.

If it were a result of matrimonial selection, it should grow from the start of this selection, or the age when young men and women begin to marry. At this point, a first difference should be noted which should increase with the progress of selection, or as marriageable persons marry and thus lose contact with the rabble naturally destined to be the class of the permanently unmarried. In short, the maximum should be reached when the good grain is completely separated from the tares, when the whole population admissible to marriage has actually been admitted, when only those are unmarried who are hopelessly committed to this condition by physical or moral inferiority. This maximum should occur between 30 and 40 years of age; few marriages are made later.

Now, the coefficient of preservation actually evolves according to quite another law. At first it is often replaced by a coefficient of aggravation. Very young married persons are more inclined to commit suicide than unmarried ones; this would not be so if their immunity were inherent and inherited. Secondly, the maximum is achieved almost at once. At the earliest age when the privileged position of married persons becomes perceptible (between 20 and 25 years), the coefficient reaches a figure which it is unlikely later to surpass. Now at this period there are only [15] 148,000 married to 1,430,000 unmarried men, and 626,000 married to 1,049,000 unmarried women (in round numbers). The ranks of the unmarried, therefore, at this time include the largest part of the elite which has been thought destined by its hereditary qualities to form later the aristocracy of the married; the difference from the point of view of suicide between the two classes should then be slight, whereas it is already considerable. Likewise, at the next age (between 25 and 30), more than a million of the two million married persons to appear between the ages of 30 and 40 are still unmarried; and yet far from the immunity of the unmarried profiting by this fact, this group cuts the poorest figure then. Never are the two parts of the population so far from one another as regards suicide. On the contrary, between the ages of 30 and 40, when the separation is complete and the married class has

[15] These figures refer to France and the census of 1891.

about reached its full complement, instead of reaching its height and thus showing that conjugal selection itself has come to a stop, the coefficient of preservation undergoes an abrupt and considerable decline. For men it falls from 3.20 to 2.77; for women the regression is still more pronounced, 1.53 instead of 2.22 or a reduction of 32 per cent.

On the other hand, however this selection is effected, it must occur equally for unmarried women as for unmarried men; for wives are recruited in the same manner as husbands. Thus, if the moral superiority of married persons is merely a result of selection, it should be the same for both sexes, and consequently the immunity from suicide should be the same. Actually, husbands are definitely more protected in France than wives. For the former, the coefficient of preservation rises as high as 3.20, falls only once below 2.04, and usually oscillates about 2.80, while for the latter the maximum does not exceed 2.22 (or at most 2.39)[16] and the minimum is below unity (0.98). Moreover, women in France are closest to men with respect to suicide, in the married state. The share of each sex in suicides, for each category of marital status, for the years 1887–91, follows below:

	Share of Each Sex			
	Per 100 Unmarried Suicides at Different Ages		Per 100 Married Suicides at Different Ages	
	Men	Women	Men	Women
From 20 to 25 years	70	30	65	35
From 25 to 30 years	73	27	65	35
From 30 to 40 years	84	16	74	26
From 40 to 50 years	86	14	77	23
From 50 to 60 years	88	12	78	22
From 60 to 70 years	91	9	81	19
From 70 to 80 years	91	9	78	22
Above 80 years	90	10	88	12

Thus at each age [17] the share of wives in the suicides of married persons is far higher than that of unmarried women in suicides of

[16] We make this reservation, because this coefficient of 2.39 relates to the period from 15 to 20 years and because, since the suicides of wives are very rare at this age, the small number of cases which form the basis of these figures makes their exactness somewhat uncertain.

[17] Usually, when the respective situation of the sexes in the two different sorts of marital status is thus compared, the effect of age is not carefully eliminated; but this produces inexact results. Following the usual method, one would find in 1887–91, 21 suicides of married women to 79 of married men and 19 suicides of unmarried women to 100 of unmarried persons of all ages. These figures would give a false impression of the situation. The above table shows that the difference be-

unmarried persons. Certainly this is not because a wife is less protected than an unmarried woman; Tables XX and XXI show the
contrary. But if women do not lose by marriage, they gain less than
men. But if immunity is here so unequal, family life must affect the
moral constitution of the two sexes differently. What proves with
real finality that the inequality has this origin is that its birth and
growth may be observed under the influence of the domestic environment. Indeed, Table XXI shows that in the beginning the coefficient
of preservation for the two sexes is hardly different (for women,
2.39 in the 15-20 age-group or 2.00 in the 20-25 age-group; for men,
2.40 in the 20-25 age-group.[18] Then, gradually, the difference increases, at first because the coefficient of married women grows less
than that of married men up to the age of the maximum, and then
because its decrease is swifter and greater.[19, 20] Thus, the coefficient
of preservation evolves in accordance with the prolongation of
family-life because it depends on this prolongation.

Still better proof is that the relative situation of the sexes as to
the degree of preservation enjoyed by married persons is not the
same in all countries. In the grand-duchy of Oldenburg women are
the favored sex and we shall find later another case of the same inversion. But on the whole, conjugal selection occurs everywhere in
the same way. So it cannot be the essential factor in matrimonial im-

tween the share of the married woman as against the unmarried woman is much
greater at every age. Thus, for both the unmarried and married, the size of the
difference between the sexes varies with the age-group, until in the age-group, 70
to 80, the size of the difference is about twice what it was at 20. Now, the unmarried population is almost wholly made up of persons below 30 years old. If,
however, no account is taken of age, the difference resulting is actually that between
unmarried men and women of about 30. But then, comparing this with the
difference between married persons without respect to age, since the latter are on
the average 50 years old, the comparison is really made with reference to married
persons of this age. Thus the comparison is falsified and the error further aggravated by the fact that the difference between the sexes does not vary in the same
way in both groups under the influence of age. Among the unmarried it increases
more than among the married.

[18] Durkheim fails to mention that in the 15–20 age-group for men the coefficient
of preservation in Table XXI is 0.22.—Ed.

[19] Thus one can also see from the preceding Table that the proportional share of
wives in the suicides of married persons increasingly surpasses, with age, the share
of unmarried women in the suicides of unmarried persons.

[20] This statement by Durkheim must be carefully appraised in the light of Table
XXI.—Ed.

munity; for how then would opposite results occur in different countries? On the contrary, the family may very well be constituted in two different societies so as to affect the sexes differently. In the constitution of the family group, accordingly, we must find the principal cause of the phenomenon of our study.

But interesting as this result is, it must be further defined; for the family environment consists of different elements. For husband and wife alike the family includes: 1. the wife or husband; 2. the children. Is the salutary effect of the family on the suicidal tendency due to the former or the latter? In other words, the family consists of two different associations: the conjugal group and the family group proper. These two societies have not the same origin, nor the same nature, nor consequently, in all probability, the same effects. One springs from a contract and elective affinity, the other from a natural phenomenon, consanguinity; the former unites two members of the same generation, the latter unites one generation to the next; the latter is as old as humanity, the former was organized at a relatively late date. Since they are here so different it is not *a priori* certain that both combine equally to produce the fact we are studying. Anyway, if both contribute to it this cannot be in the same manner, nor probably in the same measure. Thus, we must investigate whether both take part and, if so, the share of each.

A proof of the slight effect of marriage is the fact that the marriage rate has changed very little since the first of the century, while suicide has tripled. From 1821 to 1830 there were 7.8 marriages annually per 1,000 inhabitants, 8 from 1831 to 1850, 7.9 in 1851–60, 7.8 from 1861 to 1870, 8 from 1871 to 1880. During this time the suicide-rate per million inhabitants rose from 54 to 180. From 1880 to 1888 the marriage rate declined slightly (7.4 instead of 8), but this decrease is unrelated to the enormous increase of suicides, which rose more than 16 per cent [21] from 1880 to 1887.

[21] Legoyt (*op. cit.*, p. 175) and Corre (*Crime et suicide*, p. 475) nevertheless thought they could establish a relation between the variations of suicide and the marriage rate. Their error proceeds first from having considered too short a period, secondly from having compared the most recent years with an abnormal year, 1872, when the French marriage rate reached an unusual figure, unknown since 1813, because the gaps in the ranks of the married population caused by the war of 1870 had to be filled. No such reference can be a measure for the changes of the marriage

Besides, during the period 1865–88, the average marriage rate of France (7.7) is almost the same as that of Denmark (7.8) and Italy (7.6); yet these countries are as different as possible from the point of view of suicide.[22]

But we have a much more certain way of measuring exactly the real influence of conjugal association upon suicide; that of observing it when reduced to its own isolated strength, or in families without children.

During the years 1887–91, a million husbands without children accounted annually for 644 suicides.[23] To know how much the marriage status, alone and without reference to the family, insures against suicide, one has only to compare this figure with that of the unmarried men of the same average age. This comparison Table XXI permits us to make, as not the least important of its information. The average age of married men was then as now 46 years, 8 and 1/3 months. A million unmarried men of this age have about 975 suicides. Now 644 is to 975 as 100 is to 150, that is, sterile husbands have a coefficient of preservation of only 1.5; they commit suicide only a third less often than unmarried of the same age. Quite otherwise when there are children. A million husbands with children annually show during this period only 336 suicides. This number is to 975 as 100 is to 290; that is, when the marriage produces children the coefficient of preservation is almost doubled (2.90 instead of 1.5).

Conjugal society therefore plays only a slight role in the immunity of married men. We have in the preceding calculation even made this role somewhat larger than it really is. We have assumed that childless husbands have the same average age as husbands in general, whereas they are certainly younger. For among their ranks are all the youngest husbands, who are without children not because they are hopelessly sterile, but because they have married too recently to have

---

rate. The same observation applies to Germany and to almost all the European countries. Something like an electric shock seems to have affected the marriage rate at the time. A great and abrupt rise is seen, prolonged occasionally as late as 1873, in Italy, Switzerland, Belgium, England, Holland. All Europe might be said to have been contributing to repair the losses of the two war-stricken countries. A tremendous fall naturally succeeded after some time which has not the significance ascribed to it (See Oettingen, *Moralstatistik*, supplement, Tables 1, 2 and 3).

[22] See Levasseur, *Population francaise*, vol. II, p. 208.

[23] According to the census of 1886, p. 123 of the *Dénombrement*.

any. On the average, a man has his first child not before 34 years of age,[24] and yet he marries at about 28 or 29 years of age. The part of the married population from 28 to 34 years of age is thus almost entirely in the category of the childless, which lowers the average age of these latter; therefore we must certainly have exaggerated in estimating it at 46. But in that case the unmarried men with whom they should have been compared are not those of 46 but younger, who consequently commit suicide less often than the others. So the coefficient of 1.5 must be a little too high; if we knew exactly the average age of childless husbands, their aptitude for suicide would surely approach that of unmarried men still more than the above figures indicate.

The limited influence of marriage is well shown, moreover, in that widowers with children are in a better situation than husbands without them. The former indeed, show 937 suicides per million. Now they are 61 years, 8 and 1/3 months on the average. The rate of unmarried men of the same age (see Table XXI) is between 1,434 and 1,768, or about 1,504. This number is to 937 as 160 is to 100. Widowers, when they have children, thus have a coefficient of preservation of at least 1.6, superior to that of childless husbands. Moreover, we have under rather than overestimated this figure. For widowers with children are certainly older than widowers in general. The latter, indeed, include all whose marriage was without issue only because of premature end by death, that is, the youngest. Widowers with children should therefore really be compared with unmarried men above 62 years (who, because of their age, have a stronger tendency to suicide). This comparison would clearly only emphasize their immunity.[25]

To be sure, this coefficient of 1.6 is definitely below that of husbands with children, 2.9; the difference is not quite 45 per cent. Thus, matrimonial society by itself might be thought to have more effect than we have granted it, since at its conclusion the immunity of the husband surviving is so far reduced. But this loss is only in slight degree to be ascribed to the dissolution of marriage. Proof of

[24] See *Annuaire statistique de la France*, 15th vol., p. 43.

[25] For the same reason, the age of husbands with children is above that of husbands in general and, consequently, the coefficient of preservation 2.9 should be considered somewhat below reality.

this is that where there are no children widowhood produces far lesser effects. A million childless widowers show 1,258 suicides, a number related to 1,504, the contingent of sixty-two-year-old unmarried men, as 100 is to 119. Thus the coefficient of preservation is still about 1.2 which is little below that of husbands also childless, 1.5. The former of these figures is only 20 per cent less than the second. Accordingly, when a wife's death has no other effect than to break the conjugal bond, it has no strong repercussion on the suicidal tendency of the widower. Marriage during its existence must therefore only slightly aid in restraining this tendency, since the latter shows no greater increase with the end of marriage.

The reason why widowhood is relatively more disastrous when the union has been fruitful must be sought in the existence of the children.[26] Of course in a way the children attach the widower to life, but at the same time they make the crisis through which he is passing more intense. For not only is the conjugal relation destroyed; but precisely because a domestic society here exists, there is an impairment of its functioning too. An essential element is lacking and the whole machine is thrown out of gear. To reestablish the lost equilibrium the husband has to shoulder a double burden and perform functions for which he is unprepared. Thus he loses advantages which were his throughout the duration of the marriage. It is not because his marriage is ended but because the family which he heads is disorganized. The departure, not of the wife but of the mother, causes the disaster.

But the slight effect of marriage appears with special clarity in the woman's case when it does not find its natural fulfillment in children. A million childless wives show 221 suicides; a million unmarried women of the same age (between 42 and 43 years) only 150. The first of these numbers is to the second as 100 is to 67; the coefficient of preservation thus falls below unity and equals .67, that is, it has really become a coefficient of aggravation. *In France, then, married but childless women commit suicide half again as often as unmarried women of the same age.* We have already noticed that in general the wife profits less from family life than the husband. Now we see

---

[26] What Durkheim seems to mean here is that widowers with children compared to husbands with children are relatively worse off than widowers without children compared to husbands without children.—Ed.

the cause of this; in itself conjugal society is harmful to the woman and aggravates her tendency to suicide.

If most wives have, nevertheless, seemed to enjoy a coefficient of preservation, this is because childless households are the exception and consequently the presence of children in most cases corrects and reduces the evil effects of marriage. Even so these effects are only reduced. A million women having children show 79 suicides; comparing this figure with the one giving the suicide-rate of unmarried women of 42 years of age as 150, the wife is found to benefit, even when she is also a mother, only by a coefficient of preservation 1.80, 35 per cent lower,[27] therefore, than that of fathers. With respect to suicide, we must therefore disagree with the following proposition of Bertillon: "When woman enters the conjugal state she gains from the association more than man; but she necessarily suffers more than man when she leaves it." [28]

III

The immunity of married persons in general is thus due, wholly for one sex and largely for the other, to the influence not of conjugal society but of the family society. However, we have seen that even if there are no children, men at least are protected in the proportion of 1 to 1.5. A reduction of 50 suicides from 150, or 33 per cent, though considerably below that achieved when the family is complete, nevertheless is not a negligible quantity and its cause should be understood. Is it due to the special benefits bestowed by marriage on the male sex, or is it not rather a result of matrimonial selection? For although it has been shown that the latter does not play the dominant role attributed to it, it has not been proven to be wholly without influence.

One fact at first sight even seems to prove this hypothesis. We know that the coefficient of preservation of childless husbands partially survives marriage; it falls merely from 1.5 to 1.2. Now, this

---

[27] A similar difference exists between the coefficient of childless husbands and childless wives; it is much greater. The second (0.67) is 66 per cent lower than the first (1.5). The existence of children thus causes the wife to regain half the ground she loses by marriage. That is, if she benefits from marriage less than the man, she profits more than he from the family, that is, the children. She is more sensitive than he to their happy influence.

[28] Article *Mariage, Dict. Encycl.,* 2d series, vol. V, p. 36.

immunity of childless widowers evidently cannot be attributed to
widowhood, which in itself does not tend to reduce the proclivity to
suicide but on the contrary to confirm it. It thus results from an
anterior cause, though this seems unlikely to be marriage, since it
continues to act even when marriage is dissolved by the wife's death.
May it not then consist in some inherent quality of the husband
which conjugal selection makes prominent but does not create? As it
existed before marriage and is independent of it, it might well outlast
the latter. If the population of husbands is an elite, the same must be
true of widowers. To be sure, this congenital superiority has less
effect upon the latter, since they are less protected against suicide.
But the shock of widowhood may be considered as partially neutralizing this preventive influence and blocking its full results.

But for this explanation to be acceptable, it must be applicable to
both sexes. Some trace at least of this natural predisposition should
accordingly be found among married women, which, other things
being equal, would preserve them from suicide more than the unmarried. Now the very fact that they commit suicide, if childless,
more than unmarried women of the same age, is opposed to the
hypothesis that they are endowed from birth with a personal coefficient of preservation. One might, however, grant that this coefficient
exists for women as well as for men, but that it is wholly annulled
during marriage by the unfortunate effect of marriage on the wife's
moral constitution. But if its effects were only restrained and concealed by the sort of moral decline of women on entering into conjugal society, they should reappear on the dissolution of this society,
or in widowhood. Freed from the depressing influence of the matrimonial yoke, women should then recover all their advantages and
finally assert their inherent superiority to those of their sisters who
have not achieved marriage. In comparison with unmarried women,
in other words, the childless widow should have a coefficient of preservation at least approaching that of the childless widower. This is
not so. A million childless widows show annually 322 suicides; a
million unmarried women of 60 (the average age of widows) show
only between 189 and 204, or about 196. The first is to the second
number as 100 to 60. Widows without children thus have a coefficient below unity, or a coefficient of aggravation; it is 0.60, slightly
lower even than that of childless wives (0.67). It is therefore not

marriage which prevents childless wives from showing the natural indisposition to suicide attributed to them.

Perhaps it will be objected that the obstacle to the complete re-establishment of the fortunate qualities whose expression is interrupted by marriage, is that widowhood is, for women, an even worse status. Indeed the idea is widespread that a widow is in a more critical position than a widower. The moral and economic difficulties are stressed which face her when she is compelled to provide all by herself, for her own existence as well as for the needs of an entire family. This opinion has even been considered proved by facts. According to Morselli,[29] statistics prove that woman, during widowhood, is closer to man in her aptitude for suicide than she is during marriage; and since, when married, she is already nearer the male sex in this respect than when unmarried, therefore widowhood results in placing woman in the most disadvantageous position. Supporting this thesis, Morselli cites the following figures relating only to France, but to be found among all European peoples with slight variations:

Years	Share of Each Sex in 100 Suicides of Married Persons		Share of Each Sex in 100 Suicides of Widowed Persons	
	Percentage Men	Percentage Women	Percentage Men	Percentage Women
1871	79	21	71	29
1872	78	22	68	32
1873	79	21	69	31
1874	74	26	57	43
1875	81	19	77	23
1876	82	18	78	22

Woman's share in the suicides committed by both sexes in the state of widowhood seems in fact much greater than in the suicides of married persons. Does not this prove that widowhood is much more difficult for women than marriage? If so, it is not astonishing that, once a widow, the good effects of her qualities are even more prevented from appearing than before.

Unfortunately, this supposed law is based on an error of fact. Morselli has forgotten that there are everywhere twice as many widows as widowers. In France, there are in round numbers two million of the former to only one million of the latter. In Prussia, according to the census of 1890, 450,000 widowers are found and

[29] *Op. cit.,* p. 342.

1,319,000 widows; in Italy, 571,000 and 1,322,000 respectively. Under these conditions the share of widows is naturally higher than that of wives who are obviously of the same number as husbands. To obtain information from the comparison the two populations should be set up as equal. But if this precaution is taken, results contrary to those of Morselli are obtained. At the average age of the widowed or 60 years, a million wives show 154 suicides and a million husbands 577. Woman's share is therefore 21 per cent. It diminishes perceptibly in widowhood. Indeed, a million widows show 210 cases, a million widowers 1,017; whence it follows that of 100 suicides of widowed persons of both sexes women contribute only 17. The share of men on the contrary rises from 79 to 83 per cent. Man thus loses more than woman in passing from marriage to widowhood, since he does not preserve certain of the advantages which he owed to the conjugal state. There is thus no reason to assume that this change of situation is less trying or disturbing for him than for her; the opposite is the case. Besides, we know that the mortality of widowers far exceeds that of widows; and the same is true of their marriage rates. That of widowers is at every age three or four times as great as the rate of unmarried men, while that of widows is only slightly above that of unmarried women. Women are therefore as reluctant to face second marriage as men are eager.[30] It would not be so if the state of widowhood sat lightly upon men and if women, on the contrary, had in that state to face as many difficulties as has been said to be the case.[31]

But if nothing in widowhood particularly paralyzes woman's natural advantages that pertain to her solely as matrimonially elect, and if these advantages do not manifest themselves by any definite sign, there is no reason for assuming their existence. The hypothesis of matrimonial selection is therefore wholly inapplicable to the female sex. Nothing justifies the supposition that a woman entering marriage has a constitutional advantage which preserves her to a certain degree

---

[30] See Bertillon, Les célibataires, les veufs, etc., Rev. scient., 1879.

[31] Morselli also mentions in support of his thesis that on the morrow of war the suicides of widows show a much greater rise than those of unmarried women or wives. But it is merely that then the population of widows increases disproportionately; thus it naturally produces more suicides and this rise naturally persists until the restoration of equilibrium and the return to their normal level of the different sorts of marital status.

from suicide. Consequently the same supposition is just as unfounded for men. The coefficient of 1.5 of childless husbands does not result from their belonging to the healthiest portion of the population; it can only be an effect of marriage. Conjugal society, so disadvantageous for women, must, even in the absence of children, be admitted to be advantageous for men. Those who enter it are not an aristocracy of birth; they do not bring to marriage, as an existing quality, a temperament disinclining them to suicide, but acquire it by living the conjugal life. At least, if they have some natural advantages these can be only very vague and indeterminate; for they are without influence until the advent of certain other conditions. So true is it that suicide does not principally depend upon the congenital qualities of individuals but upon causes exterior to and dominating them!

There is, however, a final difficulty to be solved. If this coefficient of 1.5, independent of the family, is due to marriage, how does it survive marriage and reappear at least in attenuated form (1.2) in the childless widower? If the theory of matrimonial selection which accounted for this survival is rejected, with what shall it be replaced?

It is sufficient to assume that the habits, tastes, and tendencies formed during marriage do not disappear on its dissolution; and nothing is more plausible than this hypothesis. If the married man, then, even if childless, feels a relative security from suicide, he must inevitably preserve some of this feeling when a widower. Only, as widowhood does involve a certain moral shock and since, as we shall see later, any loss of equilibrium inclines to suicide, this disposition, though remaining, is weakened. Inversely, but for the same reason, since a childless wife more often commits suicide than if she had remained unmarried, once become a widow she retains this stronger propensity for suicide, even slightly reenforced by the distress and loss of equilibrium always accompanying widowhood. But, since the ill effects that marriage had upon her make this change of status more acceptable, the aggravation is very slight. The coefficient is lowered by only a few per cent (0.60 instead of 0.67).[32]

---

[32] When there are children, the lowering of coefficient incident to both sexes due to widowhood is almost the same. The coefficient of husbands with children is 2.9; it becomes 1.6. That of women in the same circumstances from 1.89 becomes 1.06. The diminution is 45 per cent for the former, 44 per cent for the latter. That is, as

This explanation is confirmed by the fact that it is only a particular instance of a more general proposition which may be formulated thus: *In an identical society, the tendency to suicide in the state of widowhood is for each sex a function of the suicidal tendency of the same sex in the state of marriage.* If the husband is highly protected, the widower is too, although of course to a lesser degree; if the former is only slightly protected from suicide, the latter is not thus protected at all or only very little. To assure ourselves of the accuracy of this proposition we need only refer to Tables XX and XXI and the conclusions drawn from them. We there found that one sex is always more favored than the other in both marriage and widowhood. Now, the one more privileged in the first of these conditions preserves its privilege in the second. In France, husbands have a higher coefficient of preservation than wives; that of widowers is similarly higher than that of widows. In Oldenburg the opposite is true among married couples: the wife has a higher immunity than the husband. The same inversion occurs between widowers and widows.

But as these two single cases might with some justice be considered an insufficient proof and as, on the other hand, statistical publications do not give us the necessary data to verify our proposition in other countries, we have resorted to the following procedure to extend the scope of our comparisons: we have calculated separately the suicide-rate for each age-group and marital status in the department of the Seine on the one hand, and on the other in all the rest of the departments combined. The two social groups, thus isolated from each other, are sufficiently different for us to expect their comparison to be instructive. And family life actually does have very different effects upon suicide in them (see Table XXII). In the departments the husband has much more immunity than the wife. In only four

---

we have said, widowhood produces two different effects; it disturbs 1. the conjugal society, 2. the family society. The former disturbance is much less felt by the woman than by the man, just because she profits less from marriage. But the second is felt far more by her; for she often finds it harder to take the husband's place in the direction of the family than he does to replace her in her domestic functions. When there are children, therefore, a sort of compensation occurs which makes the suicidal tendency of the two sexes vary, as a result of widowhood, in the same proportions. Thus it is especially when there are no children that a widowed woman partially recovers the ground lost in the state of marriage.

age-groups does the former's coefficient descend below 3,[33] while the wife's never reaches 2; the average is in one case 2.88, in the other 1.49. In the Seine the reverse is true; for husbands the coefficient averages only 1.56 while it is 1.79 [34] for wives. The very same inversion is found between widowers and widows. In the provinces the average coefficient of widowers is high (1.45), that of widows much lower (0.78). In the Seine, on the contrary, the second is higher, rising to 0.93, close to unity, while the other falls to 0.75. *Thus, whichever the favored sex, widowhood regularly corresponds to marriage.*

More than this, if the key is sought to the variation of the coefficient of husbands from one social group to another and if the same study is then made for widowers, the following surprising results are obtained:

$$\frac{\text{Husbands' coefficient in provinces}}{\text{Husbands' coefficient in the Seine}} = \frac{2.88}{1.56} = 1.84$$

$$\frac{\text{Widowers' coefficient in provinces}}{\text{Widowers' coefficient in the Seine}} = \frac{1.45}{0.75} = 1.93$$

and for women:

$$\frac{\text{Wives' coefficient in the Seine}}{\text{Wives' coefficient in provinces}} = \frac{1.79}{1.49} = 1.20$$

$$\frac{\text{Widows' coefficient in the Seine}}{\text{Widows' coefficient in provinces}} = \frac{0.93}{0.78} = 1.19$$

The numerical proportions are for each sex pretty nearly equal; for women, the equality, in fact, is almost absolute. Thus, not only does the coefficient of widowers follow suit when that of husbands rises or sinks, but it even increases or decreases in exactly the same measure. These relations may be expressed in a form still more clearly confirmative of the law we have stated. They imply, in fact, that

[33] From Table XXII it appears that in Paris, as in the provinces, the coefficient of husbands below 20 years is below unity; that is, for them there is aggravation. This confirms the law formulated above.

[34] Evidently, when the female sex is the one more favored by marriage, the disproportion between the sexes is much less than when the husband has the advantage; a new confirmation of a remark made above.

TABLE XXII—Comparison of the Suicide Rate per Million Inhabitants of Each Age-group and Marital Status in the Seine and the Provinces (1889-1891)

Ages	Men (Provinces)			Coefficient of Preservation with Respect to Unmarried Persons		Women (Provinces)			Coefficient of Preservation with Respect to Unmarried Persons	
	Un-married	Hus-bands	Wid-owers	Hus-bands	Wid-owers	Un-married	Wives	Wid-ows	Wives	Wid-ows
15-20	100	400	.....	0.25	....	67	36	375	1.86	0.17
20-25	214	95	153	2.25	1.39	95	52	76	1.82	1.25
25-30	365	103	373	3.54	0.97	122	64	156	1.90	0.78
30-40	590	202	511	2.92	1.15	101	74	174	1.36	0.58
40-50	976	295	633	3.30	1.54	147	95	149	1.54	0.98
50-60	1,445	470	852	3.07	1.69	178	136	174	1.30	1.02
60-70	1,790	582	1,047	3.07	1.70	163	142	221	1.14	0.73
70-80	2,000	664	1,252	3.01	1.59	200	191	233	1.04	0.85
Above 80	1,458	762	1,129	1.91	1.29	160	108	221	1.48	0.72
Averages of coefficients of preservation				2.88	1.45	Averages of coefficients of preservation			1.49	0.78
	Men (Seine)					Women (Seine)				
15-20	280	2,000	.....	0.14	....	224	...	...	....	....
20-25	487	128	.....	3.80	....	196	64	...	3.06	....
25-30	599	298	714	2.01	0.83	328	103	296	3.18	1.10
30-40	869	436	912	1.99	0.95	281	156	373	1.80	0.75
40-50	985	808	1,459	1.21	0.67	357	217	289	1.64	1.23
50-60	1,367	1,152	2,321	1.18	0.58	456	353	410	1.29	1.11
60-70	1,500	1,559	2,902	0.96	0.51	515	471	637	1.09	0.80
70-80	1,783	1,741	2,082	1.02	0.85	326	677	464	0.48	0.70
Above 80	1,923	1,111	2,089	1.73	0.92	508	277	591	1.83	0.85
Averages of coefficients of preservation				1.56	0.75	Averages of coefficients of preservation			1.79	0.93

everywhere, whichever the sex, widowhood decreases the immunity of the surviving partner in a constant proportion:

$$\frac{\text{Husbands in provinces}}{\text{Widowers in provinces}} = \frac{2.88}{1.45} = 1.98 \qquad \frac{\text{Husbands in Seine}}{\text{Widowers in Seine}} = \frac{1.56}{0.75} = 2.0$$

$$\frac{\text{Wives in provinces}}{\text{Widows in provinces}} = \frac{1.49}{0.78} = 1.91 \qquad \frac{\text{Wives in Seine}}{\text{Widows in Seine}} = \frac{1.79}{0.93} = 1.92$$

The coefficient of widowed persons is about half that of married persons. It is thus no exaggeration to say that the aptitude for suicide of widowed persons is a function of the corresponding aptitude of married persons; in other words, the former is in part a consequence of the latter. But since marriage adds to the husband's immunity, even without children, it is not surprising that the widower should retain a portion of this fortunate disposition.

At the same time that it solves the question we had asked ourselves, this result casts some light on the nature of widowhood. In fact, it teaches us that widowhood in itself is not a hopelessly disadvantageous condition. It is very often better than bachelorhood. To be truthful, the moral constitution of widowers and of widows is not at all specific, but depends on that of married people of the same sex and in the same country. It is only a prolongation of this. If you will tell me how marriage and family life in a given society affect men and women, I will tell you what widowhood does for each. Although the crisis of widowhood is more grievous where marriage and domestic society are both felicitous, by fortunate compensation people are better equipped to face it; and, inversely, this crisis is less grave where the matrimonial and family constitution leave more to be desired, but in return people are less equipped to resist it. Thus, in societies where man benefits more from the family than woman, he suffers more when left alone but is at the same time better able to endure it, because the salutary influences which he has undergone have made him more averse to desperate resolutions.

IV

The following table summarizes the facts just established: [35]

INFLUENCE OF THE FAMILY ON SUICIDE BY SEX
Men

	Suicide-rate	Coefficient of Preservation in Relation to Unmarried Men
Unmarried men 45 years old	975	...
Husbands with children	336	2.9
Husbands without children	644	1.5
Unmarried men 60 years old	1,504	...
Widowers with children	937	1.6
Widowers without children	1,258	1.2

[35] M. Bertillon (article cited in the *Revue scientifique*), had already given the suicide-rate for the different categories of marital status with and without children. He found the following results:

Husbands w. children	205 suicides per million	Widowers w. chil.	526
Husbands w. no chil.	478 suicides per million	Widowers w. no chil.	1,004
Wives w. children	45 suicides per million	Widows w. children	104
Wives w. no children	158 suicides per million	Widows w. no chil.	238

These figures refer to the years 1861–68. Given the general increase in suicides, they confirm our own figures. But as the lack of such a table as our Table XXI allowed

INFLUENCE OF THE FAMILY ON SUICIDE BY SEX—Continued
Women

	Suicide-rate	Coefficient of Preservation in Relation to Unmarried Women
Unmarried women 42 years old	150	....
Wives with children	79	1.89
Wives without children	221	0.67
Unmarried women 60 years old	196	....
Widows with children	186	1.06
Widows without children	322	0.60

From this table and the preceding remarks it appears that marriage has indeed a preservative effect of its own against suicide. But it is very limited and also benefits one sex only. Useful as it has been to attest its existence—and this usefulness will be better understood in a later chapter [36]—the fact remains that the family is the essential factor in the immunity of married persons, that is, the family as the whole group of parents and children. Of course, since husband and wife are members, they too share in producing this result, however not as husband or wife but as father or mother, as functionaries of the family association. If the disappearance of one increases the chances that the other may commit suicide, it is not because the bonds uniting them personally are broken, but because a family disaster occurs, the shock of which the survivor undergoes. Reserving the special effect of marriage for later study, we shall say that domestic society, like religious society, is a powerful counteragent against suicide.

This immunity even increases with the density of the family, that is with the increase in the number of its elements.

This proposition we have already stated and proved in an article appearing in the *Revue philosophique* of November 1888. But the insufficiency of statistical data then at our disposal did not permit as strict a proof as was desirable. We did not know the average number in family establishments either throughout France or in each department. Thus we had to assume that family density depended solely

---

no comparison of husbands and widowers with unmarried persons of the same age, no precise conclusion could be drawn as to the coefficients of preservation. We are also in doubt as to whether they refer to the entire country. Actually the French Bureau of Statistics assures us that the distinction between childless couples and those with children was never made in the census before 1886, except in 1855 for the departments exclusive of the Seine.

[36] See Book II, Chap. V, 3.

on the number of children and—this number itself not being indicated in the census—we had to estimate it indirectly by employing what demography terms the physiological increase, or the annual excess of births over a thousand deaths. To be sure, this substitution was not unreasonable, for where the increase is high, families in general can hardly be other than dense. However, this consequence is not inescapable and often does not occur. Where children habitually leave their parents early, either to emigrate, or to settle elsewhere, or for other reasons, the family density has no reference to their number. In fact, the home may be deserted no matter how fruitful the marriage has been. This happens both in cultured surroundings where the child is early sent away from home to commence or complete his education, and in impoverished neighborhoods where premature dispersion is necessitated by the hardships of existence. On the other hand, the family may include a moderate or even a larg number of elements in spite of a merely average birth rate if the unmarried adults or even the married children continue to live with their parents and form a single domestic society. For all these reasons no exact measure is possible of the relative density of family groups without knowledge of their actual composition.

The census of 1886, the results of which were not published until the end of 1888, gave us this knowledge. If we study from its data the relation in the different French departments between suicide and the actual average of family members, the following are the results:

	Suicides per Million Inhabitants (1878–1887)	Average Membership of Family Households per 100 Households (1886)
1st group (11 departments)	From 430 to 380	347
2nd group (6 departments)	From 300 to 240	360
3rd group (15 departments)	From 230 to 180	376
4th group (18 departments)	From 170 to 130	393
5th group (26 departments)	From 120 to 80	418
5th group (10 departments)	From 70 to 30	434

As suicides diminish, family density regularly increases.

Instead of comparing averages, if we analyze the content of each group we shall find only confirmation of this conclusion. In fact, for all France, the average membership is 39 persons per 10 families. If then we ask how many departments there are above or below the average in each of these 6 classes, we shall find them to be composed as follows:

What Per Cent of Each Group of Departments *

	Below Average No.	Above Average No.
1st group	100	0
2nd group	84	16
3rd group	60	30
4th group	33	63
5th group	19	81
6th group	0	100

* Figures reproduced as in original text, since errors could not be corrected.—Ed.

The group with most suicides includes only departments with family numbers below the average. Gradually and most regularly, the relation is reversed until the inversion is complete. In the last class, where suicides are few, all the departments have a family density above average.

The two maps (Appendices) also have the same general configuration. The region where families have least density definitely has the same limits as that of most frequent suicides. It also occupies the North and East and extends, on one side, to Brittany, on the other to the Loire. In the West and South, on the contrary, where there are few suicides, the family generally has large numbers. This relation even recurs in certain details. In the northern region, two departments are notable for their low aptitude for suicide, the Nord and Pas-de-Calais, a fact so much the more surprising as the Nord is highly industrial and intense industrialization favors suicide. The same peculiarity appears on the other map. In these two departments family density is high, though very low in all neighboring departments. In the South, we find on both maps the same dark area formed by the Bouches-du-Rhône, the Var, Alpes-Maritimes, and, to the West, the same light area formed by Brittany. The irregularities are exceptional and never prominent; considering the great number of factors which can affect so complex a phenomenon, such a general agreement is significant.

The same inverse relation reappears in the way both phenomena have evolved in time. Suicide has constantly increased since 1826 and the birth-rate has decreased. From 1821 to 1830 the latter was still 308 births for 10,000 inhabitants; during the period 1881–88 it was only 240, and the decrease was uninterrupted in the interval. At the same time, there appears a tendency for the family to break up and disperse more and more. From 1856 to 1886, the number of households increased by 2 millions in round figures; regularly and steadily it rose from 8,796,276 to 10,662,423. Yet, during the same time-interval, the population increased only by two million persons. Each family therefore includes a smaller membership.[37]

Facts thus are far from confirming the current idea that suicide is due especially to life's burdens, since, on the contrary, it diminishes as these burdens increase. This is a consequence of Malthusianism not foreseen by its author. When he urged control of the numbers in families, he felt that this restriction was at least in some cases necessary to general well-being. Actually, it is so much a source of the reverse condition that it diminishes the human desire to live. Far from dense families being a sort of unnecessary luxury appropriate only to the rich, they are actually an indispensable staff of daily life. However poor one is, and even solely from the point of view of personal interest, it is the worst of investments to substitute wealth for a portion of one's offspring.

This result agrees with the one we had reached before. Why does family density have this effect upon suicide? In reply one could not refer to the organic factor; for though absolute sterility has primarily physiological causes, insufficient fecundity has not, being usually voluntary and depending on a certain state of mind. Family density, moreover, measured as we have measured it, does not depend exclusively on the birth-rate; we have seen that where there are few children other elements may take their place and, vice versa, that their number may be of no significance if they do not actually and consistently share in the group life. Nor should this preservative virtue be ascribed to the special feelings of parents for their immediate descendants. Indeed, to be effective these very feelings presuppose a certain state of domestic society. They cannot be powerful if the family has broken up. It is therefore because the functioning of the family varies with its greater or less density, that the number of its component elements affects the suicidal tendency.

That is, the density of a group cannot sink without its vitality diminishing. Where collective sentiments are strong, it is because the force with which they affect each individual conscience is echoed in all the others, and reciprocally. The intensity they attain therefore depends on the number of consciences which react to them in com-

[37] See *Dénombrement de 1886*, p. 106.

mon. For the same reason, the larger a crowd, the more capable of
violence the passions vented by it. Consequently, in a family of
small numbers, common sentiments and memories cannot be very
intense; for there are not enough consciences in which they can be
represented and reenforced by sharing them. No such powerful traditions can be formed there as unite the members of a single group,
even surviving it and attaching successive generations to one another.
Small families are also inevitably short-lived; and without duration
no society can be stable. Not only are collective states weak in such
a group, but they cannot be numerous; for their number depends on
the active interchange of views and impressions, on the circulation of
these views and impressions from one person to another; and, on the
other hand, this very exchange is the more rapid the more persons
there are participating in it. In a sufficiently dense society, this circulation is uninterrupted; for some social units are always in contact,
whereas if there are few their relations can only be intermittent and
there will be moments when the common life is suspended. Likewise,
when the family is small, few relatives are ever together; so that
domestic life languishes and the home is occasionally deserted.

But for a group to be said to have less common life than another
means that it is less powerfully integrated; for the state of integration of a social aggregate can only reflect the intensity of the collective life circulating in it. It is more unified and powerful the more
active and constant is the intercourse among its members. Our previous conclusion may thus be completed to read: just as the family
is a powerful safeguard against suicide, so the more strongly it is
constituted the greater its protection.[38]

V

If statistics had not developed so late, it would be easy to show
by the same method that this law applies to political societies. His-

---

[38] The word "density" has just been used in a somewhat different sense from that
usually given it in sociology. Generally, the density of a group is defined not as a
function of the absolute number of associated individuals (which is rather called
"volume"), but of the number of individuals actually in reciprocal relationship in
one and the same social volume. (See Durkheim, E., *Régles de la Meth. sociol.*,
p. 139). But in the case of the family the distinction between volume and density
has no interest, since, due to the smallness of the group, all associated persons are
in actual relationship.

tory indeed teaches us that suicide, generally rare in young [39] societies in process of evolution and concentration, increases as they disintegrate. In Greece and Rome it makes its appearance with the overthrow of the old city-state organization and its progress marks successive stages of decadence. The same is observed in the Ottoman Empire. In France, on the eve of the Revolution, the turmoil which shook society with the disintegration of the older social system took shape in a sudden rush of suicides mentioned by contemporary authors.[40]

But beside these historical data, suicide statistics, though hardly existing for longer than the past seventy years, supply us with some proofs of this proposition which are more precise than those given above.

Great political upheavals are sometimes said to increase the number of suicides. But Morselli has conclusively shown that facts contradict this view. All the revolutions which have occurred in France during this century reduced the number of suicides at the moment of their occurrence. In 1830, the total fell to 1,756 from 1,904 in 1829, amounting to a sudden drop of nearly 10 per cent. In 1848 the drop is no less; the annual figure changes from 3,647 to 3,301. Then, during the years 1848–49, the crisis which has just shaken France spreads through Europe; everywhere suicides decrease, and this decrease is more and more perceptible the more serious and prolonged the crisis. This appears in the following table:

	Denmark	Prussia	Bavaria	Kingdom of Saxony	Austria
1847	345	1,852	217	...	611 (in 1846)
1848	305	1,649	215	398	...
1849	337	1,527	189	328	452

In Germany public feeling ran much higher than in Denmark and the struggle lasted longer even than in France, where a new government was immediately formed; accordingly, the decrease is

---

[39] Let us not confuse young societies capable of development with lower societies; in the latter, on the contrary, suicides are very frequent, as will appear in the following chapter.

[40] Helvetius wrote in 1781: "Financial disorder and the change in the constitution of the state spread general fear. Numerous suicides in the capital give sad proof of this." Quoted from Legoyt, p. 30. Mercier in his *Tableau de Paris* (1782) says that within 25 years the number of suicides tripled in Paris.

prolonged in the German states up to 1849. For that year, the decrease is 13 per cent in Bavaria, 18 per cent in Prussia; in Saxony, in a single year from 1848 to 1849, it is likewise 18 per cent.

In 1851, the same phenomenon does not occur in France, nor does it occur in 1852. Suicides remain stationary. But in France the *coup d'etat* of Louis Bonaparte has the usual effect; although it took place in December, the number of suicides fell from 483 in 1851 to 446 in 1852 (8 per cent), and even in 1853 they were 463.[41] This fact would seem to prove that this governmental revolution disturbed Paris much more than the provinces, where it seems to have had little effect. Besides, generally speaking, the influence of such crises is always more noticeable in the capital than in the departments. In 1830, the decrease in Paris was 13 per cent (269 cases instead of 307 the year before and 359 the year after); in 1848, 32 per cent (481 cases instead of 698).[42]

Mild as they are, mere election crises sometimes have the same result. Thus, in France the suicide record clearly shows the mark of the parliamentary crisis of May 16, 1877 and the resulting popular agitation, as well as of the 1889 elections which ended the Boulanger agitation. In proof, we need only compare the monthly distribution of suicides in these two years with that of the years immediately before and after.

	1876	1877	1878	1888	1889	1890
May	604	649	717	924	919	819
June	662	692	682	851	829	822
July	625	540	693	825	818	888
August	482	496	547	786	818	734
September	394	378	512	673	694	720
October	464	423	468	603	597	675
November	400	413	415	589	648	571
December	389	386	335	574	618	475

During the first months of 1877 suicides were more numerous than in 1876 (1,945 cases from January to April instead of 1,784) and the rise continues in May and June. Only at the end of the last-named month are the Chambers dissolved, the electoral period actually if not legally begun; this is probably the moment when political passions were most excited, for they were bound subsequently to subside somewhat due to time and weariness. Accordingly, in July,

[41] According to Legoyt, p. 252.
[42] According to Masaryck, *Der Selbstmord*, p. 137.

instead of continuing to surpass those of the preceding year, suicides are 14 per cent below them. Except for a slight pause in August, the drop continues to October, though less strongly. The crisis is ending. Immediately upon its conclusion, the rise, momentarily interrupted, is resumed. In 1889 the phenomenon is yet more pronounced. The Chamber is dissolved at the beginning of August; the excitement of the election period begins at once and lasts to the end of September, the time of the elections. An abrupt decrease of 12 per cent, compared with the corresponding month of 1888, occurs in August and lasts into September but stops abruptly in October when the struggle is ended.

Great national wars have the same effect as political disturbances. In 1866 war breaks out between Austria and Italy, and suicides drop 14 per cent in both countries.

	1865	1866	1867
Italy	678	588	657
Austria	1,464	1,265	1,407

In 1864 it was the turn of Denmark and Saxony. In the latter state suicides, which numbered 643 in 1863, fell to 545 in 1864 (16 per cent), only to return to 619 in 1865. As to Denmark, since we do not know the number of suicides for 1863, we cannot compare that of 1864 with it; but we do know that the figure for the second year (411) is the lowest since 1852. And as there is a rise to 451 in 1865, this figure of 411 very probably betokens a considerable drop.

The war of 1870–1871 had the same results in France and Germany:

	1869	1870	1871	1872
Prussia	3,186	2,963	2,723	2,950
Saxony	710	657	653	687
France	5,114	4,157	4,490	5,275

This decrease might perhaps be considered due to the drafting of a part of the civilian population in war-time and the fact that it is very hard to keep track of suicides in an army in the field. But women as well as men contribute to this decrease. In Italy, suicides of women drop from 130 in 1864 to 117 in 1866; in Saxony, from 133 in 1863 to 120 in 1864 and 114 in 1865 (15 per cent). In the same country there is a no less considerable drop in 1870; from 130 in 1869 suicides fall to 114 in 1870 and remain at the same level in 1871; the decrease is 13 per cent, more than that of contemporary suicides of men. While 616 women had killed themselves in Prussia in 1869, there were only 540 such suicides in 1871 (13 per cent). It is common knowledge, besides, that young men capable of bearing arms furnish only a small contingent of suicides. Only six months of 1870 were occupied by the war; at this period, in time of peace, a million Frenchmen of from 25 to 30 years of age would have showed at most about 100 suicides,[43] whereas the reduction between 1870 and 1869 is 1,057 cases.[44]

The question has also been raised whether the cause of this momentary drop at a time of crisis might not be that the record of suicides was less exactly kept because of the paralysis of administrative authority. Numerous facts, however, show that this accidental cause does not adequately explain the matter. First, the widespread occurrence of the phenomenon. It appears among conquerors as well as vanquished, invaders and invaded alike. Furthermore, when the shock was very violent, its effects persisted for a considerable time after the event. Suicides increase slowly; some years pass before their return to their point of departure; this is true even in countries where in normal times they increase with annual regularity. Though partial omissions are of course possible and even likely at such times of trouble, the drop revealed by the statistics is too steady to be attributed to a brief inadvertence of administration as its principal cause.

But the best proof that we confront a phenomenon of social psychology and not a mistake in accounting, is that not all political or national crises have this influence. Only those do which excite the passions. We have already noted that revolutions in France have always had more affect on suicide in Paris than in the departments; yet the administrative upheaval was the same in the provinces and in the capital. But this sort of event always has much less interest for the provincial than for the Parisian, its author and participant from a closer vantage point. Likewise, while great national wars

[43] Actually, the annual rate at this age in 1889–91 was only 396; the semi-annual rate about 200. From 1870 to 1890 the number of suicides at every age doubled.
[44] Durkheim's figures show a reduction from 5,114 in 1869 to 4,157 in 1870, which amounts to 957, not 1,057.—Ed.

such as that of 1870–71 have had a strong influence on the current of suicide in both France and Germany, purely dynastic wars such as the Crimean or Italian, which have not violently moved the masses, have had no appreciable effect. There even occurred a considerable rise in 1854 (3,700 cases against 3,415 in 1853). The same fact is observed in Prussia at the time of the wars of 1864 and 1866. The figures are stationary in 1864 and rise slightly in 1866. These wars were due wholly to the initiative of politicians and had not aroused public feeling like that of 1870.

From this point of view it is interesting to note that in Bavaria the year 1870 did not have the same effects as in the other countries of Germany, especially North Germany. More suicides were recorded in 1870 in Bavaria than in 1869 (452 against 425). Only in 1871 is there a slight decrease; it continues somewhat in 1872 when there are only 412 cases, which, however, entails a lowering of only 9 per cent by comparison with 1869 and 4 per cent with 1870. Yet Bavaria took the same important part as Prussia in military events; it, too, mobilized its whole army and the administrative disturbance must have been no less. It simply did not take the same moral share in events. Actually it is well known that Catholic Bavaria is, of all Germany, the country which has always lived a life most its own and been most jealous of its autonomy. It shared in the war through the will of its king but without enthusiasm. Therefore it resisted the great social movement then agitating Germany much more than the other allies; and so the reaction was felt there only later and less strongly. Enthusiasm was delayed and inconsiderable. It required the breath of glory wafted over Germany on the morrow of the victory of 1870 to warm somewhat the hitherto cold and unresponsive land of Bavaria.[45]

This fact may be compared with the following, of similar signifi-

[45] Nor is it certain that this diminution of 1872 was caused by the events of 1870. The reduction of suicides scarcely made itself felt outside of Prussia beyond the actual period of hostilities. In Saxony the reduction of 1870, only 8 per cent, is not continued in 1871 and almost completely comes to an end in 1872. In the duchy of Baden it was confined to 1870; 1871, with its 244 cases, exceeds 1869 by 10 per cent. It thus seems that Prussia alone was seized with a sort of collective euphoria on the morrow of victory. The other states had less feeling for the increased glory and power resulting from the war, and social passions subsided with the end of the great national crisis.

cance. In France during the years 1870–71, suicide diminished only
in the cities:

| | Suicides per Million Inhabitants | |
	Urban Population	Rural Population
1866–69	202	104
1870–72	161	110

Recordings of suicides must, however, have been more difficult
in the country than in the city. The true reason for this difference
accordingly lies elsewhere. The war produced its full moral effect
only on the urban population, more sensitive, impressionable and
also better informed on current events than the rural population.

These facts are therefore susceptible of only one interpretation;
namely, that great social disturbances and great popular wars rouse
collective sentiments, stimulate partisan spirit and patriotism, political and national faith, alike, and concentrating activity toward a
single end, at least temporarily cause a stronger integration of society.
The salutary influence which we have just shown to exist is due not
to the crisis but to the struggles it occasions. As they force men to
close ranks and confront the common danger, the individual thinks
less of himself and more of the common cause. Besides, it is comprehensible that this integration may not be purely momentary but
may sometimes outlive its immediate causes, especially when it is
intense.

VI

We have thus successively set up the three following propositions:

*Suicide varies inversely with the degree of integration of
religious society.*

*Suicide varies inversely with the degree of integration of
domestic society.*

*Suicide varies inversely with the degree of integration of
political society.*

This grouping shows that whereas these different societies have a
moderating influence upon suicide, this is due not to special characteristics of each but to a characteristic common to all. Religion does
not owe its efficacy to the special nature of religious sentiments, since
domestic and political societies both produce the same effects when

strongly integrated. This, moreover, we have already proved when studying directly the manner of action of different religions upon suicide.[46] Inversely, it is not the specific nature of the domestic or political tie which can explain the immunity they confer, since religious society has the same advantage. The cause can only be found in a single quality possessed by all these social groups, though perhaps to varying degrees. The only quality satisfying this condition is that they are all strongly integrated social groups. So we reach the general conclusion: suicide varies inversely with the degree of integration of the social groups of which the individual forms a part.

But society cannot disintegrate without the individual simultaneously detaching himself from social life, without his own goals becoming preponderant over those of the community, in a word without his personality tending to surmount the collective personality. The more weakened the groups to which he belongs, the less he depends on them, the more he consequently depends only on himself and recognizes no other rules of conduct than what are founded on his private interests. If we agree to call this state egoism, in which the individual ego asserts itself to excess in the face of the social ego and at its expense, we may call egoistic the special type of suicide springing from excessive individualism.

But how can suicide have such an origin?

First of all, it can be said that, as collective force is one of the obstacles best calculated to restrain suicide, its weakening involves a development of suicide. When society is strongly integrated, it holds individuals under its control, considers them at its service and thus forbids them to dispose wilfully of themselves. Accordingly it opposes their evading their duties to it through death. But how could society impose its supremacy upon them when they refuse to accept this subordination as legitimate? It no longer then possesses the requisite authority to retain them in their duty if they wish to desert; and conscious of its own weakness, it even recognizes their right to do freely what it can no longer prevent. So far as they are the admitted masters of their destinies, it is their privilege to end their lives. They, on their part, have no reason to endure life's sufferings patiently. For they cling to life more resolutely when belonging to a group they love, so as not to betray interests they put before their

46 See above, Book II, Ch. 2.

own. The bond that unites them with the common cause attaches
them to life and the lofty goal they envisage prevents their feeling
personal troubles so deeply. There is, in short, in a cohesive and
animated society a constant interchange of ideas and feelings from all
to each and each to all, something like a mutual moral support, which
instead of throwing the individual on his own resources, leads him
to share in the collective energy and supports his own when exhausted.

But these reasons are purely secondary. Excessive individualism
not only results in favoring the action of suicidogenic causes, but it
is itself such a cause. It not only frees man's inclination to do away
with himself from a protective obstacle, but creates this inclination
out of whole cloth and thus gives birth to a special suicide which
bears its mark. This must be clearly understood for this is what constitutes the special character of the type of suicide just distinguished
and justifies the name we have given it. What is there then in individualism that explains this result?

It has been sometimes said that because of his psychological constitution, man cannot live without attachment to some object which
transcends and survives him, and that the reason for this necessity
is a need we must have not to perish entirely. Life is said to be intolerable unless some reason for existing is involved, some purpose
justifying life's trials. The individual alone is not a sufficient end for
his activity. He is too little. He is not only hemmed in spatially; he
is also strictly limited temporally. When, therefore, we have no
other object than ourselves we cannot avoid the thought that our
efforts will finally end in nothingness, since we ourselves disappear.
But annihilation terrifies us. Under these conditions one would lose
courage to live, that is, to act and struggle, since nothing will remain
of our exertions. The state of egoism, in other words, is supposed
to be contradictory to human nature and, consequently, too uncertain to have chances of permanence.

In this absolute formulation the proposition is vulnerable. If the
thought of the end of our personality were really so hateful, we
could consent to live only by blinding ourselves voluntarily as to
life's value. For if we may in a measure avoid the prospect of annihilation we cannot extirpate it; it is inevitable, whatever we do. We
may push back the frontier for some generations, force our name to

endure for some years or centuries longer than our body; a moment, too soon for most men, always comes when it will be nothing. For the groups we join in order to prolong our existence by their means are themselves mortal; they too must dissolve, carrying with them all our deposit of ourselves. Those are few whose memories are closely enough bound to the very history of humanity to be assured of living until its death. So, if we really thus thirsted after immortality, no such brief perspectives could ever appease us. Besides, what of us is it that lives? A word, a sound, an imperceptible trace, most often anonymous,[47] therefore nothing comparable to the violence of our efforts or able to justify them to us. In actuality, though a child is naturally an egoist who feels not the slightest craving to survive himself, and the old man is very often a child in this and so many other respects, neither ceases to cling to life as much or more than the adult; indeed we have seen that suicide is very rare for the first fifteen years and tends to decrease at the other extreme of life. Such too is the case with animals, whose psychological constitution differs from that of men only in degree. It is therefore untrue that life is only possible by its possessing its rationale outside of itself.

Indeed, a whole range of functions concern only the individual; these are the ones indispensable for physical life. Since they are made for this purpose only, they are perfected by its attainment. In everything concerning them, therefore, man can act reasonably without thought of transcendental purposes. These functions serve by merely serving him. In so far as he has no other needs, he is therefore self-sufficient and can live happily with no other objective than living. This is not the case, however, with the civilized adult. He has many ideas, feelings and practices unrelated to organic needs. The roles of art, morality, religion, political faith, science itself are not to repair organic exhaustion nor to provide sound functioning of the organs. All this supra-physical life is built and expanded not because of the demands of the cosmic environment but because of the demands of the social environment. The influence of society is what has aroused in us the sentiments of sympathy and solidarity drawing us toward

[47] We say nothing of the ideal protraction of life involved in the belief in immortality of the soul, for (1) this cannot explain why the family or attachment to political society preserves us from suicide; and (2) it is not even this belief which forms religion's prophylactic influence, as we have shown above.

others; it is society which, fashioning us in its image, fills us with religious, political and moral beliefs that control our actions. To play our social role we have striven to extend our intelligence and it is still society that has supplied us with tools for this development by transmitting to us its trust fund of knowledge.

Through the very fact that these superior forms of human activity have a collective origin, they have a collective purpose. As they derive from society they have reference to it; rather they are society itself incarnated and individualized in each one of us. But for them to have a raison d'être in our eyes, the purpose they envisage must be one not indifferent to us. We can cling to these forms of human activity only to the degree that we cling to society itself. Contrariwise, in the same measure as we feel detached from society we become detached from that life whose source and aim is society. For what purpose do these rules of morality, these precepts of law binding us to all sorts of sacrifices, these restrictive dogmas exist, if there is no being outside us whom they serve and in whom we participate? What is the purpose of science itself? If its only use is to increase our chances for survival, it does not deserve the trouble it entails. Instinct acquits itself better of this role; animals prove this. Why substitute for it a more hesitant and uncertain reflection? What is the end of suffering, above all? If the value of things can only be estimated by their relation to this positive evil for the individual, it is without reward and incomprehensible. This problem does not exist for the believer firm in his faith or the man strongly bound by ties of domestic or political society. Instinctively and unreflectively they ascribe all that they are and do, the one to his Church or his God, the living symbol of the Church, the other to his family, the third to his country or party. Even in their sufferings they see only a means of glorifying the group to which they belong and thus do homage to it. So, the Christian ultimately desires and seeks suffering to testify more fully to his contempt for the flesh and more fully resemble his divine model. But the more the believer doubts, that is, the less he feels himself a real participant in the religious faith to which he belongs, and from which he is freeing himself; the more the family and community become foreign to the individual, so much the more does he become a mystery to himself, unable to escape the exasperating and agonizing question: to what purpose?

If, in other words, as has often been said, man is double, that is because social man superimposes himself upon physical man. Social man necessarily presupposes a society which he expresses and serves. If this dissolves, if we no longer feel it in existence and action about and above us, whatever is social in us is deprived of all objective foundation. All that remains is an artificial combination of illusory images, a phantasmagoria vanishing at the least reflection; that is, nothing which can be a goal for our action. Yet this social man is the essence of civilized man; he is the masterpiece of existence. Thus we are bereft of reasons for existence; for the only life to which we could cling no longer corresponds to anything actual; the only existence still based upon reality no longer meets our needs. Because we have been initiated into a higher existence, the one which satisfies an animal or a child can satisfy us no more and the other itself fades and leaves us helpless. So there is nothing more for our efforts to lay hold of, and we feel them lose themselves in emptiness. In this sense it is true to say that our activity needs an object transcending it. We do not need it to maintain ourselves in the illusion of an impossible immortality; it is implicit in our moral constitution and cannot be even partially lost without this losing its raison d'être in the same degree. No proof is needed that in such a state of confusion the least cause of discouragement may easily give birth to desperate resolutions. If life is not worth the trouble of being lived, everything becomes a pretext to rid ourselves of it.

But this is not all. This detachment occurs not only in single individuals. One of the constitutive elements of every national temperament consists of a certain way of estimating the value of existence. There is a collective as well as an individual humor inclining peoples to sadness or cheerfulness, making them see things in bright or sombre lights. In fact, only society can pass a collective opinion on the value of human life; for this the individual is incompetent. The latter knows nothing but himself and his own little horizon; thus his experience is too limited to serve as a basis for a general appraisal. He may indeed consider his own life to be aimless; he can say nothing applicable to others. On the contrary, without sophistry, society may generalize its own feeling as to itself, its state of health or lack of health. For individuals share too deeply in the life of society for it to be diseased without their suffering infection. What it suffers they necessarily suffer. Because it is the whole, its ills are communicated to its parts. Hence it cannot disintegrate without awareness that the regular conditions of general existence are equally disturbed. Because society is the end on which our better selves depend, it cannot feel us escaping it without a simultaneous realization that our activity is purposeless. Since we are its handiwork, society cannot be conscious of its own decadence without the feeling that henceforth this work is of no value. Thence are formed currents of depression and disillusionment emanating from no particular individual but expressing society's state of disintegration. They reflect the relaxation of social bonds, a sort of collective asthenia, or social malaise, just as individual sadness, when chronic, in its way reflects the poor organic state of the individual. Then metaphysical and religious systems spring up which, by reducing these obscure sentiments to formulae, attempt to prove to men the senselessness of life and that it is self-deception to believe that it has purpose. Then new moralities originate which, by elevating facts to ethics, commend suicide or at least tend in that direction by suggesting a minimal existence. On their appearance they seem to have been created out of whole cloth by their makers who are sometimes blamed for the pessimism of their doctrines. In reality they are an effect rather than a cause; they merely symbolize in abstract language and systematic form the physiological distress of the body social.[48] As these currents are collective, they have, by virtue of their origin, an authority which they impose upon the individual and they drive him more vigorously on the way to which he is already inclined by the state of moral distress directly aroused in him by the disintegration of society. Thus, at the very moment that, with excessive zeal, he frees himself from the social environment, he still submits to its influence. However individualized a man may be, there is always something collective remaining—the very depression and melancholy resulting from this same exaggerated individualism. He effects communion through sadness when he no longer has anything else with which to achieve it.

Hence this type of suicide well deserves the name we have given it. Egoism is not merely a contributing factor in it; it is its generating cause. In this case the bond attaching man to life relaxes because

---

[48] This is why it is unjust to accuse these theorists of sadness of generalizing personal impressions. They are the echo of a general condition.

that attaching him to society is itself slack. The incidents of private life which seem the direct inspiration of suicide and are considered its determining causes are in reality only incidental causes. The individual yields to the slightest shock of circumstance because the state of society has made him a ready prey to suicide.

Several facts confirm this explanation. Suicide is known to be rare among children and to diminish among the aged at the last confines of life; physical man, in both, tends to become the whole of man. Society is still lacking in the former, for it has not had the time to form him in its image; it begins to retreat from the latter or, what amounts to the same thing, he retreats from it. Thus both are more self-sufficient. Feeling a lesser need for self-completion through something not themselves, they are also less exposed to feel the lack of what is necessary for living. The immunity of an animal has the same causes. We shall likewise see in the next chapter that, though lower societies practice a form of suicide of their own, the one we have just discussed is almost unknown to them. Since their social life is very simple, the social inclinations of individuals are simple also and thus they need little for satisfaction. They readily find external objectives to which they become attached. If he can carry with him his gods and his family, primitive man, everywhere that he goes, has all that his social nature demands.

This is also why woman can endure life in isolation more easily than man. When a widow is seen to endure her condition much better than a widower and desires marriage less passionately, one is led to consider this ease in dispensing with the family a mark of superiority; it is said that woman's affective faculties, being very intense, are easily employed outside the domestic circle, while her devotion is indispensable to man to help him endure life. Actually, if this is her privilege it is because her sensibility is rudimentary rather than highly developed. As she lives outside of community existence more than man, she is less penetrated by it; society is less necessary to her because she is less impregnated with sociability. She has few needs in this direction and satisfies them easily. With a few devotional practices and some animals to care for, the old unmarried woman's life is full. If she remains faithfully attached to religious traditions and thus finds ready protection against suicide, it is because these very simple social forms satisfy all her needs. Man, on the contrary, is hard beset in this respect. As his thought and activity develop, they increasingly overflow these antiquated forms. But then he needs others. Because he is a more complex social being, he can maintain his equilibrium only by finding more points of support outside himself, and it is because his moral balance depends on a larger number of conditions that it is more easily disturbed.

CHAPTER 4
ALTRUISTIC SUICIDE[1]

I N THE order of existence, no good is measureless. A biological quality can only fulfill the purposes it is meant to serve on condition that it does not transgress certain limits. So with social phenomena. If, as we have just seen, excessive individuation leads to suicide, insufficient individuation has the same effects. When man has become detached from society, he encounters less resistance to suicide in himself, and he does so likewise when social integration is too strong.

I

It has sometimes[2] been said that suicide was unknown among lower societies. Thus expressed, the assertion is inexact. To be sure, egoistic suicide, constituted as has just been shown, seems not to be frequent there. But another form exists among them in an endemic state.

Bartholin, in his book, *De Causis contemptae mortis a Danis*, reports that Danish warriors considered it a disgrace to die in bed

---

[1] Bibliography.—Steinmetz, *Suicide Among Primitive Peoples*, in *American Anthropologist*, January 1894.—Waitz, *Anthropologie der Naturvoelker, passim.*— *Suicides dans les Armées*, in *Journal de la société de statistique*, 1874, p. 250.— Millar, *Statistic of military suicide*, in *Journal of the Statistical Society*, London, June 1874.—Mesnier, *Du suicide dans l'Armée*, Paris 1881.—Bournet, *Criminalité en France et en Italie*, p. 83 ff.—Roth, *Die Selbstmorde in der K. u. K. Armee, in den Jahren 1873–80*, in *Statistische Monatschrift*, 1892.—Rosenfeld, *Die Selbstmorde in der Preussischen Armee*, in *Militarwochenblatt*, 1894, 3. supplement.—By the same, *Der Selbstmord in der K. u. K. oesterreichischen Heere*, in *Deutsche Worte*, 1893.—Anthony, *Suicide dans l'armée allemande*, in *Arch. de méd. et de phar. militaire*, Paris, 1895.

[2] Oettingen, *Moralstatistik*, p. 762.

of old age or sickness, and killed themselves to escape this ignominy. The Goths likewise believed that those who die a natural death are destined to languish forever in caverns full of venomous creatures.[3] On the frontier of the Visigoths' territory was a high pinnacle called *The Rock of the Forefathers,* from the top of which old men would throw themselves when weary of life. The same custom was found among the Thracians, the Heruli, etc. Silvius Italicus says of the Spanish Celts: "They are a nation lavish of their blood and eager to face death. As soon as the Celt has passed the age of mature strength, he endures the flight of time impatiently and scorns to await old age; the term of his existence depends upon himself." [4] Accordingly they assigned a delightful abode to those who committed suicide and a horrible subterranean one to those who died of sickness or decrepitude. The same custom has long been maintained in India. Perhaps this favorable attitude toward suicide did not appear in the Vedas, but it was certainly very ancient. Plutarch says concerning the suicide of the brahmin Calanus: "He sacrificed himself with his own hands as was customary with sages of this country." [5] And Quintus Curtius: "Among them exists a sort of wild and bestial men to whom they give the name of sages. The anticipation of the time of death is a glory in their eyes, and they have themselves burned alive as soon as age or sickness begins to trouble them. According to them, death, passively awaited, is a dishonor to life; thus no honors are rendered those bodies which old age has destroyed. Fire would be contaminated did it not receive the human sacrifice still breathing." [6] Similar facts are recorded at Fiji,[7] in the New Hebrides, Manga, etc.[8] At Ceos, men who had outlived a certain age used to unite in a solemn festival where with heads crowned with flowers they joyfully drank the hemlock.[9] Like practices were found among the Troglodytes [10] and the Seri, who were nevertheless renowned for their morality.[11]

[3] Quoted from Brierre de Boismont, p. 23.
[4] *Punica,* I, 225 and ff.
[5] *Life of Alexander,* CXIII.
[6] VIII, 9.
[7] Cf. Wyatt Gill, *Myths and Songs of the South Pacific,* p. 163.
[8] Frazer, *Golden Bough,* vol. I, p. 216 and ff.
[9] Strabo, par. 486.—Elian, V. H., 337.
[10] Diodorus Siculus, III, 33, pars. 5 and 6.
[11] Pomponius Mela, III, 7.

Besides the old men, women are often required among the same peoples to kill themselves on their husbands' death. This barbarous practice is so ingrained in Hindu customs that the efforts of the English are futile against it. In 1817, 706 widows killed themselves in the one province of Bengal and in 1821, 2,366 were found in all India. Moreover, when a prince or chief dies, his followers are forced not to survive him. Such was the case in Gaul. The funerals of chiefs, Henri Martin declares, were bloody hecatombs where their garments, weapons, horses and favorite slaves were solemnly burned, together with the personal followers who had not died in the chief's last battle.[12] Such a follower was never to survive his chief. Among the Ashantis, on the king's death his officers must die.[13] Observers have found the same custom in Hawaii.[14]

Suicide, accordingly, is surely very common among primitive peoples. But it displays peculiar characteristics. All the facts above reported fall into one of the following three categories:

1. Suicides of men on the threshold of old age or stricken with sickness.

2. Suicides of women on their husbands' death.

3. Suicides of followers or servants on the death of their chiefs.

Now, when a person kills himself, in all these cases, it is not because he assumes the right to do so but, on the contrary, *because it is his duty*. If he fails in this obligation, he is dishonored and also punished, usually, by religious sanctions. Of course, when we hear of aged men killing themselves we are tempted at first to believe that the cause is weariness or the sufferings common to age. But if these suicides really had no other source, if the individual made away with himself merely to be rid of an unendurable existence, he would not be required to do so; one is never obliged to take advantage of a privilege. Now, we have seen that if such a person insists on living he loses public respect; in one case the usual funeral honors are denied, in another a life of horror is supposed to await him beyond the grave. The weight of society is thus brought to bear on him to lead him to destroy himself. To be sure, society intervenes in egoistic suicide, as well; but its intervention differs in the two cases. In one

---

[12] *Histoire de France*, I, 81, cf. Caesar, *de Bello Gallico*, VI, 19.

[13] See Spencer, *Sociology*, vol. II, p. 146.

[14] See Jarves, *History of the Sandwich Islands*, 1843, p. 108.

case, it speaks the sentence of death; in the other it forbids the choice of death. In the case of egoistic suicide it suggests or counsels at most; in the other case it compels and is the author of conditions and circumstances making this obligation coercive.

This sacrifice then is imposed by society for social ends. If the follower must not survive his chief or the servant his prince, this is because so strict an interdependence between followers and chiefs, officers and king, is involved in the constitution of the society that any thought of separation is out of the question. The destiny of one must be that of the others. Subjects as well as clothing and armor must follow their master wherever he goes, even beyond the tomb; if another possibility were to be admitted social subordination would be inadequate.[15] Such is the relation of the woman to her husband. As for the aged, if they are not allowed to await death, it is probably, at least in many instances, for religious reasons. The protecting spirit of a family is supposed to reside in its chief. It is further thought that a god inhabiting the body of another shares in his life, enduring the same phases of health and sickness and aging with him. Age cannot therefore reduce the strength of one without the other being similarly weakened and consequently without the group existence being threatened, since a strengthless divinity would be its only remaining protector. For this reason, in the common interest, a father is required not to await the furthest limit of life before transferring to his successors the precious trust that is in his keeping.[16]

This description sufficiently defines the cause of these suicides. For society to be able thus to compel some of its members to kill themselves, the individual personality can have little value. For as soon as the latter begins to form, the right to existence is the first conceded it; or is at least suspended only in such unusual circumstances as war. But there can be only one cause for this feeble individuation itself. For the individual to occupy so little place in collec-

---

[15] At the foundation of these practices there is probably also the desire to prevent the spirit of the dead man from returning to earth to revisit the objects and persons closely associated with him. But this very desire implies that servants and followers are strictly subordinated to their master, inseparable from him, and, furthermore, that to avoid the disaster of the spirit's remaining on earth they must sacrifice themselves in the common interest.

[16] See Frazer, *Golden Bough, loc. cit.,* and *passim.*

tive life he must be almost completely absorbed in the group and the latter, accordingly, very highly integrated. For the parts to have so little life of their own, the whole must indeed be a compact, continuous mass. And we have shown elsewhere that such massive cohesion is indeed that of societies where the above practices obtain.[17] As they consist of few elements, everyone leads the same life; everything is common to all, ideas, feelings, occupations. Also, because of the small size of the group it is close to everyone and loses no one from sight; consequently collective supervision is constant, extending to everything, and thus more readily prevents divergences. The individual thus has no way to set up an environment of his own in the shelter of which he may develop his own nature and form a physiognomy that is his exclusively. To all intents and purposes indistinct from his companions, he is only an inseparable part of the whole without personal value. His person has so little value that attacks upon it by individuals receive only relatively weak restraint. It is thus natural for him to be yet less protected against collective necessities and that society should not hesitate, for the very slightest reason, to bid him end a life it values so little.

We thus confront a type of suicide differing by incisive qualities from the preceding one. Whereas the latter is due to excessive individuation, the former is caused by too rudimentary individuation. One occurs because society allows the individual to escape it, being insufficiently aggregated in some parts or even in the whole; the other, because society holds him in too strict tutelage. Having given the name of *egoism* to the state of the ego living its own life and obeying itself alone, that of *altruism* adequately expresses the opposite state, where the ego is not its own property, where it is blended with something not itself, where the goal of conduct is exterior to itself, that is, in one of the groups in which it participates. So we call the suicide caused by intense altruism *altruistic suicide*. But since it is also characteristically performed as a duty, the terminology adopted should express this fact. So we will call such a type *obligatory altruistic suicide*.

The combination of these two adjectives is required to define it; for not every altruistic suicide is necessarily obligatory. Some are not so expressly imposed by society, having a more optional character.

[17] See *Division du travail social, passim.*

In other words, altruistic suicide is a species with several varieties. We have just established one; let us examine the others.

In these same societies just mentioned, or others of their sort, suicides may often be encountered with the most futile immediate and apparent motives. Titus Livy, Caesar, Valerius Maximus all tell us not without astonishment mixed with admiration, of the calmness with which the Gallic and German barbarians kill themselves.[18] Celts were known who bound themselves to suffer death in consideration of wine or money.[19] Others boasted of retreating neither before fire nor the ocean.[20] Modern travellers have noticed such practices in many lower societies. In Polynesia, a slight offense often decides a man to commit suicide.[21] It is the same among the North American Indians; a conjugal quarrel or jealous impulse suffices to cause a man or woman to commit suicide.[22] Among the Dacotas and Creeks the least disappointment often leads to desperate steps.[23] The readiness of the Japanese to disembowel themselves for the slightest reason is well known. A strange sort of duel is even reported there, in which the effort is not to attack one another but to excel in dexterity in opening one's own stomach.[24] Similar facts are recorded in China, Cochin China, Thibet and the Kingdom of Siam.

In all such cases, a man kills himself without being explicitly forced to do so. Yet these suicides are of the same nature as obligatory suicide. Though public opinion does not formally require them, it is certainly favorable to them. Since here not clinging to life is a virtue, even of the highest rank, the man who renounces life on least provocation of circumstances or through simple vainglory is praiseworthy. A social prestige thus attaches to suicide, which receives encouragement from this fact, and the refusal of this reward has effects similar to actual punishment, although to a lesser degree. What is done in one case to escape the stigma of insult is done in the other to win esteem. When people are accustomed to set no value

[18] Caesar, *Gallic War*, VI, 14.—Valerius Maximus, VI, 11 and 12.—Pliny, *Natural History*, IV, 12.
[19] Posidonius, XXIII, in Athanasius Deipnosophistes, IV, 154.
[20] Elian, XII, 23.
[21] Waitz, *Anthropologie der Naturvoelker*, vol. VI, p. 115.
[22] *Ibid.*, vol. III, Part I, p. 102.
[23] Mary Eastman, *Dacotah*, pp. 89, 169.—Lombroso, *L'Uomo delinquente*, 1884, p. 51.
[24] Lisle, *op. cit.*, p. 333.

on life from childhood on, and to despise those who value it excessively, they inevitably renounce it on the least pretext. So valueless a sacrifice is easily assumed. Like obligatory suicide, therefore, these practices are associated with the most fundamental moral characteristics of lower societies. As they can only persist if the individual has no interests of his own, he must be trained to renunciation and an unquestioned abnegation; whence come such partially spontaneous suicides. Exactly like those more explicitly prescribed by society, they arise from this state of impersonality, or as we have called it, altruism, which may be regarded as a moral characteristic of primitive man. Therefore, we shall give them, also, the name altruistic, and if *optional* is added to make their special quality clearer, this word simply means that they are less expressly required by society than when strictly obligatory. Indeed, the two varieties are so closely related that it is impossible to distinguish where one begins and the other ends.

Finally, other cases exist in which altruism leads more directly and more violently to suicide. In the preceding examples, it caused a man to kill himself only with the concurrence of circumstances. Either death had to be imposed by society as a duty, or some question of honor was involved, or at least some disagreeable occurrence had to lower the value of life in the victim's eyes. But it even happens that the individual kills himself purely for the joy of sacrifice, because, even with no particular reason, renunciation in itself is considered praiseworthy.

India is the classic soil for this sort of suicide. The Hindu was already inclined to self-destruction under Brahminic influence. Manu's laws, to be sure, command suicide only with some reservations. A man must already have attained a certain age, he must at least have left one son. But if these conditions are satisfied, he has nothing more to do with life. "The Brahmin who has freed himself from his body by one of the methods employed by the great saints, freed from grief and fear, is honorably received in the abode of Brahma." [25] Though Buddhism has often been accused of having carried this principle to its most extreme consequences and elevated suicide into a religious practice, it actually condemned it. It is true that it taught that the highest bliss was self-destruction in Nirvana;

[25] *Lois de Manu*, VI, 32 (trans. Loiseleur).

but this suspension of existence may and should be achieved even during this life without need of violent measures for its realization. Of course, the thought that one should seek to escape existence is so thoroughly in the spirit of the Hindu doctrine and so conformable with the aspirations of the Hindu temperament that it may be encountered in various forms in the chief sects sprung from Buddhism or formed simultaneously with it. It is thus with Jainism. Though one of the canonical books of the Jainist religion reproves suicide, accusing it of really augmenting life, inscriptions found in many sanctuaries show that especially among the southern Jainists religious suicide was very often practiced.[26] The believer allowed himself to die of hunger.[27] In Hinduism the custom of seeking death in the waters of the Ganges or of other sacred rivers was widespread. Inscriptions represent to us kings and ministers preparing to end their days thus [28] and we are assured that these superstitions had not wholly disappeared at the beginning of the century.[29] Among the Bhils there was a rock from the top of which men cast themselves with religious motives, to devote themselves to Shiva; [30] even as late as 1822 an officer attended one of these sacrifices. The story of the fanatics who let themselves be crushed to death in throngs under the wheels of the idol Juggernaut has become classic.[31] Charlevoix in his time had observed rites of this sort in Japan: "Nothing is commoner," he says, "than to see ships along the seashore filled with these fanatics who throw themselves into the water weighted with stones, or sink their ships and let themselves be gradually submerged while singing their idol's praises. Many of the spectators follow them with their eyes, lauding their valor to the skies and asking their blessing before they disappear. The sectarians of Amida have themselves immured in caverns where there is barely space to be seated and where they can breathe only through an air shaft. There they quietly allow themselves to die of hunger. Others climb to the top

[26] Barth, *The Religions of India*, London, 1891, p. 146.
[27] Bühler, *über die Indische Secte der Jaïna*, Vienna, 1887, pp. 10, 19, and 37.
[28] Barth, *op. cit.*, p. 279.
[29] Heber, *Narrative of a Journey through the Upper Provinces of India*, 1824–25, Chap. XII.
[30] Forsyth, *The Highlands of Central India*, London, 1871, pp. 172–175.
[31] Cf. Burnell, *Glossary*, 1886, under the word, Jagarnnath. The practice has almost disappeared; but single cases have been observed even in our days. See Stirling, *Asiatic Studies*, vol. XV, p. 324.

of very high cliffs, upon which there are sulphur mines from which flames jet from time to time. They continuously call upon their gods, pray to them to accept the sacrifice of their lives and ask that some of these flames rise. As soon as one appears they regard it as a sign of the gods' consent and cast themselves head-foremost to the bottom of the abyss. . . . The memory of these so-called martyrs is held in great reverence." [32]

There are no suicides with a more definitely altruistic character. We actually see the individual in all these cases seek to strip himself of his personal being in order to be engulfed in something which he regards as his true essence. The name he gives it is unimportant; he feels that he exists in it and in it alone, and strives so violently to blend himself with it in order to have being. He must therefore consider that he has no life of his own. Impersonality is here carried to its highest pitch; altruism is acute. But, it will be objected, do not these suicides occur simply because men consider life unhappy? Obviously, if an individual kills himself so spontaneously, he does not set much store by his life, which is consequently conceived as more or less melancholy. But in this respect all suicides are alike. Yet it would be a great mistake to make no distinction between them; for this conception has not always the same cause and thus is not identical in the different cases, appearances to the contrary notwithstanding. While the egoist is unhappy because he sees nothing real in the world but the individual, the intemperate altruist's sadness, on the contrary, springs from the individual's seeming wholly unreal to him. One is detached from life because, seeing no goal to which he may attach himself, he feels himself useless and purposeless; the other because he has a goal but one outside this life, which henceforth seems merely an obstacle to him. Thus, the difference of the causes reappears in their effects, and the melancholy of one is quite different from that of the other. That of the former consists of a feeling of incurable weariness and sad depression; it expresses a complete relaxation of activity, which, unable to find useful employment, collapses. That of the latter, on the contrary, springs from hope; for it depends on the belief in beautiful perspectives beyond this life. It even implies enthusiasm and the spur of a

[32] *Histoire du Japon*, vol. II.

226   SUICIDE

faith eagerly seeking satisfaction, affirming itself by acts of extreme energy.

Furthermore, the more or less gloomy view of life taken by a people does not in itself explain the intensity of its inclination to suicide. The Christian conceives of his abode on earth in no more delightful colors than the Jainist sectarian. He sees in it only a time of sad trial; he also thinks that his true country is not of this world. Yet the aversion to suicide professed and inspired by Christianity is well known. The reason is that Christian societies accord the individual a more important role than earlier ones. They assign to him personal duties which he is forbidden to evade; only as he has acquitted himself of the role incumbent upon him here on earth is he admitted or not admitted to the joys of the hereafter, and these very joys are as personal as the works which make them his heritage. Thus the moderate individualism in the spirit of Christianity prevents it from favoring suicide, despite its theories concerning man and his destiny.

The metaphysical and religious systems which form logical settings for these moral practices give final proof that this is their origin and meaning. It has long been observed that they coexist generally with pantheistic beliefs. To be sure, Jainism, as well as Buddhism, is atheistic; but pantheism is not necessarily theistic. Its essential quality is the idea that what reality there is in the individual is foreign to his nature, that the soul which animates him is not his own, and that consequently he has no personal existence. Now this dogma is fundamental to the doctrines of the Hindus; it already exists in Brahminism. Inversely, where the principle of being is not fused with such doctrines but is itself conceived in an individual form, that is, among monotheistic peoples like the Jews, Christians, Mahometans, or polytheists like the Greeks and the Latins, this form of suicide is unusual. It is never found there in the state of a ritual practice. There is therefore probably a relation between it and pantheism. What is this relation?

It cannot be conceded that pantheism produced suicide. Such abstract ideas do not guide men, and the course of history could not be explained through the play of purely metaphysical concepts. Among peoples as well as individuals, mental representations function above all as an expression of a reality not of their own making; they rather spring from it and, if they subsequently modify it, do so only to a limited extent. Religious conceptions are the products of the social environment, rather than its producers, and if they react, once formed, upon their own original causes, the reaction cannot be very profound. If the essence of pantheism, then, is a more or less radical denial of all individuality, such a religion could be constituted only in a society where the individual really counts for nothing, that is, is almost wholly lost in the group. For men can conceive of the world only in the image of the small social world in which they live. Religious pantheism is thus only a result and, as it were, a reflection of the pantheistic organization of society. Consequently, it is also in this society that we must seek the cause for this special suicide which everywhere appears in connection with pantheism.

We have thus constituted a second type of suicide, itself consisting of three varieties: obligatory altruistic suicide, optional altruistic suicide, and acute altruistic suicide, the perfect pattern of which is mystical suicide. In these different forms, it contrasts most strikingly with egoistic suicide. One is related to the crude morality which disregards everything relating solely to the individual; the other is closely associated with the refined ethics which sets human personality on so high a pedestal that it can no longer be subordinated to anything. Between the two there is, therefore, all the difference between primitive peoples and the most civilized nations.

However, if lower societies are the theatre par excellence of altruistic suicide, it is also found in more recent civilizations. Under this head may notably be classified the death of some of the Christian martyrs. All those neophytes who without killing themselves, voluntarily allowed their own slaughter, are really suicides. Though they did not kill themselves, they sought death with all their power and behaved so as to make it inevitable. To be suicide, the act from which death must necessarily result need only have been performed by the victim with full knowledge of the facts. Besides, the passionate enthusiasm with which the believers in the new religion faced final torture shows that at this moment they had completely discarded their personalities for the idea of which they had become the servants. Probably the epidemics of suicide which devastated the monasteries on several occasions during the Middle Ages, apparently caused by excesses of religious fervor, were of this nature.[33]

In our contemporary societies, as individual personality becomes increasingly free from the collective personality, such suicides could not be widespread. Some may doubtless be said to have yielded to altruistic motives, such as soldiers who preferred death to the humiliation of defeat, like Commandant Beaurepaire and Admiral Villeneuve, or unhappy persons who kill themselves to prevent disgrace befalling their family. For when such persons renounce life, it is for something they love better than themselves. But they are isolated and exceptional cases.[34] Yet even today there exists among us a special environment where altruistic suicide is chronic: namely, the army.

II

It is a general fact in all European countries that the suicidal aptitude of soldiers is much higher than that of the civilian population of the same age. The difference varies between 25 and 900 per cent (see Table XXIII).

TABLE XXIII—Comparison of Military and Civilian Suicides in the Chief European Countries

| | Suicides per | | |
	1 Million Soldiers	1 Million Civilians of Same Age	Coefficient of Aggravation of Soldiers Compared with Civilians
Austria (1876–90)	1,253	122	10
United States (1870–84)	680	80	8.5
Italy (1876–90)	407	77	5.2
England (1876–90)	209	79	2.6
Wurttemberg (1846–58)	320	170	1.92
Saxony (1847–58)	640	369	1.77
Prussia (1876–90)	607	394	1.50
France 1876–90)	333	265	1.25

Denmark is the only country where the contingent of the two portions of the population is substantially the same, 388 per million

[33] The moral state occasioning these suicides has been called *acedia*. See Bourquelot, *Recherches sur les opinions et la législation en matière de mort volontaire pendant le moyen âge.*

[34] Probably the frequent suicides of the men of the Revolution were at least partly due to an altruistic state of mind. At this time of civil strife and collective enthusiasm, individual personality had lost some of its value. The interests of country or party outweighed everything. Doubtless the great number of capital executions spring from the same cause. One then killed others as readily as one's self.

civilians and 382 per million soldiers during the years 1845–56. But the suicides of officers are not included in this figure.[35]

This fact is at first sight all the more surprising because it might be supposed that many causes would guard the army against suicide. First, from the physical point of view, the persons composing it represent the flower of the country. Carefully selected, they have no serious organic flaws.[36] Also, the esprit de corps and the common life should have the prophylactic effect here which they have elsewhere. What is the cause of so large an aggravation?

Since soldiers who are not officers do not marry, the fault has been ascribed to bachelorhood. But first, this should have less adverse effects in the army than in civilian life; for, as we have just remarked, the soldier is anything but isolated. He belongs to a strongly constructed society of a sort calculated partially to replace the family. However true or false this hypothesis may be, there is a way to examine this factor in isolation. One needs only compare the suicides of soldiers with those of unmarried persons of the same age; Table XXI, the importance of which again becomes clear, allows this comparison. During the years 1888–91 in France, 380 suicides per million soldiers were recorded; at the same time, unmarried men of from 20 to 25 years showed only 237. There were thus 160 military suicides per 100 unmarried civilians; which makes a coefficient of aggravation of 1.6, wholly independent of bachelorhood.

If the suicides of non-commissioned officers are separately computed, the coefficient is still higher. During the period 1867–74, a million non-commissioned officers showed an annual average of 993 suicides. According to a census made in 1866, their average age was a little over 31 years. Of course, we do not know how high suicides of unmarried men of 30 years rose at that time; the tables we have drawn up refer to a much more recent time (1889–91) and are the only ones in existence; but starting from their figures, whatever error we make can only lower the coefficient of aggravation

[35] The figures on military suicide are taken from official documents or from Wagner (*op. cit.*, p. 229 and ff.) ; those on civilian suicide from official documents, Wagner's statements, or Morselli. For the United States we have assumed that the average army age was from 20 to 30 years as in Europe.

[36] A new proof of the non-efficacy of the organic factor in general and of matrimonial selection in particular.

of the non-commissioned officers below what it really was. Actually, the number of suicides having almost doubled between the two periods, the rate of unmarried men of the age in question certainly rose. Consequently, comparing suicides of non-commissioned officers of 1867–74 with those of unmarried men of 1889–91, we may well reduce but not broaden the adverse effect of the military profession. If therefore we find a coefficient of aggravation in spite of this error, we may be sure not only that it is real but that it is quite a bit more important than the figures would make it appear. Now, in 1889–91, a million unmarried men of 31 years of age gave a number of suicides between 394 and 627, or about 510. This number is to 993 as 100 is to 194; which implies a coefficient of aggravation of 1.94 which may be increased almost to 4 without fear of exaggerating the facts.[37]

Finally, the officers' corps averaged from 1862 to 1878, 430 suicides per million persons. Their average age which cannot have varied between very wide extremes was in 1866, 37 years and 9 months. Since many of them are married, they should be compared not with unmarried men of this age but with the total of the male population, unmarried and married men combined. Now, at 37 years of age in 1863–68, a million men of every marital status gave only a little more than 200 suicides. This number is to 430 as 100 is to 215, making a coefficient of aggravation of 2.15, in no way dependent on marriage or family life.

This coefficient which varies with the different degrees of the hierarchy from 1.6 to nearly 4, can clearly be explained only by causes connected with the military status. To be sure, we have directly shown its existence only for France; for other countries we lack the data necessary to examine the influence of bachelorhood in isolation. But as the French army happens to be the very one least afflicted by suicide in Europe, with the one exception of Denmark, we may

[37] During the years 1867–74 the suicide-rate is about 140; in 1889–91 it is 210 to 220, an increase of nearly 60 per cent. If the rate of unmarried men grew in the same proportion, and there is no reason why it should not have done so, during the first of these periods it would have been only 319, which would raise the coefficient of aggravation of non-commissioned officers to 3.11. If we do not speak of non-commissioned officers after 1874, it is because from then on there were decreasingly few professional non-commissioned officers.

be sure of the general character of the above result and even that it must be much more pronounced in other European states. To what cause shall we attribute it?

Alcoholism has been suggested, which is said to afflict the army more than the civilian population. But if, in the first place, as has been shown, alcoholism has no definite influence on the suicide-rate in general, it is unlikely to have more on that of military suicides in particular. Then, the few years of service, three in France and two and a half in Prussia, could not create a large enough number of inveterate alcoholics for the enormous contingent contributed to suicide by the army to be thus explained. Finally, even according to those observers who attribute most influence to alcoholism, only a tenth of the cases can be ascribed to it. Thus, even though alcoholic suicides were two or three times as numerous among soldiers as among civilians of like age, which is not proven, a considerable excess of military suicides would still remain for which another cause would have to be sought.

The cause most often suggested is disgust with the service. This explanation agrees with the popular conception which attributes suicide to the hardships of life; for disciplinary rigor, lack of liberty, and want of every comfort makes barracks life appear especially intolerable. Actually it seems that there are many other harsher occupations which yet do not increase the inclination to suicide. The soldier is at least sure of having enough food and shelter. But whatever these considerations may be worth, the following facts show the inadequacy of this over-simple explanation:

1. It is logical to admit that disgust with the service must be much stronger during the first years and decrease as the soldier becomes accustomed to barracks life. After some time, an acclimatization must be made, either through habit or the desertion of the most refractory or their suicide; and this acclimatization must become greater the longer the stay with the colors. If, then, it were the change of habits and the impossibility of adjustment to the new life which developed in the soldier special aptitude for suicide, the coefficient of aggravation should lessen as the life under arms was prolonged. This is not so, as the following table shows:

French Army Non-commissioned Officers and Soldiers Annual Suicides per 100,000 Men (1862–69)		English Army Suicides per 100,000		
		Age	Home Stations	In India
Less than 1 year service	28	20-25 years	20	13
From 1-3 years	27	25-30 years	39	39
From 3-5 years	40	30-35 years	51	84
From 5-7 years	48	35-40 years	71	103
From 7-10 years	76			

In France, in less than 10 years of military service, the suicide-rate almost triples while for unmarried civilians during the same time it only rises from 237 to 394. In the English armies of India, it becomes eight times as high in 20 years; the civilian rate never advances so rapidly. This proves that the army's characteristic aggravation is not centered in the first years.

The situation seems to be the same in Italy. To be sure, we have not the proportional figures for the soldiers of each contingent. But the net figures are practically the same for each of the three service years, 15.1 for the first, 14.8 for the second, 14.3 for the third. It is true that the numbers diminish year by year as a result of deaths, discharges, leaves of absence, etc. The absolute figures could thus only remain at the same level if the proportional figures have considerably increased. It is not unlikely, however, that in some countries there are a certain number of suicides at the beginning of service really due to the change of life. In fact, in Prussia it is said that suicides are unusually numerous during the first six months. Likewise in Austria, of 1,000 suicides, 156 occur in the first three months,[38] which is certainly a very considerable figure. But these facts do not conflict with the preceding ones. For very possibly, besides the temporary aggravation occurring during this troubled period, there is another due to totally different causes which increases according to the same pattern we have observed in France and England. Furthermore, in France itself, the rate of the second and third years is slightly less than that of the first, which, however, does not prevent the later increase.[39]

[38] See Roth's article in the *Stat. Monatschrift*, 1892, p. 200.
[39] For Prussia and Austria, we have not the numbers of men per year of service, which prevents our computing the proportional numbers. In France, it was said that if military suicides had diminished following the war, it was because the service had become shorter (5 years instead of 7). But this decrease did not last and from 1882 the figures rose perceptibly. From 1882 to 1889 they returned to their

2. Military life is much less hard and discipline less severe for officers and non-commissioned officers than for private soldiers. The coefficient of aggravation of the first two categories should therefore be less than that of the third. The opposite is true: we have already shown it for France; the same fact is encountered in other countries. In Italy, officers during the years 1871–75 showed an annual average of 565 cases per million while the troops had only 230 (Morselli). For the non-commissioned officers the rate is still more enormous, more than 1,000 per million. In Prussia, while privates show only 560 suicides per million, non-commissioned officers show 1,140. In Austria there is one suicide of an officer for every nine of privates, while there are clearly many more than nine privates to an officer. Likewise, although there is not a non-commissioned officer for every two soldiers, there is one suicide of the former for every 2.5 of the latter.

3. Disgust with the military life should be less among those who choose it freely as a vocation. Volunteers and re-enlisted men should therefore show less aptitude for suicide. On the contrary, it is exceptionally high.

	Suicide-rate per Million	Age (Probable Average)	Suicide-rate Unmarried Civilians of the Same Age (1889–91)	Coefficient of Aggravation
Years 1875–78 Volunteers	670	25 years	Between 237 and 394, or 315	2.12
Re-enlisted	1,300	30 years	Between 394 and 627, or 510	2.54

For the reasons given, these coefficients, calculated with reference to unmarried men of 1889–91, are certainly below the correct numbers. The intensity of inclination shown by re-enlisted men is especially noteworthy, since they remain in the army after having experienced military life.

Thus the members of the army most stricken by suicide are also those who are most inclined to this career, who are best suited to its needs and are best sheltered from its disadvantages and inconveniences. The coefficient of aggravation special to this profession is then caused not by the repugnance it inspires, but, on the contrary,

number before the war, varying between 322 and 424 per million, although the length of service had again been reduced, 3 years in place of 5.

by the sum total of states, acquired habits or natural dispositions making up the military spirit. Now, the first quality of a soldier is a sort of impersonality not to be found anywhere in civilian life to the same degree. He must be trained to set little value upon himself, since he must be prepared to sacrifice himself upon being ordered to do so. Even aside from such exceptional circumstances, in peace time and in the regular exercise of his profession, discipline requires him to obey without question and sometimes even without understanding. For this an intellectual abnegation hardly consistent with individualism is required. He must have but a weak tie binding him to his individuality, to obey external impulsion so docilely. In short, a soldier's principle of action is external to himself; which is the quality of the state of altruism. Of all elements constituting our modern societies, the army, indeed, most recalls the structure of lower societies. It, too, consists of a massive, compact group providing a rigid setting for the individual and preventing any independent movement. Therefore, since this moral constitution is the natural field for altruistic suicide, military suicide may certainly be supposed to have the same character and derive from the same source.

This would explain the increase of the coefficient of aggravation with the duration of service; this aptitude for renunciation, this taste for impersonality develops as a result of prolonged discipline. Just as the military spirit must be stronger among re-enlisted men and non-commissioned officers than among mere privates, the former may be expected to be more specially inclined to suicide than the latter. This hypothesis even permits an understanding of the strange superiority of non-commissioned officers over officers in this respect. If they commit suicide more frequently, it is because no function requires so much of the habit of passive submission. However disciplined the officer, he must be capable of initiative to a certain extent; he has a wider field of action and, accordingly, a more developed individuality. The conditions favorable to altruistic suicide are thus less completely realized in him than in the non-commissioned officer; having a keener feeling of the value of his life, he is less ready to sacrifice it.

Not only does this explanation account for the facts stated above, but it is furthermore confirmed by the following facts.

1. From Table XXIII it appears that the military coefficient of

aggravation is higher the less tendency the civilian population has to
suicide and vice versa. Denmark is the classical country for suicide;
soldiers kill themselves there no more than the other inhabitants.
Next to Denmark, the states most abounding in suicides are Saxony,
Prussia and France; in them the army is not especially stricken, the
coefficient of aggravation varying between 1.25 and 1.77. On the
contrary it is very considerable for Austria, Italy, the United States
and England, countries in which civilian suicide is infrequent. Rosenfeld, in the article already cited, reached the same results, having
classified the principal European countries from the point of view
of military suicide though without thinking of drawing any theoreti-
cal conclusion from this classification. Here is the order in which he
arranges the different states and the coefficients cal. ulated by him:

	Coefficient of Aggravation of Soldiers in Proportion to Civilians of 20-30 Years	Rate of Civilian Population per Million
France	1.3	150 (1871–75)
Prussia	1.8	133 (1871–75)
England	2.2	73 (1876)
Italy	Between 3 and 4	37 (1874–77)
Austria	8	72 (1864–72)

Except that Austria should come before Italy, the inversion is
absolutely regular.[40]

It is still more strikingly clear within the Austro-Hungarian Empire. The army corps with the highest coefficient of aggravation are
those stationed in garrisons in regions where civilians have the highest immunity, and vice versa:

Military Areas	Military Coefficient of Aggravation in Propor- tion to Civilians Over 20 Years		Civilian Suicides per Million Over 20 Years	
Vienna (Lower and Upper Austria, Salzburg)	1.42		660	
Brunn (Moravia and Silesia)	2.41	Average 2.46	580	Average 480
Prague (Bohemia)	2.58		620	
Innsbruck (Tyrol, Vorarlberg)	2.41		240	
Zara (Dalmatia)	3.48	Average 3.82	250	Average 283
Graz (Steiermark, Carinthia, Carniola)	3.58		290	
Cracow (Galicia and Bukowina)	4.41		310	

There is only one exception, the territory of Innsbruck, where the
civilian rate is low and the coefficient of aggravation only average.

[40] It may be questioned whether the great size of the military coefficient of aggravation in Austria does not result from a more exact recording of military suicides
than those of the civilian population.

In Italy, likewise, Bologna is the military district where suicides of soldiers are least frequent (180 suicides per 1,000,000); and also where civilian suicides are highest (89.5). The Apulias and the Abruzzi, on the contrary, have many military suicides (370 and 400 per million) and only 15 or 16 civilian suicides. Similar facts may be observed in France. The military government of Paris with 260 suicides per million is well below the army corps of Brittany with 440. The coefficient of aggravation in Paris must really be insignificant, since in the Seine a million unmarried men of from 20 to 25 years show 214 suicides.

These facts prove that the causes of military suicide are not only different from, but in inverse proportion to, the most determining causes of civilian suicide. The latter causes in the great European societies spring from the excessive individuation characteristic of civilization. Military suicides must therefore depend on the reverse disposition, feeble individuation or what we have called the state of altruism. Actually, those peoples among whom the army is most inclined to suicide are also the least advanced, those whose customs most resemble the customs observed in lower societies. Traditionalism, the chief opponent of the spirit of individualism, is far more developed in Italy, Austria and even in England than in Saxony, Prussia and France. It is more intense in Zara, in Cracow, than in Graz or Vienna, in the Apulias than in Rome or Bologna, in Brittany than in the Seine. As it guards against egoistic suicide, one readily understands that where it still has power, the civilian population has few suicides. But it has this prophylactic influence only if it remains moderate. If it exceeds a certain degree of intensity, it becomes itself an original cause of suicide. As we know, the army necessarily tends to exaggerate this, and is the readier to do so the more its own action is aided and re-enforced by the surrounding environment. The effects of army education are more violent the more it conforms with the ideas and sentiments of the civilian population itself; for then, this education is not restrained at all. Where, on the other hand, the military spirit is steadily and strongly opposed by public morality, it cannot be as strong as where everything conspires to incline the young soldier in the same direction. It is thus readily understandable that, in countries where there is sufficient altruism to protect the population as a whole to a degree, it is easily carried by the army to a point where it becomes the cause of a considerable aggravation.[41]

2. In all armies, the coefficient of aggravation is highest among the elite troops.

	Average Age Real or Probable	Suicides per Million		Coefficient of Aggravation
Special corps of Paris	From 30 to 35	570 (1862–78)	2.45	In proportion to the male civilian population of 35 years, every marital status combined.*
Gendarmerie		570 (1873)	2.45	
Veterans (abolished in 1872)	From 45 to 55	2,860	2.37	In proportion to unmarried men of the same age of the years 1889–91.

* Because gendarmes and police are often married.

The last figure, having been calculated in proportion to unmarried men of 1889–91, is far too low and yet is far higher than that of ordinary troops. Similarly, in the army of Algeria, considered the school of military virtue, during the period 1872–78 suicide had a mortality double that of the same period for troops stationed in France (570 suicides per million instead of 280). On the other hand, the least severely affected troops are the bridge-train, the engineers, the ambulance corps, troops of administrative units, in short, those with the least pronounced military character. In Italy, similarly, while the army as a whole during the years 1878–81 provided only 430 cases per milllion, the bersaglieri had 580, the carabinieri 800, the military school and instruction battalions 1,010.

Now, what distinguishes elite troops is the intense strength of the spirit of abnegation and military renunciation among them. Suicide in the army accordingly varies with this moral state.

3. A final proof of this law is that military suicide is everywhere decreasing. In France, there were in 1862, 630 cases per million; in 1890 there are only 280. It has been claimed that this decrease was due to the laws reducing the length of service. But this tendency to decrease is much anterior to the new recruiting law. It is continuous from 1862 on, except for a fairly considerable rise from 1882 to 1888.[42] Besides, it appears everywhere. Military suicides have

[41] It is notable that the state of altruism is inherent in a region. The army corps of Brittany is not exclusively composed of Bretons, but it undergoes the influence of the moral atmosphere of its environment.

[42] This rise is too important to be accidental. If we note its occurrence at the very commencement of the period of colonial expansion, we may justly wonder whether the wars the period occasioned did not cause a reawakening of the military spirit.

fallen in Prussia from 716 per million in 1877 to 457 in 1893; in all Germany from 707 in 1877 to 550 in 1890; in Belgium from 391 in 1885 to 185 in 1891; in Italy from 431 in 1876 to 389 in 1892. In Austria and England the fall is unimportant, but there is no rise (1,209 in 1892 in the first country and 210 in the second in 1890, instead of 1,277 and 217 in 1876).

This is the way things should happen if our explanation is well founded. It is certain, indeed, that a decline in the old military spirit has occurred in all these countries at the same time. Wrongly or rightly, the habits of passive obedience, of absolute submission, of impersonalism (if this barbarism is permitted us), have proved to be more and more in contradiction with the requirements of the public conscience. Consequently, they have lost ground. To satisfy new aspirations, discipline has become less rigid, less repressive of the individual.[43] It is also noteworthy that at the very same time in these same societies civilian suicides have constantly increased. This is a new proof that their generating cause is of an opposite nature to that usually responsible for the specific aptitude of soldiers.

Everything therefore proves that military suicide is only a form of altruistic suicide. We certainly do not mean that all individual cases occurring in the regiments are of this character and origin. When he puts on his uniform, the soldier does not become a completely new man; the effects of his education and of his previous life do not disappear as if by magic; and he is also not so separated from the rest of society as not to share in the common life. The suicide he commits may therefore sometimes be civilian in its character and causes. But with the exception of these scattered cases, showing no connections with one another, a compact, homogeneous group remains, including most suicides which occur in the army and which depend on this state of altruism without which military spirit is inconceivable. This is the suicide of lower societies, in survival among us because military morality itself is in certain aspects a survival of primitive morality.[44] Influenced by this predisposition, the soldier

[43] We do not mean that individuals suffered from this repression and killed themselves because they suffered. They killed themselves in greater numbers because they were less individualized.

[44] Which does not mean that it is destined to disappear forthwith. These survivals have their own bases for existence, and it is natural for some of the past to remain in the midst of the present. Life is made of these contradictions.

kills himself at the least disappointment, for the most futile reasons, for a refusal of leave, a reprimand, an unjust punishment, a delay in promotion, a question of honor, a flush of momentary jealousy or even simply because other suicides have occurred before his eyes or to his knowledge. Such is really the source of these phenomena of contagion often observed in armies, specimens of which we have mentioned earlier. They are inexplicable if suicide depends essentially on individual causes. It cannot be chance which caused the appearance in precisely this regiment or that locality of so many persons predisposed to self-homicide by their organic constitution. It is still more inadmissible that such a spread of imitative action could take place utterly without predisposition. But everything is readily explained when it is recognized that the profession of a soldier develops a moral constitution powerfully predisposing man to make away with himself. For this constitution naturally occurs, in varying degrees, among most of those who live or who have lived under the colors, and as this is an eminently favorable soil for suicides, little is needed to actualize the tendency to self-destruction which it contains; an example is enough. So it spreads like a trail of gunpowder among persons thus prepared to follow it.

III

It may now be better understood why we insisted on giving an objective definition of suicide and on sticking to it.

Because altruistic suicide, though showing the familiar suicidal traits, resembles especially in its most vivid manifestations some categories of action which we are used to honoring with our respect and even admiration, people have often refused to consider it as self-destruction. It is to be remembered that the deaths of Cato and of the Girondins were not suicides for Esquirol and Falret. But if suicides with the spirit of renunciation and abnegation as their immediate and visible cause do not deserve the name, it can be no more appropriate for those springing from the same moral disposition, though less apparently; for the second differ by only a few shades from the first. If the inhabitant of the Canary Islands who throws himself into an abyss to do honor to his god is not a suicide, how give this name to a Jain sectary who kills himself to obtain entry to oblivion; to the primitive who, under the influence of the same

mental state, renounces life for a slight insult done him or merely
to express his contempt for existence; to the bankrupt who prefers
not to survive his disgrace; and finally to the many soldiers who
every year increase the numbers of voluntary deaths? All these cases
have for their root the same state of altruism which is equally the
cause of what might be called heroic suicide. Shall they alone be
placed among the ranks of suicides and only those excluded whose
motive is particularly pure? But first, according to what standard
will the division be made? When does a motive cease to be sufficiently praiseworthy for the act it determines to be called suicide?
Moreover, by separating these two classes of facts radically from
each other, we inevitably misjudge their nature. For the essential
characteristics of the type are clearest in obligatory altruistic suicide.
Other varieties are only derivative forms. Either a considerable number of instructive phenomena will be eliminated or, if not all are
eliminated, not only will a purely arbitrary choice be the only one
possible among them, but it will be impossible to detect the common
stock to which those that are retained belong. Such is the risk we
incur in making the definition of suicide depend on the subjective
feelings it inspires.

Besides, not even the reasons for the sentiment thought to justify
this exclusion are well founded. The fact is stressed that the motives
of certain altruistic suicides reappear in slightly different forms as
the basis of actions regarded by everyone as moral. But is egoistic
suicide any different? Has not the sentiment of individual autonomy
its own morality as well as the opposite sentiment? If the latter serves
as foundation to a kind of courage, strengthening and even harden-
ing the heart, the other softens and moves it to pity. Where altruistic suicide is prevalent, man is always ready to give his life; however, at the same time, he sets no more value on that of another. On
the contrary, when he rates individual personality above all other
ends, he respects it in others. His cult for it makes him suffer from
all that minimizes it even among his fellows. A broader sympathy
for human suffering succeeds the fanatical devotions of primitive
times. Every sort of suicide is then merely the exaggerated or de-
flected form of a virtue. In that case, however, the way they affect
the moral conscience does not sufficiently differentiate them to justify
their being separated into different types.

CHAPTER 5
ANOMIC SUICIDE

B<small>UT</small> society is not only something attracting the sentiments and activities of individuals with unequal force. It is also a power controlling them. There is a relation between the way this regulative action is performed and the social suicide-rate.

I

It is a well-known fact that economic crises have an aggravating effect on the suicidal tendency.

In Vienna, in 1873 a financial crisis occurred which reached its height in 1874; the number of suicides immediately rose. From 141 in 1872, they rose to 153 in 1873 and 216 in 1874. The increase in 1874 is 53 per cent [1] above 1872 and 41 per cent above 1873. What proves this catastrophe to have been the sole cause of the increase is the special prominence of the increase when the crisis was acute, or during the first four months of 1874. From January 1 to April 30 there had been 48 suicides in 1871, 44 in 1872, 43 in 1873; there were 73 in 1874. The increase is 70 per cent.[2] The same crisis occurring at the same time in Frankfurt-on-Main produced the same effects there. In the years before 1874, 22 suicides were committed annually on the average; in 1874 there were 32, or 45 per cent more.

The famous crash is unforgotten which took place on the Paris Bourse during the winter of 1882. Its consequences were felt not

---

[1] Durkheim incorrectly gives this figure as 51 per cent.—Ed.
[2] In 1874 over 1873.—Ed.

only in Paris but throughout France. From 1874 to 1886 the average annual increase was only 2 per cent; in 1882 it was 7 per cent. Moreover, it was unequally distributed among the different times of year, occurring principally during the first three months or at the very time of the crash. Within these three months alone 59 per cent of the total rise occurred. So distinctly is the rise the result of un-usual circumstances that it not only is not encountered in 1881 but has disappeared in 1883, although on the whole the latter year had a few more suicides than the preceding one:

	1881	1882	1883
Annual total	6,741	7,213 (plus 7%)	7,267
First three months	1,589	1,770 (plus 11%)	1,604

This relation is found not only in some exceptional cases, but is the rule. The number of bankruptcies is a barometer of adequate sensitivity, reflecting the variations of economic life. When they in-crease abruptly from year to year, some serious disturbance has cer-tainly occurred. From 1845 to 1869 there were sudden rises, symp-tomatic of crises, on three occasions. While the annual increase in the number of bankruptcies during this period is 3.2 per cent, it is 26 per cent in 1847, 37 per cent in 1854 and 20 per cent in 1861. At these three moments, there is also to be observed an unusually rapid rise in the number of suicides. While the average annual in-crease during these 24 years was only 2 per cent, it was 17 per cent in 1847, 8 per cent in 1854 and 9 per cent in 1861.

But to what do these crises owe their influence? Is it because they increase poverty by causing public wealth to fluctuate? Is life more readily renounced as it becomes more difficult? The explanation is seductively simple; and it agrees with the popular idea of suicide. But it is contradicted by facts.

Actually, if voluntary deaths increased because life was becoming more difficult, they should diminish perceptibly as comfort increases. Now, although when the price of the most necessary foods rises excessively, suicides generally do the same, they are not found to fall below the average in the opposite case. In Prussia, in 1850 wheat was quoted at the lowest point it reached during the entire period of 1848–81; it was at 6.91 marks per 50 kilograms; yet at this very time suicides rose from 1,527 where they were in 1849 to 1,736, or an increase of 13 per cent, and continued to increase during the years 1851, 1852 and 1853 although the cheap market held. In 1858–59 a new fall took place; yet suicides rose from 2,038 in 1857 to 2,126 in 1858, and to 2,146 in 1859. From 1863 to 1866 prices which had reached 11.04 marks in 1861 fell progressively to 7.95 marks in 1864 and remained very reasonable for the whole period; suicides during the same time increased 17 per cent (2,112 in 1862, 2,485 in 1866).[3] Similar facts are observed in Bavaria. According to a curve constructed by Mayr [4] for the period 1835–61, the price of rye was lowest during the years 1857–58 and 1858–59; now suicides, which in 1857 numbered only 286, rose to 329 in 1858, to 387 in 1859. The same phenomenon had already occurred during the years 1848–50; at that time wheat had been very cheap in Bavaria as well as throughout Europe. Yet, in spite of a slight temporary drop due to political events, which we have mentioned, suicides remained at the same level. There were 217 in 1847, there were still 215 in 1848, and if they dropped for a moment to 189 in 1849, they rose again in 1850 and reached 250.

So far is the increase in poverty from causing the increase in suicide that even fortunate crises, the effect of which is abruptly to enhance a country's prosperity, affect suicide like economic disasters.

The conquest of Rome by Victor-Emmanuel in 1870, by definitely forming the basis of Italian unity, was the starting point for the country of a process of growth which is making it one of the great powers of Europe. Trade and industry received a sharp stimulus from it and surprisingly rapid changes took place. Whereas in 1876, 4,459 steam boilers with a total of 54,000 horse-power were enough for industrial needs, the number of machines in 1887 was 9,983 and their horse-power of 167,000 was threefold more. Of course the amount of production rose proportionately during the same time.[5] Trade followed the same rising course; not only did the merchant marine, communications and transportation develop, but the number of persons and things transported doubled.[6] As this generally heightened activity caused an increase in salaries (an increase of 35 per cent is estimated to have taken place from 1873 to 1889),

[3] See Starck, *Verbrechen und Vergehen in Preussen*, Berlin, 1884, p. 55.
[4] *Die Gesetzmässigkeit im Gesellschaftsleben*, p. 345.
[5] See Fornasari di Verce, *La criminalita e le vicende economiche d'Italia*, Turin 1894, pp. 77-83.
[6] *Ibid.*, pp. 108-117.

the material comfort of workers rose, especially since the price of bread was falling at the same time.[7] Finally, according to calculations by Bodio, private wealth rose from 45 and a half billions on the average during the period 1875–80 to 51 billions during the years 1880–85 and 54 billions and a half in 1885–90.[8]

Now, an unusual increase in the number of suicides is observed parallel with this collective renaissance. From 1866 to 1870 they were roughly stable; from 1871 to 1877 they increased 36 per cent. There were in

1864–70	29 suicides per million	1874	37 suicides per million
1871	31 suicides per million	1875	34 suicides per million
1872	33 suicides per million	1876	36.5 suicides per million
1873	36 suicides per million	1877	40.6 suicides per million

And since then the movement has continued. The total figure, 1,139 in 1877, was 1,463 in 1889, a new increase of 28 per cent.

In Prussia the same phenomenon occurred on two occasions. In 1866 the kingdom received a first enlargement. It annexed several important provinces, while becoming the head of the Confederation of the North. Immediately this growth in glory and power was accompanied by a sudden rise in the number of suicides. There had been 123 suicides per million during the period 1856–60 per average year and only 122 during the years 1861–65. In the five years, 1866–70, in spite of the drop in 1870, the average rose to 133. The year 1867, which immediately followed victory, was that in which suicide achieved the highest point it had reached since 1816 (1 suicide per 5,432 inhabitants, while in 1864 there was only one case per 8,739).

On the morrow of the war of 1870 a new accession of good fortune took place. Germany was unified and placed entirely under Prussian hegemony. An enormous war indemnity added to the public wealth; commerce and industry made great strides. The development of suicide was never so rapid. From 1875 to 1886 it increased 90 per cent, from 3,278 cases to 6,212.

World expositions, when successful, are considered favorable events in the existence of a society. They stimulate business, bring more money into the country and are thought to increase public

---

[7] *Ibid.*, pp. 86-104.
[8] The increase is less during the period 1885–90 because of a financial crisis.

prosperity, especially in the city where they take place. Yet, quite possibly, they ultimately take their toll in a considerably higher number of suicides. Especially does this seem to have been true of the Exposition of 1878. The rise that year was the highest occurring between 1874 and 1886. It was 8 per cent, that is, higher than the one caused by the crash of 1882. And what almost proves the Exposition to have been the cause of this increase is that 86 per cent of it took place precisely during the six months of the Exposition.

In 1889 things were not identical all over France. But quite possibly the Boulanger crisis neutralized the contrary effects of the Exposition by its depressive influence on the growth of suicides. Certainly at Paris, although the political feeling aroused must have had the same effect as in the rest of the country, things happened as in 1878. For the 7 months of the Exposition, suicides increased almost 10 per cent, 9.66 to be exact, while through the remainder of the year they were below what they had been in 1888 and what they afterwards were in 1890.

	1888	1889	1890
The seven months of the Exposition	517	567	540
The five other months	319	311	356

It may well be that but for the Boulanger influence the rise would have been greater.

What proves still more conclusively that economic distress does not have the aggravating influence often attributed to it, is that it tends rather to produce the opposite effect. There is very little suicide in Ireland, where the peasantry leads so wretched a life. Poverty-stricken Calabria has almost no suicides; Spain has a tenth as many as France. Poverty may even be considered a protection. In the various French departments the more people there are who have independent means, the more numerous are suicides.

Departments Where, per 100,000 Inhabitants, Suicides Were Committed (1878–1887)		Average Number of Persons of Independent Means per 1,000 Inhabitants in Each Group of Departments (1886)
Suicides	Number of Departments	
From 48 to 43	5	127
From 38 to 31	6	73
From 30 to 24	6	69
From 23 to 18	15	59
From 17 to 13	18	49
From 12 to 8	26	49
From 7 to 3	10	42

Comparison of the maps confirms that of the averages (see Appendix V).

If therefore industrial or financial crises increase suicides, this is not because they cause poverty, since crises of prosperity have the same result; it is because they are crises, that is, disturbances of the collective order.[9] Every disturbance of equilibrium, even though it achieves greater comfort and a heightening of general vitality, is an impulse to voluntary death. Whenever serious readjustments take place in the social order, whether or not due to a sudden growth or to an unexpected catastrophe, men are more inclined to self-destruction. How is this possible? How can something considered generally to improve existence serve to detach men from it?

For the answer, some preliminary considerations are required.

II

No living being can be happy or even exist unless his needs are sufficiently proportioned to his means. In other words, if his needs require more than can be granted, or even merely something of a different sort, they will be under continual friction and can only function painfully. Movements incapable of production without pain tend not to be reproduced. Unsatisfied tendencies atrophy, and as the impulse to live is merely the result of all the rest, it is bound to weaken as the others relax.

In the animal, at least in a normal condition, this equilibrium is established with automatic spontaneity because the animal depends on purely material conditions. All the organism needs is that the supplies of substance and energy constantly employed in the vital process should be periodically renewed by equivalent quantities; that replacement be equivalent to use. When the void created by existence in its own resources is filled, the animal, satisfied, asks nothing further. Its power of reflection is not sufficiently developed to imagine other ends than those implicit in its physical nature. On the other hand,

---

[9] To prove that an increase in prosperity diminishes suicides, the attempt has been made to show that they become less when emigration, the escape-valve of poverty, is widely practiced (See Legoyt, pp. 257-259). But cases are numerous where parallelism instead of inverse proportions exist between the two. In Italy from 1876 to 1890 the number of emigrants rose from 76 per 100,000 inhabitants to 335, a figure itself exceeded between 1887 and 1889. At the same time suicides did not cease to grow in numbers.

as the work demanded of each organ itself depends on the general state of vital energy and the needs of organic equilibrium, use is regulated in turn by replacement and the balance is automatic. The limits of one are those of the other; both are fundamental to the constitution of the existence in question, which cannot exceed them.

This is not the case with man, because most of his needs are not dependent on his body or not to the same degree. Strictly speaking, we may consider that the quantity of material supplies necessary to the physical maintenance of a human life is subject to computation, though this be less exact than in the preceding case and a wider margin left for the free combinations of the will; for beyond the indispensable minimum which satisfies nature when instinctive, a more awakened reflection suggests better conditions, seemingly desirable ends craving fulfillment. Such appetites, however, admittedly sooner or later reach a limit which they cannot pass. But how determine the quantity of well-being, comfort or luxury legitimately to be craved by a human being? Nothing appears in man's organic nor in his psychological constitution which sets a limit to such tendencies. The functioning of individual life does not require them to cease at one point rather than at another; the proof being that they have constantly increased since the beginnings of history, receiving more and more complete satisfaction, yet with no weakening of average health. Above all, how establish their proper variation with different conditions of life, occupations, relative importance of services, etc.? In no society are they equally satisfied in the different stages of the social hierarchy. Yet human nature is substantially the same among all men, in its essential qualities. It is not human nature which can assign the variable limits necessary to our needs. They are thus unlimited so far as they depend on the individual alone. Irrespective of any external regulatory force, our capacity for feeling is in itself an insatiable and bottomless abyss.

But if nothing external can restrain this capacity, it can only be a source of torment to itself. Unlimited desires are insatiable by definition and insatiability is rightly considered a sign of morbidity. Being unlimited, they constantly and infinitely surpass the means at their command; they cannot be quenched. Inextinguishable thirst is constantly renewed torture. It has been claimed, indeed, that human activity naturally aspires beyond assignable limits and sets itself unattainable goals. But how can such an undetermined state be any more reconciled with the conditions of mental life than with the demands of physical life? All man's pleasure in acting, moving and exerting himself implies the sense that his efforts are not in vain and that by walking he has advanced. However, one does not advance when one walks toward no goal, or—which is the same thing —when his goal is infinity. Since the distance between us and it is always the same, whatever road we take, we might as well have made the motions without progress from the spot. Even our glances behind and our feeling of pride at the distance covered can cause only deceptive satisfaction, since the remaining distance is not proportionately reduced. To pursue a goal which is by definition unattainable is to condemn oneself to a state of perpetual unhappiness. Of course, man may hope contrary to all reason, and hope has its pleasures even when unreasonable. It may sustain him for a time; but it cannot survive the repeated disappointments of experience indefinitely. What more can the future offer him than the past, since he can never reach a tenable condition nor even approach the glimpsed ideal? Thus, the more one has, the more one wants, since satisfactions received only stimulate instead of filling needs. Shall action as such be considered agreeable? First, only on condition of blindness to its uselessness. Secondly, for this pleasure to be felt and to temper and half veil the accompanying painful unrest, such unending motion must at least always be easy and unhampered. If it is interfered with only restlessness is left, with the lack of ease which it, itself, entails. But it would be a miracle if no insurmountable obstacle were ever encountered. Our thread of life on these conditions is pretty thin, breakable at any instant.

To achieve any other result, the passions first must be limited. Only then can they be harmonized with the faculties and satisfied. But since the individual has no way of limiting them, this must be done by some force exterior to him. A regulative force must play the same role for moral needs which the organism plays for physical needs. This means that the force can only be moral. The awakening of conscience interrupted the state of equilibrium of the animal's dormant existence; only conscience, therefore, can furnish the means to re-establish it. Physical restraint would be ineffective; hearts cannot be touched by physio-chemical forces. So far as the appetites are not automatically restrained by physiological mechanisms, they can be halted only by a limit that they recognize as just. Men would never consent to restrict their desires if they felt justified in passing the assigned limit. But, for reasons given above, they cannot assign themselves this law of justice. So they must receive it from an authority which they respect, to which they yield spontaneously. Either directly and as a whole, or through the agency of one of its organs, society alone can play this moderating role; for it is the only moral power superior to the individual, the authority of which he accepts. It alone has the power necessary to stipulate law and to set the point beyond which the passions must not go. Finally, it alone can estimate the reward to be prospectively offered to every class of human functionary, in the name of the common interest.

As a matter of fact, at every moment of history there is a dim perception, in the moral consciousness of societies, of the respective value of different social services, the relative reward due to each, and the consequent degree of comfort appropriate on the average to workers in each occupation. The different functions are graded in public opinion and a certain coefficient of well-being assigned to each, according to its place in the hierarchy. According to accepted ideas, for example, a certain way of living is considered the upper limit to which a workman may aspire in his efforts to improve his existence, and there is another limit below which he is not willingly permitted to fall unless he has seriously bemeaned himself. Both differ for city and country workers, for the domestic servant and the day-laborer, for the business clerk and the official, etc. Likewise the man of wealth is reproved if he lives the life of a poor man, but also if he seeks the refinements of luxury overmuch. Economists may protest in vain; public feeling will always be scandalized if an individual spends too much wealth for wholly superfluous use, and it even seems that this severity relaxes only in times of moral disturbance.[10] A genuine regimen exists, therefore, although not always legally formulated, which fixes with relative precision the maximum degree of ease of living to which each social class may legitimately aspire. However, there is nothing immutable about such

[10] Actually, this is a purely moral reprobation and can hardly be judicially implemented. We do not consider any reestablishment of sumptuary laws desirable or even possible.

a scale. It changes with the increase or decrease of collective revenue and the changes occurring in the moral ideas of society. Thus what appears luxury to one period no longer does so to another; and the well-being which for long periods was granted to a class only by exception and supererogation, finally appears strictly necessary and equitable.

Under this pressure, each in his sphere vaguely realizes the extreme limit set to his ambitions and aspires to nothing beyond. At least if he respects regulations and is docile to collective authority, that is, has a wholesome moral constitution, he feels that it is not well to ask more. Thus, an end and goal are set to the passions. Truly, there is nothing rigid nor absolute about such determination. The economic ideal assigned each class of citizens is itself confined to certain limits, within which the desires have free range. But it is not infinite. This relative limitation and the moderation it involves, make men contented with their lot while stimulating them moderately to improve it; and this average contentment causes the feeling of calm, active happiness, the pleasure in existing and living which characterizes health for societies as well as for individuals. Each person is then at least, generally speaking, in harmony with his condition, and desires only what he may legitimately hope for as the normal reward of his activity. Besides, this does not condemn man to a sort of immobility. He may seek to give beauty to his life; but his attempts in this direction may fail without causing him to despair. For, loving what he has and not fixing his desire solely on what he lacks, his wishes and hopes may fail of what he has happened to aspire to, without his being wholly destitute. He has the essentials. The equilibrium of his happiness is secure because it is defined, and a few mishaps cannot disconcert him.

But it would be of little use for everyone to recognize the justice of the hierarchy of functions established by public opinion, if he did not also consider the distribution of these functions just. The workman is not in harmony with his social position if he is not convinced that he has his deserts. If he feels justified in occupying another, what he has would not satisfy him. So it is not enough for the average level of needs for each social condition to be regulated by public opinion, but another, more precise rule, must fix the way in which these conditions are open to individuals. There is no society in which such regulation does not exist. It varies with times and places. Once it regarded birth as the almost exclusive principle of social classification; today it recognizes no other inherent inequality than hereditary fortune and merit. But in all these various forms its object is unchanged. It is also only possible, everywhere, as a restriction upon individuals imposed by superior authority, that is, by collective authority. For it can be established only by requiring of one or another group of men, usually of all, sacrifices and concessions in the name of the public interest.

Some, to be sure, have thought that this moral pressure would become unnecessary if men's economic circumstances were only no longer determined by heredity. If inheritance were abolished, the argument runs, if everyone began life with equal resources and if the competitive struggle were fought out on a basis of perfect equality, no one could think its results unjust. Each would instinctively feel that things are as they should be.

Truly, the nearer this ideal equality were approached, the less social restraint will be necessary. But it is only a matter of degree. One sort of heredity will always exist, that of natural talent. Intelligence, taste, scientific, artistic, literary or industrial ability, courage and manual dexterity are gifts received by each of us at birth, as the heir to wealth receives his capital or as the nobleman formerly received his title and function. A moral discipline will therefore still be required to make those less favored by nature accept the lesser advantages which they owe to the chance of birth. Shall it be demanded that all have an equal share and that no advantage be given those more useful and deserving? But then there would have to be a discipline far stronger to make these accept a treatment merely equal to that of the mediocre and incapable.

But like the one first mentioned, this discipline can be useful only if considered just by the peoples subject to it. When it is maintained only by custom and force, peace and harmony are illusory; the spirit of unrest and discontent are latent; appetites superficially restrained are ready to revolt. This happened in Rome and Greece when the faiths underlying the old organization of the patricians and plebeians were shaken, and in our modern societies when aristocratic prejudices began to lose their old ascendancy. But this state of upheaval is exceptional; it occurs only when society is passing through some abnormal crisis. In normal conditions the collective order is regarded as just by the great majority of persons. Therefore, when we say that an authority is necessary to impose this order on individuals, we certainly do not mean that violence is the only means of establishing it. Since this regulation is meant to restrain individual passions, it must come from a power which dominates individuals; but this power must also be obeyed through respect, not fear.

It is not true, then, that human activity can be released from all restraint. Nothing in the world can enjoy such a privilege. All existence being a part of the universe is relative to the remainder; its nature and method of manifestation accordingly depend not only on itself but on other beings, who consequently restrain and regulate it. Here there are only differences of degree and form between the mineral realm and the thinking person. Man's characteristic privilege is that the bond he accepts is not physical but moral; that is, social. He is governed not by a material environment brutally imposed on him, but by a conscience superior to his own, the superiority of which he feels. Because the greater, better part of his existence transcends the body, he escapes the body's yoke, but is subject to that of society.

But when society is disturbed by some painful crisis or by beneficent but abrupt transitions, it is momentarily incapable of exercising this influence; thence come the sudden rises in the curve of suicides which we have pointed out above.

In the case of economic disasters, indeed, something like a declassification occurs which suddenly casts certain individuals into a lower state than their previous one. Then they must reduce their requirements, restrain their needs, learn greater self-control. All the advantages of social influence are lost so far as they are concerned; their moral education has to be recommenced. But society cannot adjust them instantaneously to this new life and teach them to practice the increased self-repression to which they are unaccustomed. So they are not adjusted to the condition forced on them, and its very prospect is intolerable; hence the suffering which detaches them from a reduced existence even before they have made trial of it.

It is the same if the source of the crisis is an abrupt growth of power and wealth. Then, truly, as the conditions of life are changed, the standard according to which needs were regulated can no longer remain the same; for it varies with social resources, since it largely determines the share of each class of producers. The scale is upset; but a new scale cannot be immediately improvised. Time is required for the public conscience to reclassify men and things. So long as the social forces thus freed have not regained equilibrium, their respective values are unknown and so all regulation is lacking for a time. The limits are unknown between the possible and the impossible, what is just and what is unjust, legitimate claims and hopes and those which are immoderate. Consequently, there is no restraint upon aspirations. If the disturbance is profound, it affects even the principles controlling the distribution of men among various occupations. Since the relations between various parts of society are necessarily modified, the ideas expressing these relations must change. Some particular class especially favored by the crisis is no longer resigned to its former lot, and, on the other hand, the example of its greater good fortune arouses all sorts of jealousy below and about it. Appetites, not being controlled by a public opinion become disoriented, no longer recognize the limits proper to them. Besides, they are at the same time seized by a sort of natural erethism simply by the greater intensity of public life. With increased prosperity desires increase. At the very moment when traditional rules have lost their authority, the richer prize offered these appetites stimulates them and makes them more exigent and impatient of control. The state of de-regulation or anomy is thus further heightened by passions being less disciplined, precisely when they need more disciplining.

But then their very demands make fulfillment impossible. Overweening ambition always exceeds the results obtained, great as they may be, since there is no warning to pause here. Nothing gives satisfaction and all this agitation is uninterruptedly maintained without appeasement. Above all, since this race for an unattainable goal can give no other pleasure but that of the race itself, if it is one, once it is interrupted the participants are left empty-handed. At the same time the struggle grows more violent and painful, both from being less controlled and because competition is greater. All classes contend among themselves because no established classification any longer exists. Effort grows, just when it becomes less productive. How could the desire to live not be weakened under such conditions?

This explanation is confirmed by the remarkable immunity of poor

SUICIDE

countries. Poverty protects against suicide because it is a restraint in itself. No matter how one acts, desires have to depend upon resources to some extent; actual possessions are partly the criterion of those aspired to. So the less one has the less he is tempted to extend the range of his needs indefinitely. Lack of power, compelling moderation, accustoms men to it, while nothing excites envy if no one has superfluity. Wealth, on the other hand, by the power it bestows, deceives us into believing that we depend on ourselves only. Reducing the resistance we encounter from objects, it suggests the possibility of unlimited success against them. The less limited one feels, the more intolerable all limitation appears. Not without reason, therefore, have so many religions dwelt on the advantages and moral value of poverty. It is actually the best school for teaching self-restraint. Forcing us to constant self-discipline, it prepares us to accept collective discipline with equanimity, while wealth, exalting the individual, may always arouse the spirit of rebellion which is the very source of immorality. This, of course, is no reason why humanity should not improve its material condition. But though the moral danger involved in every growth of prosperity is not irremediable, it should not be forgotten.

III

If anomy never appeared except, as in the above instances, in intermittent spurts and acute crisis, it might cause the social suicide-rate to vary from time to time, but it would not be a regular, constant factor. In one sphere of social life, however—the sphere of trade and industry—it is actually in a chronic state.

For a whole century, economic progress has mainly consisted in freeing industrial relations from all regulation. Until very recently, it was the function of a whole system of moral forces to exert this discipline. First, the influence of religion was felt alike by workers and masters, the poor and the rich. It consoled the former and taught them contentment with their lot by informing them of the providential nature of the social order, that the share of each class was assigned by God himself, and by holding out the hope for just compensation in a world to come in return for the inequalities of this world. It governed the latter, recalling that worldly interests are not man's entire lot, that they must be subordinate to other and higher interests, and that they should therefore not be pursued without rule or measure. Temporal power, in turn, restrained the scope of economic functions by its supremacy over them and by the relatively subordinate role it assigned them. Finally, within the business world proper, the occupational groups by regulating salaries, the price of products and production itself, indirectly fixed the average level of income on which needs are partially based by the very force of circumstances. However, we do not mean to propose this organization as a model. Clearly it would be inadequate to existing societies without great changes. What we stress is its existence, the fact of its useful influence, and that nothing today has come to take its place.

Actually, religion has lost most of its power. And government, instead of regulating economic life, has become its tool and servant. The most opposite schools, orthodox economists and extreme socialists, unite to reduce government to the role of a more or less passive intermediary among the various social functions. The former wish to make it simply the guardian of individual contracts; the latter leave it the task of doing the collective bookkeeping, that is, of recording the demands of consumers, transmitting them to producers, inventorying the total revenue and distributing it according to a fixed formula. But both refuse it any power to subordinate other social organs to itself and to make them converge toward one dominant aim. On both sides nations are declared to have the single or chief purpose of achieving industrial prosperity; such is the implication of the dogma of economic materialism, the basis of both apparently opposed systems. And as these theories merely express the state of opinion, industry, instead of being still regarded as a means to an end transcending itself, has become the supreme end of individuals and societies alike. Thereupon the appetites thus excited have become freed of any limiting authority. By sanctifying them, so to speak, this apotheosis of well-being has placed them above all human law. Their restraint seems like a sort of sacrilege. For this reason, even the purely utilitarian regulation of them exercised by the industrial world itself through the medium of occupational groups has been unable to persist. Ultimately, this liberation of desires has been made worse by the very development of industry and the almost infinite extension of the market. So long as the producer could gain his profits only in his immediate neighborhood, the restricted amount of possible gain could not much overexcite ambition. Now that he may assume to have almost the entire world as his customer, how could passions accept their former confinement in the face of such limitless prospects?

Such is the source of the excitement predominating in this part of society, and which has thence extended to the other parts. There, the state of crisis and anomy is constant and, so to speak, normal. From top to bottom of the ladder, greed is aroused without knowing where to find ultimate foothold. Nothing can calm it, since its goal is far beyond all it can attain. Reality seems valueless by comparison with the dreams of fevered imaginations; reality is therefore abandoned, but so too is possibility abandoned when it in turn becomes reality. A thirst arises for novelties, unfamiliar pleasures, nameless sensations, all of which lose their savor once known. Henceforth one has no strength to endure the least reverse. The whole fever subsides and the sterility of all the tumult is apparent, and it is seen that all these new sensations in their infinite quantity cannot form a solid foundation of happiness to support one during days of trial. The wise man, knowing how to enjoy achieved results without having constantly to replace them with others, finds in them an attachment to life in the hour of difficulty. But the man who has always pinned all his hopes on the future and lived with his eyes fixed upon it, has nothing in the past as a comfort against the present's afflictions, for the past was nothing to him but a series of hastily experienced stages. What blinded him to himself was his expectation always to find further on the happiness he had so far missed. Now he is stopped in his tracks; from now on nothing remains behind or ahead of him to fix his gaze upon. Weariness alone, moreover, is enough to bring disillusionment, for he cannot in the end escape the futility of an endless pursuit.

We may even wonder if this moral state is not principally what makes economic catastrophes of our day so fertile in suicides. In societies where a man is subjected to a healthy discipline, he submits more readily to the blows of chance. The necessary effort for sustaining a little more discomfort costs him relatively little, since he is used to discomfort and constraint. But when every constraint is hateful in itself, how can closer constraint not seem intolerable? There is no tendency to resignation in the feverish impatience of men's lives. When there is no other aim but to outstrip constantly the point arrived at, how painful to be thrown back! Now this very lack of organization characterizing our economic condition throws the door wide to every sort of adventure. Since imagination is hungry for novelty, and ungoverned, it gropes at random. Setbacks necessarily increase with risks and thus crises multiply, just when they are becoming more destructive.

Yet these dispositions are so inbred that society has grown to accept them and is accustomed to think them normal. It is everlastingly repeated that it is man's nature to be eternally dissatisfied, constantly to advance, without relief or rest, toward an indefinite goal. The longing for infinity is daily represented as a mark of moral distinction, whereas it can only appear within unregulated consciences which elevate to a rule the lack of rule from which they suffer. The doctrine of the most ruthless and swift progress has become an article of faith. But other theories appear parallel with those praising the advantages of instability, which, generalizing the situation that gives them birth, declare life evil, claim that it is richer in grief than in pleasure and that it attracts men only by false claims. Since this disorder is greatest in the economic world, it has most victims there.

Industrial and commercial functions are really among the occupations which furnish the greatest number of suicides (see Table XXIV, p. 258). Almost on a level with the liberal professions, they sometimes surpass them; they are especially more afflicted than agriculture, where the old regulative forces still make their appearance felt most and where the fever of business has least penetrated. Here is best recalled what was once the general constitution of the economic order. And the divergence would be yet greater if, among the suicides of industry, employers were distinguished from workmen, for the former are probably most stricken by the state of anomy. The enormous rate of those with independent means (720 per million) sufficiently shows that the possessors of most comfort suffer most. Everything that enforces subordination attenuates the effects of this state. At least the horizon of the lower classes is limited by those above them, and for this same reason their desires are more modest. Those who have only empty space above them are almost inevitably lost in it, if no force restrains them.

TABLE XXIV—Suicides per Million Persons of Different Occupations

	Trade	Transportation	Industry	Agriculture	Liberal * Professions
France (1878–87) †	440	.....	340	240	300
Switzerland (1876)	664	1,514	577	304	558
Italy (1866–76)	277	152.6	80.4	26.7	618 ‡
Prussia (1883–90)	754	.....	456	315	832
Bavaria (1884–91)	465	.....	369	153	454
Belgium (1886–90)	421	.....	160	160	100
Wurttemberg (1873–78)	273	.....	190	206	...
Saxony (1878)		341.59 §		71.17	...

* When statistics distinguish several different sorts of liberal occupations, we show as a specimen the one in which the suicide-rate is highest.
† From 1826 to 1880 economic functions seem less affected (see *Compte-rendu* of 1880); but were occupational statistics very accurate?
‡ This figure is reached only by men of letters.
§ Figure represents Trade, Transportation and Industry combined for Saxony. Ed.

Anomy, therefore, is a regular and specific factor in suicide in our modern societies; one of the springs from which the annual contingent feeds. So we have here a new type to distinguish from the others. It differs from them in its dependence, not on the way in which individuals are attached to society, but on how it regulates them. Egoistic suicide results from man's no longer finding a basis for existence in life; altruistic suicide, because this basis for existence appears to man situated beyond life itself. The third sort of suicide, the existence of which has just been shown, results from man's activity's lacking regulation and his consequent sufferings. By virtue of its origin we shall assign this last variety the name of *anomic suicide*.

Certainly, this and egoistic suicide have kindred ties. Both spring from society's insufficient presence in individuals. But the sphere of its absence is not the same in both cases. In egoistic suicide it is deficient in truly collective activity, thus depriving the latter of object and meaning. In anomic suicide, society's influence is lacking in the basically individual passions, thus leaving them without a check-rein. In spite of their relationship, therefore, the two types are independent of each other. We may offer society everything social in us, and still be unable to control our desires; one may live in an anomic state without being egoistic, and vice versa. These two sorts of suicide therefore do not draw their chief recruits from the same social environments; one has its principal field among intellectual careers, the world of thought—the other, the industrial or commercial world.

IV

But economic anomy is not the only anomy which may give rise to suicide.

The suicides occurring at the crisis of widowhood, of which we have already spoken [11] are really due to domestic anomy resulting from the death of husband or wife. A family catastrophe occurs which affects the survivor. He is not adapted to the new situation in which he finds himself and accordingly offers less resistance to suicide.

TABLE XXV—Comparison of European States from the Point of View of Both Divorce and Suicide

	Annual Divorces per 1,000 Marriages	Suicides per Million Inhabitants
I. COUNTRIES WHERE DIVORCE AND SEPARATION ARE RARE		
Norway	0.54 (1875–80)	73
Russia	1.6 (1871–77)	30
England and Wales	1.3 (1871–79)	68
Scotland	2.1 (1871–81)	....
Italy	3.05 (1871–73)	31
Finland	3.9 (1875–79)	30.8
Averages	2.07	46.5
II. COUNTRIES WHERE DIVORCE AND SEPARATION ARE OF AVERAGE FREQUENCY		
Bavaria	5.0 (1881)	90.5
Belgium	5.1 (1871–80)	68.5
Holland	6.0 (1871–80)	35.5
Sweden	6.4 (1871–80)	81
Baden	6.5 (1874–79)	156.6
France	7.5 (1871–79)	150
Wurttemberg	8.4 (1876–78)	162.4
Prussia	...	133
Averages	6.4	109.6
III. COUNTRIES WHERE DIVORCE AND SEPARATION ARE FREQUENT		
Kingdom of Saxony	26.9 (1876–80)	299
Denmark	38 (1871–80)	258
Switzerland	47 (1876–80)	216
Averages	37.3	257

But another variety of anomic suicide should draw greater attention, both because it is more chronic and because it will serve to illustrate the nature and functions of marriage.

[11] See above, Book II, Ch. 3.

In the *Annales de demographie internationale* (September 1882), Bertillon published a remarkable study of divorce, in which he proved the following proposition: throughout Europe the number of suicides varies with that of divorces and separations.

If the different countries are compared from this twofold point of view, this parallelism is apparent (see Table XXV, p. 259). Not only is the relation between the averages evident, but the single irregular detail of any importance is that of Holland, where suicides are not as frequent as divorces.

TABLE XXVI—Comparison of Swiss Cantons from the Point of View of Divorce and Suicide

	Divorces and Separations per 1,000 Marriages	Suicides per Million		Divorces and Separations per 1,000 Marriages	Suicides per Million
I. CATHOLIC CANTONS					
French and Italian					
Tessino	7.6	57	Freiburg	15.9	119
Valais	4.0	47			
Averages	5.8	50	Averages	15.9	119
German					
Uri	..	60	Solothurn	37.7	205
Upper Unterwalden	4.9	20	Inner Appenzell	18.9	158
Lower Unterwalden	5.2	1	Zug	14.8	87
Schwyz	5.6	70	Luzern	13.0	100
Averages	3.9	37.7	Averages	21.1	137.5
II. PROTESTANT CANTONS					
French					
Neufchâtel	42.4	560	Vaud	43.5	352
German					
Bern	47.2	229	Schaffhausen	106.0	602
Basel (city)	34.5	323	Outer Appenzell	100.7	213
Basel (country)	33.0	288	Glaris	83.1	127
			Zurich	80.0	288
Averages	38.2	280	Averages	92.4	307
III. CANTONS MIXED AS TO RELIGION					
Argau	40.0	195	Geneva	70.5	360
Grisons	30.9	116	Saint Gall	57.6	179
Averages	36.9	155	Averages	64.0	269

The law may be yet more vigorously verified if we compare not different countries but different provinces of a single country. Notably, in Switzerland the agreement between the two series of phe-

nomena is striking (see Table XXVI, p. 260). The Protestant cantons have the most divorces and also the most suicides. The mixed
cantons follow, from both points of view, and only then come the
Catholic cantons. Within each group the same agreements appear.
Among the Catholic cantons Solothurn and Inner Appenzell are
marked by the high number of their divorces; they are likewise
marked by the number of their suicides. Freiburg, although Catholic
and French, has a considerable number of both divorces and suicides.
Among the Protestant German cantons none has so many divorces
as Schaffhausen; Schaffhausen also leads the list for suicides. Finally,
the mixed cantons, with the one exception of Argau, are classed in
exactly the same way in both respects.

The same comparison, if made between French departments, gives
the same result. Having classified them in eight categories according
to the importance of their suicidal mortality, we discovered that the
groups thus formed were arranged in the same order as with reference to divorces and separations:

	Suicides per Million		Average of Divorces and Separations per 1,000 Marriages
1st group (5 departments)	Below	50	2.6
2nd group (18 departments)	From	51 to 75	2.9
3rd group (15 departments)		76 to 100	5.0
4th group (19 departments)		101 to 150	5.4
5th group (10 departments)		151 to 200	7.5
6th group (9 departments)		201 to 250	8.2
7th group (4 departments)		251 to 300	10.0
8th group (5 departments)	Above	300	12.4

Having shown this relation, let us try to explain it.

We shall mention only as a note the explanation Bertillon sum-
marily suggested. According to that author, the number of suicides
and that of divorces vary in parallel manner because both depend
on the same factor: the greater or less frequency of people with
unstable equilibrium. There are actually, he says, more divorces in a
country the more incompatible married couples it contains. The latter
are recruited especially from among people of irregular lives, persons
of poor character and intelligence, whom this temperament predisposes to suicide. The parallelism would then be due, not to the
influence of divorce itself upon suicide, but to the fact that these two
phenomena derive from a similar cause which they express differently. But this association of divorce with certain psychopathic flaws

is made arbitrarily and without proof. There is no reason to think that there are 15 times as many unbalanced people in Switzerland as in Italy and from 6 to 7 times as many as in France, and yet in the first of these countries divorces are 15 times as frequent as in the second and about 7 times as frequent as in the third. Moreover, so far as suicide is concerned, we know how far purely individual conditions are from accounting for it. Furthermore, all that follows will show the inadequacy of this theory.

One must seek the cause of this remarkable relation, not in the organic predispositions of people but in the intrinsic nature of divorce. As our first proposition here we may assert: in all countries for which we have the necessary data, suicides of divorced people are immensely more numerous than those of other portions of the population.

Suicides in a Million

	Unmarried Above 15 Years		Married		Widowed		Divorced	
	Men	Women	Men	Women	Men	Women	Men	Women
Prussia (1887–1889) *	360	120	430	90	1,471	215	1,875	290
Prussia (1883–1890) *	388	129	498	100	1,552	194	1,952	328
Baden (1885–1893)	458	93	460	85	1,172	171	1,328	...
Saxony (1847–1858)	...	...	481	120	1,242	240	3,102	312
Saxony (1876)	555.18 †		821	146	.....	...	3,252	389
Wurttemberg (1846–1860)	...	...	226	52	530	97	1,298	281
Wurttemberg (1873–1892)	251	...	218 †		405 †		796 †	

* There appears to be some error in the figures for Prussia here.—Ed
† Men and women combined.—Ed.

Thus, divorced persons of both sexes kill themselves between three and four times as often as married persons, although younger (40 years in France as against 46 years), and considerably more often than widowed persons in spite of the aggravation resulting for the latter from their advanced age. What is the explanation?

There is no doubt that the change of moral and material regimen which is a consequence of divorce is of some account in this result. But it does not sufficiently explain the matter. Widowhood is indeed as complete a disturbance of existence as divorce; it usually even has much more unhappy results, since it was not desired by husband and wife, while divorce is usually a deliverance for both. Yet divorced persons who, considering their age, should commit suicide only one half as often as widowed persons, do so more often everywhere, even twice as often in certain countries. This aggravation, to be represented by a coefficient between 2.5 and 4, does not depend on their changed condition in any way.

Let us refer to one of the propositions established above to discover the causes of this fact. In the third chapter of Book II, we saw that in a given society the tendency of widowed persons to suicide was a function of the corresponding tendency of married persons. While the latter are highly protected, the former enjoy an immunity less, to be sure, but still considerable, and the sex best protected by marriage is also that best protected in the state of widowhood. Briefly, when conjugal society is dissolved by the death of one of the couple, the effects which it had with reference to suicide continue to be felt in part by the survivor.[12] Then, however, is it not to be supposed that the same thing takes place when the marriage is interrupted, not by death, but by a judicial act, and that the aggravation which afflicts divorced persons is a result not of the divorce but of the marriage ended by divorce? It must be connected with some quality of the matrimonial society, the influence of which the couple continue to experience even when separated. If they have so strong an inclination to suicide, it is because they were already strongly inclined to it while living together and by the very effect of their common life.

Admitting so much, the correspondence between divorces and suicides becomes explicable. Actually, among the people where divorce is common, this peculiar effect of marriage in which divorce shares must necessarily be very wide-spread; for it is not confined to households predestined to legal separation. If it reaches its maximum intensity among them, it must also be found among the others, or the majority of the others, though to a lesser degree. For just as where there are many suicides, there are many attempted suicides, and just as mortality cannot grow without morbidity increasing simultaneously, so wherever there are many actual divorces there must be many households more or less close to divorce. The number of actual divorces cannot rise, accordingly, without the family condition predisposing to suicide also developing and becoming general in the same degree, and thus the two phenomena naturally vary in the same general direction.

Not only does this hypothesis agree with everything demonstrated

12 See above, Book II, Ch. 3.

TABLE XXVII—Influence of Divorce on the Immunity of Married Persons

	Suicides per Million Persons		
Country	Unmarried Men Above 15 Years	Married Men	Coefficient of Preservation of Married with Reference to Unmarried Men
Where divorce does not exist			
Italy (1884–88)	145	88	1.64
France (1863–68) *	273	245.7	1.11
Where divorce is common			
Baden (1885–93)	458	460	0.99
Prussia (1883–90)	388	498	0.77
Prussia (1887–89)	364	431	0.83

	Per one hundred suicides of every marital status.		
Where divorce is very frequent †	Unmarried men	Married men	0.63
Saxony (1879–80)	27.5	52.5	
	Per one Hundred male inhabitants of every marital status.		
	Unmarried men	Married men	
	42.10	52.47	

* We take this distant period because divorce did not exist at all at the time. The law of 1884 re-establishing it seems, however, up to the present, to have had no perceptible effects on the suicides of married men; their coefficient of preservation had not appreciably changed in 1888–92; an institution does not produce its effects in so short a time.

† For Saxony we have only the relative numbers given above and taken from Oettingen; they are enough for the purpose. In Legoyt (p. 171) other data will be found likewise proving that in Saxony married persons have a higher rate than unmarried. Legoyt himself notes this with surprise.

above but it is susceptible of direct proof. Indeed, if it is well-founded, married persons in countries where divorces are numerous must have less immunity against suicide than where marriage is indissoluble. This is the net result of the facts, at least *so far as husbands are concerned* as appears from Table XXVII above. Italy, a Catholic country in which divorce is unknown, is also the country with the highest coefficient of preservation for husbands; it is less in France, where separations have always been more frequent, and can be seen to diminish as we pass to countries where divorce is more widely practiced.[13]

[13] If we compare only these few countries from this point of view, it is because statistics for the others combine the suicides of husbands with those of wives; and we shall see below how imperative it is to keep them separate.

But one should not conclude from this table that in Prussia, Baden and Saxony husbands really kill themselves more than unmarried men. We must not forget that these coefficients were compiled independently of age and of its influence on suicide. Now, as men of the average age of the unmarried, or from 25 to 30 years, commit suicide about half as often as men of 40 to 45 years, the average age for husbands, the latter enjoy some immunity even in countries with frequent divorce; but it is less than elsewhere. For this to be considered negligible, the rate of married men with-

We were unable to obtain the number of divorces for the grand-duchy of Oldenburg. Considering, however, that it is a Protestant country, divorces may be supposed to be frequent, without being excessively so since the Catholic minority is considerable. From this point of view it should be in about the same class as Baden and Prussia. Now, it is also in the same class from the point of view of immunity of husbands; 100,000 unmarried men above 15 years of age show 52 suicides annually, 100,000 married men 66. The latter's coefficient of preservation is therefore 0.79, or very different from that found in Catholic countries where divorce is rare or unknown.

France permits us to make an observation confirming those just given, all the more so as it is still more exact. Divorces are much more frequent in the Seine than in the rest of the country. In 1885 the number of divorces issued there was 23.99 for 10,000 established households, whereas the average for all France was only 5.65. We need only refer to Table XXII to see that the coefficient of preservation for husbands is definitely less in the Seine than in the provinces. Indeed it reaches 3 there only once, for the period of 20 to 25 years; and the exactness of even this figure is uncertain, since it is calculated from too small a number of cases, since there is annually hardly more than one suicide of a husband at this age. From 30 years on, the coefficient does not exceed 2, is usually below that, and is even below unity between 60 and 70 years of age. On the average it is 1.73. In the departments, on the contrary, it is above 3, 5 times out of 8; on the average it is 2.88, or 1.66 times higher than in the Seine.

This is one more proof that the large number of suicides in countries where divorce is widespread has no reference to any organic predisposition, especially to the number of unstable people. For if

out reference to age would have to be twice that of unmarried men; which is not the case. However, this omission has no bearing on our conclusion. For the average age of husbands varies little from one country to another, only two or three years, and moreover the law of the effect of age on suicide is everywhere the same. Consequently by disregarding the effect of this factor, we have indeed reduced the absolute value of the coefficients of preservation, but as we have reduced them in the same proportion everywhere, we have not altered what is of sole importance to us— their relative value. For we are not seeking to estimate the absolute value of the immunity of married men of every country, but to classify the different countries from the point of view of this immunity. As for our reasons for making this simplification, it was first to avoid complicating the problem unnecessarily, but also because we have not in all cases the necessary data for the exact calculation of the effect of age.

such were the real cause, it would affect unmarried as well as married men. Now the latter are actually those most affected. The origin of the evil is therefore undoubtedly to be sought, as we have supposed, in some peculiarity either of marriage or of family. life. It remains for us to choose between the last two hypotheses. Is the lesser immunity of husbands due to the condition of domestic society, or to that of matrimonial society? Is the family morale inferior or the conjugal bond not all that it should be?

A first fact which makes the former explanation improbable is that among peoples where divorce is most frequent the birth-rate is very high and, consequently, the density of the domestic group is also very high. Now we know that where the family is dense, family spirit is usually strong. There is reason to believe, then, that the cause of the phenomenon is to be sought in the nature of marriage.

Actually, if it were imputable to the constitution of the family, wives should also be less protected from suicide in countries where divorce is current than in those where it is rare; for they are as much affected by the poor state of domestic relations as husbands. Exactly the reverse is the truth. The coefficient of preservation of married women rises proportionately to the fall of that of husbands, or in proportion as divorces are more frequent and vice versa. The more often and easily the conjugal bond is broken, the more the wife is favored in comparison with the husband (see Table XXVIII, p. 267).

The inversion between the two series of coefficients is remarkable. In countries where there is no divorce, the wife is less protected than the husband; but her inferiority is greater in Italy than in France, where the matrimonial tie has always been more easily broken. On the contrary, wherever divorce is practiced (Baden), the husband is less protected than the wife, and the latter's advantage increases regularly with the increase in the frequency of divorce.

Just as in the preceding instance, the grand-duchy of Oldenburg classifies from this point of view like the other sections of Germany where divorce is of average frequency. A million unmarried women show 203 suicides, a million married women 156; the latter have, therefore, a coefficient of preservation of 1.3, much above that of husbands, which was only 0.79. The first number is 1.64 times greater than the second, approximately as in Prussia.

TABLE XXVIII—Influence of Divorce on the Immunity of Married Women *

	Suicides per Million		Coefficient of Preservation		How Many Times Husbands' Coefficient Above Wives'	How Many Times Wives' Coefficient Above Husbands'
	Unmarried Women Over 16 Years	Wives	Wives	Husbands		
Italy	21	22	0.95	1.64	1.72	....
France	59	62.5	0.96	1.11	1.15	....
Baden	93	85	1.09	0.99	....	1.10
Prussia	129	100	1.29	0.77	....	1.67
Prussia (1887–89)	120	90	1.33	0.83	....	1.60

Saxony

Per 100 suicides of every marital status.

Unmarried Women	Wives
35.3	42.6

Per 100 inhabitants of every marital status.

Unmarried Women	Wives				
37.97	49.74	1.19	0.63	:...	1.73

* The periods are the same as in Table XXVII.

Comparison of the Seine with other French departments confirms this law in a striking manner. In the provinces, where there is less divorce, the average coefficient of married women is only 1.49; it is therefore only half the average coefficient of husbands, which is 2.88. In the Seine the relation is reversed. The immunity of men is only 1.56 and even 1.44 if we omit the uncertain figures referring to the period of from 20 to 25 years; the immunity of women is 1.79. The woman's situation in relation to the husband's there is thus more than twice as good as in the departments.

The same result is obtained by comparing the various provinces of Prussia:

Provinces Containing, per 100,000 Married Persons

From 810 to 405 Divorced	Coefficient of Preservation of Wives	From 371 to 324 Divorced	Coefficient of Preservation of Wives	From 229 to 116 Divorced	Coefficient of Preservation of Wives
Berlin	1.72	Pomerania	1	Posen	1
Brandenburg	1.75	Silesia	1.18	Hesse	1.44
East Prussia	1.50	West Prussia	1	Hanover	0.90
Saxony	2.08	Schleswig	1.20	Rhineland	1.25
				Westphalia	0.80

All the coefficients of the first group are distinctly above those of the second, and the lowest are found in the third. The only anomaly is Hesse, where, for unknown reasons, married women have a considerable immunity although divorced persons are few in number.[14]

In spite of these concurrent proofs, let us seek a final verification of this law. Instead of comparing the immunity of husbands with that of wives, let us discover how differently marriage in different countries modifies the respective situations of the sexes with regard to suicide. This comparison forms the subject of Table XXIX. Here

TABLE XXIX—Proportional Share of Each Sex in Suicides of Each Category of Marital Status in Different Countries of Europe

	Per 100 Suicides of Unmarried		Per 100 Suicides of Married		Average Excess per Country on the part of	
	Men	Women	Husbands	Wives	Wives Over Unmarried Women	Unmarried Women Over Wives
Italy (1871)	87	13	79	21		
Italy (1872)	82	18	78	22		
Italy (1873)	86	14	79	21	6.2	
Italy (1884–88)	85	15	79	21		
France (1863–66)	84	16	78	22		
France (1867–71)	84	16	79	21	3.6	
France (1888–91)	81	19	81	19		
Baden (1869–73)	84	16	85	15		
Baden (1885–93)	84	16	85	15		1
Prussia (1873–75)	78	22	83	17		
Prussia (1887–89)	77	23	83	17		5
Saxony (1866–70)	77	23	84	16		
Saxony (1879–90)	80	20	86	14		7

it appears that, in countries where divorce does not exist or has only recently been instituted, woman's share is greater in the suicides of married than of unmarried persons. This means that marriage here favors the husband rather than the wife, and the latter's unfavorable position is more pronounced in Italy than in France. The average excess of the proportional share of married over unmarried women is indeed twice as much in the former as in the latter of the two countries. Turning to peoples among whom the institution of divorce is widespread, the reverse is the case. Here woman gains by marriage and man loses; and her profit is greater in Prussia than in Baden, and greater in Saxony than in Prussia. Her profit is greatest in the country where divorces also are greatest.

Accordingly, the following law may be regarded as beyond dis-

[14] It has been necessary to classify these provinces by the number of divorced persons recorded, the number of annual divorces not having been available.

pute: *From the standpoint of suicide, marriage is more favorable to the wife the more widely practiced divorce is; and vice versa.*

From this proposition, two consequences flow.

First, only husbands contribute to the rise in the suicide rate observable in societies where divorces are frequent, wives on the contrary committing suicide more rarely than elsewhere. If, then, divorce can only develop with the improvement of woman's moral situation, it cannot be connected with an unfavorable state of domestic society calculated to aggravate the tendency to suicide; for such an aggravation should occur in the case of the wife, as well as of the husband. A lowering of family morale cannot have such opposite effects on the two sexes: it cannot both favor the mother and seriously afflict the father. Consequently, the cause of the phenomenon which we are studying is found in the state of marriage and not in the constitution of the family. And indeed, marriage may very possibly act in an opposite way on husband and wife. For though they have the same object as parents, as partners their interests are different and often hostile. In certain societies therefore, some peculiarity of the matrimonial institution may very well benefit one and harm the other. All of the above tends to show that this is precisely the case with divorce.

Secondly, for the same reason we have to reject the hypothesis that this unfortunate state of marriage, with which divorces and suicides are closely connected, is simply caused by more frequent domestic disputes; for no such cause could increase the woman's immunity, any more than could the loosening of the family tie. If, where divorce is common, the number of suicides really depends on the number of conjugal disputes, the wife should suffer from them as much as the husband. There is nothing in this situation to afford her exceptional immunity. The hypothesis is the less tenable since divorce is usually asked for by the wife from the husband (in France, 60 per cent of divorces and 83 per cent of separations).[15] Accordingly, domestic troubles are most often attributable to the man. Then, however, it would not be clear why, in countries of frequent divorce, the husband kills himself with greater frequency because he causes

[15] Levasseur, *Population francaise*, V. II, p. 92. Cf. Bertillon, *Annales de Dem. Inter.*, 1880, p. 460.—In Saxony, demands for divorce from men are almost as frequent as those from women.

270 SUICIDE

his wife more suffering, and the wife kills herself less often because her husband makes her suffer more. Nor is it proven that the number of conjugal dissensions increases in the same measure with divorce.[16]

If we discard this hypothesis, only one other remains possible. The institution of divorce must itself cause suicide through its effect on marriage.

After all, what is marriage? A regulation of sexual relations, including not merely the physical instincts which this intercourse involves but the feelings of every sort gradually engrafted by civilization on the foundation of physical desire. For among us love is a far more mental than organic fact. A man looks to a woman, not merely to the satisfaction of the sexual impulse. Though this natural proclivity has been the germ of all sexual evolution, it has become increasingly complicated with aesthetic and moral feelings, numerous and varied, and today it is only the smallest element of the total complex process to which it has given birth. Under the influence of these intellectual elements it has itself been partially freed from its physical nature and assumed something like an intellectual one. Moral reasons as well as physical needs impel love. Hence, it no longer has the regular, automatic periodicity which it displays in animals. A psychological impulse may awaken it at any time: it is not seasonal. But just because these various inclinations, thus changed, do not directly depend upon organic necessities, social regulation becomes necessary. They must be restrained by society since the organism has no means of restraining them. This is the function of marriage. It completely regulates the life of passion, and monogamic marriage more strictly than any other. For by forcing a man to attach himself forever to the same woman it assigns a strictly definite object to the need for love, and closes the horizon.

This determination is what forms the state of moral equilibrium from which the husband benefits. Being unable to seek other satisfactions than those permitted, without transgressing his duty, he restricts his desires to them. The salutary discipline to which he is subjected makes it his duty to find his happiness in his lot, and by doing so supplies him with the means. Besides, if his passion is forbidden to stray, its fixed object is forbidden to fail him; the obligation is reciprocal. Though his enjoyment is restricted, it is assured

[16] Bertillon, *Annales*, etc., 1882, p. 275 ff.

and this certainty forms his mental foundation. The lot of the unmarried man is different. As he has the right to form attachment
wherever inclination leads him, he aspires to everything and is satisfied with nothing. This morbid desire for the infinite which everywhere accompanies anomy may as readily assail this as any other
part of our consciousness; it very often assumes a sexual form which
was described by Musset.[17] When one is no longer checked, one
becomes unable to check one's self. Beyond experienced pleasures
one senses and desires others; if one happens almost to have exhausted the range of what is possible, one dreams of the impossible;
one thirsts for the non-existent.[18] How can the feelings not be exacerbated by such unending pursuit? For them to reach that state, one
need not even have infinitely multiplied the experiences of love and
lived the life of a Don Juan. The humdrum existence of the ordinary bachelor suffices. New hopes constantly awake, only to be
deceived, leaving a trail of weariness and disillusionment behind
them. How can desire, then, become fixed, being uncertain that it
can retain what it attracts; for the anomy is twofold. Just as the
person makes no definitive gift of himself, he has definitive title
to nothing. The uncertainty of the future plus his own indeterminate-
ness therefore condemns him to constant change. The result of it
all is a state of disturbance, agitation and discontent which inevitably increases the possibilities of suicide.

Now divorce implies a weakening of matrimonial regulation.
Where it exists, and especially where law and custom permit its
excessive practice, marriage is nothing but a weakened simulacrum
of itself; it is an inferior form of marriage. It cannot produce its
useful effects to the same degree. Its restraint upon desire is weakened; since it is more easily disturbed and superceded, it controls
passion less and passion tends to rebel. It consents less readily to
its assigned limit. The moral calmness and tranquillity which were
the husband's strength are less; they are replaced to some extent by
an uneasiness which keeps a man from being satisfied with what he
has. Besides, he is the less inclined to become attached to his present
state as his enjoyment of it is not completely sure: the future is less
certain. One cannot be strongly restrained by a chain which may be

---

[17] See *Rolla* and in *Namouna* the portrait of Don Juan.
[18] See the monologue of Faust in Goethe's work.

broken on one side or the other at any moment. One cannot help
looking beyond one's own position when the ground underfoot does
not feel secure. Hence, in the countries where marriage is strongly
tempered by divorce, the immunity of the married man is inevitably
less. As he resembles the unmarried under this regime, he inevitably
loses some of his own advantages. Consequently, the total number
of suicides rises.[19]

But this consequence of divorce is peculiar to the man and does
not affect the wife. Woman's sexual needs have less of a mental
character because, generally speaking, her mental life is less developed. These needs are more closely related to the needs of the organism, following rather than leading them, and consequently find in
them an efficient restraint. Being a more instinctive creature than
man, woman has only to follow her instincts to find calmness and
peace. She thus does not require so strict a social regulation as marriage, and particularly as monogamic marriage. Even when useful,
such a discipline has its inconveniences. By fixing the conjugal state
permanently, it prevents all retreat, regardless of consequences. By
limiting the horizon, it closes all egress and forbids even legitimate
hope. Man himself doubtless suffers from this immutability; but for
him the evil is largely compensated by the advantages he gains in
other respects. Custom, moreover, grants him certain privileges which
allow him in some measure to lessen the strictness of the regime.
There is no compensation or relief for the woman. Monogamy is
strictly obligatory for her, with no qualification of any sort, and, on
the other hand, marriage is not in the same degree useful to her for
limiting her desires, which are naturally limited, and for teaching
her to be contented with her lot; but it prevents her from changing
it if it becomes intolerable. The regulation therefore is a restraint
to her without any great advantages. Consequently, everything that
makes it more flexible and lighter can only better the wife's situation. So divorce protects her and she has frequent recourse to it.

[19] It will be objected that where marriage is not tempered by divorce the rigid
obligation of monogamy may result in disgust. This result will of course follow if
the moral character of the obligation is no longer felt. What actually matters in fact
is not only that the regulation should exist, but that it should be accepted by the
conscience. Otherwise, since this regulation no longer has moral authority and continues only through the force of inertia, it can no longer play any useful role. It
chafes without accomplishing much.

The state of conjugal anomy, produced by the institution of divorce, thus explains the parallel development of divorces and suicides. Accordingly, the suicides of husbands which increase the number of voluntary deaths in countries where there are many divorces, form a division of anomic suicide. They are not the result of the existence of more bad husbands or bad wives in these societies, that is, of more unhappy households. They result from a moral structure *sui generis,* itself caused by a weakening of matrimonial regulation. This structure, established by marriage, by surviving it produces the exceptional tendency to suicide shown by divorced men. But we do not mean that this enervation of the regulation is created out of whole cloth by the legal establishment of divorce. Divorce is never granted except out of respect for a pre-existing state of customs. If the public conscience had not gradually decided that the indissolubility of the conjugal bond is unreasonable, no legislator would ever have thought of making it easier to break up. Matrimonial anomy may therefore exist in public opinion even without being inscribed in law. On the other hand, only when it has assumed a legal form, can it produce all its consequences. So long as the marriage law is unmodified, it at least serves considerably to restrict the passions; above all, it opposes the increase of the taste for anomy merely by reproof. That is why anomy has pronounced and readily recognizable effects only where it has become a legal institution.

While this explanation accounts both for the observed parallelism between divorces and suicides [20] and the inverse variations shown by the immunity of husband and that of the wife, it is confirmed by several other facts:

1. Only where divorce applies, can there be real matrimonial instability; for it alone completely severs marriage, whereas separation merely partially suspends certain of its effects without giving the couple their liberty. If, then, this special anomy really increases the suicidal tendency, divorced people should have a far higher aptitude than those merely separated. This is in fact the gist of the only document on this matter known to us. According to a calculation by

[20] Since the wife's immunity is greater where the husband's is less, it may seem strange that there is no compensation. But as the wife's share in the total number of suicides is very slight, the decrease in female suicides is imperceptible in the whole and does not balance the increase of male suicides. Thus divorce is ultimately associated with a rise in the total number of suicides.

Legoyt,[21] in Saxony, during the period 1847–56, there were, as an annual average, 1,400 suicides for a million divorced persons and only 176 for a million separated persons. This latter rate is even below that of husbands (318).

2. If the strong suicidal tendency of the unmarried is partially connected with the sexual anomy in which they chronically exist, the aggravation they suffer must be most perceptible just when sexual feelings are most aroused. And in fact, the suicide rate of the unmarried grows between 20 and 45 years much more rapidly than after that; it quadruples during this period, while from 45 to the maximum age (after 80 years) it only doubles. But no such acceleration appears among women; the rate of unmarried women does not even double from 20 to 45 years, but merely rises from 106 to 171 (see Table XXI). The sexual period therefore does not affect the increase of female suicides. This is just what we should expect if, as we have granted, woman is not very sensitive to this form of anomy.

3. Finally, several facts established in Chapter III of this very book are explained by the theory just set forth and consequently help to verify it.

We saw in that chapter that marriage in France, by itself and irrespective of family, gives man a coefficient of preservation of 1.5. We know now to what this coefficient corresponds. It represents the advantages obtained by a man from the regulative influence exerted upon him by marriage, from the moderation it imposes on his inclinations and from his consequent moral well-being. But at the same time we noted that in the same country the condition of a married woman was, on the contrary, made worse with respect to suicide unless the advent of children corrects the ill effects of marriage for her. We have just stated the reason. Not that man is naturally a wicked and egoistic being whose role in a household is to make his companion suffer. But in France where, until recently, marriage was not weakened by divorce, the inflexible rule it imposed on women was a very heavy, profitless yoke for them. Speaking generally, we now have the cause of that antagonism of the sexes which prevents marriage favoring them equally: [22] their interests are contrary; one needs restraint and the other liberty.

[21] *Op. cit.*, p. 171.
[22] See above, Book II, Ch. 3.

Furthermore, it does seem that at a certain time of life man is affected by marriage in the same way as woman, though for different reasons. If, as we have shown, very young husbands kill themselves much more often than unmarried men of the same age, it is doubtless because their passions are too vehement at that period and too self-confident to be subjected to so severe a rule. Accordingly, this rule seems to them an unendurable obstacle against which their desire dashes and is broken. This is probably why marriage produces all its beneficent effects only when age, supervening, tempers man somewhat and makes him feel the need of discipline.[23]

Finally, in this same Chapter III we saw that where marriage favors the wife rather than the husband, the difference between the sexes is always less than when the reverse is true.[24] This proves that, even in those societies where the status of matrimony is wholly in the woman's favor, it does her less service than it does man where it is he that profits more by it. Woman can suffer more from marriage if it is unfavorable to her than she can benefit by it if it conforms to her interest. This is because she has less need of it. This is the assumption of the theory just set forth. The results obtained previously and those arising from the present chapter therefore combine and check each other mutually.

Thus we reach a conclusion quite different from the current idea of marriage and its role. It is supposed to have been originated for the wife, to protect her weakness against masculine caprice. Monogamy, especially, is often represented as a sacrifice made by man of his polygamous instincts, to raise and improve woman's condition

[23] It is even probable that marriage in itself produces a prophylactic effect only later, after the age of thirty. Actually, until that age, childless married men commit as many suicides in absolute numbers as married men with children, 6.6 from 20 to 25 years, for both, and from 25 to 30 years, 33 for the former and 34 for the latter. Of course, however, marriages with children are much more common than infertile marriages at this period. The tendency of the husbands of the latter marriages to suicide must therefore be several times as strong as that of husbands with children; or very close in intensity to that of unmarried men. Unfortunately we can only form hypotheses on the subject; for, as the census does not give the population of husbands without children for each age, as distinct from husbands with children, we cannot calculate separately the rate of each for each period of life. We can give only the absolute numbers, as we have them from the Ministry of Justice for 1889–91. We have reproduced them in a special table to be found at the close of this work. This gap in census-taking is most regrettable.

[24] See above, Book II, Ch 3.

in marriage. Actually, whatever historical causes may have made him accept this restriction, he benefits more by it. The liberty he thus renounces could only be a source of torment to him. Woman did not have the same reasons to abandon it and, in this sense, we may say that by submitting to the same rule, it was she who made a sacrifice.[25]

[25] The above considerations show that there is a type of suicide the opposite of anomic suicide, just as egoistic and altruistic suicides are opposites. It is the suicide deriving from excessive regulation, that of persons with futures pitilessly blocked and passions violently choked by oppressive discipline. It is the suicide of very young husbands, of the married woman who is childless. So, for completeness' sake, we should set up a fourth suicidal type. But it has so little contemporary importance and examples are so hard to find aside from the cases just mentioned that it seems useless to dwell upon it. However it might be said to have historical interest. Do not the suicides of slaves, said to be frequent under certain conditions (See Corre, *Le crime en pays creoles,* p. 48), belong to this type, or all suicides attributable to excessive physical or moral despotism? To bring out the ineluctible and inflexible nature of a rule against which there is no appeal, and in contrast with the expression "anomy" which has just been used, we might call it *fatalistic suicide.*

CHAPTER 6

INDIVIDUAL FORMS OF THE DIFFERENT TYPES OF SUICIDE

ONE result now stands out prominently from our investigation: namely, that there are not one but various forms of suicide. Of course, suicide is always the act of a man who prefers death to life. But the causes determining him are not of the same sort in all cases: they are even sometimes mutually opposed. Now, such difference in causes must reappear in their effects. We may therefore be sure that there are several sorts of suicide which are distinct in quality from one another. But the certainty that these differences exist is not enough; we need to observe them directly and know of what they consist. We need to see the characteristics of special suicides grouped in distinct classes corresponding to the types just distinguished. Thus we would follow the various currents which generate suicide from their social origins to their individual manifestations.

This morphological classification, which was hardly possible at the commencement of this study, may be undertaken now that an aetiological classification forms its basis. Indeed, we only need to start with the three kinds of factors which we have just assigned to suicide and discover whether the distinctive properties it assumes in manifesting itself among individual persons may be derived from them, and if so, how. Of course, not all the peculiarities which suicide may present can be deduced in this fashion; for some may exist which depend solely on the person's own nature. Each victim of suicide gives his act a personal stamp which expresses his temperament, the special conditions in which he is involved, and which, consequently, cannot be explained by the social and general causes of the phenomenon. But these causes in turn must stamp the suicides they determine with a shade all their own, a special mark expressive of them. This collective mark we must find.

To be sure, this can be done only approximately. We are not in a position to describe methodically all the suicides daily committed by men or committed in the course of history. We can only emphasize the most general and striking characteristics without even having an objective criterion for making the selection. Moreover, we can only proceed deductively in relating them to the respective causes from which they seem to spring. All that we can do is to show their logical implication, though the reasoning may not always be able to receive experimental confirmation. We do not forget that a deduction uncontrolled by experiment is always questionable. Yet this research is far from being useless, even with these reservations. Even though it may be considered only a method of illustrating the preceding results by examples, it would still have the worth of giving them a more concrete character by connecting them more closely with the data of sense-perception and with the details of daily experience. It will also introduce some little distinctiveness into this mass of facts usually lumped together as though varying only by shades, though there are striking differences among them. Suicide is like mental alienation. For the popular mind the latter consists in a single state, always identical, capable only of superficial differentiation according to circumstances. For the alienist, on the contrary, the word denotes many nosological types. Every suicide is, likewise, ordinarily considered a victim of melancholy whose life has become a burden to him. Actually, the acts by which a man renounces life belong to different species, of wholly different moral and social significance.

I

One form of suicide, certainly known to antiquity, has widely developed in our day: Lamartine's *Raphaël* offers us its ideal type. Its characteristic is a condition of melancholic languor which relaxes all the springs of action. Business, public affairs, useful work, even domestic duties inspire the person only with indifference and aversion. He is unwilling to emerge from himself. On the other hand, what is lost in activity is made up for in thought and inner life.

In revulsion from its surroundings consciousness becomes self-pre-occupied, takes itself as its proper and unique study, and undertakes as its main task self-observation and self-analysis. But by this extreme concentration it merely deepens the chasm separating it from the rest of the universe. The moment the individual becomes so enamoured of himself, inevitably he increasingly detaches himself from everything external and emphasizes the isolation in which he lives, to the point of worship. Self-absorption is not a good method of attaching one's self to others. All movement is, in a sense, altruistic in that it is centrifugal and disperses existence beyond its own limitations. Reflection, on the other hand, has about it something personal and egoistic; for it is only possible as a person becomes detached from the outside world, and retreats from it into himself. And reflection is the more intense, the more complete this retreat. Action without mixing with people is impossible; to think, on the contrary, we must cease to have connection with them in order to consider them objectively—the more so, in order to think about oneself. So the man whose whole activity is diverted to inner meditation becomes insensible to all his surroundings. If he loves, it is not to give himself, to blend in fecund union with another being, but to meditate on his love. His passions are mere appearances, being sterile. They are dissipated in futile imaginings, producing nothing external to themselves.

On the other hand, all internal life draws its primary material from without. All we can think of is objects or our conceptions of them. We cannot reflect our own consciousness in a purely undetermined state; in this shape it is inconceivable. Now consciousness becomes determined only when affected by something not itself. Therefore, if it individualizes beyond a certain point, if it separates itself too radically from other beings, men or things, it finds itself unable to communicate with the very sources of its normal nourishment and no longer has anything to which it can apply itself. It creates nothingness within by creating it without, and has nothing left upon which to reflect but its own wretched misery. Its only remaining object of thought is its inner nothingness and the resulting melancholy. It becomes addicted and abandoned to this with a kind of morbid joy which Lamartine, himself familiar with it, describes so well in the words of his hero: "The languor of all my surroundings was in marvelous harmony with my own languor. It increased this languor by its charm. I plunged into the depths of melancholy. But it was a lively melancholy, full enough of thoughts, impressions, communings with the infinite, half-obscurity of my own soul, so that I had no wish to abandon it. A human disease, but one the experience of which attracts rather than pains, where death resembles a voluptuous lapse into the infinite. I resolved to abandon myself to it wholly, henceforth; to avoid all distracting society and to wrap myself in silence, solitude and frigidity in the midst of whatever company I should encounter; my spiritual isolation was a shroud, through which I desired no longer to see men, but only nature and God." [1]

However, one cannot long remain so absorbed in contemplation of emptiness without being increasingly attracted to it. In vain one bestows on it the name of infinity; this does not change its nature. When one feels such pleasure in non-existence, one's inclination can be completely satisfied only by completely ceasing to exist. This is the element of truth in the parallelism Hartmann claims to observe between the development of consciousness and the weakening of the will to live. Ideation and movement are really two hostile forces, advancing in inverse directions, and movement is life. To think, it is said, is to abstain from action; in the same degree, therefore, it is to abstain from living. This is why the absolute reign of idea cannot be achieved, and especially cannot continue; for this is death. But this does not mean, as Hartmann believes, that reality itself is intolerable unless veiled by illusion. Sadness does not inhere in things; it does not reach us from the world and through mere contemplation of the world. It is a product of our own thought. We create it out of whole cloth; but to create it our thought must be abnormal. If consciousness sometimes constitutes unhappiness for a man, it is only by achieving a morbid development in which, revolting against its own very nature, it poses as an absolute and seeks its purpose in itself. It is so far from being a belated discovery, from being the ultimate conquest of knowledge, that we might equally well have sought the chief elements of our description in the Stoic frame of

[1] *Raphaël,* ed. Hachette, p. 6.

mind. Stoicism also teaches man to detach himself from everything external in order to live by and through himself. Only, the doctrine ends in suicide since life then has no reason.

The same characteristics reappear in the ultimate act which follows logically from this moral condition. There is nothing violent or hasty about its unfolding. The sufferer selects his own time and meditates on his plan well in advance. He is not even repelled by slow means. A calm melancholy, sometimes not unpleasant, marks his last moments. He analyzes himself to the last. Such is the case of the business man mentioned by Falret [2] who goes to an isolated forest to die of hunger. During an agony of almost three weeks he had regularly kept a journal of his impressions, which has been preserved. Another asphyxiates himself by blowing on the charcoal which is to kill him, and jots down his observations bit by bit: "I do not consider that I am showing either courage or cowardice; I simply wish to use my few remaining moments to describe the sensations felt during asphyxiation and the length of the suffering." [3] Another man, before abandoning himself to what he calls "the intoxicating perspective of rest," builds a complicated apparatus to accomplish his own death without having his blood stain the floor. [4]

It is clear how these various peculiarities are related to egoistic suicide. They are almost certainly its consequence and individual expression. This loathness to act, this melancholy detachment, spring from the over-individuation by which we have defined this type of suicide. If the individual isolates himself, it is because the ties uniting him with others are slackened or broken, because society is not sufficiently integrated at the points where he is in contact with it. These gaps between one and another individual consciousness, estranging them from each other, are authentic results of the weakening of the social fabric. And finally, the intellectual and meditative nature of suicides of this sort is readily explained if we recall that egoistic suicide is necessarily accompanied by a high development of knowledge and reflective intelligence. Indeed, it is clear that in a society where consciousness is normally compelled to extend its field

---

[2] *Hypochondrie et suicide,* p. 316.
[3] Brierre de Boismont, *Du suicide,* p. 198.
[4] *Ibid.,* p. 194.

of action, it is also much more in danger of transgressing the normal limits which shelter it from self-destruction. A mind that questions everything, unless strong enough to bear the weight of its ignorance, risks questioning itself and being engulfed in doubt. If it cannot discover the claims to existence of the objects of its questioning—and it would be miraculous if it so soon succeeded in solving so many mysteries—it will deny them all reality, the mere formulation of the problem already implying an inclination to negative solutions. But in so doing it will become void of all positive content and, finding nothing which offers it resistance, will launch itself perforce into the emptiness of inner revery.

But this lofty form of egoistic suicide is not the only one; there is another, more commonplace. Instead of reflecting sadly on his condition, the person makes his decision cheerfully. He knows his own egoism and its logical consequences; but he accepts them in advance and undertakes to live the life of a child or animal, except for his knowledge of what he is doing. He assigns himself the single task of satisfying his personal needs, even simplifying them to make this easier. Knowing that he can hope for nothing better, he asks nothing more, prepared, if unable to reach this single end, to terminate a thenceforth meaningless existence. This is Epicurean suicide. For Epicurus did not enjoin his disciples to hasten their death, but advised them on the contrary to live as long as they found any interest in doing so. Only, as he felt clearly that if a man has no other purpose in life, he risks momentarily having none at all, and as sensual pleasure is a very slight link to attach men to life, he exhorted them always to be ready to leave it, at the least stimulus of circumstance. In this case philosophic, dreamy melancholy is replaced by sceptical, disillusioned matter-of-factness, which becomes especially prominent at the final hour. The sufferer deals himself the blow without hate or anger, but equally with none of the morbid satisfaction with which the intellectual relishes his suicide. He is even more passionless than the latter. He is not surprised at the end to which he has come; he has foreseen it as a more or less impending event. He therefore makes no long preparations; in harmony with all his preceding existence, he only tries to minimize pain. Such especially is the case of those voluptuaries who, when the fatal moment arrives when they can no longer continue their easy existence, kill themselves with ironic tranquillity and a matter-of-course mood.[5]

* * *

When we established the nature of altruistic suicide, sufficient examples were given to make it superfluous to describe its characteristic psychological forms at length. They are the opposite of those characterizing egoistic suicide, as different as altruism itself from its opposite. The egoistic suicide is characterized by a general depression, in the form either of melancholic languor or Epicurean indifference. Altruistic suicide, on the contrary, involves a certain expenditure of energy, since its source is a violent emotion. In the case of obligatory suicide, this energy is controlled by the reason and the will. The individual kills himself at the command of his conscience; he submits to an imperative. Thus, the dominant note of his act is the serene conviction derived from the feeling of duty accomplished; the deaths of Cato and of Commander Beaurepaire are historic types of this. When altruism is at a high pitch, on the other hand, the impulse is more passionate and unthinking. A burst of faith and enthusiasm carries the man to his death. This enthusiasm itself is either happy or somber, depending on the conception of death as a means of union with a beloved deity, or as an expiatory sacrifice, to appease some terrible, probably hostile power. There is no resemblance between the religious fervor of the fanatic who hurls himself joyously beneath the chariot of his idol, that of the monk overcome by *acedia*, or the remorse of the criminal who puts an end to his days to expiate his crime. Yet beneath these superficially different appearances, the essential features of the phenomenon are the same. This is an active suicide, contrasting, accordingly, with the depressed suicide discussed above.

The same quality reappears in the simpler suicides of primitive man or of the soldier, who kill themselves either for a slight offense to their honor or to prove their courage. The ease with which they are performed is not to be confused with the disillusionment and

[5] Examples will be found in Brierre de Boismont, pp. 494 and 506.

matter-of-factness of the Epicurean. The disposition to sacrifice one's life is none the less an active tendency even though it is strongly enough embedded to be effected with the ease and spontaneity of instinct. A case which may be considered the model of this species is reported by Leroy. It concerns an officer, who, after having once unsuccessfully tried to hang himself, prepares to make another attempt but first takes care to record his last impressions: "Mine is a strange destiny! I have just hung myself, had lost consciousness, the rope broke, I fell on my left arm. . . . My new preparations are complete, I shall start again shortly but shall smoke a final pipe first; the last, I hope. I experienced no struggle with my feelings the first time, things went very well; I hope the second will go as well. I am as calm as though I were taking an early morning glass. It's strange, I will confess, but it is so. It is all true. I am about to die a second time with perfect tranquillity." [6] Underneath this tranquillity is neither irony nor scepticism nor the sort of involuntary wincing which the voluptuary never quite manages completely to hide when committing suicide. The man's calmness is perfect; there is no trace of effort, the action is straightforward because all the vital inclinations prepare his course.

* * *

There is, finally, a third sort of persons who commit suicide, contrasting both with the first variety in that their action is essentially passionate, and with the second because this inspiring passion which dominates their last moment is of a wholly different nature. It is neither enthusiasm, religious, moral or political faith, nor any of the military virtues; it is anger and all the emotions customarily associated with disappointment. Brierre de Boismont, who analyzed the papers left behind by 1,507 suicides, found that very many expressed primarily irritation and exasperated weariness. Sometimes they contain blasphemies, violent recriminations against life in general, sometimes threats and accusations against a particular person to whom the responsibility for the suicide's unhappiness is imputed. With this

[6] Leroy, *op. cit.*, p. 241.

group are obviously connected suicides which are preceded by a murder; a man kills himself after having killed someone else whom he accuses of having ruined his life. Never is the suicide's exasperation more obvious than when expressed not only by words but by deeds. The suicidal egoist never yields to such displays of violence. He too, doubtless, at times regrets life, but mournfully. It oppresses him, but does not irritate him by sharp conflicts. It seems empty rather than painful to him. It does not interest him, but it also does not impose positive suffering upon him. His state of depression does not even permit excitement. As for altruistic suicides, they are quite different. Almost by definition, the altruist sacrifices himself and not his fellows. We therefore encounter a third psychological form distinct from the preceding two.

This form clearly appears to be involved in the nature of anomic suicide. Unregulated emotions are adjusted neither to one another nor to the conditions they are supposed to meet; they must therefore conflict with one another most painfully. Anomy, whether progressive or regressive, by allowing requirements to exceed appropriate limits, throws open the door to disillusionment and consequently to disappointment. A man abruptly cast down below his accustomed status cannot avoid exasperation at feeling a situation escape him of which he thought himself master, and his exasperation naturally revolts against the cause, whether real or imaginary, to which he attributes his ruin. If he recognizes himself as to blame for the catastrophe, he takes it out on himself; otherwise, on some one else. In the former case there will be only suicide; in the latter, suicide may be preceded by homicide or by some other violent outburst. In both cases the feeling is the same; only its application varies. The individual always attacks himself in an access of anger, whether or not he has previously attacked another. This reversal of all his habits reduces him to a state of acute over-excitation, which necessarily tends to seek solace in acts of destruction. The object upon whom the passions thus aroused are discharged is fundamentally of secondary importance. The accident of circumstances determines their direction.

It is precisely the same whenever, far from falling below his previous status, a person is impelled in the reverse direction, constantly to surpass himself, but without rule or moderation. Sometimes he misses the goal he thought he could reach, but which was really beyond his powers; his is the suicide of the man misunderstood, very common in days when no recognized social classification is left. Sometimes, after having temporarily succeeded in satisfying all his desires and craving for change, he suddenly dashes against an invincible obstacle, and impatiently renounces an existence thenceforth too restrictive for him. This is the case of Werther, the turbulent heart as he calls himself, enamoured of infinity, killing himself from disappointed love, and the case of all artists who, after having drunk deeply of success, commit suicide because of a chance hiss, a somewhat severe criticism, or because their popularity has begun to wane.[7]

There are yet others who, having no complaint to make of men or circumstances, automatically weary of a palpably hopeless pursuit, which only irritates rather than appeases their desires. They then turn against life in general and accuse it of having deceived them. But the vain excitement to which they are prey leaves in its wake a sort of exhaustion which prevents their disappointed passions from displaying themselves with a violence equal to that of the preceding cases. They are wearied, as it were, at the end of a long course, and thus become incapable of energetic reaction. The person lapses into a sort of melancholy resembling somewhat that of the intellectual egoist but without its languorous charm. The dominating note is a more or less irritated disgust with life. This state of soul was already observed by Seneca among his contemporaries, together with the suicide resulting from it. "The evil which assails us," he writes, "is not in the localities we inhabit but in ourselves. We lack strength to endure the least task, being incapable of suffering pain, powerless to enjoy pleasure, impatient with everything. How many invoke death when, after having tried every sort of change, they find themselves reverting to the same sensations, unable to discover any new experience." [8] In our own day one of the types which perhaps best incarnate this sort of spirit is Chateaubriand's René. While Raphaël is a creature of meditation who finds his ruin within himself, René is the insatiate type. "I am accused," he exclaims unhappily, "of being inconstant in my desires, of never long enjoying the same fancy, of being prey to an imagination eager to sound the depth of my pleasures as though it were overwhelmed by their persistence; I am accused of always miss-

---

[7] See cases in Brierre de Boismont, pp. 187-189.
[8] *De tranquillitate animi*, II, *sub fine*. Cf. Letter XXIV.

ing the goal I might attain. Alas! I only seek an unknown good, the instinct for which pursues me. *Is it my fault if I everywhere find limits, if everything once experienced has no value for me?"* [9]

This description conclusively illustrates the relations and differences between egoistic and anomic suicide, which our sociological analysis had already led us to glimpse.[10] Suicides of both types suffer from what has been called the disease of the infinite. But the disease does not assume the same form in both cases. In one, reflective intelligence is affected and immoderately overnourished; in the other, emotion is over-excited and freed from all restraint. In one, thought, by dint of falling back upon itself, has no object left; in the other, passion, no longer recognizing bounds, has no goal left. The former is lost in the infinity of dreams, the second in the infinity of desires.

Thus, not even the psychological formula concerning the suicide has the simplicity commonly attributed to it. It is no definition to say of him that he is weary of life, disgusted with life, etc. There are really very different varieties of suicides, and these differences appear in the way suicide is performed. Acts and agents may thus be classified in a certain number of species; these species also correspond in essential traits with the types of suicide we have established previously in accordance with the nature of the social causes on which they rest. They are like prolongations of these causes inside of individuals.

We should add, to be sure, that they are not always found in actual experience in a state of purity and isolation. They are very often combined with one another, giving rise to composite varieties; characteristics of several types will be united in a single suicide. The reason for this is that different social causes of suicide themselves may simultaneously affect the same individual and impose their combined effects upon him. Thus invalids fall a prey to deliria of different sorts, involved with one another but all converging in a single direction so as to cause a single act, despite their different origins. They mutually re-enforce each other. Thus again, widely different fevers may coexist in one person and contribute each in its own way and manner to raising the temperature of the body.

[9] *René*, ed. Vialat, Paris, 1849, p. 112.
[10] See above, p. 258.

Two factors of suicide, especially, have a peculiar affinity for one another: namely, egoism and anomy. We know that they are usually merely two different aspects of one social state; thus it is not surprising that they should be found in the same individual. It is, indeed, almost inevitable that the egoist should have some tendency to non-regulation; for, since he is detached from society, it has not sufficient hold upon him to regulate him. If, nevertheless, his desires are not usually excited, it is because in his case the life of the passions languishes, because he is wholly introverted and not attracted by the world outside. But he may be neither a complete egoist nor a pure victim of agitation. In such cases he may play both roles concurrently. To fill up the gap he feels inside himself, he seeks new sensations; he applies, to be sure, less ardour than the passionate temperament properly so-called, but he also wearies sooner and this weariness casts him back upon himself, thus re-enforcing his original melancholy. Inversely, an unregulated temperament does not lack a spark of egoism; for if one were highly socialized one would not rebel at every social restraint. Only, this spark cannot develop in cases where the action of anomy is preponderant; for, by casting its possessor outside himself, it prevents him from retiring into himself. If anomy is less intense, however, it may permit egoism to produce certain characteristic effects. The obstacle, for example, against which the victim of insatiate desires dashes may cause him to fall back upon himself and seek an outlet for his disappointed passions in an inner life. Finding there nothing to which he can attach himself, however, the melancholy inspired by this thought can only drive him to new self-escape, thus increasing his uneasiness and discontent. Thus are produced mixed suicides where depression alternates with agitation, dream with action, transports of desire with reflective sadness.

Anomy may likewise be associated with altruism. One and the same crisis may ruin a person's life, disturb the equilibrium between him and his surroundings, and, at the same time, drive his altruistic disposition to a state which incites him to suicide. Such is notably the case of what we have called suicides of the besieged. If, for example, the Jews killed themselves en masse upon the capture of Jerusalem, it was both because the victory of the Romans, by making them subjects and tributaries of Rome, threatened to transform the sort of life to which they were accustomed and because they loved their city and cult too much to survive the probable destruction of both. Thus it often happens that a bankrupt man kills himself as much because he cannot live on a smaller footing, as to spare his name and family the disgrace of bankruptcy. If officers and non-commissioned officers readily commit suicide just when forced to re-tire, it is also doubtless because of the sudden change about to occur in their way of living, as well as because of their general disposition to attach little value to life. The two causes operate in the same di-rection. There then result suicides where either the passionate exul-tation or the courageous resolution of altruistic suicide blends with the exasperated infatuation produced by anomy.

Finally, egoism and altruism themselves, contraries as they are, may combine their influence. At certain epochs, when disaggregated society can no longer serve as an objective for individual activities, individuals or groups of individuals will nevertheless be found who, while experiencing the influence of this general condition of egoism, aspire to other things. Feeling, however, that a constant passage from one egoistic pleasure to another is a poor method of escaping them-selves, and that fugitive joys, even though constantly renewed, could never quiet their unrest, they seek some durable object to which to attach themselves permanently and which shall give meaning to their lives. Since they are contented with nothing real, however, they can find satisfaction only in creating out of whole cloth some ideal reality to play this role. So in thought they create an imaginary being whose slaves they become and to which they devote themselves the more ex-clusively the more they are detached from everything else, themselves included. To it they assign all the attachment to existence which they ascribe to themselves, since all else is valueless in their eyes. So they live a twofold, contradictory existence: individualists so far as the real world is concerned, they are immoderate altruists in everything that concerns this ideal objective. Both dispositions lead to suicide.

Such are the sources and the nature of Stoic suicide. Immediately above we pointed out its reproduction of certain essential qualities of egoistic suicide; but it may be considered under a totally different as-pect. Though the Stoic professes absolute indifference to everything beyond the range of the individual personality, though he exhorts the individual to be self-sufficient, he simultaneously assigns the in-dividual a close dependence on universal reason, and even reduces him to nothing more than the instrument through which this reason is realized. He thus combines two antagonistic conceptions: the most radical moral individualism and an immoderate pantheism. The suicide he commits is thus both apathetic, like that of the egoist, and performed as a duty like that of the altruist.[11] The former's melancholy and the active energy of the latter appear in this form of suicide; egoism here mingles with mysticism. This same combination also distinguishes the mysticism characteristic of periods of decadence, which, contrary to appearances, is so different from that observed among young, formative peoples. The latter springs from the collective enthusiasm which carries individual wills along with it on its own way, from the self-abnegation with which citizens forget themselves to share in a common work; the former is mere self-conscious egoism, conscious also of its own nothingness, striving to surpass itself but succeeding only artificially and in appearance.

II

One might think *a priori* that some relation existed between the nature of suicide and the kind of death chosen by the one who commits it. It seems quite natural that the means he uses to carry out his resolve should depend on the feelings urging him on and thus express these feelings. We might therefore be tempted to use the data concerning this matter supplied us by statistics to describe the various sorts of suicides more closely, by their external form. But our researches into this matter have given only negative results.

Social causes, however, certainly determine the choice of these means; for the relative frequency of the various ways of committing suicide is invariable for long periods in a given society, while varying very perceptibly from one society to another, as Table XXX shows.

Thus, each people has its favorite sort of death and the other of its preferences changes very rarely. It is even more constant than the total number of suicides; events which sometimes transiently modify the latter do not always affect the former. Moreover, social causes are so preponderant that the influence of cosmic factors does not appear to be appreciable. Thus suicides by drowning, contrary to all presumptions,

---

[11] Seneca praises Cato's suicide as the triumph of the human will over material things (See *De Prov.* 2, 9 and *Ep.* 71, 16).

TABLE XXX—Distribution of the Different Kinds of Death Among 1,000 Suicides (Both Sexes Combined)

Countries & Years		Strangula-tion and Hanging	Drowning	Fire-arms	Leaping from a High Spot	Poison	Asphyxia-tion
France	1872	426	269	103	28	20	69
France	1873	430	298	106	30	21	67
France	1874	440	269	122	28	23	72
France	1875	446	294	107	31	19	63
Prussia	1872	610	197	102	6.9	25	3
Prussia	1873	597	217	95	8.4	25	4.6
Prussia	1874	610	162	126	9.1	28	6.5
Prussia	1875	615	170	105	9.5	35	7.7
England	1872	374	221	38	30	91	....
England	1873	366	218	44	20	97	....
England	1874	374	176	58	20	94	....
England	1875	362	208	45	...	97	....
Italy	1874	174	305	236	106	60	13.7
Italy	1875	173	273	251	104	62	31.4
Italy	1876	125	246	285	113	69	29
Italy	1877	176	299	238	111	55	22

do not vary from one season to another in accordance with any special law. Here is their monthly distribution in France for 1872–78 compared with that of suicides in general:

Share of Each Month in 1,000 Annual Suicides

	Jan.	Feb.	Mar.	Apr.	May	June	July	Aug.	Sept.	Oct.	Nov.	Dec.
Of all sorts	75.8	66.5	84.8	97.3	103.1	109.9	103.5	86.3	74.3	74.1	65.2	59.2
By drowning	73.5	67.0	81.9	94.4	106.4	117.3	107.7	91.2	71.0	74.3	61.0	54.2

Suicides by drowning increase very little more than others during the fine season; the difference is insignificant. Yet it would seem that Summer should favor them exceptionally. It has, to be sure, been said that drowning was less employed in the North than in the South, and this fact has been attributed to climate.[12] But at Copenhagen during the period from 1845 to 1856 this form of suicide was no less common than in Italy, (281 cases per thousand as against 300). None was more common in St. Petersburg during the years 1873–74. So temperature affords no obstacle to this sort of death.

The social causes on which suicides in general depend, however, differ from those which determine the way they are committed; for no relation can be discovered between the types of suicides which we have distinguished and the most common methods of performance.

[12] Morselli, pp. 445-446.

Italy is a fundamentally Catholic country where scientific culture was relatively little developed until recent times. Thus it is very probable that altruistic suicides are more frequent there than in France and Germany, since they occur somewhat in inverse ratio to intellectual development; several reasons to be found in the remainder of this work will confirm this hypothesis. Consequently, as suicide by fire-arms is much more common there than in the central European countries, it might be thought not unconnected with the state of altruism. In support of this supposition, it might also be noted that this is also the sort of suicide preferred by soldiers. Unfortunately, it happens that in France it is the most intellectual classes, authors, artists, officials, who kill themselves oftenest in this way.[13] It might likewise seem that suicide from melancholy finds its natural expression in hanging. Actually, it is most employed in the country, yet melancholy is a state of mind more characteristic of the city.

The causes impelling a man to kill himself are therefore not those determining him to do so in one way rather than in another. The motives which set his choice are of a totally different sort. First, the totality of customs and usages of all kinds, placing one instrument of death rather than another at his disposal. Always following the line of least resistance so long as no opposing factor intervenes, he tends to employ the means of destruction lying nearest to his hand and made familiar to him by daily use. That, for example, is why suicides by throwing one's self from a high place are oftener committed in great cities than in the country: the buildings are higher. Likewise, the more the land is covered with railroads the more general becomes the habit of seeking death by throwing one's self under a train. The table showing the relative share of the different methods of suicide in the total number of voluntary deaths thus partly reproduces the state of industrial technology, of the most wide-spread forms of architecture, of scientific knowledge, etc. As the use of electricity becomes commoner, suicides by means of electric processes will become commoner also.

But perhaps the most powerful cause is the relative dignity attributed by each people, and by each social group within each people, to the different sorts of death. They are far from being regarded as

13 See Lisle, *op. cit.*, p. 94.

all on the same plane. Some are considered nobler, others repel as being vulgar and degrading; and the way opinion classifies them varies with the community. In the army, decapitation is considered an infamous death; elsewhere, it is hanging. This is why suicide by strangulation is much commoner in the country than in the city and in small cities than in large ones. It is because it connotes something gross and violent which conflicts with the gentleness of urban manners and the regard of the cultivated classes for the human body. Perhaps this revulsion is also associated with the dishonorable repute clinging for historical reason to this sort of death, one which is felt more keenly by refined urban populations than is possible for the simpler rural sensibility.

The form of death chosen by the suicide is therefore something entirely foreign to the very nature of suicide. Intimately related as these two elements of a single act seem, they are actually independent of each other. At least, there are only external relations of juxtaposition between them. For while both depend on social causes, the social conditions expressed by them are widely different. The first has nothing to teach us about the second; it was discovered by a wholly different study. That is why we shall not dwell on these various forms longer, though they are customarily treated at some length relative to suicide. To do so would add nothing to the results given by our preceding studies and summarized in the following table:

AETIOLOGICAL AND MORPHOLOGICAL CLASSIFICATION OF THE SOCIAL TYPES OF SUICIDE

Individual Forms Assumed

	Fundamental Character		Secondary Varieties
Basic types	Egoistic suicide	Apathy	Indolent melancholy with self-complacence. The sceptic's disillusioned sangfroid.
	Altruistic suicide	Energy of passion or will	With calm feeling of duty. With mystic enthusiasm. With peaceful courage.
	Anomic suicide	Irritation, disgust	Violent recriminations against life in general. Violent recriminations against one particular person (homicide-suicide).
Mixed types	Ego-anomic suicide		Mixture of agitation and apathy, of action and revery.
	Anomic-altruistic suicide		Exasperated effervesence.
	Ego-altruistic suicide		Melancholy tempered with moral fortitude.

Such are the general characteristics of suicide, that is, those which result directly from social causes. Individualized in particular cases, they are complicated by various nuances depending on the personal temperament of the victim and the special circumstances in which he finds himself. But beneath the variety of combinations thus produced, these fundamental forms are always discoverable.

BOOK THREE
GENERAL NATURE OF SUICIDE AS A SOCIAL PHENOMENON

CHAPTER 1
THE SOCIAL ELEMENT OF SUICIDE

Now that we know the factors in terms of which the social suicide-rate varies, we may define the reality to which this rate corresponds and which it expresses numerically.

I

The individual conditions on which suicide might, *a priori*, be supposed to depend, are of two sorts.

There is first the external situation of the agent. Sometimes men who kill themselves have had family sorrow or disappointments to their pride, sometimes they have had to suffer poverty or sickness, at others they have had some moral fault with which to reproach themselves, etc. But we have seen that these individual peculiarities could not explain the social suicide-rate; for the latter varies in considerable proportions, whereas the different combinations of circumstances which constitute the immediate antecedents of individual cases of suicide retain approximately the same relative frequency. They are therefore not the determining causes of the act which they precede. Their occasionally important role in the premeditation of suicide is no proof of being a causal one. Human deliberations, in fact, so far as reflective consciousness affects them are often only purely formal, with no object but confirmation of a resolve previously formed for reasons unknown to consciousness.

Besides, the circumstances are almost infinite in number which are supposed to cause suicide because they rather frequently accompany it. One man kills himself in the midst of affluence, another in

297

the lap of poverty; one was unhappy in his home, and another had just ended by divorce a marriage which was making him unhappy. In one case a soldier ends his life after having been punished for an offense he did not commit; in another, a criminal whose crime has remained unpunished kills himself. The most varied and even the most contradictory events of life may equally serve as pretexts for suicide. This suggests that none of them is the specific cause. Could we perhaps at least ascribe causality to those qualities known to be common to all? But are there any such? At best one might say that they usually consist of disappointments, of sorrows, without any possibility of deciding how intense the grief must be to have such tragic significance. Of no disappointment in life, no matter how insignificant, can we say in advance that it could not possibly make existence intolerable; and, on the other hand, there is none which must necessarily have this effect. We see some men resist horrible misfortune, while others kill themselves after slight troubles. Moreover, we have shown that those who suffer most are not those who kill themselves most. Rather it is too great comfort which turns a man against himself. Life is most readily renounced at the time and among the classes where it is least harsh. At least, if it really sometimes occurs that the victim's personal situation is the effective cause of his resolve, such cases are very rare indeed and accordingly cannot explain the social suicide-rate.

Accordingly, even those who have ascribed most influence to individual conditions have sought these conditions less in such external incidents than in the intrinsic nature of the person, that is, his biological constitution and the physical concomitants on which it depends. Thus, suicide has been represented as the product of a certain temperament, an episode of neurasthenia, subject to the effects of the same factors as neurasthenia. Yet we have found no immediate and regular relationship between neurasthenia and the social suicide-rate. The two facts even vary at times in inverse proportion to one another, one being at its minimum just when and where the other is at its height. We have not found, either, any definite relation between the variations of suicide and the conditions of physical environment supposed to have most effect on the nervous system, such as race, climate, temperature. Obviously, though the neuropath may show some inclination to suicide under certain conditions, he is not necessarily destined to kill himself; and the influence of cosmic factors is not enough to determine in just this sense the very general tendencies of his nature.

Wholly different are the results we obtained when we forgot the individual and sought the causes of the suicidal aptitude of each society in the nature of the societies themselves. The relations of suicide to certain states of social environment are as direct and constant as its relations to facts of a biological and physical character were seen to be uncertain and ambiguous. Here at last we are face to face with real laws, allowing us to attempt a methodical classification of types of suicide. The sociological causes thus determined by us have even explained these various concurrences often attributed to the influence of material causes, and in which a proof of this influence has been sought. If women kill themselves much less often than men, it is because they are much less involved than men in collective existence; thus they feel its influence—good or evil—less strongly. So it is with old persons and children, though for other reasons. Finally, if suicide increases from January to June but then decreases, it is because social activity shows similar seasonal fluctuations. It is therefore natural that the different effects of social activity should be subject to an identical rhythm, and consequently be more pronounced during the former of these two periods. Suicide is one of them.

The conclusion from all these facts is that the social suicide-rate can be explained only sociologically. At any given moment the moral constitution of society establishes the contingent of voluntary deaths. There is, therefore, for each people a collective force of a definite amount of energy, impelling men to self-destruction. The victim's acts which at first seem to express only his personal temperament are really the supplement and prolongation of a social condition which they express externally.

This answers the question posed at the beginning of this work. It is not mere metaphor to say of each human society that it has a greater or lesser aptitude for suicide; the expression is based on the nature of things. Each social group really has a collective inclination for the act, quite its own, and the source of all individual inclination, rather than their result. It is made up of the currents of egoism, altruism or anomy running through the society under consideration with the tendencies to languorous melancholy, active renunciation or exasperated weariness derivative from these currents. These tendencies of the whole social body, by affecting individuals, cause them to commit suicide. The private experiences usually thought to be the proximate causes of suicide have only the influence borrowed from the victim's moral predisposition, itself an echo of the moral state of society. To explain his detachment from life the individual accuses his most immediately surrounding circumstances; life is sad to him because he is sad. Of course his sadness comes to him from without in one sense, however not from one or another incident of his career but rather from the group to which he belongs. This is why there is nothing which cannot serve as an occasion for suicide. It all depends on the intensity with which suicidogenetic causes have affected the individual.

II

Besides, the stability of the social suicide-rate would itself sufficiently show the truth of this conclusion. Though we have, for methodological reasons, delayed the problem until now, it will nevertheless admit of no other solution.

When Quételet drew to the attention of philosophers [1] the remarkable regularity with which certain social phenomena repeat themselves during identical periods of time, he thought he could account for it by his theory of the average man—a theory, moreover, which has remained the only systematic explanation of this remarkable fact. According to him, there is a definite type in each society more or less exactly reproduced by the majority, from which only the minority tends to deviate under the influence of disturbing causes. For example, there is a sum total of physical and moral characteristics represented by the majority of Frenchmen and not found in the same

[1] Especially in his two works *Sur l'homme et le développement de ses facultés ou Essai de physique sociale*, 2 vol., Paris, 1835, and *Du système social et des lois qui le régissent*, Paris 1848. If Quételet is the first to try to give a scientific explanation of this regularity, he is not the first to have observed it. The true founder of moral statistics is Pastor Süssmilch, in his work, *Die Göttliche Ordnung in den Veränderungen des menschlichen Geschlechts, aus der Geburt, dem Tode und der Fortpflanzung desselben erwiesen*, 3 vol., 1742.

See on the same question: Wagner, *Die Gesetzmässigkeit*, etc., first part; Drobisch, *Die Moralische Statistik und die menschliche Willensfreiheit*, Leipzig, 1867 (especially pp. 1-58) ; Mayr, *Die Gesetzmässigkeit im Gesellschaftsleben*, Munich, 1877; Oettingen, *Moralstatistik*, p. 90 and ff.

manner or degree among the Italians or the Germans, As these characteristics are by definition much the mo the actions deriving from them are also much the mo these constitute the great groups. Those, on the contrary, by divergent qualities are relatively rare, like these qua ....nem- selves. Again, though not absolutely unchangeable, this general type varies much more slowly than an individual type; for it is much more difficult for a society to change en masse than for one or a few individuals, singly, to do so. This stability naturally recurs in the acts derived from the characteristic attributes of this type; the former remain the same in quantity and quality so long as the latter do not change, and as these same ways of behaviour are also the commonest, stability must necessarily be the general law of those manifestations of human activity described by statistics. The statistician, in fact, takes into account all events of an identical nature which occur within a given society. Therefore, since most of them remain invariable so long as the general type of the society is unchanged, and since, on the other hand, its changes are unusual, the results of statistical enumerations must necessarily remain the same for fairly long series of consecutive years. Facts derived from special qualities and individual occurrences are not, to be sure, subject to the same regularity; therefore, stability is never absolute. But they are the exception; this is why invariability is the rule, while change is exceptional.

Quételet gave the name *average type* to this general type, because it is obtained almost exactly by taking the arithmetic mean of the individual types. If, for example, after having determined the height of all persons in a given social group, one adds them and divides by the number of individuals measured, the result arrived at expresses with quite sufficient accuracy the most common height. For the differences of greater or less, the giants and dwarfs, probably are about equal in number. Thus they offset each other, annul each other mutually and accordingly have no effect on the quotient.

The theory seems very simple. But first, it can only be considered as an explanation if it shows how the average type is realized in the great majority of individuals. For the average type to remain constantly equal to itself while they change, it must be to some extent independent of them; and yet it must also have some way of insinuating itself into them. Of course, the question ceases to be significant if the average type is admitted to be the same as the ethnic type. For the constituent elements of the race, having their origin outside the individual, are not subject to the same variations as he; and yet they are realized only in him. They can thus well be supposed to penetrate the truly individual elements and even act as their base. Only, for this explanation to apply to suicide, the tendency impelling a man to kill himself must depend strictly on race; but we know that the facts contradict this hypothesis. Shall we suppose that the general condition of the social environment, being the same for most individuals, affects nearly all in the same way and so partially bestows a common appearance on them. But the social environment is fundamentally one of common ideas, beliefs, customs and tendencies. For them to impart themselves thus to individuals, they must somehow exist independently of individuals; and this approaches the solution we suggested. For thus is implicitly acknowledged the existence of a collective inclination to suicide from which individual inclinations are derived, and our whole problem is to know of what it consists and how it acts.

But there are still other considerations. However the preponderance of the average man is explained, this conception could never account for the regularity of the reproduction of the social suicide-rate. Actually, by definition, the only possible characteristics this type involves are those found in the major part of the population. But suicide is the act of a minority. In the countries where it is most common, 300 or 400 cases per million inhabitants at most are found. It is radically excluded by the average man's instinct of self-preservation; the average man does not kill himself. But in that case, if the inclination to self-destruction is rare and anomalous, it is wholly foreign to the average type and so, even a profound knowledge of the latter could not even explain the source of suicides, still less help us understand the stability of the number of suicides in a given society. In short, Quételet's theory rests on an inaccurate observation. He thought it certain that stability occurs only in the most general manifestations of human activity; but it is equally found in the sporadic manifestations which occur only at rare and isolated points of the social field. He thought he had met all the requirements by showing how, as a last resort, one could explain the invariability of what is not exceptional; but the exception itself has its own invariability, inferior to none. Everyone dies; every living organism is so made up that it cannot escape dissolution. There are, on the contrary, very few people who kill themselves; the great majority of men have no inclination to suicide. Yet the suicide-rate is even more stable than that of general mortality. The close connection which Quételet sees between the commonness of a quality and its permanence therefore does not exist.

Besides, the results to which his own method leads confirm this conclusion. By his principle, in order to calculate the intensity of any quality belonging to the average type, one must divide the sum of the items displaying this quality within the society under consideration by the number of individuals capable of producing them. Thus, in a country like France, where for a long time there have not been more than 150 suicides per million inhabitants, the average intensity of the suicidal inclination would be expressed by the proportion 150/1,000,000 or 0.00015; and in England, where there are only 80 cases for an equal number, this proportion would be only 0.00008. There would therefore be an inclination to suicide, of this strength, in the average individual. But such figures practically amount to zero. So weak an inclination is so far from an act that it may be considered non-existent. It has not strength enough to occasion a single suicide unaided. It is not, therefore, the commonness of such an inclination which can explain why so many suicides are committed annually in one or the other of these two societies.

Even this estimate is infinitely exaggerated. Quételet reached it only by arbitrarily ascribing a certain affinity for suicide to men on the average, and by estimating the strength of this affinity according to manifestations not observed in the average man, but only among a small number of exceptional persons. Thus, the abnormal was used to determine the normal. To be sure, Quételet thought to escape this objection by noting that abnormal cases, which occur sometimes in one and sometimes in the other direction, mutually compensate and offset each other. But such compensation occurs only for qualities which are found in varying degrees in everybody, such as height. We may in fact assume that unusually tall and unusually short persons are about numerically equal to each other. The average of these exceptional heights may therefore practically be equal to the most usual height: so that only the latter appears at the end of the total calculation. The contrary actually takes place in regard to a naturally exceptional fact, such as the suicidal inclination. In this case Quételet's procedure can only artificially introduce into the average type an element which falls outside the average. To be sure, as we have just seen, it occurs there only in a very dilute state, precisely because the number of individuals among whom it is distributed is far greater than it should be. But if the mistake is of little practical importance, it none the less exists.

In reality, the meaning of the relation calculated by Quételet is simply the probability that a single man belonging to a definite social group will kill himself during the year. If there are 15 suicides annually in a population of 100,000 souls, we may well conclude that there are 15 chances in 100,000 that some person will commit suicide during this same unit of time. But this probability in no sense gives us a measure of the average inclination to suicide, or helps prove the existence of such an inclination. The fact that so many individuals out of 100 kill themselves does not imply that the others are exposed to any degree and can teach us nothing concerning the nature and intensity of the causes leading to suicide.[2]

Thus the theory of the average man does not solve the problem. Let us take the problem up again, then, and see how it presents itself. Victims of suicide are in an infinite minority, which is widely dispersed; each one of them performs his act separately, without knowing that others are doing the same; and yet, so long as society remains unchanged the number of suicides remains the same. Therefore, all these individual manifestations, however independent of one another they seem, must surely actually result from a single cause or a single group of causes, which dominate individuals. Other-

[2] These considerations are one more proof that race cannot account for the social suicide-rate. The ethnic type, indeed, is itself also a generic type; it includes only characteristics common to a considerable mass of individuals. Suicide, on the contrary, is an exceptional occurrence. Race therefore contains nothing which could determine suicide; otherwise it would be more general than it actually is. Shall it be said that though none of the elements constituting race could be regarded as a sufficient cause of suicide, race according to its nature may nevertheless make men more or less accessible to the causes giving rise to suicide? But then, even if facts verified this hypothesis, which is not the case, one would at least have to recognize that the ethnic type is a factor of very mediocre efficacy, since its supposed influence could not manifest itself in the vast majority of cases and would appear only very exceptionally. In brief, race cannot explain how out of a million persons all of whom belong to the same race, only 100 or 200 at most kill themselves annually.

wise how could we explain that all these individual wills, ignorant of one another's existence, annually achieve the same end in the same numbers? At least for the most part they have no effect upon one another; they are in no way conjoined; yet everything takes place as if they were obeying a single order. There must then be some force in their common environment inclining them all in the same direction, whose greater or lesser strength causes the greater or less number of individual suicides. Now the effects revealing this force vary not according to organic and cosmic environments but solely according to the state of the social environment. This force must then be collective. In other words, each people has collectively an inclination of its own to suicide, on which the size of its contribution to voluntary death depends.

From this point of view there is no longer anything mysterious about the stability of the suicide-rate, any more than about its individual manifestations. For since each society has its own temperament, unchangeable within brief periods, and since this inclination to suicide has its source in the moral constitution of groups, it must differ from group to group and in each of them remain for long periods practically the same. It is one of the essential elements of social coenaesthesia. Now this coenaesthetic state, among collective existences as well as among individuals, is their most personal and unchangeable quality, because nothing is more fundamental. But then the effects springing from it must have both the same personality and the same stability. It is even natural for them to possess a higher stability than that of general mortality. For temperature, climatic and geological influences, in a word the various conditions on which public health depends, change much more readily from year to year than the temperament of peoples.

There is however another hypothesis, apparently different from the above, which might be tempting to some minds. To solve the difficulty, might we not suppose that the various incidents of private life considered to be preeminently the causes determining suicide, regularly recur annually in the same proportions? Let us suppose [3] that every year there are roughly the same number of unhappy marriages, bankruptcies, disappointed ambitions, cases of poverty, etc. Numerically the same and analogously situated, individuals would

[3] This is fundamentally Drobisch's opinion in his work cited above.

then naturally form the resolve suggested by their situation, in the same numbers. One need not assume that they yield to a superior influence; but merely that they reason generally in the same way when confronted by the same circumstances.

But we know that these individual events, though preceding suicides with fair regularity, are not their real causes. To repeat, no unhappiness in life necessarily causes a man to kill himself unless he is otherwise so inclined. The regularity of possible recurrence of these various circumstances thus cannot explain the regularity of suicide. Whatever influence is ascribed to them, moreover, such a solution would at best change the problem without solving it. For it remains to be understood why these desperate situations are identically repeated annually, pursuant to a law peculiar to each country. How does it happen that a given, supposedly stable society always has the same number of disunited families, of economic catastrophes, etc.? This regular recurrence of identical events in proportions constant within the same population but very inconstant from one population to another would be inexplicable had not each society definite currents impelling its inhabitants with a definite force to commercial and industrial ventures, to behaviour of every sort likely to involve families in trouble, etc. This is to return under a very slightly different form to the same hypothesis which had been thought refuted.[4]

III

Let us make an effort to grasp the meaning and import of the terms just employed.

[4] This line of argument holds true not only of suicide, though more striking in that than in any other case. It is identically applicable to crime in its different forms. The criminal indeed is an exceptional being like the suicide, and thus the nature of the average type cannot explain the trends of criminality. But this is no less true of marriage, although the tendency to marry is more general than that to kill or to kill one's self. At each period of life the number of people who marry is only a small minority with reference to the unmarried population of the same age. Thus in France, from 25 to 30 years of age or when the marriage rate is at its highest, only 176 men and 135 women per year marry per 1,000 unmarried of each sex (period 1877–81). If, therefore, the tendency to marriage, which must not be confused with the taste for sexual intercourse, has sufficient strength to find satisfaction among only a few, the marriage rate at a given moment cannot be explained by the strength of this tendency in the average type. In truth, here as in the case of suicide, statistical figures express not the mean intensity of individual dispositions but that of the collective impulse to marriage.

Usually when collective tendencies or passions are spoken of, we tend to regard these expressions as mere metaphors and manners of speech with no real signification but a sort of average among a certain number of individual states. They are not considered as things, forces *sui generis* which dominate the consciousness of single individuals. None the less this is their nature, as is brilliantly [5] shown by statistics of suicide. The individuals making up a society change from year to year, yet the number of suicides is the same so long as the society itself does not change. The population of Paris renews itself very rapidly; yet the share of Paris in the total of French suicides remains practically the same. Although only a few years suffice to change completely the personnel of the army, the rate of military suicides varies only very slowly in a given nation. In all countries the evolution of collective life follows a given rhythm throughout the year; it grows from January to about July and then diminishes. Thus, though the members of the several European societies spring from widely different average types, the seasonal and even monthly variations of suicide take place in accordance with the same law. Likewise, regardless of the diversity of individual temperaments, the relation between the aptitude for suicide of married persons and that of widowers and widows is identically the same in widely differing social groups, from the simple fact that the moral condition of widowhood everywhere bears the same relation to the moral constitution characteristic of marriage. The causes which thus fix the contingent of voluntary deaths for a given society or one part of it must then be independent of individuals, since they retain the same intensity no matter what particular persons they operate on. One would think that an unchanging manner of life would produce unchanging effects. This is true; but a way of life is something, and its unchanging character requires explanation. If a way of life is unchanged while changes occur constantly among those who practise it, it cannot derive its entire reality from them.

It has been thought that this conclusion might be avoided through the observation that this very continuity was the work of individuals and that, consequently, to account for it there was no need to ascribe to social phenomena a sort of transcendency in relation to individual

---

[5] However, such statistics are not the only ones to do so. All the facts of moral statistics imply this conclusion, as the preceding note suggests.

SUICIDE

life. Actually, it has been said, "anything social, whether a word of a language, a religious rite, an artisan's skill, an artistic method, a legal statute or a moral maxim is transmitted and passes from an individual parent, teacher, friend, neighbor, or comrade to another individual."[6]

Doubtless if we had only to explain the general way in which an idea or sentiment passes from one generation to another, how it is that the memory of it is not lost, this explanation might as a last resort be considered satisfactory.[7] But the transmission of facts such as suicide and, more broadly speaking, such as the various acts reported by moral statistics, has a very special nature not to be so readily accounted for. It relates, in fact, not merely in general to a certain way of acting, *but to the number of cases in which this way of acting is employed.* Not merely are there suicides every year, but there are as a general rule as many each year as in the year preceding. The state of mind which causes men to kill themselves is not purely and simply transmitted, but—something much more remarkable—transmitted to an equal number of persons, all in such situations as to make the state of mind become an act. How can this be if only individuals are concerned? The number as such cannot be directly transmitted. Today's population has not learned from yesterday's the size of the contribution it must make to suicide; nevertheless, it will make one of identical size with that of the past, unless circumstances change.

Are we then to imagine that, in some way, each suicide had as his initiator and teacher one of the victims of the year before and that he is something like his moral heir? Only thus can one conceive the pos-

---

[6] Tarde, *La sociologie élémentaire,* in *Annales de l'Institut international de sociologie,* p. 213.

[7] We say "as a last resort" for the essence of the problem could not be solved in this way. The really important thing if this continuity is to be explained is to show not merely how customary practices of a certain period are not forgotten in a subsequent one, but how they preserve their authority and continue to function. The mere fact that new generations may know by way of transmissions solely between individuals, what their ancestors did, does not mean that they have to do the same. What does oblige them, then? The respect for custom, the authority of past generations? In that case the cause of the continuity is no longer individuals serving as vehicles for ideas or practices, but the highly collective state of mind which causes ancestors to be regarded with an especial respect among a certain people. And this state of mind is imposed on individuals. Like the tendency to suicide, this state of mind in a given society even has a definite intensity, depending on the greater or lesser degree with which individuals conform to tradition.

sibility that the social suicide-rate is perpetuated by way of inter-individual traditions. For if the total figure cannot be transmitted as a whole, the units composing it must be transmitted singly. According to this idea, each suicide would have received his tendency from some one of his predecessors and each act of suicide would be something like the echo of a preceding one. But not a fact exists to permit the assumption of such a personal filiation between each of these moral occurrences statistically registered this year, for example, and a similar event of the year before. As has been shown above, it is quite exceptional for an act to be inspired in this way by another of like nature. Besides, why should these ricochets occur regularly from year to year? Why should the generating act require a year to produce its counterpart? Finally, why should it inspire a single copy only? For surely each model must be reproduced only once on the average, or the total would not be constant. Such an hypothesis, as arbitrary as it is difficult to conceive, we need discuss no longer. But if it is dropped, if the numerical equality of annual contingents does not result from each particular case producing its counterpart in the ensuing period, it can only be due to the permanent action of some impersonal cause which transcends all individual cases.

The terms therefore must be strictly understood. Collective tendencies have an existence of their own; they are forces as real as cosmic forces, though of another sort; they, likewise, affect the individual from without, though through other channels. The proof that the reality of collective tendencies is no less than that of cosmic forces is that this reality is demonstrated in the same way, by the uniformity of effects. When we find that the number of deaths varies little from year to year, we explain this regularity by saying that mortality depends on the climate, the temperature, the nature of the soil, in brief on a certain number of material forces which remain constant through changing generations because independent of individuals. Since, therefore, moral acts such as suicide are reproduced not merely with an equal but with a greater uniformity, we must likewise admit that they depend on forces external to individuals. Only, since these forces must be of a moral order and since, except for individual men, there is no other moral order of existence in the world but society, they must be social. But whatever they are called, the important thing is to recognize their reality and conceive of them as a totality of forces which cause us to act from without, like the physico-chemical forces to which we react. So truly are they things *sui generis* and not mere verbal entities that they may be measured, their relative sizes compared, as is done with the intensity of electric currents or luminous foci. Thus, the basic proposition that social facts are objective, a proposition we have had the opportunity to prove in another work [8] and which we consider the fundamental principle of the sociological method, finds a new and especially conclusive proof in moral statistics and above all in the statistics of suicide. Of course, it offends common sense. But science has encountered incredulity whenever it has revealed to men the existence of a force that has been overlooked. Since the system of accepted ideas must be modified to make room for the new order of things and to establish new concepts, men's minds resist through mere inertia. Yet this understanding must be reached. If there is such a science as sociology, it can only be the study of a world hitherto unknown, different from those explored by the other sciences. This world is nothing if not a system of realities.

But just because it encounters traditional prejudices this conception has aroused objections to which we must reply.

First, it implies that collective tendencies and thoughts are of a different nature from individual tendencies and thoughts, that the former have characteristics which the latter lack. How can this be, it is objected, since there are only individuals in society? But, reasoning thus, we should have to say that there is nothing more in animate nature than inorganic matter, since the cell is made exclusively of inanimate atoms. To be sure, it is likewise true that society has no other active forces than individuals; but individuals by combining form a psychical existence of a new species, which consequently has its own manner of thinking and feeling. Of course the elementary qualities of which the social fact consists are present in germ in individual minds. But the social fact emerges from them only when they have been transformed by association since it is only then that it appears. Association itself is also an active factor productive of special effects. In itself it is therefore something new. When the consciousness of individuals, instead of remaining isolated, becomes grouped and combined, something in the world has been altered. Naturally

[8] See *Règles de la méthode sociologique,* ch. II.

this change produces others, this novelty engenders other novelties, phenomena appear whose characteristic qualities are not found in the elements composing them.

This proposition could only be opposed by agreeing that a whole is qualitatively identical with the sum of its parts, that an effect is qualitatively reducible to the sum of its productive causes; which amounts to denying all change or to making it inexplicable. Someone has, however, gone so far as to sustain this extreme thesis, but only two truly extraordinary reasons have been found for its defense. First, it has been said that "in sociology we have through a rare privilege intimate knowledge both of that element which is our individual consciousness and of the compound which is the sum of consciousness in individuals"; secondly, that through this two-fold introspection "we clearly ascertain that if the individual is subtracted nothing remains of the social." [9]

The first assertion is a bold denial of all contemporary psychology. Today it is generally recognized that psychical life, far from being directly cognizable, has on the contrary profound depths inaccessible to ordinary perception, to which we attain only gradually by devious and complicated paths like those employed by the sciences of the external world. The nature of consciousness is therefore far from lacking in mystery for the future. The second proposition is purely arbitrary. The author may of course state that in his personal opinion nothing real exists in society but what is individual, but proofs supporting this statement are lacking and discussion is therefore impossible. It would be only too easy to oppose to this the contrary feeling of a great many persons, who conceive of society not as the form spontaneously assumed by individual nature on expanding outwardly, but as an antagonistic force restricting individual natures and resisted by them! What a remarkable intuition it is, by the way, that lets us know directly and without intermediary both the element—the individual—and the compound, society? If we had really only to open our eyes and take a good look to perceive at once the laws of the social world, sociology would be useless or at least very simple. Unfortunately, facts show only too clearly the incompetence of consciousness in this matter. Never would consciousness have dreamt, of its own accord, of the necessity which annually reproduces demo-

[9] Tarde, *op. cit.*, in *Annales de l'Institut de sociol.*, p. 222.

SUICIDE

graphic phenomena in equal numbers, had it not received a suggestion from without. Still less can it discover their causes, if left to its own devices.

But by separating social from individual life in this manner, we do not mean that there is nothing psychical about the former. On the contrary, it is clear that essentially social life is made up of representations. Only these collective representations are of quite another character from those of the individual. We see no objection to calling sociology a variety of psychology, if we carefully add that social psychology has its own laws which are not those of individual psychology. An example will make the thought perfectly clear. Usually the origin of religion is ascribed to feelings of fear or reverence inspired in conscious persons by mysterious and dreaded beings; from this point of view, religion seems merely like the development of individual states of mind and private feelings. But this over-simplified explanation has no relation to facts. It is enough to note that the institution of religion is unknown to the animal kingdom, where social life is always very rudimentary, that it is never found except where a collective organization exists, that it varies with the nature of societies, in order to conclude justifiably that exclusively men in groups think along religious lines. The individual would never have risen to the conception of forces which so immeasurably surpass him and all his surroundings, had he known nothing but himself and the physical universe. Not even the great natural forces to which he has relations could have suggested such a notion to him; for he was originally far from having his present knowledge of the extent of their dominance; on the contrary, he then believed that he could control them under certain conditions.[10] Science taught him how much he was their inferior. The power thus imposed on his respect and become the object of his adoration is society, of which the gods were only the hypostatic form. Religion is in a word the system of symbols by means of which society becomes conscious of itself; it is the characteristic way of thinking of collective existence. Here then is a great group of states of mind which would not have originated if individual states of consciousness had not combined, and which result from this union and are superadded to those which derive from individual natures. In spite of the minutest possible analysis of the

[10] See Frazer, *Golden Bough*, p. 9 ff.

latter, they will never serve to explain the foundation and development of the strange beliefs and practices from which sprang totemism, the origin of naturism from it and how naturism itself became on the one hand the abstract religion of Jahwe, on the other, the polytheism of the Greeks and Romans, etc. All we mean by affirming the distinction between the social and the individual is that the above observations apply not only to religion, but to law, morals, customs, political institutions, pedagogical practices, etc., in a word to all forms of collective life.[11]

Another objection has been made, at first glance apparently more serious. Not only have we admitted that the social states of mind are qualitatively different from individual ones, but that they are in a sense exterior to individuals. We have not even hesitated to compare this quality of being external with that of physical forces. But, it is objected, since there is nothing in society except individuals, how could there be anything external to them?

If the objection were well founded we should face an antinomy. For we must not lose sight of what has been proved already. Since the handful of people who kill themselves annually do not form a natural group, and are not in communication with one another, the stable number of suicides can only be due to the influence of a common cause which dominates and survives the individual persons involved. The force uniting the conglomerate multitude of individual cases, scattered over the face of the earth, must necessarily be external to each of them. If it were really impossible for it to be so, the problem would be insoluble. But the impossibility is only apparent.

First, it is not true that society is made up only of individuals; it also includes material things, which play an essential role in the common life. The social fact is sometimes so far materialized as to become an element of the external world. For instance, a definite type of architecture is a social phenomenon; but it is partially em-

---

[11] Let us add, to avoid any misunderstanding, that despite all the above we do not admit that there is a precise point at which the individual comes to an end and the social realm commences. Association is not established and does not produce its effects all at once; it requires time and there are consequently moments at which the reality is indeterminate. Thus we pass without interval from one order of facts to the other; but this is no reason for not distinguishing them. Otherwise nothing in the world would be distinct, since there are no distinct genera and evolution is continuous.

bodied in houses and buildings of all sorts which, once constructed, become autonomous realities, independent of individuals. It is the same with the avenues of communication and transportation, with instruments and machines used in industry or private life which express the state of technology at any moment in history, of written language, etc. Social life, which is thus crystallized, as it were, and fixed on material supports, is by just so much externalized, and acts upon us from without. Avenues of communication which have been constructed before our time give a definite direction to our activities, depending on whether they connect us with one or another country. A child's taste is formed as he comes into contact with the monuments of national taste bequeathed by previous generations. At times such monuments even disappear and are forgotten for centuries, then, one day when the nations which reared them are long since extinct, reappear and begin a new existence in the midst of new societies. This is the character of those very social phenomena called Renaissances. A Renaissance is a portion of social life which, after being, so to speak, deposited in material things and remaining long latent there, suddenly reawakens and alters the intellectual and moral orientation of peoples who had had no share in its construction. Doubtless it could not be reanimated if living centers of consciousness did not exist to receive its influence; but these individual conscious centers would have thought and felt quite differently if this influence were not present.

The same remark applies to the definite formulae into which the dogmas of faith are precipitated, or legal precepts when they become fixed externally in a consecrated form. However well digested, they would of course remain dead letters if there were no one to conceive their significance and put them into practice. But though they are not self-sufficient, they are none the less in their own way factors of social activity. They have a manner of action of their own. Juridical relations are widely different depending on whether or not the law is written. Where there is a constituted code, jurisprudence is more regular but less flexible, legislation more uniform but also more rigid. Legislation adapts itself less readily to a variety of individual cases, and resists innovations more strongly. The material forms it assumes are thus not merely ineffective verbal combinations but active realities, since they produce effects which would not occur without their existence. They are not only external to individual consciousness, but this very externality establishes their specific qualities. Because these forms are less at the disposal of individuals, individuals cannot readily adjust them to circumstances, and this very situation makes them more resistant to change.

Of course it is true that not all social consciousness achieves such externalization and materialization. Not all the aesthetic spirit of a nation is embodied in the works it inspires; not all of morality is formulated in clear precepts. The greater part is diffused. There is a large collective life which is at liberty; all sorts of currents come, go, circulate everywhere, cross and mingle in a thousand different ways, and just because they are constantly mobile are never crystalized in an objective form. Today, a breath of sadness and discouragement descends on society; tomorrow, one of joyous confidence will uplift all hearts. For a while the whole group is swayed towards individualism; a new period begins and social and philanthropic aims become paramount. Yesterday cosmopolitanism was the rage, today patriotism has the floor. And all these eddies, all these fluxes and refluxes occur without a single modification of the main legal and moral precepts, immobilized in their sacrosanct forms. Besides, these very precepts merely express a whole sub-jacent life of which they partake; they spring from it but do not supplant it. Beneath all these maxims are actual, living sentiments, summed up by these formulae but only as in a superficial envelope. The formulae would awake no echo if they did not correspond to definite emotions and impressions scattered through society. If, then, we ascribe a kind of reality to them, we do not dream of supposing them to be the whole of moral reality. That would be to take the sign for the thing signified. A sign is certainly something; it is not a kind of supererogatory epiphenomenon; its role in intellectual development is known today. But after all it is only a sign.[12]

But because this part of collective life has not enough consistency to become fixed, it none the less has the same character as the formu-

[12] We do not expect to be reproached further, after this explanation, with wishing to substitute the exterior for the interior in sociology. We start from the exterior because it alone is immediately given, but only to reach the interior. Doubtless the procedure is complicated; but there is no other unless one would risk having his research apply to his personal feeling concerning the order of facts under investigation, instead of to this factual order itself.

lated precepts of which we were just speaking. *It is external to each average individual taken singly.* Suppose some great public danger arouses a gust of patriotic feeling. A collective impulse follows, by virtue of which society as a whole assumes axiomatically that private interests, even those usually regarded most highly, must be wholly effaced before the common interest. And the principle is not merely uttered as an *ideal;* if need be it is literally applied. Meanwhile, take a careful look at the average body of individuals. Among very many of them you will recapture something of this moral state of mind, though infinitely attenuated. The men who are ready to make freely so complete a self-abnegation are rare, even in time of war. *Therefore there is not one of all the single centers of consciousness who make up the great body of the nation, to whom the collective current is not almost wholly exterior, since each contains only a spark of it.*

The same thing is observable in respect to even the stablest, most fundamental moral sentiments. Every society, for example, has a respect for the life of man in general, the intensity of which is determined by and commensurate with, the relative [13] weight of the penalties attached to homicide. The average man, on the other hand, certainly feels something of the same sort, but far less and in a quite different way from society. To appreciate this difference, we need only compare the emotion one may individually feel at sight of the murderer or even of the murder, and that which seizes assembled crowds under the same circumstances. We know how far they may be carried if unchecked. It is because, in this case, anger is collective. The same difference constantly appears between the manner in which society resents these crimes and the way in which they affect individuals; that is, between the individual and the social form of the sentiment offended. Social indignation is so strong that it is very often satisfied only by supreme expiation. The private person, however, provided that the victim is unknown or of no interest to him,

[13] To discover whether this sentiment of respect is stronger in one society or another, not only the intrinsic violence of the repressive measures should be considered, but the position of the penalty in the penal scale. Premeditated murder is punished solely by death, today as in past centuries. But today unadorned punishment by death has a greater relative significance; for it is the supreme punishment, whereas heretofore it could be aggravated. And since these aggravations were not then applied to ordinary murder, it follows that the latter was the object of lesser reprobation.

that the criminal does not live near and thus constitute a personal threat to him, though thinking it proper for the crime to be punished, is not strongly enough stirred to feel a real need for vengeance. He will not take a step to discover the guilty one; he will even hesitate to give him up. Only when public opinion is aroused, as the saying goes, does the matter take on a different aspect. Then we become more active and demanding. But it is opinion speaking through us; we act under the pressure of the collectivity, not as individuals.

Indeed, the distance between the social state and its individual repercussions is usually even greater. In the above case, the collective sentiment, in becoming individualized, retained, at least among most people, strength enough to resist acts by which it is offended; horror at the shedding of human blood is sufficiently deeply enrooted in most consciences today to prevent the outburst of homicidal thoughts. But mere misappropriation, quiet, non-violent fraud, are far from inspiring us with equal aversion. Not many have enough respect for another's rights to stifle in the germ every wish to enrich themselves fraudulently. Not that education does not develop a certain distaste for all unjust actions. But what a difference between this vague, hesitant feeling, ever ready for compromise, and the categorical, unreserved and open stigma with which society punishes theft in all shapes! And what of so many other duties still less rooted in the ordinary man, such as the one that bids us contribute our just share to public expense, not to defraud the public treasury, not to try to avoid military service, to execute contracts faithfully, etc.? If morality in all these respects were only guaranteed by the uncertain feelings of the average conscience, it would be extremely unprotected.

So it is a profound mistake to confuse the collective type of a society, as is so often done, with the average type of its individual members. The morality of the average man is of only moderate intensity. He possesses only the most indispensable ethical principles to any decided degree, and even they are far from being as precise and authoritative as in the collective type, that is, in society as a whole. This, which is the very mistake committed by Quételet, makes the origin of morality an insoluble problem. For since the individual is in general not outstanding, how has a morality so far surpassing him succeeded in establishing itself, if it expresses only the average of individual temperaments? Barring a miracle, the greater cannot arise from the lesser. If the common conscience is nothing but the most general conscience, it cannot rise above the vulgar level. But then whence come the lofty, clearly imperative precepts which society undertakes to teach its children, and respect for which it enforces upon its members? With good reason, religions and many philosophies with them have regarded morality as deriving its total reality only from God. For the pallid, inadequate sketch of it contained in individual consciences cannot be regarded as the original type. This sketch seems rather the result of a crude, unfaithful reproduction, the model for which must therefore exist somewhere outside individuals. This is why the popular imagination, with its customary over-simplicity assigns it to God. Science certainly could waste no time over this conception, of which it does not even take cognizance.[14] Only, without it no alternative exists but to leave morality hanging unexplained in the air or make it a system of collective states of conscience. Morality either springs from nothing given in the world of experience, or it springs from society. It can only exist in a conscience; therefore, if it is not in the individual conscience it is in that of the group. But then it must be admitted that the latter, far from being confused with the average conscience, everywhere surpasses it.

Observation thus confirms our hypothesis. The regularity of statistical data, on the one hand, implies the existence of collective tendencies exterior to the individual, and on the other, we can directly establish this exterior character in a considerable number of important cases. Besides, this exteriority is not in the least surprising for anyone who knows the difference between individual and social states of consciousness. By definition, indeed, the latter can reach none of us except from without, since they do not flow from our personal predispositions. Since they consist of elements foreign to us [15] they express something other than ourselves. To be sure in so far as

[14] Just as the science of physics involves no discussion of the belief in God, the creator of the physical world, so the science of morals involves no concern with the doctrine which beholds the creator of morality in God. The question is not of our competence; we are not bound to espouse any solution. Secondary causes alone need occupy our attention.

[15] See above, p. 39 and p. 310.

we are solidary with the group and share its life, we are exposed to their influence; but so far as we have a distinct personality of our own we rebel against and try to escape them. Since everyone leads this sort of double existence simultaneously, each of us has a double impulse. We are drawn in a social direction and tend to follow the inclinations of our own natures. So the rest of society weighs upon us as a restraint to our centrifugal tendencies, and we for our part share in this weight upon others for the purpose of neutralizing theirs. We ourselves undergo the pressure we help to exert upon others. Two antagonistic forces confront each other. One, the collective force, tries to take possession of the individual; the other, the individual force, repulses it. To be sure, the former is much stronger than the latter, since it is made of a combination of all the individual forces; but as it also encounters as many resistances as there are separate persons, it is partially exhausted in these multifarious contests and reaches us disfigured and enfeebled. When it is very strong, when the circumstances activating it are of frequent recurrence, it may still leave a deep impression on individuals; it arouses in them mental states of some vivacity which, once formed, function with the spontaneity of instinct; this happens in the case of the most essential moral ideas. But most social currents are either too weak or too intermittently in contact with us to strike deep roots in us; their action is superficial. Consequently, they remain almost completely external. Hence, the proper way to measure any element of a collective type is not to measure its magnitude within individual consciences and to take the average of them all. Rather, it is their sum that must be taken. Even this method of evaluation would be much below reality, for this would give us only the social sentiment reduced by all its losses through individuation.

So there is some superficiality about attacking our conception as scholasticism and reproaching it for assigning to social phenomena a foundation in some vital principle or other of a new sort. We refuse to accept that these phenomena have as a substratum the conscience of the individual, we assign them another; that formed by all the individual consciences in union and combination. There is nothing substantival or ontological about this substratum, since it is merely a whole composed of parts. But it is just as real, nevertheless, as the elements that make it up; for they are constituted in this very way.

They are compounds, too. It is known today that the ego is the resultant of a multitude of conscious states outside the ego; that each
of these elementary states, in turn, is the product of unconscious
vital units, just as each vital unit is itself due to an association of inanimate particles. Therefore if the psychologist and the biologist correctly regard the phenomena of their study as well founded, merely
through the fact of their connection with a combination of elements
of the next lower order, why should it not be the same in sociology?
Only those have the right to consider such a basis inadequate who
have not renounced the hypothesis of a vital force and of a substan-
tive soul. Nothing is more reasonable, then, than this proposition at
which such offense has been taken; [16] that a belief or social practice
may exist independently of its individual expressions. We clearly
did not imply by this that society can exist without individuals, an
obvious absurdity we might have been spared having attributed to
us. But we did mean: 1. that the group formed by associated individuals has a reality of a different sort from each individual considered singly; 2. that collective states exist in the group from whose
nature they spring, before they affect the individual as such and establish in him in a new form a purely inner existence.

Such a way of considering the individual's relations to society also
recalls the idea assigned the individual's relations with the species or
the race by contemporary zoologists. The very simple theory has been
increasingly abandoned that the species is only an individual perpetuated chronologically and generalized spacially. Indeed it conflicts
with the fact that the variations produced in a single instance become specific only in very rare and possibly doubtful cases.[17] The
distinctive characteristics of the race change in the individual only as
they change in the race in general. The latter has therefore some
reality whence come the various shapes it assumes among individual
beings, far from its consisting simply of a generalization of these
beings. We naturally cannot regard these doctrines as finally demonstrated. But it is enough for us to show that our sociological conceptions, without being borrowed from another order of research, are
indeed not without analogies to the most positive sciences.

[16] See Tarde, *op. cit.*, p. 212.
[17] See Delage, *Structure du protoplasme, passim;* Weissmann, *L'hérédité* and all
the theories akin to Weissmann's.

IV

Let us apply these ideas to the question of suicide; the solution we gave at the beginning of this chapter will become more precise if we do so.

No moral idea exists which does not combine in proportions varying with the society involved, egoism, altruism and a certain anomy. For social life assumes both that the individual has a certain personality, that he is ready to surrender it if the community requires, and finally, that he is to a certain degree sensitive to ideas of progress. This is why there is no people among whom these three currents of opinion do not co-exist, bending men's inclinations in three different and even opposing directions. Where they offset one another, the moral agent is in a state of equilibrium which shelters him against any thought of suicide. But let one of them exceed a certain strength to the detriment of the others, and as it becomes individualized, it also becomes suicidogenetic, for the reasons assigned.

Of course, the stronger it is, the more agents it contaminates deeply enough to influence them to suicide, and inversely. But this very strength can depend only on the three following sorts of causes: 1. the nature of the individuals composing the society; 2. the manner of their association, that is, the nature of the social organization; 3. the transitory occurrences which disturb the functioning of the collective life without changing its anatomical constitution, such as national crises, economic crises, etc. As for the individual qualities, they can play a role only if they exist in all persons. For strictly personal ones or those of only small minorities are lost in the mass of the others; besides, from their differences from one another they neutralize one another and are mutually eradicated during the elaboration resulting in the collective phenomenon. Only general human characteristics, accordingly, can have any effect. Now these are practically immutable; at least, their change would require more centuries than the life of one nation can occupy. So the social conditions on which the number of suicides depends are the only ones in terms of which it can vary; for they are the only variable conditions. This is why the number of suicides remains stable as long as society does not change. This stability does not exist because the state of mind which generates suicide is found through some chance in a definite number of individuals who transmit it, for no recognizable reason, to an equal number who will imitate the act. It exists because the impersonal causes which gave it birth and which sustain it are the same. It is because nothing has occurred to modify either the grouping of the social units or the nature of their concurrence. The actions and reactions interchanged among them therefore remain the same; and so the ideas and feelings springing from them cannot vary.

To be sure, it is very rare, if not impossible, for one of these currents to succeed in exerting such preponderant influence over all points of the society. It always reaches this degree of energy in the midst of restricted surroundings containing conditions specially favorable to its development. One or another social condition, occupation, or religious faith stimulates it more especially. This explains suicide's twofold character. When considered in its outer manifestations, it seems as though these were just a series of disconnected events; for it occurs at separated places without visible interrelations. Yet the sum of all these individual cases has its own unity and its own individuality, since the social suicide-rate is a distinctive trait of each collective personality. That is, though these particular environments where suicide occurs most frequently are separate from one another, dispersed in thousands of ways over the entire territory, they are nevertheless closely related; for they are parts of a single whole, organs of a single organism, as it were. The condition in which each is found therefore depends on the general condition of society. There is a close solidarity between the virulence achieved by one or another of its tendencies and the intensity of the tendency in the whole social body. Altruism is more or less a force in the army depending on its role among the civilian population,[18] intellectual individualism is more developed and richer in suicides in Protestant environments the more pronounced it is in the rest of the nation, etc. Everything is tied together.

But though there is no individual state except insanity which may be considered a determining factor of suicide, it seems certain that no collective sentiment can affect individuals when they are absolutely indisposed to it. The above explanation might be thought inadequate for this reason, until we have shown how the currents giving rise to suicide find at the very moment and in the very environments in

[18] See above, Book II, Ch. 4.

which they develop a sufficient number of persons accessible to their influence.

If we suppose, however, that this conjunction is really always necessary and that a collective tendency cannot impose itself by brute force on individuals with no preliminary predisposition, then this harmony must be automatically achieved; for the causes determining the social currents affect individuals simultaneously and predispose them to receive the collective influence. Between these two sorts of factors there is a natural affinity, from the very fact that they are dependent on, and expressive of the same cause: this makes them combine and become mutually adapted. The hypercivilization which breeds the anomic tendency and the egoistic tendency also refines nervous systems, making them excessively delicate; through this very fact they are less capable of firm attachment to a definite object, more impatient of any sort of discipline, more accessible both to violent irritation and to exaggerated depression. Inversely, the crude, rough culture implicit in the excessive altruism of primitive man develops a lack of sensitivity which favors renunciation. In short, just as society largely forms the individual, it forms him to the same extent in its own image. Society, therefore, cannot lack the material for its needs, for it has, so to speak, kneaded it with its own hands.

The role of individual factors in the origin of suicide can now be more precisely put. If, in a given moral environment, for example, in the same religious faith or in the same body of troops or in the same occupation, certain individuals are affected and certain others not, this is undoubtedly, in great part, because the formers' mental constitution, as elaborated by nature and events, offers less resistance to the suicidogenetic current. But though these conditions may share in determining the particular persons in whom this current becomes embodied, neither the special qualities nor the intensity of the current depend on these conditions. A given number of suicides is not found annually in a social group just because it contains a given number of neuropathic persons. Neuropathic conditions only cause the suicides to succumb with greater readiness to the current. Whence comes the great difference between the clinician's point of view and the sociologist's. The former confronts exclusively particular cases, isolated from one another. He establishes, very often, that the victim was either nervous or an alcoholic, and explains the act by one or the other of these psychopathic states. In a sense he is right; for if this person rather than his neighbors committed suicide, it is frequently for this reason. But in a general sense this motive does not cause people to kill themselves, *nor, especially, cause a definite number to kill themselves in each society in a definite period of time.* The productive cause of the phenomenon naturally escapes the observer of individuals only; for it lies outside individuals. To discover it, one must raise his point of view above individual suicides and perceive what gives them unity. It will be objected that if enough neurasthenics did not exist, social causes would not produce all their effects. But no society exists in which the various forms of nervous degeneration do not provide suicide with more than the necessary number of candidates. Only certain ones are called, if this manner of speech is permitted. These are the ones who through circumstances have been nearer the pessimistic currents and who consequently have felt their influence more completely.

But a final question remains. Since each year has an equal number of suicides, the current does not strike simultaneously all those within its reach. The persons it will attack next year already exist; already, also, most of them are enmeshed in the collective life and therefore come under its influence. Why are they provisionally spared? It may indeed be understood why a year is needed to produce the current's full action; for since the conditions of social activity are not the same according to season, the current too changes in both intensity and direction at different times of the year. Only after the annual cycle is complete have all the combinations of circumstances occurred, in terms of which it tends to vary. But since, by hypothesis, the next year only repeats the last and causes the same combinations, why was not the first enough? Why, to use the familiar expression, does society pay its bill only in installments?

What we think explains this delay is the way time affects the suicidal tendency. It is an auxiliary but important factor in it. Indeed, we know that the tendency grows incessantly from youth to maturity,[19] and that it is often ten times as great at the close of life as at its beginning. The collective force impelling men to kill them-

---

[19] Let us note, to be sure, that this progression has been proved only for European societies, where altruistic suicide is relatively rare. Perhaps it does not apply to the altruistic type. Altruistic suicide may attain its height towards the period of matur-

selves therefore only gradually penetrates them. All things being equal, they become more accessible to it as they become older, probably because repeated experiences are needed to reveal the complete emptiness of an egoistic life or the total vanity of limitless ambition. Thus, victims of suicide complete their destiny only in successive layers of generations.[20]

---

ity, when a man is most zealously involved in social life. The relations of this form of suicide to homicide, to be mentioned in the following chapter, confirm this hypothesis.

[20] Without wishing to raise a question of metaphysics outside our province, we must note that this theory of statistics does not deny men every sort of freedom. On the contrary, it leaves the question of free will much more untouched than if one made the individual the source of social phenomena. Actually, whatever the causes of the regularity of collective manifestations, they are forced to produce their effects wherever they occur; because otherwise these effects would vary at random, whereas they are uniform. If they are inherent in individuals, they must therefore inevitably determine their possessors. Consequently, on this hypothesis, no way is found to avoid the strictest determinism. But it is not so if the stability of demographic data results from a force external to the individual. Such a force does not determine one individual rather than another. It exacts a definite number of certain kinds of actions, but not that they should be performed by this or that person. It may be granted that some people resist the force and that it has its way with others. Actually, our conception merely adds to physical, chemical, biological and psychological forces, social forces which like these act upon men from without. If the former do not preclude human freedom, the latter need not. The question assumes the same terms for both. When an epidemic center appears, its intensity predetermines the rate of mortality it will cause, but those who will be infected are not designated by this fact. Such is the situation of victims of suicide with reference to suicidogenetic currents.

CHAPTER 2
RELATIONS OF SUICIDE WITH OTHER
SOCIAL PHENOMENA

SINCE suicide is a social phenomenon by virtue of its essential element, it is proper to discuss the place it occupies among other social phenomena.

The first and most important question which concerns the subject is to discover whether or not suicide should be classed among the actions permitted by morality or among those proscribed by it. Should it be regarded to any degree whatever as a criminal act? The question, as is well known, has always been warmly discussed. For its solution a certain conception of ideal morality is usually first formulated and then the question is raised whether or not suicide logically contradicts it. For reasons elsewhere set forth [1] this cannot be our method. An uncontrolled deduction is always suspect, and as such, moreover, starts from a pure postulate of individual feeling; for everyone conceives in his own way the ideal morality so axiomatically assumed. Instead, let us first seek to discover how peoples actually have estimated suicide morally in the course of history; then try to find the reasons for this estimate. Then, we will have only to see whether and how far these reasons are founded in the nature of present-day societies. [2]

[1] See *Division du travail social*, Introduction.

[2] Bibliography on the question. Appiano Buonafede, *Histoire critique et philosophique du suicide*, 1762, Fr. trans., Paris, 1843.—Bourquelot, *Recherches sur les opinions de la législation en matière de morts volontaires*, in *Bibliothèque de l'Ecole des Chartes*, 1842 and 1843.—Guernesey, *Suicide, History of the Penal Laws*, New York, 1883.—Garrison, *Le suicide en droit romain et en droit francais*, Toulouse, 1883.—Wynn Westcott, *Suicide*, London, 1885, pp. 43-58.—Geiger, *Der Selbstmord im klassischen Altertum*, Augsburg, 1888.

I

As soon as Christian societies were formed, suicide was formally forbidden in them. In 452 the council of Arles declared suicide a crime and that it could only be caused by a diabolically inspired fury. But this order received a penal sanction only in the following century, at the council of Prague in 563. There it was decided that victims of suicide would be "honored with no memorial in the holy sacrifice of the mass, and the singing of psalms should not accompany their bodies to the grave." Civil legislation followed the lead of canon law, adding material penalties to religious penalties. A chapter of St. Louis' institutions especially regulates the matter; the body of the suicide was tried before the authorities otherwise competent in cases of the homicide of one person by another; the deceased's property was diverted from the usual heirs and reverted to the baron. Many customs did not stop at confiscation but prescribed various tortures in addition. "At Bordeaux the corpse was hung by the feet; at Abbeville it was dragged through the streets on a hurdle; at Lille, if it was a man, the corpse was hung after being dragged to the crossroads, if a woman, burned.[3] Even insanity was not always considered an excuse. The criminal ordinance issued by Louis XIV in 1670 codified these usages without much modification. A regular sentence of condemnation was spoken *ad perpetuam rei memoriam;* the body drawn on a hurdle, face down, through the streets and squares, was then hung or thrown upon the garbage heap. The property was confiscated. Nobles incurred the loss of nobility and were declared commoners; their woods were cut, their castles demolished, their escutcheons broken. We still have a decree of the Parliament of Paris, given January 31, 1749, in agreement with this legislation.

By an abrupt reaction the revolution of 1789 abolished all these repressive measures and erased suicide from the list of legal crimes. But all the religions numbering Frenchmen among their followers still prohibit and punish it, and common morality reproves it. It still inspires an aversion in popular consciousness extending to the place where the suicidal act was performed and to all persons closely related to the victim. It constitutes a moral flaw although opinion seems tending to become more indulgent on this point than formerly.

[3] Garrison, *op. cit.*, p. 77.

But, it has preserved something of its old criminological character. According to the most widespread jurisprudence, an accomplice of suicide is prosecuted as a homicide. This would not be so if suicide were considered an act indifferent to morality.

This same legislation is found among all Christian peoples and has remained more severe almost everywhere else than in France. In England, in the 10th century, King Edward in one of his Canons associated suicides with robbers, assassins and criminals of every kind. Up to 1823 it was customary to drag the suicide's body, pierced crossways with a stick, through the streets and bury it on a highway without any ceremony. Even today burial is separate. The suicide was declared a felon (*felo de se*) and his property reverted to the Crown. Only in 1870 was this provision abolished together with all confiscations for felony. To be sure, the excessive character of the punishment had made it inapplicable for a long time before; the jury evaded the law, usually by declaring that the suicide had acted in a moment of insanity and was therefore irresponsible. But the act is still designated as a crime; whenever committed it is regularly reported and sentenced, and the attempt is punished in principle. According to Ferri,[4] even in 1889, 106 legal proceedings were instituted for the offence and 84 sentences of condemnation passed in England alone. This is still more the case with complicity.

Michelet relates that at Zurich the corpse was formerly subject to horrible treatment. If the man had stabbed himself, a bit of wood in which the dagger was fixed was driven into the body near the head; if he had drowned himself, he was buried under five feet of water in the sand.[5] In Prussia until the Penal Code of 1871, burial had to be without any display and without religious ceremony. The new German penal code still punishes complicity with three years of imprisonment (art. 216). In Austria, the old canonical prescriptions are almost completely observed.

Russian law is more severe. If the suicide seems not to have acted under the influence of mental disturbance, chronic or temporary, his will is annulled and all the material dispositions he made in anticipation of death are likewise annulled. Christian burial is refused

[4] *Omicidio-suicidio*, pp. 61-62.
[5] *Origines du droit français*, p. 371.

him. The mere attempt is punished by a fine which is fixable by ecclesiastical authority. Finally, whoever incites another to kill himself or helps him carry out his resolve in any way, as by supplying him with the necessary instruments, is treated as an accomplice of premeditated homicide.[6] The Spanish Code, besides religious and moral penalties, imposes confiscation of property and punishes any complicity.[7]

Finally, the Penal Code of the State of New York, though of recent date (1881), terms suicide a crime. To be sure, in spite of this, punishment has been given up for practical reasons, since the penalty could in no way affect the guilty person. But the attempt may incur a sentence either of imprisonment up to 2 years, a fine up to $200.00 or both penalties. The mere fact of advising the suicide or favoring its performance is associated with complicity in murder.[8]

Mahometan societies prohibit suicide with equal vigor. "Man," says Mahomet, "dies only by the will of God according to the book which fixes the term of his life." [9] "When the term has arrived they cannot delay or hasten it by a single moment." [10] "We have decreed that death shall strike you each in turn and no one shall anticipate us." [11] Nothing, in fact, is more contrary to the general spirit of Mahometan civilization than suicide; for the virtue set above all others is absolute submission to the divine will, the docile resignation "which makes one endure all patiently." [12] As an act of insubordination and revolt suicide could therefore only be regarded as a grave offense to fundamental duty.

If we turn from modern societies to the historically earlier ones of the Greco-Latin city-states, we find legislation concerning suicide there also, but not based wholly on the same principle. Suicide was only considered illegal if it was not authorized by the state. Thus at Athens a man who had killed himself was punished with "atimia"

[6] Ferri, op. cit., p. 62.
[7] Garrison, op. cit., pp. 144, 145.
[8] Ferri, op. cit., pp. 63 and 64.
[9] Koran, III, v. 139.
[10] Ibid., XVI, v. 63.
[11] Ibid., LVI, v. 60.
[12] Ibid., XXXIII, v. 33.

for having committed an injustice to the city; [13] the honors of regular
burial were denied him; also his hand was cut from his body and
buried separately.[14] It was the same at Thebes with variations in detail, and also at Cyprus.[15] The rule was so severe at Sparta that Aristodemus was punished for the way he sought and found death at the
battle of Plataea. But these punishments were applicable only when
the person had killed himself without having previously asked permission of the proper authorities. At Athens, if he asked authority of
the Senate before killing himself, stating the reasons which made
life intolerable to him, and if his request was regularly granted, suicide was considered a legitimate act. Libanius [16] reports some precepts on the matter, the period of which he does not state, but which
were really enforced at Athens; besides, he praises these laws very
highly and asserts that they had the desired effects. They read as follows: "Whoever no longer wishes to live shall state his reasons to
the Senate, and after having received permission shall abandon life.
If your existence is hateful to you, die; if you are overwhelmed by
fate, drink the hemlock. If you are bowed with grief, abandon life.
Let the unhappy man recount his misfortune, let the magistrate supply him with the remedy, and his wretchedness will come to an end."
The same law is found at Ceos.[17] It was carried to Marseilles by the
Greek colonists who founded the city. The magistrates had a supply
of poison, the necessary quantity of which they gave to all who, after
having told the Council of the Six Hundred the reasons they thought
they had for killing themselves received its authorization.[18]

We are less well informed concerning the provisions of early
Roman law: the fragments of the law of the XII Tables which have
come down to us do not mention suicide. But since this Code was
largely inspired by Greek legislation it probably contained similar
provisions. At least, in his commentary on the Aeneid,[19] Servius tells
us that according to the laws of the pontiffs, whoever had hung himself was deprived of burial. The statutes of a religious confraternity

---

[13] Aristotle, *Eth. Nic.*, V. 11, 3.
[14] Aeschines, *Against Ctesiphon.*—Plato, *Laws,* IX, 12.
[15] Dion Chrysostom, *Orations,* 4, 14 (Teubner ed. V, 2, p. 207).
[16] *Melet.* Ed. Reiske, Altenburg, 1797, p. 198 ff.
[17] Valerius Maximus, 2, 6, 8.
[18] Valerius Maximus, 2, 6, 7.
[19] XII, 603.

of Lanuvium prescribed the same penalty.[20] According to the annalist Cassius Hermina, quoted by Servius, Tarquin the Proud, to combat an epidemic of suicides, ordered the bodies of the dead crucified after torture and left a prey to birds and wild beasts.[21] The custom of denying burial to suicides seems to have persisted, at least in principle, for in the Digest one reads: *Non solent autem lugeri suspendiosi nec qui manus sibi intulerunt, non taedio vitae, sed mala conscientia.*[22]

But according to a text of Quintilian [23] until a rather late period there was an institution at Rome similar to the one just mentioned in Greece, intended to modify the severity of the above provisions. The citizen who wished to kill himself had to submit his reasons to the Senate, which decided upon their acceptability and even determined the kind of death. What makes it probable that some such practice really existed at Rome is that something like it survived in the army even under the emperors. The soldier who tried to kill himself to avoid service was punished with death; but if he could prove that he was impelled by some plausible reason, he was only dismissed from the army.[24] If, finally, his act was one of remorse for some military fault, his will was annulled and his property reverted to the public treasury.[25] There is certainly no doubt that at Rome consideration of the motives leading to suicide always played a preponderant role in the moral or judicial estimation of it. Hence the precept: *"Et merito, si sine causa sibi manus intulit, puniendus est: qui enim sibi non pepercit, multo minus aliis parcet.*[26] The public conscience, while reproving it as a general rule, reserved the right to authorize it in certain cases. Such a principle is close kin to that which forms the basis of the institution of which Quintilian speaks; and it was so fundamental in Roman legislation concerning suicide that it remained even under the emperors. In time, however, the list of legitimate excuses lengthened. Finally there was practically only one *causa injusta:* the wish to

---

[20] See Lasaulx, *Ueber die Bücher des Koenigs Numa,* in his *Etudes d'antiquité classique.* We quote from Geiger, p. 63.

[21] Servius, *loc. cit.*—Pliny, *Natural History,* XXXVI, 24.

[22] III, title II, bk. II, par. 3.

[23] *Inst. orat.* VII, 4, 39.—*Orations,* 337.

[24] *Digest,* bk. XLIX, title XVI, law 6, par. 7.

[25] *Ibid.,* bk. XXVIII, title III, law 6, par. 7.

[26] *Digest,* bk. XLVIII, title XXI, law 3, par. 6.

escape the consequences of a criminal sentence. There was even a moment when the law excluding this from tolerance seems not to have been applied.[27]

If from the level of the city-state, we descend to the primitive peoples among whom altruistic suicide flourishes, it is hard to state anything exactly concerning the legislation that may obtain there. The complacency with which suicide is considered there, however, makes it probable that it is not formally forbidden. Yet it is possible that it is not absolutely tolerated in all cases. But however this may be, the fact remains that among all the societies above this lower level, none is known where the individual is unreservedly granted the right to kill himself. In both Greece and Italy, to be sure, there was a time when the old regulations concerning suicide became almost entirely a dead letter. But this was not until the city-state regime itself began to decline. This belated tolerance cannot be referred to as an example for imitation; for it is clearly interrelated with the serious disturbances which then afflicted these societies. It is the symptom of a morbid condition.

Such general reprobation, except for these cases of retrogression, is even in itself an instructive fact which should check moralists too much inclined to indulgence. An author must have great faith in the strength of his logic to venture such a revolt, in the name of a system, against the moral conscience of humanity; or, if he considers the prohibition of suicide founded on the past and advocates its abolition only for the immediate present, he should first prove that some profound change in the basic conditions of collective life has occurred recently.

A more striking conclusion springs from our sketch, practically excluding the possibility of such a proof. Regardless of differences in detail in repressive measures of different peoples, legislation on the subject clearly passed through two chief phases. In the first, the individual is forbidden to destroy himself on his own authority; but the State may permit him to do so. The act is immoral only when it is wholly private and without collaboration through the organs of collective life. Under specific circumstances, society yields slightly and absolves what it condemns on principle. In the second period, con-

[27] Towards the end of the Republic and the beginning of the Empire; see Geiger, p. 69.

demnation is absolute and universal. The power to dispose of a human life, except when death is the punishment for a crime,[28] is withheld not merely from the person concerned but from society itself. It is henceforth a right denied to collective as well as to private disposition. Suicide is thought immoral in and for itself, whoever they may be who participate in it. Thus, with the progress of history the prohibition, instead of being relaxed, only becomes more strict. If the public conscience seems less assured in its opinion of this matter today, therefore, this uncertainty may rise from fortuitous and passing causes; for it is wholly unlikely that moral evolution should so far reverse itself after having developed in a single direction for centuries.

The ideas that set it in this direction are in fact still alive. It has occasionally been said that if suicide is and should be forbidden, it is because a man evades his obligations towards society by killing himself. But if we were moved only by this thought we, like the Greeks, should leave society free to abrogate a prohibition issued only for its own benefit. If we refuse it this authority, it is because we see in the suicide more than an unscrupulous debtor to society. A creditor may always remit a debt by which he benefits. Besides, if this were the only reason for disapproving suicide, the reprobation should be more formal the more strictly the individual is subject to the State; so that it would be at its height in lower societies. On the contrary, its rigor increases with the growth of individual as contrasted with State rights. If it has become so formal and severe in Christian societies, this is not because of the idea of the State held by these people but because of their new conception of the human personality. It has become sacred, even most sacred in their eyes, something which no one is to offend. Of course, even under the city-state regime the individual's existence was no longer as self-effacing as among primitive tribes. Then it was accorded a social value, but one supposed to belong wholly to the State. The city-state could therefore dispose of him freely without the individual having the same right over himself. But today he has acquired a kind of dignity which places him above himself as well as above society. So long as his conduct has not caused him to forfeit the title of man, he seems to us to share in some degree in that quality *sui generis* ascribed by every religion to its gods

[28] And even in this case the right of society is beginning to be disputed.

which renders them inviolable by everything mortal. He has become tinged with religious value; man has become a god for men. Therefore, any attempt against his life suggests sacrilege. Suicide is such an attempt. No matter who strikes the blow, it causes scandal by violation of the sacrosanct quality within us which we must respect in ourselves as well as in others.

Hence, suicide is rebuked for derogating from this cult of human personality on which all our morality rests. Proof of this explanation is the difference between our view and that of the nations of antiquity. Once suicide was thought only a simple civil wrong committed against the State; religion had little or no interest in the matter.[29] Now it has become an act essentially involving religion. The judges condemning it have been church councils, and lay power in punishing it has only followed and imitated ecclesiastical authority. Because we have an immortal soul in us, a spark of divinity, we must now be sacred to ourselves. We belong completely to no temporal being because we are kin to God.

But if this is why suicide has been classed among illicit actions, should we not henceforth consider the condemnation to be without basis? It seems that scientific criticism cannot concede the least value to these mystical conceptions, nor admit that man contains anything whatever that is superhuman. Reasoning thus, Ferri in his *Omicidio-suicidio* thought himself justified in regarding all prohibitions of suicide as survivals from the past, doomed to disappear. Considering it absurd from the rationalist point of view that the individual could have an extra-personal aim, he deduces that we are always free to renounce the advantages of community existence by renouncing life itself. The right to live seems to him logically to imply the right to die.

But this method of argument draws its conclusion too abruptly from form to content, from the verbal expression through which we translate our feeling to the feeling itself. It is true that, both intrinsically and abstractly, the religious symbols by means of which we explain the respect inspired in us by human personality are not adequate to reality, and this is easily proveable; but from all this it does not follow that this respect is itself unreasonable. On the contrary, its preponderant role in our law and in our morality must warn us

[29] See Geiger, *op. cit.*, pp. 58-59.

against such an interpretation. Instead of taking a literal interpretation of this conception, let us examine it in itself, let us discover its make-up, and we shall see that in spite of the crudeness of the popular formula the conception nevertheless has objective value.

Indeed, the sort of transcendency we ascribe to human personality is not a quality peculiar to it. It is found elsewhere. It is nothing but the imprint of all really intense collective sentiments upon matters related to them. Just because these feelings derive from the collectivity, the aims to which they direct our actions can only be collective. Society has needs beyond our own. The acts inspired in us by its needs therefore do not depend on our individual inclinations; their aim is not our personal interest, but rather involves sacrifices and privations. When I fast, when I accept mortification to be pleasing in God's sight, when I undertake some inconvenience out of respect for a tradition the meaning and import of which are usually unknown to me, when I pay my taxes, when I give any labor or life to the State, I renounce something of myself; and by the resistance offered by our egoism to these renunciations, we readily see that they are forced from us by a power to which we have submitted. Even when we defer gladly to its commands we feel that our conduct is guided by a sentiment of reverence for something greater than ourselves. However willingly we obey the voice dictating this abnegation, we feel sure that its tone is imperative beyond that of instinct. That is why we cannot indisputably consider it our own, though it speaks within our consciences. We ascribe it to other sources, as we do our sensations; we project it outside of ourselves, referring it to an existence we think of as exterior and superior to ourselves, since it commands us and we obey. Of course, whatever seems to us to come from the same origin shares the same quality. Thus we have been forced to imagine a world beyond this one and to people it with realities of a different order.

Such is the source of all the ideas of transcendency which form the bases of religions and morals; for moral obligation is explicable only in this way. To be sure, the definite form in which we usually clothe these ideas is without scientific value. Whether we ascribe them to a personal being of a special nature or to some abstract force which we vaguely hypostasize under the title of moral ideal, they are solely metaphorical conceptions, giving no adequate explanation of the facts. But the process which they symbolize is none the less real. It remains true that in every case we are urged to act by an authority exceeding ourselves, namely society, and that the aims to which it attaches us thus enjoy real moral supremacy. If so, all the objections applicable to the common conceptions by which men have tried to represent this sensed supremacy to themselves cannot lessen its reality. Such criticism is superficial, not reaching to the basis of things. If it is demonstrable that exaltation of human personality is one of the aims pursued, and which should be pursued, by modern societies, all moral regulation deriving from this principle is justified by that fact itself, whatever the manner of its usual justification. Though the reasons satisfying the crowd are open to criticism, they need only be transposed into another idiom to be given their full import.

Now, not only is this aim really one of the aims of modern societies, but it is a law of history that peoples increasingly detach themselves from every other objective. Originally society is everything, the individual nothing. Consequently, the strongest social feelings are those connecting the individual with the collectivity; society is its own aim. Man is considered only an instrument in its hands; he seems to draw all his rights from it and has no counter-prerogative, because nothing higher than it exists. But gradually things change. As societies become greater in volume and density, they increase in complexity, work is divided, individual differences multiply,[30] and the moment approaches when the only remaining bond among the members of a single human group will be that they are all men. Under such conditions the body of collective sentiments inevitably attaches itself with all its strength to its single remaining object, communicating to this object an incomparable value by so doing. Since human personality is the only thing that appeals unanimously to all hearts, since its enhancement is the only aim that can be collectively pursued, it inevitably acquires exceptional value in the eyes of all. It thus rises far above all human aims, assuming a religious nature.

This cult of man is something, accordingly, very different from the egoistic individualism above referred to, which leads to suicide. Far from detaching individuals from society and from every aim beyond themselves, it unites them in one thought, makes them servants of one work. For man, as thus suggested to collective affection and re-

[30] See my *Division du travail social*, bk. II.

spect, is not the sensual, experiential individual that each one of us represents, but man in general, ideal humanity as conceived by each people at each moment of its history. None of us wholly incarnates this ideal, though none is wholly a stranger to it. So we have, not to concentrate each separate person upon himself and his own interests, but to subordinate him to the general interests of humankind. Such an aim draws him beyond himself; impersonal and disinterested, it is above all individual personalities; like every ideal, it can be conceived of only as superior to and dominating reality. This ideal even dominates societies, being the aim on which all social activity depends. This is why it is no longer the right of these societies to dispose of this ideal freely. While we recognize that they too have their reason for existence, they have subjected themselves to the jurisdiction of this ideal and no longer have the right to ignore it; still less, to authorize men themselves to do so. Our dignity as moral beings is therefore no longer the property of the city-state; but it has not for that reason become our property, and we have not acquired the right to do what we wish with it. How could we have such a right if society, the existence greater than ourselves, does not have it?

Under these conditions suicide must be classed among immoral acts; for in its main principle it denies this religion of humanity. A man who kills himself, the saying goes, does wrong only to himself and there is no occasion for the intervention of society; for so goes the ancient maxim *Volenti non fit injuria.* This is an error. Society is injured because the sentiment is offended on which its most respected moral maxims today rest, a sentiment almost the only bond between its members, and which would be weakened if this offense could be committed with impunity. How could this sentiment maintain the least authority if the moral conscience did not protest its violation? From the moment that the human person is and must be considered something sacred, over which neither the individual nor the group has free disposal, any attack upon it must be forbidden. No matter that the guilty person and the victim are one and the same; the social evil springing from the act is not affected merely by the author being the one who suffers. If violent destruction of a human life revolts us as a sacrilege, in itself and generally, we cannot tolerate it under any circumstances. A collective sentiment which yielded so far would soon lose all force.

Of course, this does not mean that we must revert to the ferocious penalties imposed on suicide during the past centuries. They were established at a time when, under the influence of temporary circumstances, the entire system of public repression was enforced with excessive severity. But the principle that homicide of one's self should be reproved must be maintained. It remains to determine by what external tokens this reprobation is to be shown. Are moral sanctions enough or must there be juridical ones, and if so, what? This is a question of application which shall be treated in the next chapter.

II

But in order better to decide to what extent suicide partakes of immorality, let us examine first its relation with other immoral acts, especially crimes and misdemeanors.

According to Lacassagne there is consistently an inverse relation between the variations of suicide and those of crimes against property (qualified thefts, incendiarism, fraudulent bankruptcies, etc.). This thesis was defended in his name by one of his pupils, Dr. Chaussinand, in his *Contribution a l'étude de la statistique criminelle*.[31] But there are absolutely no proofs for it. According to the author, the two curves need only to be compared to show that they vary inversely with one another. Actually, no trace of relation, direct or inverse, can be seen between them. No doubt, property crimes have decreased since 1854 while suicides are increasing. But this decrease is in part fictitious; it is due merely to the fact that at about that time judges began to send certain crimes before courts of summary jurisdiction, in order to remove them from the jurisdiction of courts of assizes, by which they had hitherto been judiciable. A certain number of offences therefore vanished from then on from the list of crimes, only to reappear in that of misdemeanors. Crimes against property have benefited most by this now established departure in jurisprudence. So that, if statistics suggest a smaller number, this decrease is probably due merely to a procedure in bookkeeping.

But no one can decide whether the decrease was real; for though starting from 1854 the two curves follow an inverse direction, from

[31] Lyons, 1881. At the Congress on Criminology held at Rome in 1887, Lacassagne claimed responsibility for this theory.

1826 to 1854 the curve of crimes against property either rises con-jointly with that of suicides; though less rapidly, or is stationary. From 1831 .to 1835 an average of 5,095 indicted was annually re-corded; this rose to 5,732 during the following period, was still 4,918 in 1841–45, 4,992 from 1846 to 1850, a reduction of only 2 per cent from 1830. Besides, the general shape of the two curves precludes any thought of comparison. That of property-crimes is very erratic; it makes abrupt leaps from year to year; its apparently capricious changes clearly depend on a quantity of fortuitous circum-stances. That of suicide, on the contrary, rises regularly and uniformly; with rare exceptions there are neither abrupt jumps nor sudden falls. Ascent is steady and progressive. Between phenomena the develop-ment of which is so different no connection of any sort can exist.

Moreover, Lacassagne seems to have been alone in his opinion. But it is otherwise with another idea, relating suicide with crimes against persons and especially with homicide. It numbers many de-fenders and deserves serious examination.[32]

As early as 1833 Guerry pointed out that crimes against persons are twice as numerous in the southern as in the northern depart-ments, while the reverse is true of suicide. Later, Despine estimated that in the 14 departments where sanguinary crimes are most fre-quent there were only 30 suicides per million inhabitants, whereas 82 occurred in 14 other departments where such crimes were much more infrequent. The same author adds that in the Seine only 17 crimes against persons are found per 100 proceedings and an average of 427 suicides per million, while in Corsica the proportion of the former is 83 per cent and that of the latter only 18 per million inhabitants.

These remarks, however, had attracted no notice until the Italian school of criminology took them up. Ferri and Morselli especially made them the basis of an entire theory.

According to them the polar character of suicide and homicide

[32] Bibliography.—Guerry, *Essai sur la statistique morale de la France.*—Cazau-vieilh, *Du suicide, de l'aliénation mentale et des crimes contre les personnes, com-parés dans leurs rapports reciproques,* 2 vols., 1840.—Despine, *Psychologie natur.,* p. 111.—Maury, *Du mouvement moral des sociétés,* in *Revue des Deux-Mondes,* 1860.—Morselli, *Il suicidio,* p. 243 ff.—*Actes du premier congrès international d'Anthropologie criminelle,* Turin, 1886–87, p. 202 ff.—Tarde, *Criminalité com-parée,* p. 152 ff.—Ferri, *Omicidio-suicidio,* 4th ed., Turin, 1895, p. 253 ff.

is an absolutely general law. Whether as regards their geographical distribution or their evolution in time, they are always found changing inversely with one another. But this antagonism, once granted, may be explained in either of two ways. Either homicide and suicide form two opposite currents, so opposed that one can gain only through the other's loss, or they are two different channels of a single stream, fed by a single source, which consequently cannot move in one direction without receding to an equal extent in the other. The Italian criminologists adopted the second of these explanations. In suicide and homicide they see two manifestations of the same state, two effects of the same cause, expressing itself at times in one form, at times in another, but unable to assume both simultaneously.

They chose this interpretation because, according to them, the inversion of the phenomena in certain respects does not exclude a certain parallelism. While they vary inversely in terms of some conditions, other conditions make them vary not inversely. Thus, says Morselli, temperature has the same effect on both; they reach their maximum at the same time of year, the beginning of the hot season; both occur more frequently among men than among women; both, finally, according to Ferri, increase with age. Therefore, while opposite in certain aspects they are partially of the same nature. Now, the factors under the influence of which they react similarly, are all individual; for they either consist directly of certain organic states (such as age or sex), or belong to the cosmic environment which can affect the moral individual only through the medium of the physical individual. Individual conditions would thus serve to bind suicide and homicide together. The psychological constitution predisposing to one or the other is supposed to be the same: the two inclinations are one. Following Lombroso, Ferri and Morselli have even tried to define this temperament. It is supposedly characterized by a decay of the organism, which puts the person at a disadvantage in the struggle of life. Both the murderer and the suicide accordingly are degenerates and impotents. Equally unable to play a useful part in society, they are consequently doomed to defeat.

But, supposedly, this single predisposition which itself inclines no more one way than the other prefers the form of homicide or of suicide depending on the nature of the social environment; and so these contrasting phenomena are produced which, though real, nevertheless conceal a fundamental identity. Where customs generally are gentle and pacific, where the shedding of blood is abhorred, the defeated person will resign himself, confess his impotence, and anticipating the effects of natural selection will withdraw from the fight by withdrawing from life. Where average morality has a ruder character and human life is less respected, he will revolt, declare war on society and kill, instead of killing himself. In short, the murder of one's self and of another are two violent acts. But sometimes the violence which is their source, finding no resistance in the social environment, overruns it and then it becomes homicide. Sometimes, incapable of outward expression because of the pressure of the public conscience, it reverts to its source, and then the same person from whom it springs is its victim.

Suicide is, then, a transformed and attenuated homicide. In this view, it seems almost salutary; for if it is not a good, it is at least a lesser evil, which spares us a greater. It would even seem that one should not try to restrain its scope by prohibitive measures; for by so doing one would be giving rein to homicide. It is a safety-valve which is useful to leave open. In short, suicide would have the very great advantage of ridding us of a number of useless or harmful persons without social intervention, and hence in the most simple and economical way. Is it not better to let them put themselves out of the way voluntarily and quietly, than to force society to eject them from its midst by violence?

Is this ingenious thesis well-founded? The question is twofold and each part must be examined separately. Are the psychological conditions of crime and suicide the same? Is there a polarity between the social conditions on which they depend?

III

Three facts have been alleged to prove the psychological unity of the two phenomena.

First there is the similar effect which sex is supposed to have upon suicide and homicide. To be exact, this influence of sex is an effect rather of social than of organic causes. Woman kills herself less, and she kills others less, not because of physiological differences from man but because she does not participate in collective life in the same way. Moreover, she is far from having the same antipathy

to these two forms of immorality. Indeed we are inclined to forget
that there are murders of which she has a monopoly, infanticides,
abortions and poisonings. Whenever homicide is within her range
she commits it as often or more often than man. According to
Oettingen,[33] half the total number of domestic murders is attributable
to her. So there is no reason to suppose that she has greater respect
for another's life because of her congenital constitution; she merely
lacks as frequent opportunities, being less deeply involved in the
struggle of life. The causes impelling to sanguinary crimes affect her
less than man because she is less within their sphere of influence.
For the same reason she is less exposed to accidental forms of death;
out of 100 of this sort, only 20 are women.

Besides, if a single classification is made to cover all sorts of intentional homicide—premeditated and unpremeditated murders,[34] parricides, infanticides, poisonings—woman's share in the total is still
very high. In France, 38 or 39 out of 100 such crimes are committed
by women, and even 42 if abortions are included. In Germany, the
proportion is 51 per cent, in Austria 52 per cent. To be sure, involuntary homicides are omitted in this calculation, but homicide is truly
homicide only when it is intentional. On the other hand, the characteristically feminine forms of murder, such as infanticides, abortions,
and domestic murders, are by their nature hard to discover. Many
therefore are committed which escape justice and, accordingly, statistics. Remembering that woman must probably benefit by the same
indulgence in preliminary investigations as she certainly does in sentences, where she is much more often acquitted than man, it is clear,
finally, that aptitude for homicide cannot be very different in the
two sexes. On the contrary, we know how great is woman's immunity to suicide.

---

[33] *Moralstatistik*, p. 526.

[34] Throughout this chapter, Durkheim uses several technical, French legal terms
for the varieties of homicide. These terms are somewhat different from those employed in English and American law. In French law there are five varieties of what
is called *homicide volontaire;* they are *assassinat, meurtre, parricide, infanticide,
empoisonnement.* The two most important for Durkheim's analysis are *assassinat* and
meurtre. Assassinat is intentional homicide with aggravating circumstances such as
premeditation or prearrangement. *Meurtre* is simple intentional homicide (*homicide
volontaire simple*) without aggravating circumstances such as premeditation or prearrangement. *Assassinat* has been translated, therefore, as "premeditated murder,"
while *meurtre* has been translated as "unpremeditated murder."—Ed.

The influence of age on each phenomenon shows equal differences. According to Ferri, homicide and suicide both become more frequent as man advances in life. To be sure, Morselli expresses the opposite view.[35] The truth is that there is neither inversion nor agreement. While suicide increases regularly until old age, premeditated and unpremeditated murder reach their height in maturity, at about 30 or 35 years of age, and then decrease. This appears in Table XXXI. Not the shadow of proof appears here that suicide and sanguinary crime are of identical or opposite character.

The effect of temperature remains to be considered. If all crimes against persons are combined, the curve thus obtained seems to confirm the theory of the Italian school. It rises until June and descends regularly to December, like that of suicides. But this results merely from the fact that under this common expression of crimes against persons not only homicides, but indecent assaults and rape are included. Since these crimes reach their maximum in June and are

TABLE XXXI—Comparative Development of Murders (Premeditated and Unpremeditated) and Suicides at Different Ages, in France (1887)

Age	Per 100,000 Individuals of Each Age, Number of		Per 100,000 Individuals of Each Sex and Age, Number of Suicides	
	Unpremeditated Murders	Premeditated Murders	Men	Women
From 16 to 21 *	6.2	8	14	9
21 to 25	9.7	14.9	23	9
25 to 30	15.4	15.4	30	9
30 to 40	11	15.9	33	9
40 to 50	6.9	11	50	12
50 to 60	2	6.5	69	17
Above 60	2.3	2.5	91	20

* The figures for the first two periods are not strictly exact for homicide, since criminal statistics begin their first period at 16 years and carry it to 21, while the census gives the total figure of the population from 15 to 20. But this slight inexactness does not in the least affect the general results apparent in the table. For infanticide the maximum is reached earlier, towards 25 years, and the decrease is much more rapid. The reason is readily surmised.

much more numerous than attempts against life, they give the curve its shape. But they have no relation to homicide; so that if we wish to know the variations of the latter at different times of year, we must isolate it from the others. If this is done, and especially if we carefully distinguish from each other the different forms of homicidal

[35] *Op. cit.*, p. 333.—In the *Actes du congrès de Rome*, p. 205, the same author expresses doubt, however, as to the reality of this antagonism.

TABLE XXXII—Monthly Variations of the Different Forms of Homicidal Criminality * (1827–1870)

	Unpremeditated Murders	Premeditated Murders	Infanticides	Manslaughter
January	560	829	647	830
February	**664**	**926**	750	937
March	600	766	**783**	840
April	574	712	662	867
May	587	809	666	983
June	644	853	552	938
July	614	776	491	919
August	**716**	849	501	**997**
September	665	839	495	**993**
October	653	815	478	892
November	650	**942**	497	960
December	591	866	542	886

* According to Chaussinand.

criminality, no trace of the supposed parallelism is found (see Table XXXII).

Indeed, while the growth of suicide is constant and regular from January to about June, like its decrease during the rest of the year, premeditated and unpremeditated murder, and infanticide oscillate from month to month most capriciously. Not only is the general development different, but neither the maxima nor the minima coincide. Unpremeditated murders have two maxima, one in February and the other in August. Premeditated murders also have two, one being the same, February, but the other is in November. The maximum for infanticides is in May; for manslaughter [36] in August and September. If the seasonal, not the monthly variations are calculated, the divergencies are equally striking. Autumn has almost as many unpremeditated murders as Summer (1,968 as against 1,974) and Winter has more than Spring. For premeditated murder, Winter leads (2,621), Autumn follows (2,596), then Summer (2,478) and finally Spring (2,287). For infanticide Spring surpasses the other seasons (2,111) and is followed by Winter (1,939). For manslaughter, Summer and Autumn are on the same level (2,854 for one and 2,845 for the other); then comes Spring (2,690) and, not far away, Winter (2,653). The distribution of suicide is entirely different, as we have seen.

Besides, if the tendency to suicide were only a repressed tendency

[36] The French legal terms "coups mortel" and "blessures mortels"—mortal blows and mortal wounds—refer in this context to that variety of homicide which we know as "manslaughter" and they are so translated here. They constitute unintentional homicide resulting from an act of violence itself not unintentional.—Ed.

to murder, as soon as murderers and assassins are arrested and their violent instincts can no longer find external expression, they should become their own victims. The homicidal tendency should therefore be transformed into the suicidal tendency under the influence of imprisonment. On the contrary, it seems from the testimony of several observers that great criminals rarely kill themselves. Cazauvieilh gathered from the physicians of our different convict prisons information concerning the frequency of suicide among convicts.[37] At Rochefort only a single case had been observed in thirty years; none at Toulon, where the population was usually from 3,000 to 4,000 (1818–1834). At Brest the results obtained were a little different; in seventeen years, in an average population of about 3,000, 13 suicides had been committed, making an annual rate of 21 per 100,000. Although higher than the preceding, this figure is not excessive, since it refers to a population chiefly male and adult. According to Dr. Lisle, "out of 9,320 deaths registered in convict prisons from 1816 to 1837 inclusively, only 6 suicides were recorded." [38] From a study by Dr. Ferrus it appears that only 30 suicides occurred in seven years in the different regional jails, in an average population of 15,111 prisoners. But the proportion was still lower in the convict prisons, where only 5 suicides were recorded from 1838 to 1845 in an average population of 7,041.[39] Brierre de Boismont confirms the fact last mentioned, adding: "Professional assassins and great criminals have less frequent recourse to this violent means of escaping penal atonement than prisoners of less perversity." [40] Dr. Leroy similarly remarks that "professional rogues, habitual convicts" rarely make attempts upon their own lives.[41]

Two statistical records, one quoted by Morselli [42] and the other by Lombroso,[43] do indeed tend to prove that prisoners are in general unusually disposed to suicide. But as these documents do not distinguish murderers and assassins from other criminals, nothing can be concluded as to the question before us. They even seem rather to con-

[37] Op. cit., pp. 310 ff.
[38] Op. cit., p. 67.
[39] Des prisonniers, de l'imprisonnement et des prisons, Paris, 1850, p. 133.
[40] Op. cit., p. 95.
[41] Le suicide dans le département de Seine-et-Marne.
[42] Op. cit., p. 377.
[43] L'homme criminel, Fr. trans. p. 338.

firm the above observations. In fact they prove that imprisonment by itself develops a very strong tendency to suicide. Even if no account is made of persons who kill themselves immediately upon arrest and before condemnation, a considerable number of suicides remains which can only be attributed to the influence of prison life.[44] But then the imprisoned murderer ought to have a very pronounced disposition for voluntary death, if the aggravation resulting from his mere imprisonment were reenforced by the congenital predisposition ascribed to him. The fact that, from this point of view, he is rather below than above the average, is therefore hardly favorable to the hypothesis that merely because of his temperament he has a natural affinity for suicide, ever ready to manifest itself as soon as circumstances favor its development. Besides, we do not mean to affirm that he enjoys a real immunity; the information at our disposal is not sufficient to settle the question. Possibly, under certain conditions, great criminals hold their lives fairly cheaply and surrender them without great reluctance. But at least the fact does not have the generality and inevitability that the Italian thesis logically involves. And this is all we had to establish.[45]

IV

But it remains to discuss this school's second proposition. Granted that homicide and suicide do not stem from the same psychological state, we must see if there is any real antagonism between the social conditions on which they depend.

The question is more complex than the Italian authors and several of their adversaries have thought. Certainly, the law of inversion is not verified in a number of cases. Fairly often the two phenomena

[44] Of what does this influence consist? It seems due in part, certainly, to cell life. But we should not be surprised if the community-life of the prison were apt to have the same effects. The society of evil-doers and prisoners is known to be very coherent; the individual disappears completely and prison discipline has the same effacing tendency. Something similar to what we have observed in the army may take place. What confirms this hypothesis is that epidemics of suicide are frequent in prisons as well as in barracks.

[45] Statistics reported by Ferri (*Omicidio*, p. 373) are no more conclusive. From 1866 to 1876, 17 suicides were committed in Italian convict prisons by convicts condemned for crimes against persons, and only 5 committed by convicts guilty of crimes against property. But the former are much more numerous in convict prisons than the latter. These figures are therefore wholly inconclusive. Besides, we do not know whence the author of these statistics took the data he uses.

develop in a parallel manner instead of repulsing and excluding one another. Thus in France unpremeditated murders have shown a certain tendency to increase since the end of the war of 1870. In annual average they numbered only 105 during the years 1861–65; from 1871 to 1876 they rose to 163 and during the same time premeditated murders rose from 175 to 201. Now suicides were increasing in considerable proportions at the same time. The same phenomenon had occurred during the years 1840–50. In Prussia suicides, which from 1865 to 1870 had not gone beyond 3,658, reached 4,459 in 1876, 5,042 in 1878, an increase of 36 per cent. Premeditated and unpremeditated murders followed the same course; from 151 in 1869 they rose successively to 166 in 1874, 221 in 1875, 253 in 1878, an increase of 67 per cent.[46] The same thing happened in Saxony. Before 1870 suicides oscillated between 600 and 700; only once, in 1868, there were 800. Beginning with 1876 they rose to 981, then to 1,114, to 1,126, until finally in 1880 they were 1,171.[47] In parallel manner attempts at murder rose from 637 in 1873 to 2,232 in 1878.[48] In Ireland, from 1865 to 1880, suicide increased 29 per cent, and homicide also increased and in almost the same degree (23 per cent).[49] In Belgium, from 1841 to 1885, homicides increased from 47 to 139 and suicides from 240 to 670; an increase of 195 per cent for the first and 178 per cent for the second. These figures agree so little with the law that Ferri is reduced to questioning the exactness of the Belgian statistics. But even if we confine ourselves to the most recent years, the data for which are least suspect, the same result is reached. From 1874 to 1885 the increase for homicides is 51 per cent (139 cases as against 92) and, for suicides, 79 per cent (670 cases as against 374).

The geographical distribution of the two phenomena gives rise to similar comment. The French departments with most suicides are: the Seine, Seine-et-Marne, Seine-et-Oise, Marne. Now, though they are not also highest in homicide, they still occupy a fairly high rank, the Seine being 26th in unpremeditated murders and 17th in premeditated murders, Seine-et-Marne 33rd and 14th, Seine-et-Oise

[46] According to Oettingen, *Moralstatistik,* supplement, table 61.
[47] *Ibid.,* table 109.
[48] *Ibid., table* 65.
[49] According to Ferri's own tables.

15th and 24th, Marne 27th and 21st respectively. Var, which is 10th for suicides, is 5th for premeditated and 6th for unpremeditated murders. In Bouches-du-Rhône, where suicides are frequent, murders are likewise so; it is in the 5th rank for unpremeditated and the 6th for premeditated.[50] On the suicide-map as on that for homicide, Ile-de-France is represented by a dark area like that of the strip containing the Mediterranean departments, with the only difference that the former region is of a less deep shade on the map of homicides than on the suicide-map and that the reverse is true of the second region. Likewise in Italy, Rome which is the third judicial district for suicides is also the fourth for qualified homicides. Finally, as we have seen, suicides are often very numerous in lower societies where there is little respect for life.

But incontestable as these facts are, and important as it is not to lose sight of them, there are contradictory facts equally stable and even much more numerous. If the two phenomena agree at least partially in certain cases, in others they are obviously in opposition:

1. Although at certain moments during the century they move in the same direction, the two curves taken as wholes contrast very clearly, at least where they can be followed for any considerable period. In France, from 1826 to 1880, suicide regularly increases, as we have seen; homicide on the contrary tends to decrease, though less rapidly. In 1826–30 there were on the average 279 annual indictments for unpremeditated murder, only 160 in 1876–80 and, during the interval, the number had fallen to 121 in 1861–65 and to 119 in 1856–60. At two periods, about 1845 and just after the war, there was a tendency to rise; but if these secondary oscillations are disregarded, the general tendency to decrease is clear. The diminution is 43 per cent, all the more noticeable since the population increased by 16 per cent at the same time.

Regression is less clear for premeditated murder. There were 258 indicted in 1826–30, there were still 239 in 1876–80. The fall is notable only if the increase in population is taken into account. This difference in the evolution of this type of murder has nothing surprising about it. It is actually a crime of mixed nature, having elements in common with unpremeditated murder but also different

[50] This classification of departments is from Bournet, *De la Criminalité en France et en Italie*, Paris, 1884, pp. 41 and 51.

ones; in part it springs from other causes. Sometimes it is merely a more deliberate and intentional murder, sometimes only the incident of a crime against property. On the last score it depends on other factors than those determining homicide. These are not the sum of the varied tendencies which lead to the shedding of blood but the very different motives which lie at the root of robbery. The dual nature of both crimes was obvious even in the table of their monthly and seasonal variations. Premeditated murder reaches its height in Winter and especially in November, just as do attempts at robbery. The evolution of the trend of homicide cannot therefore be best observed through the variations of premeditated murder; its general orientation is better brought out by the curve of unpremeditated murder.

The same phenomenon is observed in Prussia. In 1834, 368 preliminary investigations were instituted for murders or manslaughter, or one per 29,000 inhabitants; in 1851 there were only 257, one for 53,000 inhabitants. The movement then continued though a little more slowly. In 1852 there was still one preliminary investigation for 76,000 inhabitants; in 1873 only one for 109,000.[51] In Italy, from 1875 to 1890, the decrease in simple and qualified homicides was 18 per cent (2,660 as against 3,280) while suicides increased 80 per cent.[52] Where homicide does not lose, neither does it gain. In England, from 1860 to 1865, there were annually 359 cases, but only 329 in 1881–85; in Austria there were 528 in 1866–70, but only 510 in 1881–85,[53] and if in these countries homicide were differentiated from premeditated murder, the regression would probably be more marked. During the same time, suicide was increasing in all these States.

Nevertheless, Tarde undertook to show that this diminution of homicide in France was only apparent.[54] It is supposed to be due simply to the failure to combine cases judged by the courts of assize and those classified by the lawyers as not to be carried further, which ended in decrees of insufficient grounds. According to Tarde, the number of murders which were thus not prosecuted and which for this reason do not figure in the totals of judicial statistics has grown

[51] Starke, *Verbrechen und Verbrecher in Preussen,* Berlin, 1884, pp. 144 ff.
[52] According to Ferri's tables.
[53] See Bosco, *Gli Omicidii in alcuni Stati d'Europa,* Rome, 1889.
[54] *Philosophie pénale,* pp. 347-48.

constantly; by adding them to like crimes on which judgment has been passed, a constant increase would appear instead of the regression above mentioned. Unfortunately, his proof of this assertion depends on too ingenious an arrangement of the figures. He merely compares the number of premeditated and unpremeditated murders not deferred to jurisdiction at the courts of assize during the five years 1861–65 with that of the years 1876–80 and 1880–85, and shows that the second and especially the third is greater than the first. But it happens that the period 1861–65 is the one of all the century when there were much the fewest such cases estopped before judgement; the number is exceptionally minute, for unknown reasons. So it was the most improper period for comparison possible. Moreover, a law cannot be arrived at from the comparison of two or three figures. If Tarde, instead of choosing such a starting point, had observed the variations of the number of these cases over a longer period, he would have reached a wholly different conclusion. The following is the result suggested by doing so.

Number of Cases Not Prosecuted [55]

	1835–38	1839–40	1846–50	1861–65	1876–80	1880–85
Unpremeditated murders	442	503	408	223	322	322
Premeditated murders	313	320	333	217	231	252

The variation of the figures is not very regular; but from 1835 to 1885 they have perceptibly decreased in spite of the rise about 1876. The diminution is 37 per cent for unpremeditated murders and 24 per cent for premeditated. Nothing therefore permits the conclusion that there was an increase in the criminality in question.[56]

[55] Certain of these cases are not prosecuted because they are neither crimes nor delicts. They should therefore be deducted. However we avoided this in order to follow our author on his own ground; besides, we are confident that this deduction would change nothing in the results shown by the above figures.

[56] A secondary consideration, offered by the same author in support of his thesis, is no less unconvincing. According to this, one should also consider the homicides erroneously classed among voluntary or accidental deaths. Now, since the number of both has increased since the beginning of the century, he concludes that the sum of homicides under one or the other of these two classifications must have grown equally. Here, he says, is another serious increase which we must consider in order to estimate the course of homicide correctly.—But his reasoning is based on a confusion of ideas. It does not follow from the fact that the number of accidental and voluntary deaths has grown, that the same is true of the homicides wrongly assigned to this classification. From the increase in suicides and accidents it does not follow that there are also more false suicides and false accidents. For such a hypothesis to possess any probability, it would have to be shown that the ad-

2. If there are countries which accumulate suicides and homicides, it is never in the same proportions; the two manifestations never reach their maximum intensity at the same point. It is even a general rule that *where homicide is very common it confers a sort of immunity against suicide.*

Spain, Ireland and Italy are the three countries of Europe where there is least suicide; the first has 17 cases per million inhabitants, the second 21 and the third 37. Inversely, nowhere else is murder so common. *These are the only countries where the number of murders exceeds that of voluntary deaths.* Spain has thrice as many of one as of the other (1,484 homicides on the average during the years 1885–89 and only 514 suicides); Ireland twice as many (225 of one and 116 of the other); Italy one and a half times as many (2,322 as against 1,437). On the contrary, France and Prussia abound in suicides (160 and 260 cases per million); homicides there are only one-tenth as numerous: France has only 734 cases and Prussia 459 per average year for the period 1882–88.

The same proportions appear within each country. In Italy, on the map of suicides, the entire North is dark, the South absolutely clear; but exactly the reverse is true on the map of homicides. Moreover, if the Italian provinces are divided into two classes according to their suicide-rates and if the average rate of homicides in each is sought, the contrast appears most strikingly:

1st class	From 4.1 suicides to 30 per million	271.9 homicides per million
2nd class	From 30 suicides to 80 per million	95.2 homicides per million

The province where there are most murders is Calabria, with 69 qualified homicides per million; there is none where suicide is so rare.

In France, the departments where most murders are committed are Corsica, Pyrénées-Orientales, Lozère and Ardèche. With respect to

ministrative or judicial inquests in the doubtful cases are more poorly conducted than formerly; a supposition for which we know of no foundation. Tarde, to be sure, is surprised at the contemporary increase in deaths by submersion, and in this increase is inclined to see a hidden increase in the number of homicides. But the number of deaths by lightning has increased much more; it has doubled. Criminal malevolence had nothing to do with this. The truth is, first, that statistical tabulations are computed more exactly and, as for the cases of submersion, that more frequent sea bathing, more active harbors and more numerous river vessels occasion more accidents.

suicides, Corsica falls from first place to 85th, Pyrénées-Orientales to 63rd, Lozère to 83rd and Ardèche to 68th.[57]

In Austria suicide is at its maximum in Lower Austria, in Bohemia and in Moravia, while it is rare in Carniola and Dalmatia. On the contrary Dalmatia has 79 homicides per million inhabitants and Carniola 57.4, while Lower Austria has only 14, Bohemia 11 and Moravia 15.

3. We have shown that wars have a restraining effect on the development of suicide. They have the same effect on robberies, frauds, abuses of confidence, etc. But one crime is an exception: homicide. In France, in 1870, unpremeditated murders which averaged 119 for the years 1866–69 rose abruptly to 133 and then to 224 in 1871, an increase of 88 per cent,[58] falling to 162 in 1872. This increase will appear still more important if we reflect that the age at which most murders are committed is about thirty and that all young men were then with the colors. So that the crimes they would have committed in time of peace do not appear in statistical calculations. No doubt moreover, the confusion of judicial administration must have prevented more than one crime from being known or more than one preliminary investigation from ending in prosecution. If the number of homicides increased in spite of these two causes of diminution, the seriousness of the real rise may be surmised.

In Prussia, likewise, when war broke out against Denmark in 1864, homicides rose from 137 to 169, a level they had not reached since 1854; in 1865 they fell to 153, but rose again in 1866 (159), although the Prussian army had been mobilized. In 1870 a slight fall in comparison with 1869 is registered (151 cases as against 185) which is accentuated in 1871 (136 cases), but how much less than for other crimes! At the same time, robberies qualified as crimes sank by one half, 4,599 in 1870 as against 8,676 in 1869. Moreover, unpremeditated and premeditated murders are included together in these figures; but these two crimes do not have the same significance and we know that in France also only the former increase in wartime. So that if the whole decrease of all sorts of homicides is not greater, one

[57] The inversion is less marked for premeditated murder; which confirms what was said above of the mixed character of this crime.
[58] Premeditated murders, on the contrary, which were 200 in 1869, 215 in 1868, fall to 162 in 1870. The great difference between these two kinds of crime is clear.

may believe that if premeditated murders were eliminated the unpremeditated would show a considerable rise. Besides, if all cases undoubtedly omitted for the two reasons above mentioned were added, this apparent fall would be reduced to very little. Finally, it is very strange that involuntary murders rose then very perceptibly, from 268 in 1869 to 303 in 1870 and 310 in 1871.[59] Does this not prove that less value was set upon life at that time than in time of peace?

Political crises have the same effect. In France, while the curve of unpremeditated murders had remained stationary from 1840 to 1846, it rose abruptly in 1848 and reached a maximum of 240 in 1849.[60] The same thing had already happened during the first years of Louis Philippe's reign. The struggles of political parties were then very violent. It was just then that unpremeditated murders reached their highest point throughout the entire century. From 204 in 1830 they rose to 264 in 1831, a figure never exceeded; in 1832 they were still 253 and in 1833, 257. In 1834 an abrupt fall occurred which increased steadily; in 1838 there were only 145 cases, a reduction of 44 per cent. During this time suicide was developing in the opposite direction. In 1833 it was at the same level as in 1829 (1,973 cases on the one hand, 1,904 on the other); then in 1834 a very rapid rise began. In 1838 the increase was 30 per cent.

4. Suicide is much more urban than rural. The opposite is true of homicide. By combining unpremeditated murders, parricides and infanticides, we find that in 1887, 11.1 crimes of this nature were committed in the country and only 8.6 in cities. In 1880 the figures are about the same; respectively 11.0 and 9.3.

5. We have seen that Catholicism reduces the tendency to suicide while Protestantism increases it. Inversely, homicides are much more frequent in Catholic countries than among Protestant peoples:

Catholic Countries	Simple Homicides per Million	Premeditated Murders per Million	Protestant Countries	Simple Homicides per Million	Premeditated Murders per Million
Italy	70	23.1	Germany	3.4	3.3
Spain	64.9	8.2	England	3.9	1.7
Hungary	56.2	11.9	Denmark	4.6	3.7
Austria	10.2	8.7	Holland	3.1	2.5
Ireland	8.1	2.3	Scotland	4.4	0.70
Belgium	8.5	4.2			
France	6.4	5.6			
Averages	32.1	9.1	Averages	3.8	2.3

[59] According to Starke, op. cit., p. 133.
[60] Premeditated murders remain about stationary.

The contrast between these two groups of societies is especially striking as regards simple homicide.

The same contrast appears within Germany. The districts most above the average are all Catholic: Posen (18.2 premeditated and unpremeditated murders per million inhabitants), Donau (16.7), Bromberg (14.8), Upper and Lower Bavaria (13.0). Within Bavaria, likewise, the fewer Protestants in a province, so much the greater its abundance in homicides:

Catholic Minority	Premeditated & Unpremeditated Murders per Million	Catholic Majority	Premeditated and Unpremeditated Murders per Million	More Than 90% Catholic	Premeditated and Unpremeditated Murders per Million
Rhine Palatinate	2.8	Lower Franconia	9	Upper Palatinate	4.3
Central Franconia	6.9			Upper Bavaria	13.0
Upper Franconia	6.9	Swabia	9.2	Lower Bavaria	13.0
Average	5.5	Average	9.1	Average	10.1

Only the Upper Palatinate is an exception to the law. Besides, we need only compare the above table with that on page 353 for the inverse proportion between the distribution of suicide and that of homicide to appear clearly.

6. Finally, while family life has a moderating effect upon suicide, it rather stimulates murder. During the years 1884–87, a million married men showed on the average 5.07 murders per year; a million unmarried above 15 years, 12.7. The former therefore seem to enjoy a coefficient of preservation with relation to the latter of about 2.3. Only we must remember that the two categories of persons are not of the same age and that the intensity of the homicidal tendency varies at the different periods of life. The unmarried average from 25 to 30 years, married men about 45. Now the tendency to murder is maximal between 25 and 30 years; a million individuals of this age show 15.4 murders annually while at 45 years the rate is only 6.9. The proportion of the first to the second number is 2.2. Thus, merely because of their greater age, married men would commit only half as many murders as unmarried. Their apparently privileged situation therefore does not depend on the fact that they are married, but on the fact that they are older. Domestic life gives them no immunity.

Not only does it furnish no protection against homicide but it more probably supplies a stimulus to it. It is probable indeed that the married population has, on principle, a higher morality than the unmarried. We believe that it owes this superiority less to matrimonial selection, the effects of which however are not negligible, than to the actual influence of the family on each of its members. A person is almost certainly less well insured morally when isolated and left to himself than when constantly under the beneficent discipline of family surroundings. If then, so far as homicide is concerned, married men are not better off than unmarried men, it is because the moralizing influence they undergo, which should deflect them from all sorts of crime, is partly neutralized by an aggravating influence, which impels them to murder and which must be connected with family life.[61]

By way of summary, then, suicide sometimes coexists with homicide, sometimes they are mutually exclusive; sometimes they react under the same conditions in the same way, sometimes in opposite ways, and the antagonistic cases are the most numerous. How explain these apparently contradictory facts?

The only way to reconcile them is by admitting that there are different sorts of suicide, some of which have a certain kinship to homicide, while it is repugnant to others. For the identical phenomenon cannot possibly behave so differently under the same circumstances. The suicide which varies in the same proportion with murder and that which varies inversely with it cannot be of like nature.

Actually we have shown that there are different types of suicide, the characteristics of which are not at all the same. The conclusion of the preceding book is thus confirmed, while also serving to explain the facts just set forth. They would have sufficed by themselves to suggest the inner diversity of suicide; but the hypothesis ceases to be only an hypothesis when confronted with the results just previously obtained, while these receive a supplementary confirmation from this interconnection. Now that we know the different sorts of suicide and of what they consist, we may even easily perceive which are incompatible with homicide; which, on the contrary, depend partly on the

[61] These remarks, however, are intended rather to raise than to settle the question. It could be settled only if the influences of age and of marital status were isolated, as we have done for suicide.

same causes; and why incompatibility is the more common phenomenon.

The type of suicide actually the most widespread and which con-
tributes most to raise the annual total of voluntary deaths is egoistic
suicide. It is characterized by a state of depression and apathy produced by exaggerated individuation. The individual no longer cares
to live because he no longer cares enough for the only medium which
attaches him to reality, that is to say, for society. Having too keen a
feeling for himself and his own value, he wishes to be his own only
goal, and as such an objective cannot satisfy him, drags out languidly
and indifferently an existence which henceforth seems meaningless to
him. Homicide depends on opposite conditions. It is a violent act inseparable from passion. Now, whenever society is integrated in such
a way that the individuation of its parts is weakly emphasized, the
intensity of collective states of conscience raises the general level of
the life of the passions; it is even true that no soil is so favorable to
the development of the specifically homicidal passions. Where family
spirit has retained its ancient strength, offences against the family
are regarded as sacrileges which cannot be too cruelly avenged and
the vengeance for which cannot be left to third persons. This is the
source of the practice of *vendetta* which still leaves its bloody trace
on our Corsica and certain southern countries. Where religious faith
is very intense, it often inspires murders and this is also true of political faith.

Moreover and above all, the homicidal current, generally speaking,
is more violent the less it is restrained by the public conscience, that
is, the more venial attempts against life are considered; and since,
less weight is attached to them, the less value common morality attaches to the individual and his interests, weak individuation or, to
use our term again, a state of excessive altruism, impels to homicides.
This is why they are both frequent and little repressed in lower socities. This frequency and the relative indulgence accorded homicides
spring from one and the same cause. The less respect there is for individual persons, the more they are exposed to violence, while this
violence at the same time appears less criminal. Egoistic suicide and
homicide, therefore, spring from antagonistic causes, and consequently it is impossible for the one to develop readily where the
other flourishes. Where social passions are strong, men are much less

inclined either to idle revery or to cold, epicurean calculation. When man is used to set little value on individual destinies, he is not inclined to much self-interrogation concerning his own destiny. When he cares little for human pain, he feels the weight of his personal sufferings less.

On the contrary, and for the same reasons, altruistic suicide and homicide may get along very well together; for they depend on conditions different only in degree. When one is trained to think little of his own life, he cannot have much regard for another's. For this reason homicides and voluntary deaths are equally endemic among certain primitive peoples. But the cases of parallelism which we have found among civilized nations probably cannot be attributed to the same source. A state of exaggerated altruism cannot have produced the suicides which we have occasionally found to coexist in great numbers with murders in the most cultivated environments. For altruism must be extraordinarily strong to impel to suicide, even stronger than to give the impulse to homicide. In fact, however low an estimate I put on individual life in general, I shall always value my own individual life more than that of others. All things being equal, the average man tends to respect human personality in himself more than in his fellows; consequently, a more powerful cause is required to destroy this sentiment of respect in the first case than in the second. Now today, outside of some few special environments like the army, the taste for impersonality and renunciation is too little pronounced and the opposite feelings too strong and general to make self-immolation so easy as this. There must therefore be another, more modern form of suicide, equally capable of combination with homicide.

This is anomic suicide. Anomy, in fact, begets a state of exasperation and irritated weariness which may turn against the person himself or another according to circumstances; in the first case, we have suicide, in the second, homicide. The causes determining the direction of such over-excited forces probably depend on the agent's moral constitution. According to its greater or less resistance, it will incline one way rather than the other. A man of low morality will kill another rather than himself. We have even seen that these two manifestations sometimes occur one after the other and that they are only two aspects of a single act, which shows their close relationship. The exacerbated condition of the individual is then such that it requires two victims to be assuaged.

This is why there exists today, especially in great centers and regions of intense civilization, a certain parallelism between the development of homicide and that of suicide. It is because anomy is in an acute state there. The same cause prevents murders from decreasing as rapidly as suicides increase. Though the advance of individualism closes off one of the sources of homicide, anomy, accompanying economic development, opens another. It is particularly probable that if in France and especially in Prussia the slaying of one's self and the slaying of others have increased simultaneously since the war, the reason is the increase of moral instability in both countries, though for different causes. This is, finally, also the explanation why antagonism is the commoner relation, in spite of these partial correspondences. Anomic suicide occurs in large numbers only at special points, where industrial and commercial activity are very great. Egoistic suicide is probably the most widespread; but this precludes sanguinary crime.

We thus reach the following conclusion. If suicide and homicide often vary inversely to one another, it is not because they are two different aspects of the same phenomenon; but because in some respects they form two opposed social currents. In these respects they are as mutually exclusive as day and night, just as the diseases of extreme drought preclude those of extreme humidity. If this general opposition still does not completely prevent harmony, it is because certain types of suicide, instead of depending on causes opposed to those which occasion homicide, are on the contrary expressions of the same social condition and develop in the midst of the same moral environment. Besides, it may be anticipated that homicides which coexist with anomic suicide and those which are reconcilable with altruistic suicide cannot be of the same nature; that homicide, therefore, like suicide is not a single, indivisible criminological entity, but must include a variety of species very different from one another. But this is not the place to dwell on this important proposition of criminology.

It is inexact, then, to say that suicide has desirable counter-effects which lessen its immorality, and that it may therefore be well not to interfere with its spread. It is not a derivative of homicide.

Doubtless, the moral constitution on which egoistic suicide depends and that which retards murder among the most civilized peoples are closely related. But the victim of this sort of suicide, far from being an abortive murderer, has nothing of the murderer about him. He is a sad, depressed person. His act may accordingly be condemned without transforming those in the same class with him into assassins. Will it be objected that condemning suicide is a simultaneous condemnation, and consequent weakening of the state of mind which gives rise to it, that is, a condemnation and weakening of that hyperaesthesia for everything relating to the individual? And that by so doing we risk strengthening the taste for impersonality and for the homicide which springs from this impersonality? But to restrain the inclination to murder, individualism need not attain this excessive intensity which makes it a source of suicide. For the individual to be averse to shedding the blood of his fellows, it is not imperative that he care for nothing but himself. He need only love and respect human personality generally. The tendency to individuation may therefore be restrained within proper limits without the tendency to homicide being thereby strengthened.

As for anomy, since it produces both homicide and suicide, whatever checks it checks both of these. There need be no fear that, if prevented from appearing in the form of suicide, it may be translated into more numerous murders; for a man sensitive enough to moral discipline to renounce suicide out of respect for the public conscience and its prohibitions will be much less inclined to homicide which is more severely reproved and repressed. Besides, we have seen that the best types kill themselves in such cases, so that there is no reason to favor a selection which would be retrogressive.

This chapter may help to solve an often debated problem.

The discussions are well-known that are occasioned by the question whether our feelings for our fellow-men are only extensions of egoistic sentiments or, on the contrary, independent of them. We have just seen that both hypotheses are baseless. Certainly, pity for another and pity for ourselves are not foreign to each other, since their development or recession is parallel; but one does not spring from the other. If a bond of kinship exists between them, it is their common derivation from a single state of the collective conscience, of which they are only different aspects. What they express is the manner in which public opinion estimates the moral value of the individual in general. If the individual looms large in public estimation, we apply this social judgement to others as well as to ourselves; their persons, as well as our own, assume more value in our eyes, and we become more sensitive to whatever concerns each of them individually as well as to what concerns us particularly. Their griefs, like our own, are more readily intolerable to us. Our sympathy for them is not, accordingly, a mere extension of what we feel for ourselves. But both are effects of one cause and constituted by the same moral state. Of course this varies, depending on whether it is applied to ourselves or to others; in the first case our egoistic instincts reenforce it, in the second, weaken it. But it exists and is active in both cases. So true is it that even the feelings apparently most associated with the individual's personal temperament depend on causes greater than himself! Our very egoism is in large part a product of society.

CHAPTER 3
PRACTICAL CONSEQUENCES

Now that we know what suicide is, its species and its principal laws, we must seek to find what attitude present-day societies should take toward it.

But this question itself presupposes another. Should the present state of suicide among civilized peoples be considered as normal or abnormal? According to the solution one adopts, he will consider reforms necessary and possible with a view to restraining it, or, on the contrary, will agree, not without censure, to accept it as it is.

I

Some are perhaps astonished that this question could be raised.

It is true, we usually regard everything immoral as abnormal. Therefore, if suicide offends the public conscience, as has been established, it seems impossible not to see in it a phenomenon of social pathology. But we have shown elsewhere [1] that even the preeminent form of immorality, crime itself, need not necessarily be classed among morbid manifestations. To be sure, this declaration shocked certain persons and may have seemed, on superficial examination, to shake the foundations of morality. Nevertheless there is nothing subversive about it. To assure one's self one need only refer to the argument on which it rests, which may be summarized as follows.

Either the word disease means nothing or it means something avoidable. Doubtless, not everything avoidable is morbid, but whatever is morbid may be avoided, at least by most people. Without

---

[1] See *Règles de la Méthode sociologique,* chap. III.

abandoning all distinctions of ideas and terms alike, one cannot call a state or characteristic morbid which members of a species cannot avoid having, one necessarily implied in their constitution. On the other hand, we have only one objective and empirically determinable sign, controllable by others, by which we may recognize the existence of this necessity: universality. When two facts always and everywhere occur together without a single cited exception, it is contrary to all methodology to suppose that they can be separated. Not that one is always the other's cause. The bond between them may be mediate,[2] but it exists and is necessary, none the less.

Now there is no society known where a more or less developed criminality is not found under different forms. No people exists whose morality is not daily infringed upon. We must therefore call crime necessary and declare that it cannot be non-existent, that the fundamental conditions of social organization, as they are understood, logically imply it. Consequently it is normal. It is useless to invoke the inevitable imperfections of human nature and maintain that evil does not cease to be evil even though it cannot be prevented; this is the preacher's language, not the scholar's. A necessary imperfection is not a disease; otherwise disease would have to be postulated everywhere, since imperfection is everywhere. No organic function, no anatomical form exists, some further perfection of which may not be conceived. It has been said that an oculist would blush to have constructed so crude an instrument of vision as the human eye. But from this it has not been and could not be concluded that the structure of this organ is abnormal. Moreover, to employ the somewhat theological language of our adversaries, whatever is necessary must have some perfection in it. *Whatever is an indispensable condition of life cannot fail to be useful, unless life itself is not useful.* The proposition is inescapable. And we have actually shown how crime may be of service. But it serves only when reproved and repressed. The mere fact of cataloguing it among the phenomena of normal sociology has been wrongly thought to imply its absolution. If it is normal that there should be crimes, it is normal that they should be punished. Punishment and crime are two terms of an in-

---

[2] And is not every logical connection thus mediate? Close as the two terms it connects may be, they are always distinct, and thus there is always a space, a logical interval between them.

separable pair. One is as indispensable as the other. Every abnormal relaxation of the system of repression results in stimulating criminality and giving it an abnormal intensity.

Let us apply these ideas to suicide.

We have not sufficient data, it is true, to be sure that there is no society where suicide is not found. Statistics on suicide are available to us for only a small number of peoples. For the rest, the existence of chronic suicide can be proved only by the traces it leaves in legislation. Now, we do not know with certainty that suicide has everywhere been the object of juridical regulation. But we may affirm that this is usually the case. It is sometimes proscribed, sometimes reproved; sometimes its interdiction is formal, sometimes it includes reservations and exceptions. But all analogies permit the belief that it can never have remained a matter of indifference to law and morality; that is, it has always been sufficiently important to attract the attention of the public conscience. At any rate, it is certain that suicidogenetic currents of different intensity, depending on the historical period, have always existed among the peoples of Europe; statistics prove it ever since the last century, and juridical monuments prove it for earlier periods. Suicide is therefore an element of their normal constitution, and even, probably, of any social constitution.

It is also possible to see their mutual connection.

This is especially true of altruistic suicide with respect to lower societies. Precisely because the strict subordination of the individual to the group is the principle on which they rest, altruistic suicide is there, so to speak, an indispensable procedure of their collective discipline. If men, there, did not set a low value on life, they would not be what they should be; and from the moment they value it so lightly, everything inevitably becomes a pretext for them to abandon it. So there is a close connection between the practice of this sort of suicide and the moral organization of this sort of society. It is the same today in those special settings where abnegation and impersonality are essential. Even now, military esprit can only be strong if the individual is self-detached, and such detachment necessarily throws the door open to suicide.

For opposite reasons, in societies and environments where the dignity of the person is the supreme end of conduct, where man is a God to mankind, the individual is readily inclined to consider the man in himself as a God and to regard himself as the object of his own cult. When morality consists primarily in giving one a very high idea of one's self, certain combinations of circumstances readily suffice to make man unable to perceive anything above himself. Individualism is of course not necessarily egoism, but it comes close to it; the one cannot be stimulated without the other being enlarged. Thus, egoistic suicide arises. Finally, among peoples where progress is and should be rapid, rules restraining individuals must be sufficiently pliable and malleable; if they preserved all the rigidity they possess in primitive societies, evolution thus impeded could not take place promptly enough. But then inevitably, under weaker restraint, desires and ambitions overflow impetuously at certain points. As soon as men are inoculated with the precept that their duty is to progress, it is harder to make them accept resignation; so the number of the malcontent and disquieted is bound to increase. The entire morality of progress and perfection is thus inseparable from a certain amount of anomy. Hence, a definite moral constitution corresponds to each type of suicide and is interconnected with it. One cannot exist without the other, for suicide is only the form inevitably assumed by each moral constitution under certain conditions, particular, to be sure, but inescapably arising.

We shall be answered that these varied currents cause suicide only if exaggerated; and asked whether they might not have everywhere a single, moderate intensity? This is wishing for the conditions of life to be everywhere the same, which is neither possible nor desirable. There are special environments in every society which are reached by collective states only through the latter being modified; according to circumstances, they are strengthened or weakened. For a current to have a certain strength in most of the country, it therefore has to exceed or fail to reach this strength at certain points.

But not only are these excesses in one or the other direction necessary; they have their uses. For if the most general state is also the one best adapted to the most general circumstances of social life, it cannot be so related with unusual circumstances; yet society must be capable of being adapted to both. A man in whom the taste for activity never surpassed the average could not maintain himself in situations requiring an unusual effort. Likewise, a society in which intellectual individualism could not be exaggerated would be unable to shake off the yoke of tradition and renew its faiths, even when this became necessary. Inversely, where this same spiritual state could not on occasion be reduced enough to allow the opposite current to develop, what would happen in time of war, when passive obedience is the highest duty? But, for these forms of activity to be produced when they are needed, society must not have totally forgotten them. Thus, it is indispensable that they have a place in the common existence; there must be circles where an unrelenting spirit of criticism and free examination is maintained, others, like the army, where the old religion of authority is preserved almost intact. Of course, in ordinary times, the influence of these special foci must be restricted to certain limits; since the sentiments which flourish there relate to particular circumstances, they must not be generalized. But if they must remain localized, it is equally important that they exist. This need will seem still clearer if we remember that societies not only are required to confront different situations in the course of a single period, but that they cannot even endure without transformation. Within one century, the normal proportions of individualism and altruism fitting for modern peoples will no longer be the same. But the future would be impossible if its germs were not contained in the present. For a collective tendency to be able to grow weaker or stronger through evolution, it must not become set once for all in a single form, from which it could not free itself; it could not vary in time if it were incapable of variation in space.[3]

The different currents of collective sadness which derive from these three moral states have their own reasons for existence so long as they are not excessive. Indeed, it is wrong to believe that unmixed joy is the normal state of sensibility. Man could not live if he were entirely impervious to sadness. Many sorrows can be endured only by being embraced, and the pleasure taken in them naturally has a somewhat melancholy character. So, melancholy is morbid only

[3] What helps make this question unclear is the failure to observe how relative these ideas of sickness and health are. What is normal today will no longer be so tomorrow, and vice versa. The large intestines of primitive man are normal for his environment but would not be so today. What is morbid for individuals may be normal for society. Neurasthenia is a sickness from the point of view of individual physiology; but what would a society be without neurasthenics? They really have a social role to play. When a state is said to be normal or abnormal, one must add, "With reference to this or that," or else one is misunderstood.

when it occupies too much place in life; but it is equally morbid for it to be wholly excluded from life. The taste for happy expansiveness must be moderated by the opposite taste; only on this condition will it retain measure and harmonize with reality. It is the same with societies as with individuals. Too cheerful a morality is a loose morality; it is appropriate only to decadent peoples and is found only among them. Life is often harsh, treacherous or empty. Collective sensibility must reflect this side of existence, too. This is why there has to be, beside the current of optimism which impels men to regard the world confidently, an opposite current, less intense, of course, and less general than the first, but able to restrain it partially; for a tendency does not limit itself, it can never be restrained except by another tendency. From certain indications it even seems that the tendency to a sort of melancholy develops as we rise in the scale of social types. As we have said in another work,[4] it is a quite remarkable fact that the great religions of the most civilized peoples are more deeply fraught with sadness than the simpler beliefs of earlier societies. This certainly does not mean that the current of pessimism is eventually to submerge the other, but it proves that it does not lose ground and that it does not seem destined to disappear. Now, for it to exist and maintain itself, there must be a special organ in society to serve as its substratum. There must be groups of individuals who more especially represent this aspect of the collective mood. But the part of the population which plays this role is necessarily that where ideas of suicide easily take root.

But it does not follow from the fact that a suicidogenetic current of a certain strength must be considered as a phenomenon of normal sociology, that every current of the same sort is necessarily of the same character. If the spirit of renunciation, the love of progress, the taste for individuation have their place in every kind of society, and cannot exist without becoming generators of suicide at certain points, it is further necessary for them to have this property only in a certain measure, varying with various peoples. It is only justified if it does not pass certain limits. Likewise, the collective penchant for sadness

[4] *Division du travail social,* p. 266.

is only wholesome as long as it is not preponderant. So the above remarks have not settled the question whether the present status of suicide among civilized nations is or is not normal. We need further to consider whether its tremendous aggravation during the past century is not pathological in origin.

It has been called the ransom-money of civilization. Certainly, it is general in Europe and more pronounced the higher the culture of European nations. In fact, it rose 411 per cent in Prussia from 1826 to 1890, 385 per cent in France from 1826 to 1888, 318 per cent in German Austria from 1841–45 to 1877, 238 per cent in Saxony from 1841 to 1875, 212 per cent in Belgium from 1841 to 1889, only 72 per cent in Sweden from 1841 to 1871–75, 35 per cent in Denmark during the same period. Italy, since 1870, or since it became an active sharer in European civilization, saw the number of its suicides rise from 788 cases to 1,653, an increase of 109 per cent in twenty years. Moreover, suicide is most widespread everywhere in the most cultivated regions. Thus it was conceivable that a link might exist between the progress of intelligence and of suicide, that one went hand in hand with the other; [5] this is a thesis similar to that of an Italian criminologist, that the increase of crimes was caused and compensated by the parallel increase of economic transactions.[6] If it were admitted, one would have to conclude that the characteristic constitution of higher societies implies an exceptional stimulation of suicidogenetic currents; so that their actual extreme violence would be normal because necessary, and there would be no way of taking special measures against it without simultaneously taking them against civilization.[7]

But one fact especially should throw us on our guard against this reasoning. In Rome, at the very height of the empire, a veritable hecatomb of voluntary deaths likewise occurred. So that one might

[5] Oettingen, *Ueber acuten und chronischen Selbstmord*, pp. 28-32 and *Moralstatistik*, p. 761.

[6] Poletti; we know his theory, however, only through its exposition by Tarde, in his *Criminalité comparée*, p. 72.

[7] To escape this conclusion, to be sure, it is said (Oettingen) that suicide is only one of the evil aspects (*Schattenseiten*) of civilization, and that it may be diminished without affecting civilization. But this is playing with words. If suicide springs from the same causes on which culture depends, we cannot diminish one without reducing the other; for the only means of combatting it effectively is to attack its causes.

have concluded then as now that this was the price of the intellectual development achieved and that it is a law of cultivated peoples that they must furnish a greater number of victims to suicide than others. But the historical sequel showed how unfounded such an induction would have been; for this epidemic of suicides lasted only for a time, while Roman culture survived. Not only did the Christian societies assimilate its best fruits, but from the 16th century on, after the discovery of printing, after the Renaissance and the Reformation, these societies had far surpassed the highest level ever attained by the socities of antiquity. Yet suicide had developed only slightly until the 18th century. Progress was not therefore the necessary cause of so much bloodshed, since its results could be preserved and even surpassed with no continuation of these homicidal effects. Is it not probable, therefore, that the same is true today, that the course of our civilization and that of suicide do not logically involve one another, and that the latter may accordingly be checked without the other stopping simultaneously? Besides, we have seen that suicide is found in the first stages of evolution and that it is even, sometimes, of the utmost virulence. If, then, it exists among the crudest peoples, there is no reason to suppose it to be necessarily related to extreme refinement of manners. Those types of suicide observed at these distant periods have, of course, partly disappeared; but this very disappearance should somewhat reduce our annual tribute and it is thus much more surprising that it keeps becoming heavier.

Thus, we may believe that this aggravation springs not from the intrinsic nature of progress but from the special conditions under which it occurs in our day, and nothing assures us that these conditions are normal. For we must not be dazzled by the brilliant development of sciences, the arts and industry of which we are the witnesses; this development is altogether certainly taking place in the midst of a morbid effervescence, the grievous repercussions of which each one of us feels. It is then very possible and even probable that the rising tide of suicide originates in a pathological state just now accompanying the march of civilization without being its necessary condition.

The rapidity of the growth of suicides really permits no other hypothesis. Actually, in less than fifty years, they have tripled, quadrupled, and even quintupled, depending on the country. On the other hand, we know their connection with the most ineradicable element in the constitution of societies, since they express the mood of societies, and since the mood of peoples, like that of individuals, reflects the state of the most fundamental part of the organism. Our social organization, then, must have changed profoundly in the course of this century, to have been able to cause such a growth in the suicide-rate. So grave and rapid an alteration as this must be morbid; for a society cannot change its structure so suddenly. Only by a succession of slow, almost imperceptible modifications does it achieve different characteristics. The possible changes, even then, are limited. Once a social type is fixed it is no longer infinitely plastic; a limit is soon reached which cannot be passed. Thus the changes presupposed by the statistics of contemporary suicides cannot be normal. Without even knowing exactly of what they consist, we may begin by affirming that they result not from a regular evolution but from a morbid disturbance which, while able to uproot the institutions of the past, has put nothing in their place; for the work of centuries cannot be remade in a few years. But if the cause is so abnormal, the effect must be so, as well. Thus, what the rising flood of voluntary deaths denotes is not the increasing brilliancy of our civilization but a state of crisis and perturbation not to be prolonged with impunity.

To these various reasons another may be added. Though it is true that collective sadness has, normally, a role to play in the life of societies, it is not ordinarily general or intense enough to reach the higher centers of the social body. It remains a submerged current, felt vaguely by the collective personality, which therefore undergoes its influence without clearly taking it into account. At least, if these vague dispositions do affect the common conscience, it is only by tentative and intermittent thrusts. Generally they are expressed merely by fragmentary judgments, isolated maxims, unrelated to one another and which, in spite of their intransigeant aspect, are intended to convey only one side of reality, to be corrected and supplemented by contradictory maxims. Thence come the melancholy sayings and proverbial sallies at life's expense in which sometimes is put the wisdom of nations, but without being more frequent than their opposite numbers. Clearly they convey passing impressions, which have transiently touched consciousness without taking full possession of it. Only when such sentiments acquire unusual strength do

they sufficiently absorb public attention to be seen as a whole, co-
ordinated and systematized, and then become the bases of complete
theories of life. In fact, in Rome and in Greece, it was when society
felt itself seriously endangered that the discouraging theories of Epicurus and Zeno appeared. The formation of such great systems is
therefore an indication that the current of pessimism has reached a
degree of abnormal intensity which is due to some disturbance of the
social organism. We well know how these systems have recently multiplied. To form a true idea of their number and importance it is not
enough to consider the philosophies avowedly of this nature, such as
those of Schopenhauer, Hartmann, etc. We must also consider all
the others which derive from the same spirit under different names.
The anarchist, the aesthete, the mystic, the socialist revolutionary,
even if they do not despair of the future, have in common with the
pessimist a single sentiment of hatred and disgust for the existing
order, a single craving to destroy or to escape from reality. Collective
melancholy would not have penetrated consciousness so far, if it had
not undergone a morbid development; and so the development of
suicide resulting from it is of the same nature.[8]

All proofs combine therefore to make us consider the enormous
increase in the number of voluntary deaths within a century as a pathological phenomenon becoming daily a greater menace. By what
means shall we try to overcome it?

II

Some authors have recommended the reestablishment of the com-
minatory penalties formerly in use.[9]

It is willingly accepted that our present indulgence towards suicide
is really excessive. Since it offends morality, it should be repulsed
more energetically and precisely, and this reprobation should be expressed by definite external signs, that is, penalties. The relaxation of

[8] This argument is open to an objection. Buddhism and Jainism are systematically
pessimistic doctrines of life; should the indication of a morbid state of the peoples
who have practiced them be assumed? The author knows too little of them to decide the question. But let our reasoning be considered only with reference to the
European peoples, and even to the societies of a metropolitan type. Within these
limits we think it open to little dispute. It is still possible that the spirit of renunciation characteristic of certain other societies may be formulated into a system
without anomaly.
[9] Among others, Lisle, *op. cit.*, p. 327 and ff.

our repressive system at this point is in itself an abnormal phenomenon. Yet somewhat severe punishments are impossible; they would not be tolerated by the public conscience. For as we have seen, suicide is a close kin to genuine virtues, which it simply exaggerates. So public opinion is easily divided in its judgment. Since suicide, up to a certain point, emanates from sentiments respected by public opinion, the latter's blame is tempered with reserve and hesitation. Thus arise the ever-recurring controversies between theorists as to whether or not it is contrary to morality. Since a continuous series of graduated, intermediary acts connects it with other acts approved or tolerated by morality, it has naturally enough been regarded at times as of the same nature as they and been apt to benefit by the same tolerance. Far more rarely have such doubts been aroused in behalf of homicide and robbery, because the line of demarcation is more clearly drawn here.[10] Moreover, the mere fact of the death which the victim has inflicted on himself inspires, in spite of everything, too much pity for the censure to be implacable.

For all these reasons only moral penalties could be decreed. The only possible thing would be to refuse the suicide the honors of a regular burial, to deprive the author of the attempt of certain civic, political or family rights, such as certain attributes of the paternal power and eligibility to public office. We believe that public opinion would readily agree that whoever tried to evade his fundamental duties should be deprived of his corresponding rights. But however legitimate these measures were, they could never have more than a very secondary influence; it is childish to suppose that they could check so violent a current.

Besides, all by themselves, they would not touch the evil at its source. Actually, if we have renounced the legal prohibition of suicide, it is because its immorality is too little felt. We let it develop freely because it no longer revolts us to the same extent as formerly. But our moral sensitiveness will never be aroused by legislative measures. It does not depend on the legislator that a fact shall ap-

[10] It is not that the distinction between moral and immoral acts is absolute, even in these cases. The opposition between good and evil lacks the radical character ascribed to it by the popular conscience. Imperceptible gradations lead from one to the other and frontiers are often unclear. Only when acknowledged crimes are involved is the distance great, and the relation between extremes less evident than in the case of suicide.

pear morally hateful or not. When the law forbids acts which public sentiment considers inoffensive, we are indignant with the law, not with the act it punishes. Our excessive tolerance with regard to suicide is due to the fact that, since the state of mind from which it springs is a general one, we cannot condemn it without condemning ourselves; we are too saturated with it not partly to excuse it. But then the only way of making ourselves more severe is to act directly on the current of pessimism, to lead it back to its normal bed and confine it there, to relieve most consciences from its influence and to strengthen them. Once they have recovered their moral equilibrium they will react appropriately against whatever offends them. A repressive system will no longer have to be created out of nothing; it will take shape itself under the pressure of need. Until then it will be artificial and of little use for that reason.

Would not education be the surest means of obtaining this result? As characters may be influenced through it, would it not suffice for them to be so shaped as to become braver and thus less indulgent towards those who willingly give themselves up? This is Morselli's opinion. For him, the prophylactic treatment for suicide entirely consists of the following precept: [11] "To develop in man the power of coordinating his ideas and feelings, so that he may be able to follow a definite purpose in life; in brief, to give strength and energy to the moral character." A thinker of quite a different school reaches the same conclusion: "How," asks Franck, "shall we attack suicide at its source? By improving the great work of education, by striving to improve character as well as intelligence, convictions as well as ideas." [12]

But this is to ascribe to education a power it lacks. It is only the image and reflection of society. It imitates and reproduces the latter in abbreviated form; it does not create it. Education is healthy when peoples themselves are in a healthy state; but it becomes corrupt with them, being unable to modify itself. If the moral environment is affected, since the teachers themselves dwell in it they cannot avoid being influenced; how then should they impress on their pupils a different orientation from what they have received? Each new generation is reared by its predecessor; the latter must therefore improve in order to improve its successor. The movement is circular. It may well

[11] *Op. cit.*, p. 499.
[12] Art. *Suicide*, in *Diction. Philos.*

happen that at great intervals a person emerges whose ideas and aspirations go beyond those of his fellows; but isolated individuals are not enough to remake the moral constitution of peoples. Of course, we enjoy believing that an eloquent voice is enough to transform magically the material of society; but here as elsewhere nothing comes from nothing. The strongest wills cannot elicit non-existent forces from nothingness and the shocks of experience constantly dissipate these facile illusions. Besides, even though through some incomprehensible miracle a pedagogical system were constituted in opposition to the social system, this very antagonism would rob it of all effect. If the collective organization whence comes the moral state it is desired to combat, is intact, the child is bound to feel its effect from the moment he first has contact with it. The school's artificial environment can protect him only briefly and weakly. To the extent that real life increasingly takes possession of him, it will come to destroy the work of the teacher. Education, therefore, can be reformed only if society itself is reformed. To do that, the evil from which it suffers must be attacked at its sources.

Now, these sources we know. We discovered them when we showed the springs from which the chief suicidogenetic currents flow. There is one, however, which certainly has no share in the present progress of suicide: the altruistic current. Today, indeed, it is losing much more ground than it gains; it appears principally in lower societies. Though persisting in the army it does not seem to be of an abnormal intensity there; for to a certain extent it is required to maintain military spirit. Besides, even there it is constantly declining. Egoistic suicide and anomic suicide are the only forms, therefore, whose development may be regarded as morbid, and so we have only them to consider.

Egoistic suicide results from the fact that society is not sufficiently integrated at all points to keep all its members under its control. If it increases inordinately, therefore, it is because the state on which it depends has itself excessively expanded; it is because society, weak and disturbed, lets too many persons escape too completely from its influence. Thus, the only remedy for the ill is to restore enough consistency to social groups for them to obtain a firmer grip on the individual, and for him to feel himself bound to them. He must feel himself more solidary with a collective existence which precedes him in time, which survives him, and which encompasses him at all points. If this occurs, he will no longer find the only aim of his conduct in himself, and, understanding that he is the instrument of a purpose greater than himself, he will see that he is not without significance. Life will resume meaning in his eyes, because it will recover its natural aim and orientation. But what groups are best calculated constantly to reimpress on man this salutary sentiment of solidarity?

Not political society. Especially today; in our great modern States, it is too far removed from the individual to effect him uninterruptedly and with sufficient force. Whatever connection there may be between our daily tasks and the whole of public life, it is too indirect for us to feel it keenly and constantly. Only when matters of serious import are at stake do we feel our dependence on the body politic strongly. Of course, the idea of country is rarely wholly obscured among the moral elite of the people; but in ordinary times it is overshadowed, barely perceptible, and even wholly eclipsed. Such unusual circumstances as a great national or political crisis are necessary for it to assume primary importance, invade the consciences of men, and become the guiding motive of action. No such intermittent influence as this can regularly restrain the suicidal tendency. Not only occasionally but continually the individual must be able to realize that his activity has a goal. For his existence not to seem empty to him, he must constantly see it serving an end of immediate concern to him. But this is possible only if a simpler and less extensive social environment enwraps him with real intimacy and offers his activity a nearer aim.

Religious society is equally unadapted to this function. Of course, it has been able to exert a beneficent influence under given conditions; but the necessary conditions are no longer given. In reality, it secures against suicide only if powerfully enough constructed to have a close grip on the individual. Because the Catholic religion imposes on its faithful a vast system of dogmas and practices, and so penetrates all the details of even their earthly life, it attaches them to this life with greater force than Protestantism. The Catholic is much less likely to lose sight of the ties binding him to the confessional group of which he is part, because at every moment this group is recalled to him in the shape of imperative precepts applying to different circumstances of life. He need not anxiously watch his step; he refers each step to God because most of them are divinely regulated, that is, by the Church which is the visible body of God. But furthermore, because these commands supposedly emanate from superhuman authority, human reflection has no right to bring itself to bear on them. It would be actual contradiction to attribute such an origin to them and permit free criticism of them. Religion, therefore, modifies the inclination to suicide only to the extent that it prevents men from thinking freely. This seizure of possession of human intelligence is difficult at present and will become more and more so. It offends our dearest sentiments. We increasingly refuse to admit that limits may be set to reason and that one may say: Thou shalt go no further. And this is no movement of yesterday; the history of the human mind is the very history of the progress of free thought. It is childish to wish to check a current which everything proves irresistible. Unless the great societies of today helplessly crumble and we return to the little social groups of long ago,[13] that is, unless humanity returns to its starting-point, religions will no longer be able to exert very deep or wide sway on consciences. This does not mean that new ones will not be founded. But the only viable ones will be those permitting more freedom to the right of criticism, to individual initiative, than even the most liberal Protestant sects. So they could not have the strong effect on their members necessary to set up an obstacle to suicide.

Though many authors have considered religion the only remedy for the evil, they are mistaken as to the sources of its power. They make it consist almost wholly of a number of lofty thoughts and noble maxims which are capable, on the whole, of accommodating themselves to rationalism, and which they think need only be rooted in the heart and mind of men to prevent weakness. But this is an error, both as to the essence of religion and especially as to the causes of the immunity it has sometimes conferred against suicide. Actually, this privilege belonged to religion, not because it encouraged in men

[13] Let us not be misunderstood. Of course, the time will come for our present societies to perish; they will therefore decompose into smaller groups. But, if the future is to be judged by the past, this situation will be merely temporary and these partial groups will be the material of new societies, much larger than those of today. One may even foresee that these partial groups will be much greater than those whose combination formed present-day societies.

some vague sentiment of a more or less mysterious beyond, but from the powerful and scrupulous discipline to which it subjected thought and conduct. When religion is merely a symbolic idealism, a traditional philosophy, subject to discussion and more or less a stranger to our daily occupations, it can hardly have much influence upon us. A God relegated by his majesty outside of the universe and everything temporal, cannot serve as a goal for our temporal activity, which is thus left without an objective. From that moment on, too many things are unrelated to him for him to give a sense to life. Abandoning the world to us, as unworthy of himself, he simultaneously abandons us to ourselves in everything respecting the world's life. Men cannot be prevented from taking their lives through meditations on the mysteries surrounding us, nor even through belief in an all-powerful being, but one infinitely removed from ourselves, to whom we shall have to give account only in an undetermined future. In a word, we are only preserved from egoistic suicide in so far as we are socialized; but religions can socialize us only in so far as they refuse us the right of free examination. They no longer have, and probably will never again have, enough authority to wring such a sacrifice from us. We therefore cannot count on them to rear barriers to suicide. Besides, if those who see our only cure in a religious restoration were self-consistent, they would demand the reestablishment of the most archaic religions. For against suicide Judaism preserves better than Catholicism, and Catholicism better than Protestanism. Yet the Protestant religion is the freest from material practices and consequently the most idealistic. On the contrary, Judaism, in spite of its great historic role, still clings to the most primitive religious forms in many respects. How true it is that moral and intellectual superiority of dogma counts for naught in its possible influence on suicide!

We are left with the family, the prophylactic virtue of which is assured. But it would be delusive to believe that one need only reduce the number of the unmarried to stop the growth of suicide. For if married persons have less tendency to kill themselves, this tendency itself increases with the same regularity and in the same proportions as that in the case of unmarried persons. From 1880 to 1887 suicides of married persons grew 35 per cent (3,706 cases as against 2,735); suicides of unmarried persons only 13 per cent (2,894 cases as against 2,554). In 1863–68, according to Bertillon's calculations, the rate of the former was 154 per million; it was 242 in 1887, an increase of 57 per cent. During the same time the rate for unmarried persons rose very little more; it went from 173 to 289, an increase of 67 per cent. *The aggravation appearing in the course of the century is therefore independent of marital status.*

Changes have actually occurred in the constitution of the family which no longer allow it to have the same preservative influence as formerly. While it once kept most of its members within its orbit from birth to death and formed a compact mass, indivisible and endowed with a quality of permanence, its duration is now brief. It is barely formed when it begins to disperse. As soon as the children's first growth is over, they very often leave to complete their education away from home; moreover, it is almost the rule that as soon as they are adult they establish themselves away from their parents and the hearth is deserted. For most of the time, at present, the family may be said to be reduced to the married couple alone, and we know that this union acts feebly against suicide. Consequently, since it plays a smaller role in life, it no longer suffices as an object for life. Not, certainly, that we care less for our children; but they are entwined less closely and continuously with our existence and so this existence needs some other basis for being. Since we have to live without them, we also have to attach our thoughts and acts to other objects.

But it is especially the family as a collective being which this periodic dispersion reduces to non-entity. Formerly, domestic society was not just a number of individuals united by bonds of mutual affection; but the group itself, in its abstract and impersonal unity. It was the hereditary name, together with all the memories it recalled, the family house, the ancestral field, the traditional situation and reputation, etc. All this is tending to disappear. A society momentarily dissolving, only to reform elsewhere but under wholly new conditions and with quite new elements, has not sufficient continuity to acquire a personal aspect, a history of its own, to which its members may feel attachment. If men therefore do not replace this age-old objective of their activity, as it little by little disappears from among them, a great void must inevitably appear in existence.

This cause multiplies the suicides not only of married but of unmarried persons. For this state of the family forces the young people to leave their native home before they are able to found another; partly for this reason, households of a single person become increasingly numerous, and this isolation has been shown to increase the tendency to suicide. Yet nothing can stop the movement. Once, when each local environment was more or less closed to others by usages, traditions, the scarcity of communications, each generation remained perforce in its place of origin or at least could not move far from it. But as these barriers vanish, as these small environments are levelled and blended with one another, the individuals inevitably disperse in accordance with their ambitions and to further their interests into the wider spaces now open to them. No scheme can therefore offset this inevitable swarming of the bees and restore the indivisibility which was once the family's strength.

III

Is the evil then incurable? At first glance one might think so, because not one of all the societies whose beneficent influence we have demonstrated above seems able to afford a genuine remedy. But we have shown that, while religion, the family and the nation are preservatives against egoistic suicide, the cause of this does not lie in the special sort of sentiments encouraged by each. Rather, they all owe this virtue to the general fact that they are societies and they possess it only in so far as they are well integrated societies; that is, without excess in one direction or the other. Quite a different group may, then, have the same effect, if it has the same cohesion. Besides the society of faith, of family and of politics, there is one other of which no mention has yet been made; that of all workers of the same sort, in association, all who cooperate in the same function, that is, the occupational group or corporation.

Its aptness for this role is proved by its definition. Since it consists of individuals devoted to the same tasks, with solidary or even combined interests, no soil is better calculated to bear social ideas and sentiments. Identity of origin, culture and occupation makes occupational activity the richest sort of material for a common life. Moreover, in the past the corporation has proved that it could form a collective personality, jealous, even excessively so, of its autonomy and its authority over its members; so there is no doubt of its capacity to be a moral environment for them. There is no reason for the corporative interest not acquiring in its workers' eyes the respectable character and supremacy always possessed by social interests, as contrasted with private interests, in a well-organized society. From another point of view, the occupational group has the three-fold advantage over all others that it is omnipresent, ubiquitous and that its control extends to the greatest part of life. Its influence on individuals is not intermittent, like that of political society, but it is always in contact with them by the constant exercise of the function of which it is the organ and in which they collaborate. It follows the workers wherever they go; which the family cannot do. Wherever they are, they find it enveloping them, recalling them to their duties, supporting them at need. Finally, since occupational life is almost the whole of life, corporative action makes itself felt in every detail of our occupations, which are thus given a collective orientation. Thus the corporation has everything needed to give the individual a setting, to draw him out of his state of moral isolation; and faced by the actual inadequacy of the other groups, it alone can fulfil this indispensable office.

But for it to have this influence it must be organized on wholly different bases from those of today. First, it is essential that it become a definite and recognized organ of our public life, instead of remaining a private group legally permitted, but politically ignored. By this we do not mean that it must necessarily be made obligatory, but the important thing is for it to be so constituted as to play a social role instead of expressing only various combinations of particular interests. This is not all. For the frame not to remain empty, all the germs of life of such a nature as to flourish there must find their places in it. For this grouping to remain no mere label, it must be given definite functions, and there are some which it can fulfil better than any other agency.

At present, European societies have the alternative either of leaving occupational life unregulated, or of regulating it through the State's mediation, since no other organ exists which can play this role of moderator. But the State is too far removed from these complex manifestations to find the special form appropriate to each of them. It is a cumbersome machine, made only for general and clear-cut tasks. Its ever uniform action cannot adapt and adjust itself to the infinite variety of special circumstances. It is therefore necessarily

compressive and levelling in its action. On the other hand, we feel
how impossible it is to leave unorganized all the life thus unattached.
In so doing, by an endless series of oscillations we alternately pass
from authoritarian regulation made impotent by its excessive rigidity
to systematic abstention which cannot last because it breeds anarchy.
Whether the question is one of hours of work, or health, or wages,
or social insurance and assistance, men of good will constantly encounter the same difficulties. As soon as they try to set up some rules,
they prove inapplicable to experience because they lack pliability; or
at least, they apply to the matter for which they are made only by
doing violence to it.

The only way to resolve this antinomy is to set up a cluster of collective forces outside the State, though subject to its action, whose
regulative influence can be exerted with greater variety. Not only will
our reconstituted corporations satisfy this condition, but it is hard to
see what other groups could do so. For they are close enough to the
facts, directly and constantly enough in contact with them, to detect
all their nuances, and they should be sufficiently autonomous to be
able to respect their diversity. To them, therefore, falls the duty of
presiding over companies of insurance, benevolent aid and pensions,
the need of which are felt by so many good minds but which we
rightly hesitate to place in the hands of the State, already so powerful
and awkward; theirs it should likewise be to preside over the disputes
constantly arising between the branches of the same occupation, to
fix conditions—but in different ways according to the different sorts
of enterprise—with which contracts must agree in order to be valid, in
the name of the common interest to prevent the strong from unduly
exploiting the weak, etc. As labor is divided, law and morality
assume a different form in each special function, though still resting
everywhere on the same general principles. Besides the rights and
duties common to all men, there are others depending on qualities
peculiar to each occupation, the number of which increases in importance as occupational activity increasingly develops and diversifies.
For each of these special disciplines an equally special organ is
needed, to apply and maintain it. Of whom could it consist if not
of the workers engaged in the same function?

Here, in broad outlines, is what corporations should be in order
to render the services rightly to be expected of them. When their

present state is considered, of course, it is somewhat hard to conceive of their ever being elevated to the dignity of moral powers. Indeed, they are made up of individuals attached to one another by no bond, with only superficial and intermittent relations, even inclined to treat each other rather as rivals and enemies than as cooperators. But when once they have so many things in common, when the relations between themselves and the group to which they belong are thus close and continuous, sentiments of solidarity as yet almost unknown will spring up, and the present cold moral temperature of this occupational environment, still so external to its members, would necessarily rise. And these changes would occur not only among the agents of economic life, as the above examples might lead one to believe. Every occupation in society would demand such an organization and be capable of receiving it. Thus the social fabric, the meshes of which are so dangerously relaxed, would tighten and be strengthened throughout its entire extent.

This restoration, the need of which is universally felt, unfortunately has to contend with the bad name left in history by the corporations of the ancient regime. Yet is there not more proof of their indispensability in the fact that they have lasted not merely since the Middle Ages but since Greco-Roman antiquity,[14] than of their uselessness in the fact of their recent abrogation? If occupational activity has been corporatively organized, except for a single century, wherever it has developed to any extent, is it not most probable that such organization is necessary, and that if it was no longer equal to its role a hundred years ago, the remedy was to restore and improve, not radically to suppress it? Certainly, it had finally become an obstacle to the most urgent progress. The old, narrowly local corporation, closed to all outside influence, had become an anomaly in a morally and politically unified nation; the excessive autonomy it enjoyed, making it a State within a State, could not be retained while the governmental organ, ramifying itself in all directions, was more and more subordinating all secondary organs of society to itself. So the base on which the institution rested had to be enlarged and the institution itself reconnected with the whole of national life. But if similar corporations of different localities had been connected with one

---

[14] The first colleges of artisans go back to imperial Rome. See Marquardt, *Privatleben der Roemer*, II, p. 4.

another, instead of remaining isolated, so as to form a single system, if all these systems had been subject to the general influence of the State and thus kept in constant awareness of their solidarity, bureaucratic despotism and occupational egoism would have been kept within proper limits. It is true, tradition is not preserved with such facile invariability in a great association, spread over an immense territory, as in a little coterie not exceeding the boundaries of a municipality; [15] but at the same time each particular group is less inclined to see and pursue only its own interest, once it is in regular relationship with the directive center of public life. Only on this condition, indeed, could awareness of the public welfare be kept constantly alert in the individual consciousness. For, as communications would then be uninterrupted between each single organ and the power charged with representing general interests, society would no longer be recalled only intermittently or vaguely to the individual; we should feel it present in the whole course of our daily life. But by overthrowing existing order without putting anything in its place, corporative egoism has only been replaced by a still more corrosive individual egoism. For this reason, this is the only demolition of all those then accomplished which we have to regret. By dispersing the only groups which could persistently unite individual wills, we ourselves have broken the appointed instrument of our moral reorganization.

But not only egoistic suicide would be combatted in this way. Anomic suicide, closely related to it, might be dealt with by the same treatment. Anomy indeed springs from the lack of collective forces at certain points in society; that is, of groups established for the regulation of social life. Anomy therefore partially results from the same state of disaggregation from which the egoistic current also springs. But this identical cause produces different effects, depending on its point of incidence and whether it influences active and practical functions, or functions that are representative. The former it agitates and exasperates; the latter it disorients and disconcerts. In both cases the remedy is therefore the same. And as a matter of fact we have just seen that the chief role of corporations, in the future as in the past, would be to govern social functions, especially economic func-

---

[15] See the reasons in my *Division du travail social*, Bk. II, ch. III, especially p. 335 ff.

tions, and thus to extricate them from their present state of disorganization. Whenever excited appetites tended to exceed all limits, the corporation would have to decide the share that should equitably revert to each of the cooperative parts. Standing above its own members, it would have all necessary authority to demand indispensable sacrifices and concessions and impose order upon them. By forcing the strongest to use their strength with moderation, by preventing the weakest from endlessly multiplying their protests, by recalling both to the sense of their reciprocal duties and the general interest, and by regulating production in certain cases so that it does not degenerate into a morbid fever, it would moderate one set of passions by another, and permit their appeasement by assigning them limits. Thus, a new sort of moral discipline would be established, without which all the scientific discoveries and economic progress in the world could produce only malcontents.

Clearly, in no other environment could this urgent law of distributive justice be developed, nor could it be applied by any other organ. Religion, which once partially assumed this role, would now be unadapted to it. For the essential principle of the only regulation to which it can subject economic life is contempt for riches. If religion exhorts its followers to be satisfied with their lot, it is because of the thought that our condition on earth has nothing to do with our salvation. If religion teaches that our duty is to accept with docility our lot as circumstances order it, this is to attach us exclusively to other purposes, worthier of our efforts; and in general religion recommends moderation in desires for the same reason. But this passive resignation is incompatible with the place which earthly interests have now assumed in collective existence. The discipline they need must not aim at relegating them to second place and reducing them as far as possible, but at giving them an organization in harmony with their importance. The problem has increased in complexity, and while it is no remedy to give appetites free rein, neither is it enough to suppress them in order to control them. Though the last defenders of the old economic theories are mistaken in thinking that regulation is not necessary today as it was yesterday, the apologists of the institution of religion are wrong in believing that yesterday's regulation can be useful today. It is precisely its lack of present usefulness which causes the evil.

These easy solutions have no relation to the difficulties of the situation. Of course, nothing but a moral power can set a law for men; but this must also be sufficiently associated with affairs of this world to be able to estimate them at their true value. The occupational group has just this two-fold character. Being a group, it sufficiently dominates individuals to set limits to their greed; but sees too much of their life not to sympathize with their needs. Of course, it remains true that the State itself has important functions to fulfill. It alone can oppose the sentiment of general utility and the need for organic equilibrium to the particularism of each corporation. But we know that its action can be useful only if a whole system of secondary organs exists to diversify the action. It is, above all, these secondary organs that must be encouraged.

*   *   *

There is one form of suicide, however, which could not be halted by this means; the form springing from conjugal anomy. We seem here confronted by an antinomy which is insoluble.

As we have said, its cause is divorce with all the ideas and customs from which this institution arises and which it merely establishes more firmly. Does it follow that where divorce exists it must be abrogated? This question is too complex to be treated here; it can be profitably approached only after a study of marriage and its evolution. At present we need only concern ourselves with the relations of divorce and suicide. From this point of view we shall say: The only way to reduce the number of suicides due to conjugal anomy is to make marriage more indissoluble.

What makes the problem especially disturbing and lends it an almost dramatic interest is that the suicides of husbands cannot be diminished in this way without increasing those of wives. Must one of the sexes necessarily be sacrificed, and is the solution only to choose the lesser of the two evils? Nothing else seems possible as long as the interests of husband and wife in marriage are so obviously opposed. As long as the latter requires above all, liberty, and the former, discipline, the institution of matrimony cannot be of equal benefit to both. But this antagonism which just now makes the solution impossible is not without remedy, and it may be hoped that it will disappear.

It originates in fact because the two sexes do not share equally in social life. Man is actively involved in it, while woman does little more than look on from a distance. Consequently man is much more highly socialized than woman. His tastes, aspirations and humor have in large part a collective origin, while his companion's are more directly influenced by her organism. His needs, therefore, are quite different from hers, and so an institution intended to regulate their common life cannot be equitable and simultaneously satifying to such opposite needs. It cannot simultaneously be agreeable to two persons, one of whom is almost entirely the product of society, while the other has remained to a far greater extent the product of nature. But it is by no means certain that this opposition must necessarily be maintained. Of course, in one sense it was originally less marked than now, but from this we cannot conclude that it must develop indefinitely. For the most primitive social states are often reproduced at the highest stages of evolution, but under different forms, forms almost the opposites of their original ones. To be sure, we have no reason to suppose that woman may ever be able to fulfill the same functions in society as man; but she will be able to play a part in society which, while peculiarly her own, may yet be more active and important than that of today. The female sex will not again become more similar to the male; on the contrary, we may foresee that it will become more different. But these differences will become of greater social use than in the past. Why, for instance, should not aesthetic functions become woman's as man, more and more absorbed by functions of utility, has to renounce them? Both sexes would thus approximate each other by their very differences. They would be socially equalized, but in different ways.[16] And evolution does seem to be taking place in this direction. Woman differs from man much

---

[16] It may be foreseen that this differentiation would probably no longer have the strictly regulative character that it has today. Woman would not be officially excluded from certain functions and relegated to others. She could choose more freely, but as her choice would be determined by her aptitudes it would generally bear on the same sort of occupations. It would be perceptibly uniform, though not obligatory.

more in cities than in the country; and yet her intellectual and moral constitution is most impregnated with social life in cities.

In any case, this is the only way to reduce the unhappy moral conflict actually dividing the sexes, definite proof of which the statistics of suicide have given us. Only when the difference between husband and wife becomes less, will marriage no longer be thought, so to speak, necessarily to favor one to the detriment of the other. As for the champions today of equal rights for woman with those of man, they forget that the work of centuries cannot be instantly abolished; that juridical equality cannot be legitimate so long as psychological inequality is so flagrant. Our efforts must be bent to reduce the latter. For man and woman to be equally protected by the same institution, they must first of all be creatures of the same nature. Only then will the indissolubility of the conjugal bond no longer be accused of serving only one of the two parties pleading.

IV

In resume, just as suicide does not proceed from man's difficulties in maintaining his existence, so the means of arresting its progress is not to make the struggle less difficult and life easier. If more suicides occur today than formerly, this is not because, to maintain ourselves, we have to make more painful efforts, nor that our legitimate needs are less satisfied, but because we no longer know the limits of legitimate needs nor perceive the direction of our efforts. Competition is of course becoming keener every day, because the greater ease of communication sets a constantly increasing number of competitors at loggerheads. On the other hand, a more perfected division of labor and its accompanying more complex cooperation, by multiplying and infinitely varying the occupations by which men can make themselves useful to other men, multiplies the means of existence and places them within reach of a greater variety of persons. The most inferior aptitudes may find a place here. At the same time, the more intense production resulting from this subtler cooperation, by increasing humanity's total resources, assures each worker an ampler pay and so achieves a balance between the greater wear on vital strength and its recuperation. Indeed, it is certain that average comfort has increased on all levels of the social hierarchy, although perhaps not always in equal proportions. The maladjustment from

which we suffer does not exist because the objective causes of suffering have increased in number or intensity; it bears witness not to
greater economic poverty, but to an alarming poverty of morality.

We must not, however, mistake the meaning of the word. When
an individual or social ill is said to be entirely moral, the usual meaning is that it does not respond to any actual treatment but can be
cured only be repeated exhortations, methodical objurgations, in a
word, by verbal influence. We reason as though a system of ideas had
no reference to the rest of the universe and as if it were enough,
consequently, to utter some particular formulae in a particular way
in order to destroy or change it. We fail to see that this is applying to
things of the spirit the beliefs and methods applied by primitive man
to things of the physical world. Just as he believes in the existence
of magical words capable of changing one being into another, we
implicitly admit without seeing the grossness of our own conception
that men's undertakings and characters can be transformed by appropriate words. Like the savage, who by vehement declaration of
his will to see some cosmic phenomenon occur, believes he can make
it happen through the use of sympathetic magic, we think that if
we warmly state our wish to see such a change accomplished, it will
spontaneously take place. In reality, a people's mental system is a system of definite forces not to be disarranged or rearranged by simple
injunctions. It depends really on the grouping and organization of
social elements. Given a people composed of a certain number of individuals arranged in a certain way, we obtain a definite total of collective ideas and practices which remain constant so long as the conditions on which they depend are themselves the same. To be sure, the
nature of the collective existence necessarily varies depending on
whether its composite parts are more or less numerous, arranged on
this or that plan, and so its ways of thinking and acting change; but
the latter may be changed only by changing the collective existence
itself and this cannot be done without modifying its anatomical constitution. By calling the evil of which the abnormal increase in suicides is symptomatic a moral evil, we are far from thinking to reduce
it to some superficial ill which may be conjured away by soft words.
On the contrary, the change in moral temperament thus betrayed
bears witness to a profound change in our social structure. To cure
one, therefore, the other must be reformed.

We have explained what, it seems to us, this reform should be. But the final proof of its urgency is that it is forced on us not only by the actual state of suicide but by the whole of our historical development.

The latter's chief characteristic is to have swept cleanly away all the older social forms of organization. One after another, they have disappeared either through the slow usury of time or through great disturbances, but without being replaced. Society was originally organized on the family basis; it was formed by the union of a number of smaller societies, clans, all of whose members were or considered themselves kin. This organization seems not to have remained long in a pure state. The family quite soon ceases to be a political division and becomes the center of private life. Territorial grouping then succeeds the old family grouping. Individuals occupying the same area gradually, but independently of consanguinity, contract common ideas and customs which are not to the same extent those of their neighbors who live farther away. Thus, little aggregations come to exist with no other material foundation than neighborhood and its resultant relations, each one, however, with its own distinct physiognomy; we have the village, or better, the city-state and its dependent territory. Of course, they do not usually shut themselves off in savage isolation. They become confederated, combine under various forms and thus develop more complex societies which they enter however without sacrificing their personalities. They remain the elemental segments of which the whole society is merely an enlarged reproduction. But bit by bit, as these confederations become tighter, the territorial surroundings blend with one another and lose their former moral individuality. From one city or district to another, the differences decrease.[17] The great change brought about by the French Revolution was precisely to carry this levelling to a point hitherto unknown. Not that it improvised this change; the latter had long since been prepared by the progressive centralization to which the ancient regime had advanced. But the legal suppression of the former provinces and the creation of new, purely artificial and nominal divisions definitely made it permanent. Since then the development

[17] Of course, we can only show the chief stages of this evolution. We do not mean to imply that modern societies succeeded directly from the city-state; we omit intermediate stages.

of means of communication, by mixing the populations, has almost eliminated the last traces of the old dispensation. And since what remained of occupational organization was violently destroyed at the same time, all secondary organs of social life were done away with.

Only one collective form survived the tempest: the State. By the nature of things this therefore tended to absorb all forms of activity which had a social character, and was henceforth confronted by nothing but an unstable flux of individuals. But then, by this very fact, it was compelled to assume functions for which it was unfitted and which it has not been able to discharge satisfactorily. It has often been said that the State is as intrusive as it is impotent. It makes a sickly attempt to extend itself over all sorts of things which do not belong to it, or which it grasps only by doing them violence. Thence the expenditure of energy with which the State is reproached and which is truly out of proportion with the results obtained. On the other hand, individuals are no longer subject to any other collective control but the State's, since it is the sole organized collectivity. Individuals are made aware of society and of their dependence upon it only through the State. But since this is far from them, it can exert only a distant, discontinuous influence over them; which is why this feeling has neither the necessary constancy nor strength. For most of their lives nothing about them draws them out of themselves and imposes restraint on them. Thus they inevitably lapse into egoism or anarchy. Man cannot become attached to higher aims and submit to a rule if he sees nothing above him to which he belongs. To free him from all social pressure is to abandon him to himself and demoralize him. These are really the two characteristics of our moral situation. While the State becomes inflated and hypertrophied in order to obtain a firm enough grip upon individuals, but without succeeding, the latter, without mutual relationships, tumble over one another like so many liquid molecules, encountering no central energy to retain, fix and organize them.

To remedy this evil, the restitution to local groups of something of their old autonomy is periodically suggested. This is called decentralization. But the only really useful decentralization is one which would simultaneously produce a greater concentration of social energies. Without loosening the bonds uniting each part of society with the State, moral powers must be created with an influence, which the State cannot have, over the multitude of individuals. To-day neither the commune, the department nor the province has enough ascendency over us to exert this influence; we see in them only conventional labels without meaning. Of course, other things being equal, people usually prefer to live where they were born and have been reared. But local patriotisms no longer exist nor can they exist. The general life of the country, permanently unified, rebels at all dispersion of this sort. We may regret the past—but in vain. It is impossible to artificially resuscitate a particularist spirit which no longer has any foundation. Henceforth it will be possible to lighten somewhat the functioning of the machinery of government by various ingenious combinations; but the moral stability of society can never be affected in this way. By so doing the burden of overloaded ministries can be reduced or a little more scope given to the activity of regional authorities; but not in this way will so many moral environments be constructed from the different regions. For in addition to the fact that administrative measures would be inadequate to achieve such a result, the result itself is neither possible nor desirable.

The only decentralization which would make possible the multiplication of the centers of communal life without weakening national unity is what might be called *occupational decentralization*. For, as each of these centers would be only the focus of a special, limited activity, they would be inseparable from one another and the individual could thus form attachments there without becoming less solidary with the whole. Social life can be divided, while retaining its unity, only if each of these divisions represents a function. This has been understood by the ever growing number [18] of authors and statesmen, who wish to make the occupational group the base of our political organization, that is, divide the electoral college, not by sections of territory but by corporations. But first the corporation must be organized. It must be more than an assemblage of individuals who meet on election day without any common bond. It can fulfill its destined role only if, in place of being a creature of convention, it becomes a definite institution, a collective personality, with its customs and traditions, its rights and duties, its unity. The great difficulty is not to decree that the representatives shall be selected by

[18] See on this point Benoist, *L'organisation du suffrage universel*, in *Revue des Deux-Mondes*, 1886.

occupation and what each occupation's share shall be, but to make each corporation become a moral individuality. Otherwise, only another external and artificial subdivision will be added to the existing ones which we wish to supplant.

Thus a monograph on suicide has a bearing beyond the special class of facts which it particularly embraces. The questions it raises are closely connected with the most serious practical problems of the present time. The abnormal development of suicide and the general unrest of contemporary societies spring from the same causes. The exceptionally high number of voluntary deaths manifests the state of deep disturbance from which civilized societies are suffering, and bears witness to its gravity. It may even be said that this measures it. When these sufferings are expressed by a theorist they may be considered exaggerated and unfaithfully interpreted. But in these statistics of suicide they speak for themselves, allowing no room for personal interpretation. The only possible way, then, to check this current of collective sadness is by at least lessening the collective malady of which it is a sign and a result. We have shown that it is not necessary, in order to accomplish this, to restore, artificially, social forms which are outworn and which could be endowed with only an appearance of life, or to create out of whole cloth entirely new forms without historical analogies. We must seek in the past the germs of new life which it contained, and hasten their development.

As for determining more exactly the special forms under which these germs are destined to develop from now on, that is, the details of the occupational organization that we shall need, this cannot be attempted within the compass of this work. Only after a special study of the corporative regime and the laws of its development would it be possible to make the above conclusions more precise. Nor must one exaggerate the importance of the too definite programs generally embraced by our political philosophers. They are imaginative flights, too far from the complexity of facts to be of much practical value; social reality is not neat enough and is too little understood as yet to be anticipated in detail. Only direct contact with things can give the teachings of science the definiteness they lack. Once the existence of the evil is proved, its nature and its source, and we consequently know the general features of the remedy and its point of application, the important thing is not to draw up in advance a plan anticipating everything, but rather to set resolutely to work.

SUICIDES AND ALCOHOLISM

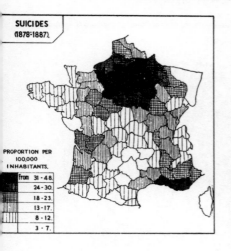

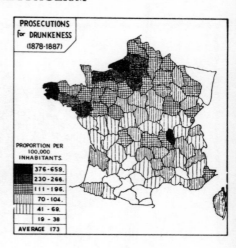

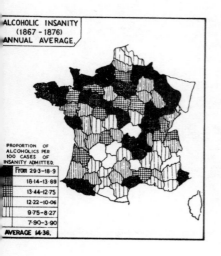

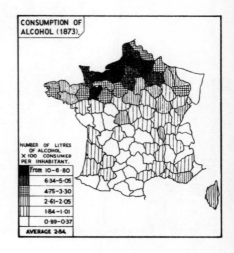

SUICIDES IN FRANCE BY ARRONDISSEMENTS (1887-91)

APPENDIX III

SUICIDES IN CENTRAL EUROPE
(AFTER MORSELLI)

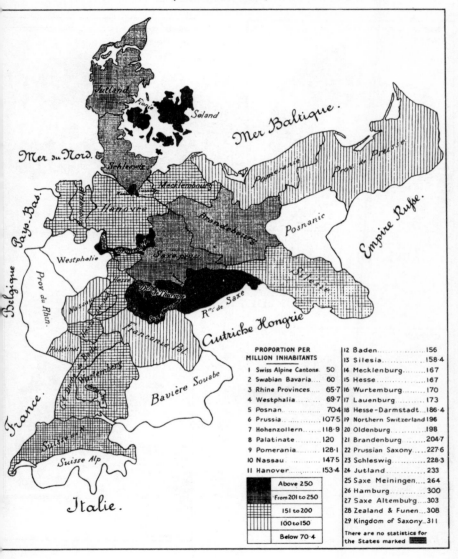

PROPORTION PER MILLION INHABITANTS

1	Swiss Alpine Cantons.	50
2	Swabian Bavaria...	60
3	Rhine Provinces....	65·7
4	Westphalia........	69·7
5	Posnan...........	70·4
6	Prussia...........	107·5
7	Hohenzollern......	118·9
8	Palatinate........	120
9	Pomerania........	128·1
10	Nassau...........	147·5
11	Hanover..........	153·4
12	Baden............	156
13	Silesia...........	158·4
14	Mecklenburg......	167
15	Hesse............	167
16	Wurtemburg......	170
17	Lauenburg........	173
18	Hesse-Darmstadt...	186·4
19	Northern Switzerland	196
20	Oldenburg........	198
21	Brandenburg......	204·7
22	Prussian Saxony...	227·6
23	Schleswig.........	228·3
24	Jutland..........	233
25	Saxe Meiningen....	264
26	Hamburg.........	300
27	Saxe Altemburg....	303
28	Zealand & Funen...	308
29	Kingdom of Saxony..	311

Above 250
From 201 to 250
151 to 200
100 to 150
Below 70·4

There are no statistics for the States marked ▨

395

SUICIDES AND THE SIZE OF FAMILIES

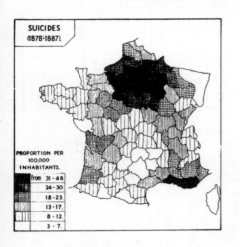

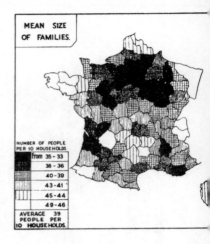

SUICIDES AND WEALTH

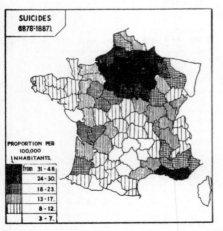

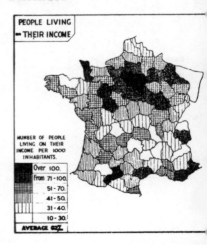

APPENDIX VI—Suicides, by Ages, of Married and Widowed Persons, Classified as with or without Children (French Departments Minus the Seine) *

ABSOLUTE NUMBERS (YEARS 1889–91)

Age	Married No Children	Married with Children	Widowed No Children	Widowed with Children
		Men		
From 0 to 15	1.3	0.3	0.3	.....
15 to 20	0.3	0.6	....	.....
20 to 25	6.6	6.6	0.6	.....
25 to 30	33	34	2.6	3
30 to 40	109	246	11.6	20.6
40 to 50	137	367	28	48
50 to 60	190	457	48	108
60 to 70	164	385	90	173
70 to 80	74	187	86	212
80 and above	9	36	25	71
		Women		
From 0 to 15	.....	.....	....	.....
15 to 20	2.3	0.3	0.3	.....
20 to 25	15	15	0.6	0.3
25 to 30	23	31	2.6	2.3
30 to 40	46	84	9	12.6
40 to 50	55	98	17	19
50 to 60	57	106	26	40
60 to 70	35	67	47	65
70 to 80	15	32	30	68
80 and above	1.3	2.6	12	19

* This table was made with the aid of unpublished documents of the Ministry of Justice. We have been able to make little use of it, because the census of population does not tell the number of married and widowed persons without children at each age. We publish the results of our work nevertheless, hoping that it will be of use later when this omission of the census is rectified.

INDEX